Praise for We, Pro

"I, like Uncle Bob, spent much of my career consulting, teaching, and going to computer conferences. The importance of this is that I got to meet and dine with many of the characters in this book. So this book is about my professional friends, and I can tell you that it is a faithful story. In fact, it is incredibly well-written and researched. That is how it *really* was."

—*From the Afterword by Tom Gilb*

"I can't think of any other book that provides such a sweeping overview of the early history of programming."

—*Mark Seeman*

"*We, Programmers* is a fascinating romp through the history of computers and programming. Wonderful glimpses into the lives of some of the greats. And an enjoyable ride with Uncle Bob's career as a programmer."

—*Jon Kern, co-author of the Agile Manifesto*

"In *We, Programmers*, Bob successfully weaves together a highly entertaining history of programmers, giving us a wealth of historical context, humanizing stories, and eye-opening revelations about the foundational folks in our industry, all bolstered with just the right amount of low-level detail. Bob, being a small piece of this rich history, finds a way to pepper the history with his own relevant observations and critiques. We also get Bob's full story this time out, as well as his own thoughts about what's coming next. A fun, quick read."

—*Jeff Langr*

We, Programmers

A Chronicle of Coders from Ada to AI

Robert C. Martin

♦♦ Addison-Wesley

Hoboken, New Jersey

Cover image: agsandrew/Shutterstock
Page xxxi: Author photo courtesy of Robert C. Martin
Page 31: Jacquard Loom, gorosan/Shutterstock
Page 46: David Hilbert, INTERFOTO/Alamy Stock Photo
Page 53: Hilbert's tomb, Kassandro, licensed under CC BY-SA 3.0
Page 82: Harvard Mark I, Arnold Reinhold, licensed under CC BY-SA 3.0
Page 116: John Backus, courtesy of Lawrence Berkeley National Laboratory
Page 119: SSEC mainframe computer, Everett Collection/Shutterstock
Page 139: ARRA, Internationaal Instituut voor Sociale Geschiedenis (IISG), licensed under CC BY-SA 2.0
Page 147: ARMAC, Gabriele Sowada, licensed under CC BY 3.0
Page 210: Newspaper article with photo of Judith Allen; *The Oregon Journal*'s archive is the property of Oregonian Publishing Co.
Page 213: Second gen computers, courtesy of Paul Pierce
Page 224: Operator working with early CAD program, courtesy of the Computer History Museum
Page 245: Digi-Comp, Pierre Terre, licensed under CC BY-SA 3.0
Page 259: Varian 620, J R Spigot, licensed under CC0 1.0
Page 262: Tri-data Cartridge, Museum of Obsolete Media, by Jason Curtis licensed under CC BY SA 4.0
Page 267: System7, Mike Ross/corestore.org
Page 373: Grace Murray Hopper, official U.S. Navy Photograph, from the collections of the Naval History and Heritage Command; photo # NH 96919-KN
Page 392: IBM 026 Keypunch illustration, Jennifer Kohnke
Page 393: IBM Selectric typewriter, Steve lodefink, licensed under CC BY 2.0
Page 393: IBM Selectric Type Ball, David Whidborne/Shutterstock
Page 394: Intel 8080, the Board of Trustees of the Science Museum; image licensed under CC BY-SA 4.0
Page 398: PDP-7, Tore Sinding Bekkedal, licensed under CC BY-SA 1.0
Page 399: PDP-11, Don P. Mitchell/mentallandscape.com
Page 400: Plugboard, Chris Shrigley, licensed under CC BY 2.5
Page 401: Rk07drive, Gunkies.org/Computer History Wiki, licensed under the GNU Free Documentation License 1.2
Page 401: Rk07 Packs, Gunkies.org/Computer History Wiki, licensed under the GNU Free Documentation License 1.2
Page 404: Transistors, Jules Selmes/Pearson Education Ltd.
Page 406: Vacuum tube, bearwu/Shutterstock
Page 407: VT100, Living Computer Museum, Seattle by Jason "Textfiles" Scott, licensed under CC BY 2.0

Library of Congress Control Number: 2024947905

ISBN-13: 978-0-13-534426-2
ISBN-10: 0-13-534426-3

2 2024

For Timothy Michael Conrad

CONTENTS

FOREWORD

```
vim .
```

Five simple characters launch my favorite text editor. This isn't just any text editor, it's NeoVim. Today's NeoVim experience sports keybinds, LSPs, syntax highlighting, in-editor error diagnostics, and more. With all of this customization, NeoVim launches in mere milliseconds, allowing file editing in what feels like an instant. Even with thousands of files, LSPs quickly report the state of the project, and errors are loaded into quickfix menus for speedy navigation. A couple keystrokes allow me to build and launch or run tests. My computer produces code from plain English via the AI! Furthermore, that same AI can code alongside me as I type, providing large amounts of (highly questionable) code in a flash. This all sounds *impressive*. The NeoVim experience is wonderful, smooth, and blazingly fast. However, using NeoVim is considered *primitive*, and by some, profane. "Luddite!" some developers shout for choosing to use NeoVim and spending time configuring my editor when full-batteries-included *environments* exist. IntelliJ supports actions that my NeoVim mind cannot even comprehend!

I tell you all of this because it is shocking. No, not shocking that I use what some would call antiquated technologies. Not shocking how software engineers argue over preferences—all that is par for the course. What truly boggles my mind is how the sheer power of editing is mundane to us engineers. A mere blip in the daily grind of coding, meetings, and Slack messages. Text editing is ordinary. Autocompletes, syntax highlighting, reliable (sometimes) docs are just things we expect. Before text editors, engineers spent decades without a high-level language, even longer without syntax highlighting, and practically 70 years without LSPs to give autocomplete and refactoring tools in almost any language. Text editing is truly a marvel of humankind.

Besides living in the past with my text editor, I also love reading about the past. The "real programmers" who could time their code with the drum memory for optimal reading speeds. What I wouldn't give to see one of the greats, experts of their craft, in action. Perhaps it's just nostalgia, but the past adventures seem more grand, discoveries more significant, and work more meaningful. In *We, Programmers*, I got the chance to walk that past, side by side, with the creator(s) of each significant leap in computing history. I could see the dinner parties of Charles Babbage, who inspired and terrified his guests with the Difference Engine. That giant mechanical monster clinking and clanking as it produced what must have appeared as magic. Seeing the Difference Engine in action was likely similar to what we experienced with our first LLM prompt or Copilot autocomplete. I bet you could have heard dinner guests exclaiming "Machines can really think." I got to feel the pressure of teams working around the clock and the urgent need for better computing during the critical calculations of World War II that allowed for the atom bomb. No, they did not have Herman Miller chairs and fancy standing desks. Hell, they didn't even have a monitor or a keyboard! Yet they achieved the unimaginable and changed the course of history. *We, Programmers* is one of the most compelling tellings of computing history.

I would be very surprised to meet a programmer who hasn't heard the name Uncle Bob or isn't familiar with his work. He is absolutely prolific in our industry. For many years, I only knew of Uncle Bob by name, by

Twitter PFP, and his notable works on clean code and Agile. In my mind, he was the Avatar of AbstractBuilderFactory. That all changed when one day we started interacting on Twitter, which resulted in emails, phone calls, and even a podcast. Through these exchanges, my whole perspective changed. Robert C. Martin is so much more than what my university studies lead me to believe. He is pragmatic and willing to make concessions when needed. During and after our podcast, one of the most consistent comments went along the lines of "He laughs and smiles a lot!" It's a testament to his character and a life well lived. He is a genuine Software Engineer and somebody that we can all learn from.

I am personally tired of the countless arguments over whitespace, text editors, and the OOP vs. FP debates that rage across X in 280 characters or less. What I think is interesting is who created the technologies behind the arguments that have shaped so many of us. *We, Programmers* delivers something many times more meaningful, a connection to the past and hope for the future, and Uncle Bob is perhaps the perfect mediator for this story.

—The name is ThePrimeagen

PREFACE

I am about to tell you the story of how it all began. It's a twisty-turny tale of the lives and challenges of some remarkable people, the remarkable times in which they lived, and the remarkable machines they mastered.

But before we dive headlong into those twisty little passages all different, a little preview is likely appropriate—just to whet your appetite.

Necessity may be the mother of invention, but nothing breeds necessity like war. The impetus for our industry was created by the paroxysms of war—especially World War II.

In the 1940s, the technology of warfare had outstripped our computational resources. There was simply no way that battalions of humans operating desk calculators could keep up with the computational demands coming from all sectors of the war.

The problem was the vast amount of additions, subtractions, multiplications, and divisions required to approximate the path of a shell fired from a gun to its target. Such problems could not be solved by a simple mathematical formula like $d=rt$ or $s=\frac{1}{2}at^2$. These problems required that time and distance be broken down into thousands of tiny segments and that the path of the projectile be simulated and approximated from segment to segment. Such simulation requires a vast amount of brute-force grade-school calculation.

In centuries past, all that calculation was performed by armies of humans equipped with pen and paper. It was only in the last century that they were given adding machines to assist in that task. Organizing the calculations, and the teams of people who performed them, was a herculean task.[1] The calculations themselves could take such teams weeks, or even months.

Machines that could perform such feats had been dreamed of in the 1800s. Some anemic prototypes had even been built. But they were playthings and oddities. They were devices to be shown at the dinner parties of the elite. Few considered them to be tools worthy of use—especially considering their cost.

But WWII changed all that. The need was dire. The cost was irrelevant. And so those early dreams became reality, and vast calculating engines were built.

The people who programmed and operated those machines were the pioneers of our field. At first, they were forced into the most primitive of conditions. Programming instructions were literally punched, one hole at a time, into long ribbons of paper tape that the machine would consume and execute. This style of programming was overwhelmingly laborious, hideously detailed, and utterly unforgiving. Moreover, the execution of such programs could span weeks that required detailed monitoring and constant intervention. A loop in a program, for example, was executed by manually repositioning the paper tape for every iteration of the loop, and

---

1. To see such a task in action, I recommend the 2024 Pi Day celebration, where over 100 digits were calculated by hand by a very well-coordinated team of a few hundred individuals over the period of a week. At the time of writing, "The biggest hand calculation in a century! [Pi Day 2024]", posted to YouTube by Stand-up Maths, Mar. 13, 2024.

manually inspecting the state of the machine to see if the loop should be terminated or not.

As the years wore on, electromechanical machines gave way to electronic vacuum tube machines that stored their data in sound waves traveling through long tubes of mercury. Paper tape gave way to punched cards and eventually to stored programs. These new technologies were driven by those early pioneers, and enabled further innovations.

The first compilers of the early 1950s were little more than assemblers with special keywords that loaded and invoked prewritten subroutines— sometimes from paper tape, or magnetic tape. Later compilers experimented with expressions and data types but remained primitive and slow. By the late '50s, John Backus's FORTRAN and Grace Hopper's COBOL introduced a whole new mindset. The binary code that programmers had previously written by hand could now be generated by a computer program that could read and parse abstract text.

In the early '60s, Dijkstra's ALGOL drove the level of abstraction higher. A few years later Dahl's and Nygaard's SIMULA 67 drove it higher again.

Structured programming and object-oriented programming emerged from those beginnings.

Meanwhile, John Kemeny and crew brought computing to the common person by creating BASIC and time-sharing in 1964. BASIC was a language almost anyone could understand and use. Time-sharing allowed many people to conveniently and simultaneously use a single, expensive computer.

And then came Ken Thompson and Dennis Ritchie, who, in the late '60s and early '70s, blew open the world of software development by creating C and Unix. After that, we were off to the races.

The mainframe computer revolution of the '60s was followed by the minicomputer revolution of the '70s and the microcomputer revolution of the '80s. The personal computer took the industry by storm in the '80s, followed quickly by the object-oriented revolution, and then the internet revolution, and then the Agile revolution. Software was beginning to dominate *everything*.

9/11 and the dotcom bust slowed us down for a few years, but then came the Ruby/Rails revolution, and then the mobile revolution. And then the internet was *everywhere*. The social networks blossomed and then decayed while AI reared up to threaten everything.

And that brings us to now and to thoughts of the future. All of that, and more, is what we will be talking about in the pages of this book. So, if you are ready, buckle up—because the ride is going to be a wild one.

Register your copy of *We, Programmers* on the InformIT site for convenient access to updates and/or corrections as they become available. To start the registration process, go to informit.com/register and log in or create an account. Enter the product ISBN (9780135344262) and click Submit. If you would like to be notified of exclusive offers on new editions and updates, please check the box to receive email from us.

TIMELINE

The people and events described through the stories in this book are depicted upon this timeline. As you read the stories and encounter the events, you can place them in context by finding them here. For example, you may find it interesting to know that FORTRAN and Sputnik are coincident in time, or that Ken Thompson joined Bell Labs before Dijkstra said that GOTO statements were harmful.

WW2   Korean War   Vietnam War

1930   1940   1950   1960   1970

Events
- Pearl Harbor
- IBM 701
- IBM 7090
- VAX
- IBM 704
- UNIVAC 1107
- Trinity
- UNIVAC 1108
- CP/M
- Manchester Baby
- PDP7
- Apple][
- PDP8
- 8080
- Sputnik
- PDP11
- ECP-18
- DN30&335
- H200

Hilbert
- Hilbert's Challenge
- Hilbert Dies
- Von Neumann Dies
- Gödel's Incompleteness
- Hilbert: No Math in Gottingen
- Turing Decideability
- Turing Dies
- Von Neumann Meets Turing
- Turing to Bletchley Park
- Von Neumann to London (NCR)
- Von Neumann to Los Alamos
- Von Neumann sees Mark I & ENIAC. Writes EDVAC draft.

Hopper
- Hopper Joins Mark I
- Betty Snyder's Merge Sort
- Mark I Symposium
- Hopper Joins UNIVAC
- Hopper: Automatic Programming
- A-O
- Symposium: Automatic Programming
- B-O Flowmatic
- CODASYL
- COBOL

Backus
- SSEC
- Speedcoding
- Fortran
- BNF ALGOL

Dijkstra
- Cambridge EDSAC
- THE
- MCC ARRA
- Gatlinburg
- Programmer
- Go to Harmful
- FERTA
- ARMAC
- Min Path
- XI
- First ALGOL
- Dark Future

Nygaard
- Nygaard NDRE
- Dahl NDRE
- Monte Carlo Compiler
- Simula Spec
- Nygaard pitches UNIVAC
- 1107 Delivered
- Simula I
- Simula 67
- Simula 67 Commercialized
- Stroustrup Arrhus

Kemeny
- Kemeny Hears Von Neumann on EDVAC
- Hired at Dartmouth
- LGP-30
- DN30 & DN235
- BASIC & Timesharing

Ritchie
- Ken Thompson Bell
- Dennis Ritchie Bell
- Dennis Ritchie No Thesis
- Brian Kernighan Bell
- MULTICS Killed
- UNIX PDP7
- UNIX PDP11
- C
- K&R

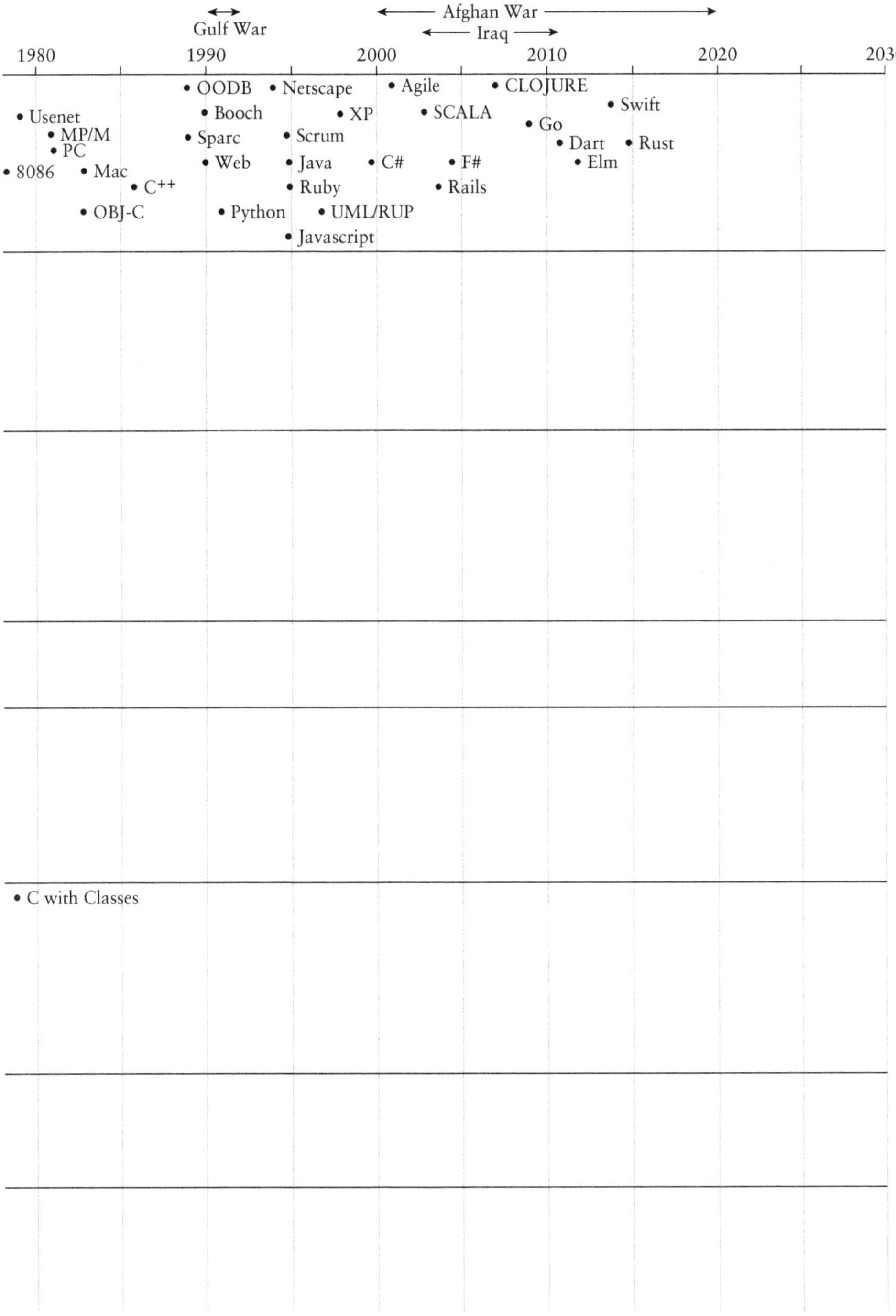
Gulf War
Afghan War
Iraq
1980
1990
2000
2010
2020
2030
• OODB
• Netscape
• Agile
• CLOJURE
• Swift
• Usenet
• Booch
• XP
• SCALA
• Go
• MP/M
• PC
• Sparc
• Scrum
• Dart
• Rust
• 8086
• Mac
• Web
• Java
• C#
• F#
• Elm
• C++
• Ruby
• Rails
• OBJ-C
• Python
• UML/RUP
• Javascript
• C with Classes

ABOUT THIS BOOK

Before we get started, there are a few points about the book, and its author, that I think you should be aware of.

- At the time of this writing, I have been a programmer for 60 years, although perhaps the years from ages 12 to 18 should be counted differently. Still, from 1964 until today, I have participated in the vast majority of the "computer age." I have seen and lived many of the important and even foundational events within this field. And so what you are about to read was written by someone who is part of a small and shrinking group of early travelers in this field. And though that group cannot claim to be among the earliest of travelers, we *can* claim to have accepted the baton from their hands.

- This work spans two centuries of time. Many may find the names and ideas mentioned in the telling of these stories to be unfamiliar—lost in the shadows of time. Therefore, at the end of this work, there is a *Glossary of Terms* and a *Cast of Supporting Characters*.

- The *Glossary of Terms* contains a description of most of the hardware mentioned in the text. If you see a computer or a device that you don't recognize, see if you can find it there.

- The *Cast of Supporting Characters* is a list of the people mentioned in passing in the pages that follow. The list is quite long, and yet it is far too short. It names just some of the people who had either a direct or indirect influence on the industry of computer programming. Some of the folks mentioned in the book have been lost in the mist of time and in the fog of internet search engines. Look through those names and be amazed at who you find there. Look again and realize that the list just barely scratches the surface. Look yet again at the dates when these people passed. Most of them passed very recently indeed.

ACKNOWLEDGMENTS

Yet again, I offer my thanks to the folks at Pearson who have worked so hard to publish this book: Julie Phifer, Harry Misthos, Julie Nahil, Menka Mehta, and Sandra Schroeder. And thanks also to the production team who polished the content: Maureen Forys, Audrey Doyle, Chris Cleveland, and others. Working with them is always a pleasure.

Thank you to Andy Koenig and Brian Kernighan for helping me to make connections.

A special thanks to Bill and John Ritchie for providing me with so many wonderful insights into their brother "Dear old DMR".

Thanks to Michael Paulson (aka, The name is ThePrimeagen) for the lovely Foreword.

Thanks to Tom Gilb for your hospitality, your insight, and for one of the most entertaining Afterwords I have ever read.

Thanks to Grady Booch, Martin Fowler, Tim Ottinger, Jeff Langr, Tracy Brown, John Kern, Mark Seeman, and Heather Kanser for reviewing the manuscript when it was in much rougher shape. Their help made it much better.

As always, I thank my wonderful and beautiful wife—the love of my life—and my four spectacular children and my ten equally spectacular grandchildren. They are my life. Writing about software is just for fun.

Lastly, I must offer thanks that my life is perfect—I live in paradise.

ABOUT THE AUTHOR

Robert C. Martin (Uncle Bob) has been a programmer since 1970. He is founder of Uncle Bob Consulting, LLC, and cofounder with his son Micah Martin of Clean Coders, LLC. Martin has published dozens of articles in various trade journals and is a regular speaker at international conferences and trade shows. He has authored and edited many books, including *Designing Object-Oriented C++ Applications Using the Booch Method*; *Pattern Languages of Program Design 3*; *More C++ Gems*; *Extreme Programming in Practice*; *Agile Software Development: Principles, Patterns, and Practices*; *UML for Java Programmers*; *Clean Code*; *The Clean Coder*; and *Functional Design: Principles, Patterns, and Practices*. A leader in the industry of software development, Martin served for three years as editor-in-chief of *The C++ Report*, and he served as the first chairman of the Agile Alliance.

SETTING **I** THE STAGE

Who are we programmers, and why are we here? And what are these machines that we try so hard to dominate?

WHO ARE WE?

We, programmers, are the ones who speak to the machines and make them work. We are the ones who breathe life into them, and into our economies and societies. Nothing happens in this world without us. We—rule the world!

Other people think they rule the world and then they hand those rules to us and we write the rules that execute in the machines that govern everything.

But this ascendant and necessary position was not always the case. In the earliest days of programming, programmers were invisible. All eyes were on the computers and their great promise. It was the machines, and those who built them, that were ascendant and impressive. No eyes were on the programmers who merely made those machines work. We were little more than background noise.

Of those earliest times, Dijkstra said:[1]

> "Because [each computer] was a unique machine, [the programmer] knew only too well that his programs had only local significance and also, because it was patently obvious that this machine would have a limited lifetime, he knew that very little of his work would have lasting value."

1. *The Humble Programmer*, ACM Turing Lecture, 1972.

What's more, what we did back in those days could hardly be called a profession, or a discipline, or even a well-defined job. We were, for all intents and purposes, gremlins. We somehow got those unreliable, cantankerous, and hideously expensive behemoths, with slow processing speeds and tiny memories, to actually do something useful—sometimes. And we did this through the ugliest and most bedeviled of ways. Again, Dijkstra said:[2]

> "And in those days many a clever programmer derived an immense intellectual satisfaction from the cunning tricks by means of which he contrived to squeeze the impossible into the constraints of his equipment."

This image of programmers was slow to change. Indeed, throughout the '60s and into the '70s, the image worsened. We went from white lab coats in the back room to blue-collar nerds kept out of sight within vast cube farms. It is only in more recent years that programmers have ascended, once again, to white-collar status. And even now, our civilization does not quite realize how much it depends upon us, and we don't quite realize the power that we wield.

For years, we were necessary evils. Executives and product managers dreamed of the days when programmers would no longer be necessary. And they had reason for hope, because the machines kept on growing in power and capability. Not just a little bit, but by dozens of orders of magnitude.

And yet the dream of the programmer-free society never materialized. Indeed, the need for programmers never shrank; it only grew in order to keep pace with the power of the machines. Rather than become less necessary and less skilled, programmers have become more necessary and require ever more skill. Indeed, programmers have specialized, like doctors. Nowadays, you have to hire the *right kind* of programmer.

Despite their best efforts to eliminate the need for programmers, that need has only increased and diversified. And now, they think the solution will be AI. But, trust me, the outcome will be the same. With greater power, the need for and stature of programmers can only increase.

---

2. Ibid.

This transition from the transparent to the significant can be seen in the popular movies of the time. Robby, the robot from *Forbidden Planet* (1956), was the stiff-upper-lip British butler. The machine was the character. The fact that his code was written by the mad scientist was barely even considered.

The robot from *Lost in Space* (1965) is similar. Ostensibly programmed by Dr. Smith, the robot was his own character. The character was the machine.

HAL 9000, of *2001: A Space Odyssey* (1968), was the central character. Dr. Chandra, the programmer, was mentioned once: as the machine sang "Daisy Bell" while being disconnected.

This pattern repeats over and over. In *Colossus: The Forbin Project* (1970), it is the machine that is the dominant character. The programmers are powerless victims who eventually become slaves.

In *Short Circuit* (1986), the machine is the lead character. The programmer offers only gullible, hapless, and bumbling support.

In *WarGames* (1983), we see the beginnings of a transition. The computer, Joshua (or WOPR), is the character, but the programmer is there helping to resolve the situation, though he plays second to a teenager who is the true hero of the story.

The real change came with *Jurassic Park* (1993). The computers were important, but they were not characters. Dennis Nedry, the chief programmer, was the character—and the villain, in that story.

How times have changed. In August of 2014, I gave a talk to the programmers at Mojang in Stockholm. Mojang is the company that gave us *Minecraft*. After the talk, we all went to get a beer, and sat in a pleasant beer garden surrounded by a hedge. A young boy on the street, perhaps 12 years of age, ran over to the hedge and called to one of the programmers: *"Are you Jeb?"* The long-red-haired, bespectacled Jens Bergensten nodded stoically, and gave the boy his autograph.

Programmers have become the heroes of our young who grow up *wanting* to be like us.

WHY ARE WE HERE?

Why are we here? We programmers—why do we exist?

Perhaps that question is too existential. OK, then: Why are we needed? Why do people pay us to do what we do? Why don't they do it themselves?

Perhaps you think that it's because we are smart. We are, of course, but that's not the reason. Perhaps you think it's because we are techies. And it's true we are, but again, that's also not the reason. The reason may surprise you. It's likely not what you expect. In fact, it's an aspect of our personalities that'll likely cause you to cringe when you accept the obvious truth of it.

We love details. We revel in details. We swim upstream in rivers of details. We slog through marshes and swamplands of details. And we love it. We live for it. We work joyously hard at it. We are . . . detail managers.

But that doesn't answer the question of why we are needed. The answer to that is that society can no longer function without phones.

Phones. Why do we call them phones? They're not phones! They have nothing to do with telephones. Alexander Graham Bell would not point to an iPhone and accept that it is the straight-line descendant of his and Watson's invention.

They are not phones; they are handheld supercomputers. They are the portals and gateways to information and gossip and entertainment and . . . everything. And we cannot imagine life without them. We would curl up into little balls of desperate depression without our screen time.

Of course I'm making fun of the situation, but the fun comes from the fact that it is inalterably true. If our phones suddenly stopped working, our civilization would end at that moment.

OK, so what does that have to do with us? Why are we needed to manage all the details of phones? Why can't everybody manage their own details?

I'm sure you know someone who has had *The Killer App Idea* and wanted you to program it for them. They knew they'd make a gazillion dollars with their idea, and they'd be willing to split that gazillion with you 20–80 if you would *just write the code*.

Yeah, that's all. Just write the code. No biggie.

Why don't *they* write the code? After all, it's *their* idea. Why don't they *just* write the code?

The obvious answer is that they don't know how. But that's not true. They do. They can unambiguously describe the behavior they are seeking—albeit in somewhat abstract terms. Why can't they turn those abstract ideas into reality?

Let's say that Jimmy, our eager entrepreneur, is utterly convinced that a gazillion dollars awaits him if he can just draw one red line[3] on the screen. Just that. I mean, everyone wants a red line, right? So how should Jimmy proceed?

Jimmy looks at his phone and all he sees is a rectangular prism with some minor protuberances, indentations, and cavities. What the hell is he to make of that? Of course he needs a programmer, because programmers know about that kind of thing.

But wait. Have you ever sneezed while holding your phone? Have you ever looked at the little droplets as they magnified the details of that screen? A mere moment's reflection on what appears within those globules of exudate would reveal *dots*. *Colored* dots. Indeed, red, green, and blue dots arranged in what appears to be a rectangular grid.

---

3. Lauris Beinerts. "The Expert (Short Comedy Sketch)". Posted on YouTube on Mar. 23, 2014. (Available at the time of writing.)

So Jimmy sneezes and sees those dots, and for the briefest of all moments he comes to an awareness. His red line will be drawn from the red dots!

If he allows himself to think one moment more, he'll realize that those three colors can be combined. If he thinks a bit further, he'll realize that there must be some way to control the brightness of those individual dots in order to create various colors. Oh, he probably doesn't know about RGB colors, but every schoolchild knows that you can mix some colors to make others. So the concept isn't that difficult.

If he allows himself yet another moment of consideration, he'll realize that the rectangular grid means that the dots have coordinates. Oh, he may not remember much about first-year algebra, and he may not remember about Cartesian coordinates. But, again, every schoolchild understands the concept of a rectangular grid. I mean, for God's sake, when you dial your phone, the buttons are arranged in a rectangular grid!

OK, I know, nobody dials their phones anymore, and nobody knows why the word *dial* is used. But never mind that. With just a few precious moments of consideration, Jimmy has realized that he can draw his red line by turning on the red dots that line up, um, linearly.

"How do you do that?" Jimmy wonders. Does he remember the old linear formula: $y=mx+b$? Probably not. But with a few more moments of consideration, he would certainly realize that the dots on his red line would have a fixed ratio of vertical to horizontal. He probably does not realize that he's reinventing the roots of calculus; but that's OK. Rise over run is just not that difficult a concept to grasp.

If Jimmy continues his reflection, he'll realize that the only reason he can see those dots is because the snot on his screen is acting like Leeuwenhoek's microscope. Those dots must be *small*! And that means he's going to have to draw *a lot* of them, and their coordinates will all have to follow his rise over run formula. How's he going to do *that*?

What's more, if he draws just one line of dots, then that line is going to be very thin. It might not even be visible! So he's going to have to draw his line with some *thickness*.

At this point, Jimmy's sequence of reflective moments have consumed an hour or so, and he realizes that he has stopped thinking about the gazillion dollars that his red line will make him and has been focusing on *dots* for the last hour. He may also realize that he has only just scratched the surface of the problem before him. After all, he doesn't know how to tell the phone to turn on dots. He doesn't know how to communicate coordinates to the phone. He doesn't know how to tell the phone to do something over and over and over so that he can turn on all those damned dots!

And, most important of all, *he doesn't want to think about this anymore*! He wants to go back to thinking about how his red line is going to make him a gazillion dollars and about how he's going to position his red line advertisements on the X platform, and . . .

So to hell with the damned dots. Jimmy will let some programmer worry about that. He doesn't *want* to think about that level of detail.

But we do! That's our personality defect and our superpower. We love all those details. We revel in working out how to assemble a bunch of dots on the screen into a red line. We don't so much care about the red line itself.

What we love is the challenge of assembling all those little teensy-weensy details into a red line.

So why are we needed? Because society needs people who love to worry about details. Those people (us) free society to think about other things, like the Ice Bucket Challenge or *Angry Birds* or playing solitaire while waiting in the dentist's office.

So long as the vast majority of people run away from the details, they will need those of us who run toward them. That's who we are. We are the detail managers for the whole world.

THE GIANTS

> "We have a long history in computing and we tend to forget it and ignore it. But in fact there are giants who came before us who gave us examples of how to act ethically in our profession."
>
> —Kent Beck, 2023 (in reference to the recent passing of Barry Dwolatzky)

Here in Part II, I'm going to regale you with tales about some of those giants. The stories I'm going to relate are about programmers who achieved a level of greatness and had a profound effect upon our industry. Those stories will describe some of the technical, and some of the personal, challenges that they faced. My goal for these stories is to get you to know these remarkable people both at a more personal level and at a more technical level.

The personal part should convince you that these people were human, like you and like me. They felt pain and joy like you and me. They made mistakes like you and me. And they overcame obstacles and enjoyed successes like you and me.

The technical part is there because you are a programmer, and only a programmer can truly understand the technical challenges that these people faced. My goal is that you learn to respect the accomplishments of these individuals at a deep level—a level that only a fellow programmer could appreciate.

There are many pioneers of the past that I have not included in this part. Their omission is not due to any lack of greatness or worth. It's just that, for reasons of space and time, I had to choose. I hope I chose wisely.

BABBAGE: THE FIRST COMPUTER ENGINEER

A common lore among programmers and computer aficionados is that Charles Babbage was the father of the general-purpose computer and Ada King Lovelace was the first programmer. Many colorful stories, both fictional and quasi-factual, have been told. But, as always, the truth is far more interesting than the lore.

THE MAN

Charles Babbage was born in Walworth, Surrey, on December 26, 1791. The son of a well-to-do banker, he was part of the upper crust of early nineteenth-century British society and inherited a sizable fortune[1] that freed him to indulge his interests—which were legion.

Over his life, Babbage wrote six books and 86 scientific and miscellaneous papers on topics such as math, chess, lock picking, taxation, life insurance, geology, politics, philosophy, electricity and magnetism, instrumentation, statistics, railways, machine tools, political economics, diving apparatus, submarines, navigation, travel, philology, cryptanalysis, industrial arts, astronomy, and archeology—just to mention a few.

---

1. An estate worth £100,000, which made him independently wealthy and well able to keep his family in comfort while financing his scientific investigations.

But, above all, Babbage was a tinkerer—an inventor of mechanisms of all kinds. He invented a forced-air heating system, an ophthalmoscope, a cable-driven mail delivery system, a machine to play tic-tac-toe, and any number of other devices that struck his fancy. But, in all his tinkering, he failed to create anything that made him a profit. In most cases, his inventions were drawings that never left the drafting table.

Babbage was also a social butterfly. He was a storyteller and an entertainer par excellence. He hosted many dinner soirées of his own, and his presence at others' parties was greatly to be desired. At one point, in 1843, his social calendar included 13 invitations for every day of the month, Sundays included.[2]

His social contacts included the likes of Charles Dickens, Charles Darwin, Charles Lyell, Charles Wheatstone (lots of Charleses), George Boole, George Biddell Airy, Augustus De Morgan, Alexander von Humboldt, Peter Mark Roget, John Herschel, and Michael Faraday.

He also achieved a great deal of recognition in his life. He was elected a Fellow of the Royal Society in 1816. He was presented with the first Gold Medal of the Astronomical Society in 1824 for his invention of the calculating engine that we are soon to discuss. He was elected to the Lucasian Chair of Mathematics at Cambridge[3] in 1828, and held it until 1839.

Suffice it to say that he was a popular and well-connected dude.

Despite his popularity in society, and the recognition of his peers, Babbage was not a particularly successful person. The vast majority of his endeavors came to naught. Nor was he a delight to work with. His contemporaries

---

2. Swade, p. 173.

3. The Lucasian Chair was held by many other significant characters including Isaac Newton (1669–1702), Paul Dirac (1932–1969), Stephen Hawking (1979–2009), and Data sometime after 2395.

considered him to be petulant and cantankerous, given to nasty and self-serving outbursts—an irascible genius.[4]

He was given to publishing letters that lambasted the people in power; the very people from whom he would then ask for financial help with his projects. Let us say that genteel discretion was not one of his primary virtues.

In the end, even Sir Robert Peel, the prime minister, asked: "What shall we do to get rid of Mr. Babbage and his calculating machine?"

TABLES

The story of Charles Babbage the programmer begins in the summer of 1821. Babbage and his lifelong friend, John Herschel, are collaborating to review a set of tables for the Astronomical Society. There are two sets of tables created by two independent teams. If the two teams did all their calculations correctly, the two tables should be identical. Babbage and Herschel are comparing them one against the other to spot, and resolve, any differences. There are thousands of numbers, each with a dozen digits or more. The two men are engaged in hours of tedious, laborious, highly focused work reciting numbers to each other and verifying that they are identical. Every time there is an error in a written digit or a number is misread, they must pause, check again, and either resolve or annotate the discrepancy. The work is mind-numbing, frustrating, and exhausting.

In the end, Babbage exclaims: "I wish to God these calculations had been executed by steam!"[5]

And with that, Babbage the programmer was hooked. Before a year had ended, he had paid some artisans to build parts, and then assembled a small working model of a machine that could calculate. It was a tiny prototype of his vision of a much, much larger machine. A machine that would do the horrible grunt work of calculating mathematical tables.

4. *Irascible Genius* is the title of a book about Babbage, written by Maboth Moseley in 1964. See https://archive.org/details/irasciblegeniusl00mose/mode/2up.

5. Swade, p. 10.

MAKING TABLES

The need for mathematical tables was ubiquitous. Mathematicians needed them. Navigators needed them. Astronomers, engineers, and surveyors needed them. The kinds of tables they needed were tables of logarithms, tables of trigonometry, tables of ballistics, tables of tides. The list was endless. What's more, they needed both accuracy and precision. Every entry in the table had to be accurate, and precise to several decimal digits.

How are such tables made? How do you calculate tens of thousands of logarithms to six or eight or ten decimal places? How do you determine the sines and cosines and tangents of arc-second after arc-second of angle to such precision? At first blush, the problem seems insurmountable.

But, despite some evidence to the contrary, humans are clever beasts. It turns out, there is a way.

The first part of the trick is to bring the transcendent back to Earth. Logarithms, sines, and cosines are transcendental functions; which means that they cannot be calculated by using a polynomial. But they *can* be *approximated* with a polynomial.

Consider a sine wave on a Cartesian coordinate plane. It undulates on the *y*-axis between 1 and –1 with a period of 2π on the *x*-axis.

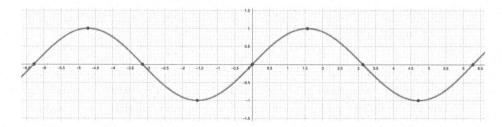

Now consider the graph of $y = -0.1666x^3 + x$ superimposed upon that sine wave.

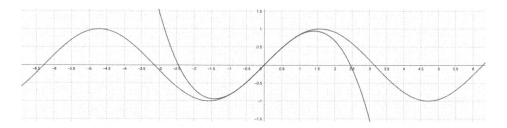

That's pretty good when x is close to zero. But we can do better. Consider $y = 0.00833x^5 - 0.1666x^3 + x$.

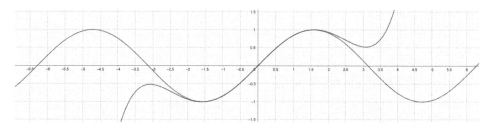

Hey! We're cooking with gas here! But let's do even better. Consider the following:

$y = -0.0001984x^7 + 0.00833x^5 - 0.1666x^3 + x$

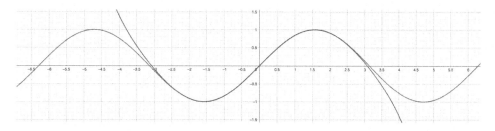

Wow! Between $-\pi/2$ and $\pi/2$, that's really, really close. Indeed, for $-\pi/2$, the value of the polynomial is -1.00007. That's pretty close to four decimal digits of precision.

Of course, what I'm using to get all those interesting coefficients is the simple Taylor expansion:

$\sin(x) = x - x^3/3! + x^5/5! - x^7/7!\ldots$

OK, so now that we've pulled the sine function out of the transcendental realm, how are we going to calculate all those nasty polynomials without driving ourselves to distraction and delusion?

I mean, let's just say we want to build a table of sines for each arc-second between 0 and $\pi/2$. There are 324,000 arc-seconds within that range. And the value of one arc-second is 0.000004848136811 radians. Do you really feel like taking a number like that to the third power, the fifth power, and the seventh power; dividing them by 6, 120, and 5,040; and then adding and subtracting them—340,000 times?

Fortunately, there is a better way: the method of finite differences.

FINITE DIFFERENCES

Imagine a simple polynomial like $f(x) = x^2 + 3x - 2$. Let's evaluate this from 1 to 5.

x	x²+3x-2
1	2
2	8
3	16
4	26
5	38

Now let's take the first difference between those values.

x	x²+3x-2	d1
1	2	
2	8	6
3	16	8
4	26	10
5	38	12

And now the second difference.

x	x^2+3x-2	d1	d2
1	2		
2	8	6	
3	16	8	2
4	26	10	2
5	38	12	2

Aha! The second difference is the constant 2. Indeed, for any polynomial of degree n, the nth difference will be constant.

OK, so what is the value of our function if x is 6? Before you bother to calculate the polynomial, notice that the first difference should be 14 because we just add the second difference (2) to the first difference (12). But now we can add the new first difference to 38 to get 52, which is the right answer. All it took was two additions!

And this can continue: $f(7)$ is 68 because 14+2 is 16 and 16+52 is 68; $f(8)$ is 86 because 16+2 is 18 and 18+68 is 86. If we want a table of all the values of f, we only need to add two numbers to get each successive entry in that table. No multiplying, no subtracting: just two simple additions!

Does this work for sines? Let's say we wanted a table of sines from 0 to ~π/2 by 0.005. Let's also say we are using our Taylor expansion of degree 7. All we need to do is calculate the first eight values, and then we should be able to just add up the differences for the remaining values.

So let's first evaluate our polynomial for 0.005:

```
0.005 - 0.005³/6 + 0.005⁵/120 - 0.005⁷/5040
```

Rather than expanding these fractions into decimals, and thereby losing precision, let's keep the fractions intact until the last moment:

```
0.005 - 0.000000125/6 + 3.125E-12/120 - 7.8125E-17/5040
5/1000 - 125/6000000000 + 3125/120000000000000000 - 78125/5040000000000000000000000
1/200 - 1/48000000 + 1/38400000000000 - 1/64512000000000000000
322558656001679999/64512000000000000000
```

The decimal expansion of that last fraction is:

0.004999979166692708

And that's the value of *sin(0.005)* to within 12 digits or so.

But now we see something important. Those denominators are big. That drives the final numerator to have a lot of significant digits (18). That means we're going to have to take all our calculations out far and work hard to not lose precision.

Working with a bunch of fractions with large denominators doesn't seem all that much easier than evaluating the Taylor expansion. So let's try something different. Let's multiply all those fractions by 10^{30} and reduce all those denominators down to something more reasonable.

Now our first value is 3149986875016406240234375000000/63. If we do that division, and ignore the fractional part, we get the following integer: 49999791666927083178323341269. That's very close to *sin(0.005)* times 10^{30}.

So, by reducing the denominators so much, we can ignore the fractional parts without losing much significance. Now let's use this technique to calculate the next seven sines, giving us the first eight.

```
3149986875016406240234375000000/63
3149908125508592509765625000000/63
3149750628461698642578125000000/63
3149514387813142607421875000000/63
3149199409468928310546875000000/63
3148805701303497939453125000000/63
3148333273159535087890625000000/63
3147782136847718662109375000000/63
```

Now we can calculate the seven first differences.

```
-1249992187519531250000000
-7499859375898437500000000/3
-11249554693144531250000000/3
-14998968772109375000000000/3
-18748007877636718750000000/3
-22496578283945312500000000/3
-26244586276972656250000000/3
```

Then the second, third, fourth, fifth, and sixth differences—which end in constants, as they should.

```
-3749882813339843750000000/3
-12498984390820312500000000
-12498046929882812500000000
-37490391055273437500000000/3
-12495234687695312500000000
-12493359976757812500000000
18749609375000000000000/3
9374609375000000000000
37497343750000000000000/3
46869921875000000000000/3
18747109375000000000000

93742187500000000000000/3
93735156250000000000000/3
93725781250000000000000/3
93714062500000000000000/3

-234375000000000
-312500000000000
-390625000000000

-78125000000000
-78125000000000
```

So the first seven differences are:

```
3149986875016406240234375000000/63
-1249992187519531250000000
-374988281333984375000000/3
18749609375000000000000/3
9374218750000000000000/3
-234375000000000
-78125000000000
```

Once again, with such large numerators and small denominators, we are likely safe ignoring the fractional part and considering just the integer part, because the repeating decimals in the low-order positions are unlikely to do very much damage when we do the additions. So those differences become the following integers:

```
49999791666927083178323412269
-1249992187519531250000000
-12499609377799479166666
6249869791666666666
3124739583333333333
-234375000000000
-78125000000000
```

And now all we have to do is add these integers to fill out each successive row of the table. This gives us a very nice set of sines multiplied by 10^{30}.

0.005	49999791666927083178323412269
0.01	99998333341666646825396682538
0.01	149994375063280910993303357141
0.02	199986666933330793650793650078
0.025	249973959147123306516617063348
0.03	299955002024956607142857142822
0.035	349928546043361925998263888876
0.04	399893341866341587301587301245
0.045	449848140376602342354910713515
0.05	499791692706783234126984125464
0.055	549722750270677211836557536954
0.06	599964006479445714285714281149

This is more or less the way tables were built back before automatic computers. Master mathematicians, who were responsible for the generation of the tables, would work out the polynomials that would best fit the transcendental functions they wanted to approximate. They'd farm those polynomials out to a half dozen or so skilled mathematicians, who divided those functions into relatively small ranges and computed the difference tables for each range. Finally, they'd farm the difference tables out to an army of many dozens of individuals whose skills were sufficient to do simple addition and subtraction. Those folks were known as "computers,"[6] and they would crank through all the additions, building up the table entries within each range.

Thousands upon thousands upon more thousands of rows. Tens of thousands of additions carried out to a large number of places. The pay was low, the work was drudgery, and it was all done with pen[7] and paper.

Typically, the "computers" were divided into two teams, each of which was given the same job. If they both did their jobs perfectly, the two results would match. And that's what Babbage and Herschel were checking on that fateful day in the summer of 1821.

BABBAGE'S VISION

The meaning of his frustrated exclamation regarding steam should now be clear. If the "computers" could be replaced by a reliable machine, then he and Herschel would never need to cross-check the "computers" again.

But more than that, Babbage could see a future where the use of computational mechanisms would be essential for the advancement of science.

---

6. In the early 1800s, they were often French ex-hairdressers who had lost their customers because their customers had lost their heads.

7. The first pencil factory opened in the US in 1861. There were predecessors, of course; but it would take mass production to make the pencil a household device.

In 1822, shortly after his "steam" complaint, he presciently wrote:

> "I will yet venture to predict, that a time will arrive, when the accumulating labour which arises from the arithmetical application of mathematical formulae, acting as a constantly retarding force, shall ultimately impede the useful progress of the science, unless this[8] or some equivalent method is devised for relieving it from the overwhelming incumbrance [sic] of numerical detail."

Unfortunately for Babbage, that time was over a century in the future. But it came. And as we'll see in later chapters, it came with a vengeance.

THE DIFFERENCE ENGINE

The machine that Babbage originally envisioned was a big adding machine—with a twist. It would have had six registers of 20 decimal digits to represent six differences. As such, it could have handled sixth-order polynomials. Each cycle of the machine (each turn of the crank) would cause the sixth register to be added to the fifth, then the fifth to the fourth, then the fourth to the third, and so on. Adding. Only adding.

The machine would have had 25,000 individual parts and would have been 8 feet high, 7 feet long, and 3 feet wide, weighing in at around 4 tons.

Why was adding such a difficult task? Why would it require an industrial-scale machine to accomplish?

The problem was twofold. First, the machine had to be *accurate*. Any moving part had to be restrained from moving unless that motion was necessary at the moment. No vibration, nor friction, nor any other kind of parasitic motion could be allowed to accidentally move a part. Thus, Babbage added many mechanisms for locking and unlocking parts to maintain the integrity of the machine through the thousands of crank cycles it would have to endure.

---

8. Referring to his ideas for a Difference Engine.

The second problem was the schoolchild problem of carrying. When a 9 goes to a 0, we carry a 1 to the next position to the left. In the traditional mechanisms of the day, this was done by representing each digit with a wheel, and by having a tab on each wheel engage the next wheel over when the first was moved from 9 to 0. Thus, the amount of effort required to turn a wheel depended upon how many carries would be propagated. Adding 1 to 999999999999 would require *a lot* of force. High-force loads are a source of error and wear. Also, since the machine was to be hand cranked, the poor operator would experience wildly varying force loads on their arms.

So Babbage conceived of a very clever mechanism to remember carries, and then propagate them one at a time during a different part of the cycle. That memory was in the form of a little lever associated with each wheel. The lever could be in one of two states: carry or no-carry. The carries were then propagated by a set of rods, each of which interrogated the state of its corresponding lever and added 1 to the wheel above if its lever was in the carry state. Those rods were splayed out in a kind of spiral staircase form so that each carry took place after the previous carry was finished.

It was all quite ingenious.

Babbage was a programmer. The program he wrote was in the form of levers and wheels and gears and cranks. But still, a programmer he was. His machine executed a lovely little procedure of successive additions.

The code we might use today for that program could look something like this:

```
(defn crank [xs]
  (let [dxs (concat (rest xs) [0])] (map + xs dxs)))
```

Yes, three lines of code, ~74 characters, replace 25,000 mechanical parts weighing 4 tons.

But perhaps that's not fair. After all, I'm running that code on a MacBook Pro. And although that laptop weighs only about a pound or two, it is vastly more complicated than Babbage's poor Difference Engine.

By the way, you may have noticed that some of the differences in the sine example in the previous section were negative. Yet Babbage's machine could only represent positive integers. So how did Babbage handle that?

I don't know for a fact how he did it; but I was able to do it by using the nine's complement. If you only have 20 digits, and you ignore the carry of the 20th digit, then you can represent negative numbers by "nine-ing them out."

For example, the ten's complement of 1 is 99999999999999999999. Add those two together, ignore the final carry, and you get 0. Thus, the ten's complement of 1 behaves like -1.

The general procedure is to take each digit of the number and subtract it from 9, making that the corresponding digit of the complement. Then, when you have done that to all the digits, add 1 to the final number.

So, given the number 31415926535887932384, we would "nine-out" each digit, creating the nine's complement, 68584073464112067615, and then we'd add 1, giving the ten's complement, 68584073464112067616. When you add those two numbers together and ignore the final carry, you get 0.

Thus, the ten's complement is an effective way to create a negative number, and turn a subtraction into an addition.

MECHANICAL NOTATION

Another indication that Babbage was a programmer was that he had a problem the scale of which no other mechanical engineer had faced: dynamics. The parts in his engine moved in complicated ways and at complicated times. They also engaged and disengaged with each other in similarly complicated ways. This scale of mechanical complexity was entirely new, and required some form of representation.

So Babbage created a notational formalism for the dynamics of his machine. This formalism included timing diagrams, logical flow diagrams, and a variety of symbolic conventions to identify parts in motion, not in motion, and in any other state necessary to describe his intention. Babbage considered this notation to be a "universal abstract language" of interacting parts. Indeed, he felt it was applicable to any form of interaction, mechanical or otherwise.

Of this notation, he said:[9]

> "The difficulty of retaining in the mind all the contemporaneous and successive movements of a complicated machine, and the still greater difficulty of properly timing movements which had already been provided for, induced me to seek for some method by which I might at a glance of the eye select any particular part, and find at any given time its state of motion or rest, its relation to the motions of any other part of the machine, and if necessary trace back the sources of its movement through all its successive states to the original moving power."

It has often been said that Babbage failed to realize that the numbers his engines manipulated could represent symbols of other formalisms. But here we see that Babbage was quite comfortable inventing a whole new symbolic formalism of dynamics. So symbol manipulation was not something that was foreign to him.

PARTY TRICKS

Yet another indication that Babbage was a programmer was his ability to program the prototypes of his engines to play parlor tricks on his dinner guests.

As a contrived example of his pranks, let's say he gathered a group of London's glitterati around the small prototype machine in his parlor. He'd show them a 0 in the final register and then turn the crank. The number increased from 0 to 2. He'd ask his guests what number would appear the next time he turned the crank, and those who guessed 4 would be pleasantly surprised. He'd query again, and everyone would

---

9. Swade, p. 119.

guess 6, and then 8, and then 10. But before they became too bored, the next turn of the crank would yield 42.

Once you understand how a difference engine works, it's not too hard to set up surprises like that. After all, the sequence 0, 2, 4, 6, 8, 10, 42 has a set of differences that, when added forward, will reproduce that sequence.

Babbage then told his guests that the machine was obeying hidden laws that he alone knew. He would go on to tell them that the "miracle" of the 42 was similar to miracles such as the parting of the Red Sea or the healing of the sick. God, you see, is a programmer who built the universe with hidden laws that only He knew.[10]

THE ENGINE'S DEMISE

In 1823, Babbage, being a member in good standing of the Astronomical Society and the Royal Society of London, and with a sympathetic contact in Parliament, managed to secure a government-funded commission to build his machine.

The funding decision was controversial. Some thought his device would be useful, others thought the expense was not worth the benefit. After all, out-of-work hairdressers were not very expensive—and they could add.

But Babbage was an ardent advocate and a charismatic speaker. He would often regale people with the advantages of the machine and the incredible powers that it would possess. He even claimed that he himself did not know all these powers. He could hold an audience spellbound with his enthusiasm and articulation for the project.

And, of course, there is something magical about the idea that by simply applying a physical force to a machine, that machine would do something that had previously belonged to the domain of *thinking*. Then, as today, a machine that could think was something everyone would be amazed to see.

---

10. Swade, p. 79.

Through these efforts, and the enthusiastic backing of his friends and supporters, Babbage won the day and secured a promise of funding. That funding started at £1,500 and grew to over £17,000 over time. Babbage himself put in quite a bit of his own monies as well.

The effort started well, and prototypes were forthcoming. Over the next decade, many parts were made, and small demonstration machines were produced. However, the scale of the device was large, and Babbage was easily distracted and rather unpleasant to work with. He was touchy and proud, he never forgot a slight or an injury, and he ruffled a few good feathers. After a decade of delays, disputes with his contractor, work stoppages, and significant cost overruns, his funding was eventually pulled.

His friends and backers who supported him at the start were all dismayed and embarrassed by this eventual failure. A rather large amount of public monies were spent, and there was nothing to show for it. It was not likely that any of them would back him again.

So Babbage's engine was never built.[11] Oh, parts of it certainly were. Indeed, that machine he entertained his guests with was made from parts intended for the full-scale machine.

In the end, however, at the recommendation of George Bidell Airy, the Astronomer Royal, the government refused any more funding. The letter from the prime minister's office read:[12]

> "Mr. Babbage's projects appear to be so indefinitely expensive, the ultimate success so problematic, and the expenditure certainly so large and so utterly incapable of being calculated, that the Government would not be justified in taking upon itself any further liability."

---

11. His much-improved design, the Difference Engine 2, was finally built at the London Science Museum in the late 1980s and early 1990s. It is on display there, and it works as Babbage designed—though debugging it was a challenge.

12. Swade, p. 176.

So, after the expenditure of a decade, and £17,000, the effort was abandoned.

In my humble view, though I think Babbage would likely deny it, I believe much of the ultimate failure was caused by the fact that his attention was continually drawn away to other, more ambitious ideas. For Babbage, finishing was not nearly so much fun as starting.

THE TECHNOLOGY ARGUMENT

It has been said that the failure to complete the Difference Engine was due to the inability of early nineteenth-century metalworking technology to create parts with the necessary precision. However, there is no real evidence to support this. The surviving parts are very accurate, and there are prototype machines that function to this day.

Had Babbage had the will, the focus, and the resources to finish that machine, there is every reason to believe that it would have worked as designed. Though, as we shall see, getting the machine to actually work is a very different thing than simply building it.

THE ANALYTICAL ENGINE

> *"...and yet in my teeming circuitry I can navigate the infinite delta streams of future probability and see that there must one day come a computer whose merest operational parameters I am not worthy to calculate, but which it will be my fate eventually to design."*
>
> —Deep Thought, *The Hitchhiker's Guide to the Galaxy*

What was it that was distracting Babbage from the completion of the Difference Engine?

Imagine a machine the size of a railroad locomotive. Instead of 6 columns of 20 digits, it has 1,000 columns of 50 digits. It has a mechanical bus that transfers the values of those columns to the two input channels of *the mill*. The mill can add, subtract, multiply, and divide those numbers in single or double (100-digit) precision. The bus then transfers the resultant values back into the 1,000-column store.

Imagine that this machine is driven by a set of instructions on punched cards that are strung together into a chain, like the punched cards on a Jacquard loom. Those instruction cards direct the bus to fetch values from particular columns in the store and move them over the bus to the inputs of the mill. They instruct the mill to operate on the values provided by the bus. They instruct the bus to move results from the mill back into the store.

They load constants into the store. They instruct values to be printed on a printer, or plotted on a curve plotter, or to enact the simple ringing of a bell.

Most critically of all, there are cards that instruct the card reader to skip forward or backward *n* cards *if* the last mill operation ended in an overflow.

With two giant exceptions, this is the architecture of a modern computer. Those two exceptions are that the program is stored on cards rather than in the 1,000-column store, and that the machine is entirely mechanical, driven by . . . you guessed it . . . steam.

Babbage took great pains to increase the efficiency of the mill beyond that of the Difference Engine. In the end, he estimated 50-digit numbers could be added or subtracted in under a second. Babbage designed the mill to multiply using a shift-and-add technique and to divide using a shift-and-subtract technique. Thus, even double-precision multiplications and divisions could be executed within a minute.[13]

Imagine this steampunk monstrosity working. Imagine the grinding and clanking and growling of its internal organs driven by the clicking and scraping of the cards through the readers. Imagine following values from the store, over the bus, and to the mill and back. You could *see them move*!

Imagine the mill, shifting and adding, shifting and adding, rasping out products and clanging out quotients and remainders. Imagine watching a program run, and run, and run, while the machine moved values hither and yon through store and mill, occasionally to print a value, move the stylus on the plotter, or ring a bell.

Would you ever look away?

Babbage could not. Babbage saw the operation of this machine in his mind; and he understood the implications. He said that "the whole of arithmetic now appears within the grasp of mechanism."[14] He reasoned that the machine could even be programmed to play chess.[15] In 1832 he

---

13. Swade, p. 111.

14. Swade, p. 91.

15. Swade, p. 179.

wrote in *The Life of a Philosopher*: "Every game of skill is susceptible of being played by an automaton."

Of course, this machine was never built. Babbage built small prototypes of the mill, and he tinkered around with various mechanisms that he wanted to prove out. But he knew in his heart of hearts that he could never find the nearly infinite funds, time, and energy that building this beast would require.

In the end, all his tinkering and optimization led him to look back on the inadequacies of the Difference Engine; and he designed the Difference Engine 2, which had one-third of the parts, was three times as fast, and had more than double the capacity of the original. Even then, the spirit of Moore[16] was alive and well.

Of course, Babbage never built that machine either; but it was this machine, the Difference Engine 2, that the folks at the London Science Museum built at the end of the last century.[17]

SYMBOLS

Once again, we must refute the claim that Babbage did not realize that his engines could manipulate symbols. First, the fact that he thought that the Analytical Engine could be programmed to play chess indicates his ability to symbolize a chessboard, and pieces, and moves.

Babbage also realized that the machine, properly programmed, might be able to do symbolic algebra. In his own words:[18]

> "This day I had for the first time a general but very indistinct conception
> of the possibility of making an engine work out algebraic development,
> I mean without any reference to the value of the letters."

---

16. Gordon Moore, the originator of "Moore's Law," which predicted that integrated circuit density would double every year.

17. Swade, p. 221.ff.

18. Swade, p. 169.

No. Babbage was a programmer. He understood the connection between symbols and numbers and that any machine that could manipulate numbers could, by that connection, manipulate those symbols.

ADA: THE COUNTESS OF LOVELACE

If, fallen in evil days on evil tongues, Milton appealed to the avenger, Time . . .

It was, perhaps, an evil day when George Gordon Byron was born. He was a talented and prolific writer and poet: one of England's best. He wrote such masterpieces as *Don Juan* and *Hebrew Melodies*. At the age of 10, he inherited the Barony of Rochdale, and so became Lord Byron.

Byron was not a savory character. He was an ill-tempered womanizer who fathered many illegitimate children, including with the stepsister of Mary Shelley[19] and with his own half-sister Augusta Maria Leigh.

In order to assuage the pressure of his accumulating debts, he sought a suitable marriage. Among the many targets of this search was Annabella Milbanke,[20] the likely heiress of a rich uncle. Though she refused him at first, she eventually relented and married Lord Byron in January of 1815. He sired his only legitimate child by her. Born that December, the child's name was Augusta Ada Byron.

Byron was not pleased by this birth; he had expected a "glorious boy." Whether as an insult or an honor, he named her after his lover and half-sister; but he always referred to her as Ada.

---

19. Mary was visiting Byron's home near Lake Geneva in Switzerland during the summer of 1816—the year without a summer. The globe had been plunged into a devastating volcanic cold spell by the explosion of Mount Tambora the year before. During those rainy days and nights, they and an elite group of friends sat around campfires and read ghost stories. Byron challenged them all to write a ghost story, which inspired Mary to write *Frankenstein*.

20. Anne Isabella Milbanke; Annabella was her nickname.

A biographer[21] of Byron once described his marriage to Annabella as among the most infamously wretched in history.[22] Byron's behavior was atrocious. He continued his affair with his half-sister, and had many other sexual escapades with various other women, including some well-known actresses.

Byron tried to force himself upon Annabella on four different occasions, so she had her servants lock her doors against him.

He continued his drunken abuse and, in the end, even tried to evict Annabella from their home. She considered him to be insane, and left, taking the 5-week-old Ada with her.

It was a highly public scandal. London society was all aflutter. In April, Byron fled to the Continent, never to return, and never to lay eyes on his daughter Ada again.

But public reaction to Ada was the opposite of her father's neglect. The public could not get enough. Ada was an instant celebrity, and the association with her famous lothario father was always front and center.

Annabella was trained in mathematics, and she used that training as a way to deflect Ada's interests away from her father and his insanity. Ada had the gift, and she grew to love math, perhaps more than her mother; but she never lost interest in her father, and eventually named her children after him and requested that her grave be set next to his.

Her affinity for the memory of her father may have been amplified by Annabella's frequent absences and apparent lack of affection. When Annabella spoke of Ada, she sometimes used the pronoun *it*. For the most part, she left Ada in the care of her maternal grandmother,[23] who doted upon her, and effectively raised her.

---

21. Benita Eisler, *Byron: Child or Passion, Fool of Fame*.

22. Swade, p. 156.

23. The Hon. Judith Lamb Noel.

Ada was a sickly child. She experienced headaches and blurred vision. In her adolescence, she was paralyzed after contracting measles and was bedridden for the better part of a year. But she continued her mathematical studies—perhaps too well. When she was 17, she ran away and tried to elope with one of her tutors.[24]

Another of her tutors, Mary Somerville, introduced her to many important figures in math and science of the day—including Charles Babbage.

Subsequently, at one of Babbage's many dinner parties, Ada saw the prototype Difference Engine and became fascinated by its workings. Thereafter, she visited Babbage frequently to see and talk about his Engines and his greater plans. He spoke to her of the high goal of the Analytical Engine. She reveled in the intricacies and possibilities.

The hook was set. She was a programmer.

At the age of 19, she married William King, the eighth Lord Ockham and the first Earl of Lovelace. And so Ada became the Countess of Lovelace. Though burdened with illnesses and the responsibilities of children and domestic life, she continued to pursue both mathematics and Babbage's ideas. She asked Babbage to recommend a tutor, and he arranged for Augustus De Morgan[25] to fill that role.

Shortly thereafter, Babbage received an invitation from the mathematician Giovanni Plana to present the concept of his Analytical Engine at a convention of Italian scientists in Turin, Italy. Babbage gleefully agreed. It was to be the first, and last, time he would describe this grand idea in public.

The talk was well received, and Plana promised to publish a report on the session. Babbage waited for that report for nearly two years.

---

24. William Turner. Ada claimed the affair was never consummated.

25. Yeah, THAT De Morgan. You know: $AB = \sim(\sim A + \sim B)$.

The delay was possibly the result of complications in Plana's life, and possibly also because Plana was not quite as enthusiastic as he had let on. So, in the end, he delegated the task to Luigi Menabrea, a 31-year-old engineer who had attended the session. The report, written in French, was eventually published in a Swiss journal in 1842.

Charles Wheatstone,[26] friends with both Ada and Babbage, read the report and suggested that he and Ada should collaborate to produce an English translation to be published in *Scientific Memoirs*.[27] Ada agreed, and made use of her proficiency in French and her deep understanding of the Analytical Engine. Under Wheatstone's watchful eye, the translation was accomplished and presented to Babbage as a surprise—an effort of friends on his behalf.

Babbage was pleased, but he told Ada that she was more than capable of writing an original paper on the topic, and then suggested that she use that capability to add some notes to the translation.

Thrilled by the prospect, Ada and Babbage entered into a frenetic collaboration involving visits, letters, and messages. Indeed, she "worked with frantic energy [becoming] demanding, bossy, coquettish, and irritable."[28] The more she worked, the more enthusiastic she became.

And this is where things take a strange turn. Ada, the Countess of Lovelace, had a manic streak to her. She once wrote, in a letter to her mother, a bizarrely monomaniacal description of herself. It included the following excerpts:[29]

> "I believe myself to possess a most singular combination of qualities exactly fitted to make me *pre-eminently* a discoverer of the *hidden realities* of nature."

---

26. Yeah, THAT Wheatstone. You know: the Wheatstone Bridge.

27. A journal specializing in foreign papers on science.

28. Swade, p. 161.

29. Swade, p. 158.

". . . Owing to some peculiarity in my nervous system, I have *perceptions* of some things, which no one else has..."

"... my immense reasoning faculties..."

"... [I have] the power not only of throwing my whole energy & existence into whatever I choose, but also bringing to bear on any one subject or idea, a vast apparatus from all sorts of apparently irrelevant & extraneous sources. I can throw *rays* from every quarter of the universe into one vast focus . . ."

Of this letter, she finally says that though they appear *mad*, they were "the most logical, sober-minded, cool, pieces of composition, (I believe), that I ever penned; the result of much accurate, matter-of-fact, reflection & study."

In light of this, consider the following excerpts from the letters she wrote to Babbage during the frenzy of activity over the notes—letters that she would sometimes sign *Your Lady Fairy*:

"The more I study, the more insatiable do I feel my genius for it to be."[30]

"I do *not* believe that my father was (or ever could have been) such a *Poet* as I shall be an *Analyst* (& Metaphysician)."

In the end, there were seven notes, lettered A to G. Combined, they are three times the size of the original article. They were published in 1843, and they are brilliant. Indeed, they are effusive. She writes in note A, for example:

"The Analytical Engine does not occupy common ground with mere 'calculating machines.' It holds a position wholly its own; and the considerations it suggests are most interesting in their nature. In enabling mechanism to combine together general symbols."

For this, and for several other references to the ability of the Engine to represent symbols as opposed to purely numerical values, Ada is often called "The First Programmer."

---

30. Swade, p. 161.

THE FIRST PROGRAMMER?

If you read through the notes, you can clearly see that Ada Lovelace was a programmer. She understood the machine. Indeed, she was captivated by the machine. She could envision its operation and follow its execution. If she could have touched it, she would likely have mastered it.

Imagine knowing—knowing!—what that machine could do; and yet also knowing that you would *never* see it work—never see it *at all*. What a frustrating admixture of joy and disappointment, of grand vision and forlorn hope that must have been.

But, despite her competence, Ada, the Countess of Lovelace, was *not* the first programmer. Babbage certainly came before her; and he was no less able to see the symbolic nature of the machine than she. There is no significant insight that she had, that he did not.

Yes, the notes are brilliant. Yes, she formally describes programs that the Engine could execute. And though she did debug one of them, she did not write those programs—Babbage did.

What's more, it's very clear that she was not the sole author of the notes. The collaboration between her and Babbage was so intense that there is no way that could be true.

But, because of that collaboration, we *might* be able to say something different. Ada, the Countess of Lovelace, may not have been the first programmer, but Ada and Babbage were almost certainly *the first pair programmers*.

ONLY THE GOOD DIE YOUNG

Nine years later, after a long physical and emotional ordeal, Ada succumbed to cervical cancer at the age of 36. She was buried according to her wishes: next to the father who had abandoned her.

A MIXED END

In the end, the conclusions of the efforts of Babbage and Lovelace are mixed. In their own time, they came to nothing at all. Ada never published again, and Babbage did not attempt any further expositions of his ideas. The grand vision languished for a century.

It is tempting to suggest that the ideas of those star-crossed pair programmers were the spark that ignited the information age—that the pioneers who came more than a century later were inspired by their writings and their visions. But, alas, this is not exactly the case. If mentioned at all by those later pioneers, it is as an afterthought, or a salute across a gulf of time to like-minded folk.

Babbage, for his part, responded to that salute with a message sent forward in time from 1851. A message that reveals a hint of the pain and disappointment he must have felt knowing that his grand ideas were ignored by his peers:

> "The certainty that a future age will repair the injustice of the present, and the knowledge that the more distant the day of preparation, the more he has outstripped the efforts of his contemporaries, may well sustain him against the sneers of the ignorant, or the jealousy of rivals."

As we shall see in the chapters that follow, much reverence was paid by the latter pioneers to Babbage and Lovelace. We shall even see a repeat, of sorts, of their relationship in the collaboration between Howard Aiken and Grace Hopper, who built and programmed the electromechanical analog of Babbage's Analytical Engine: the Harvard Mark I. Still, it is too much of a stretch to say that those pioneers were influenced or guided by Babbage and Lovelace in any significant way.

Babbage was not a finisher. He started the Difference Engine. He started the Analytical Engine. He started the Difference Engine 2. He drew the designs. He tinkered with bits and pieces. He even assembled portions. But he never finished a one. His contemporaries complained that he would eagerly show them one idea, but then would show them his next, better idea and his next, better idea, using each as an excuse as to why the previous was left unfinished.

Had Babbage actually driven the first Difference Engine project to completion, who knows what might have happened. We know now that the machine would have worked. Might that success have led to other, grander machines? Might he, in the end, have seen his Analytical Engine in one form or another?

THE REALIZATION OF THE DIFFERENCE ENGINE 2

Had Babbage finished that first engine, he would certainly have discovered that he had provided no means to debug and test the machine during its assembly.

In the late '80s and early '90s, the folks at the London Science Museum built a working instance of the Difference Engine 2. It is a lovely machine, a *glittering metallic framework* of brass and steel. As the crank is turned, the number columns do gyre and gimble in the ranks, and the mimsy carry spindles outgrabe their tallies upon the totals. It is a wonder to watch.

But the story told, by those who built it, was one of significant frustration.

Upon assembly, the machine simply jammed after the handle was turned more than a degree or two. Each part needed to be perfectly aligned with each other part according to the timing of the machine, and this is not something Babbage had allowed for. It's not clear that he had even anticipated the problem.

The very gradual debugging, aligning, and repairing of the machine took 11 months. It sometimes involved a small turn of the crank until it jammed, and then poking around in the guts with screwdrivers or pliers to find a bit of play here or a lack of play there. Sometimes it involved purposely breaking parts to find the locus of the resistance. Sometimes it even involved minor redesigns.

Doron Swade, the curator of computing at the London Science Museum and the guy who drove that project from beginning to end, had this to say about Babbage's design:

> "Babbage had made no provision for debugging. There is no easy way of isolating one section of the Engine from another so as to localise the source of a jam. The whole machine is one monolithic 'hard wired' unit. Drive rods and links are pinned or riveted permanently into position and are difficult to dismantle once assembled."

But in the end, with all 4,000 parts aligned and all the minor improvements installed, the machine operated perfectly.

There are some truly mesmerizing videos of the machine's operation. To get started, I recommend searching YouTube. (At the time of writing, Computer History Museum. "The Babbage Difference Engine #2 at CHM". Posted on YouTube on Feb. 17, 2016.)

CONCLUSION

Babbage was an inventor, a tinkerer, a visionary, and . . . a programmer. Unfortunately, like many of us, he allowed the perfect to be the enemy of the good. Like many of us, he was overconfident in his designs and gave little or no thought to incrementalism. Like many of us, he was easily enthralled by an idea, and was happy to think that idea 80% of the way through, but did not maintain that enthusiasm when it came to the last 20%, which requires 80% of the effort.

Edison has been quoted as saying that invention is 1% inspiration, 99% perspiration. Babbage was great at the 1%, but he never managed to get past the 99%. He liked to think about things. He even liked to build bits of things. He liked to talk about things, and demo the bits he had built. But when it came to the truly hard work of getting something done, he was more interested in *the Next Big Thing*™.

REFERENCES

Adam, Douglas. 1979. *The Hitchhiker's Guide to the Galaxy.* Pan Books.

Beyer, Kurt W. 2009. *Grace Hopper and the Invention of the Information Age.* MIT Press.

Eisler, Benita. 1999. *Byron: Child or Passion, Fool of Fame.* Knopf.

Jollymore, Amy. 2013. "Ada Lovelace, an Indirect and Reciprocal Influence." Posted by O'Reilly Media, Inc., October 14, 2013. www.oreilly.com/content /ada-lovelace-an-indirect-and-reciprocal-influence.

Moseley, Maboth. 1964. *Irascible Genius: The Life of Charles Babbage.* Hutchinson.

Scoble, Robert. "A Demo of Charles Babbage's Difference Engine," 24:09. Posted on YouTube on June 17, 2010. (Available at the time of writing.)

Swade, Doron. 2000. *The Difference Engine.* Penguin Books.

University of St Andrews. "The early history of computing | Professor Ursula Martin (Lecture 1)," 1:01:46. Posted on YouTube on Feb. 26, 2020. (Available at the time of writing.)

Wikipedia. "Sketch of the Analytical Engine Invented by Charles Babbage, L. F. Menabrea, translated and annotated by Ada Augusta, the Countess of Lovelace." https://en.wikisource.org/wiki/Scientific_Memoirs/3/Sketch_of_the_Analytical _Engine_invented_by_Charles_Babbage,_Esq.

Other significant resources include the Wikipedia pages for Babbage, the Difference Engine, the Analytical Engine, Ada Lovelace, Lord Byron, and others.

HILBERT, TURING, AND VON NEUMANN: THE FIRST COMPUTER ARCHITECTS

One important aspect of Babbage's Analytical Engine was the fact that instructions and data were stored in very different places. Data were kept in Babbage's registers made of rotating counters. Instructions were encoded in the holes punched into a train of wooden cards.

This separation of instructions and data made a lot of sense both philosophically and pragmatically. Instructions are verbs. Data are nouns. The data change during execution, but the instructions do not. So they are very obviously different both in nature and intent. Perhaps more importantly, changeable memory was expensive and holes in wooden cards were cheap. A program with hundreds of cards required very little material and mechanism, whereas the storage of a hundred numbers required vast amounts of expensive and complex machinery.

It is therefore somewhat remarkable that the idea that instructions and data should be stored in the same memory appeared as early as it did. In fact, it appeared long before any machine could be built to use that idea.

The man who came up with the computer architecture combining instructions and data was Alan Turing; but it was the influence of John von Neumann that drove the adoption of that architecture.

The story of these two men, and the synergy of their ideas, is a tale worthy of campfires and marshmallows. And in the smoke above the campfire broods the ghost of David Hilbert.

DAVID HILBERT

The rise of computation in the twentieth century can be traced to the abject failure of one particular man: David Hilbert.

Of all the mathematicians of the early twentieth century, perhaps none was more highly regarded than Hilbert. From 1895 until the rise of the Nazi party, the University of Göttingen, where Hilbert was a professor of mathematics, was the center of the mathematical world. His circle of collaborators and students included such luminaries as Felix Klein, Hermann Weyl, Emanuel Lasker, Alonzo Church, Emmy Noether, Hermann Minkowski, and John von Neumann.

Hilbert adopted and defended Georg Cantor's set theory, and transfinite numbers. This was not a popular position at the time, and Hilbert took quite a bit of heat for it. But, in the end, it is the view that prevailed.

I'm sure most of you remember the rudiments of set theory. It was all the rage among elementary school math teachers in the '60s. It was part of the "new math." Probably fewer of you remember what transfinite numbers are—if, indeed, you ever learned.

Cantor showed that there is more than one kind of infinity. In fact, he showed that there are an infinite number of infinities, each somehow larger than the next. The two infinities that we are most accustomed to are the infinity of the counting numbers and the infinity of the continuum.

It is possible to place all the rational and algebraic numbers into a one-to-one correspondence with the natural numbers, thus showing that the set of all such numbers is countably infinite. Cantor showed that no such one-to-one correspondence is possible with the set of all real numbers, thus proving that the size of the set of all real numbers is larger than the size of the set of all natural numbers.

NOTE: As an aside, I find it entertaining that our two primary theories of reality, quantum mechanics and general relativity, are each aligned with one of these two infinities, and that it is that alignment that makes the two theories so frustratingly incompatible. As you will see later on, it was von Neumann who bridged the gap between these two infinities in the very specific case of the mismatch between the Schrödinger equation and Heisenberg's matrix analysis.

Hilbert was fascinated by the idea of axiomatizing[1] mathematics the way Euclid had axiomatized plane geometry. In 1899 Hilbert published *The Foundations of Geometry*, which axiomatized non-Euclidian geometries with a formality far exceeding Euclid and which set the standard for mathematical formalisms from then on.

But Hilbert was not satisfied with simply axiomatizing geometry. He wanted to apply the same level of formalism to *all of mathematics*, deriving it from just a few foundational axioms. He argued that every mathematical question had a definite answer that could be derived from those axioms.

The words engraved upon his tombstone are: *Wir müssen wissen. Wir werden wissen.* (We must know. We will know.)

But in the wake of Hilbert's success with geometry, the first cracks in his goal for mathematics were starting to appear. In 1901 Bertrand Russell showed that it was possible, using the formalism of set theory, to express a statement that was neither true nor false. Flying in the face of Hilbert's

---

1. Axiomatizing is the creation of a set of axioms or postulates, and a set of logical rules, from which the area under study can be completely derived.

demand that "we will know," Russell created a statement[2] that was unknowable.

Hilbert desperately encouraged mathematicians everywhere to rescue set theory from Russell's catastrophe, exclaiming, "No one will drive us out of this paradise that Cantor has created for us." The issue became so poignant for Hilbert that he reacted angrily to mathematicians who thought there might be no solution, and even tried to damage[3] their careers.

Einstein weighed in, saying, in effect, that the whole affair was too trivial to warrant such angst, but Hilbert disagreed: "If mathematical thinking is defective, where are we to find truth and certitude?"

After a decade or so, in 1921, a 17-year-old John von Neumann created a ray of hope for Hilbert. In a mathematical paper that displayed his brilliance, he applied Hilbert's axiomatic approach to show that natural numbers, at least, are not subject to Russell's paradox. This was the first step in the long and enduring affection that Hilbert developed for John von Neumann.

Four years later, von Neumann cemented that affection by publishing his doctoral thesis with the unassuming title "The Axiomatization of Set Theory."[4] This paper rescued set theory from Russell's paradox by creating the concept of—wait for it—wait for it—classes.[5]

Hilbert was, of course, delighted. He felt vindicated in his demand that "we will know." Meanwhile, Russell and Alfred North Whitehead had shown, in a massive tome titled *Principia Mathematica*, that virtually all of mathematics could be axiomatized within logic and set theory. And so, in 1928, Hilbert challenged mathematicians to prove the final axiomatic

---

2. That statement can be paraphrased as: Does the set of all sets that do not contain themselves, contain itself? Or, to put it more simply: This statement is false.

3. Cancel culture is as old as human society.

4. The formal German title was *Die Axiomatisierung der Mengenlehre*.

5. It would be another four decades before Nygaard and Dahl recognized that they needed von Neumann classes in SIMULA.

goal: that mathematics was *complete*, *consistent*, and *decidable*. Once those challenges had been met, mathematics would be the language of pure truth, a language that described everything that was true, that never led to contradiction or ambiguity, and that possessed a mechanism for identifying all statements that could be proven.

And it was upon this grand and glorious goal that Hilbert met his defeat. And it was in that defeat that the era of automatic computation found its beginnings.

Gödel

In late February 1930, Kurt Gödel hinted at the demise of Hilbert's challenge of *completeness* at a conference in Königsberg. In a 20-minute talk, Gödel outlined his proof that the system of first-order logic,[6] developed by Hilbert and his student Wilhelm Ackermann, was indeed complete. This was not a surprise to anyone there—everyone had expected this to be proved.[7]

It was at a roundtable discussion on the final day of the conference, and upon the very eve of Hilbert's "Wir müssen wissen, wir werden wissen" retirement address, that Gödel quietly dropped this bomb: "One can even give examples of propositions (and in fact of those of the type of Goldbach[8] or Fermat[9]) that, while contentually true, are unprovable in the formal system of classical mathematics." In other words, there are true statements in mathematics that cannot be proven *by* mathematics—mathematics is *incomplete*.

Gödel might have expected that bomb to wreak havoc on the conference, but it fizzled instead. Only one attendee at the conference truly grasped the import of Gödel's statement. That person, one of Hilbert's chief acolytes,

---

6. That is, predicate calculus.

7. Bhattacharya, p. 112.

8. Christian Goldbach, Prussian mathematician (1690–1764).

9. Pierre de Fermat, French mathematician (1607–1665).

was John von Neumann. Von Neumann was thunderstruck and took Gödel aside to grill him about his methods.

Von Neumann thought deeply about the issue for several months and concluded that the very foundation of Hilbert's mathematical edifice was shattered. He declared Gödel to be the greatest logician since Aristotle, and that Hilbert's program was "essentially hopeless."

Thereafter, von Neumann abandoned his pursuit of the foundations of mathematics. He had moved to Princeton and, as we shall see, found quantum mechanics a more interesting endeavor.

Gödel published his incompleteness proof[10] the next year. His approach should be familiar to every computer programmer, because what he did in that proof is what we do with every program we write. He came up with a way to represent Russell and Whitehead's *Principia Mathematica* logical notation using only natural numbers: that is, positive integers.

We programmers use integers to represent characters, coordinates, colors, cars, trains, birds, or whatever else we might be writing our programs for. *Angry Birds* is nothing more than a rather complex manipulation of integers.

This must be true, since all the data in a computer are held in integers. A byte is an integer. A string of text is an integer. A program is an integer. Everything in a computer is an integer. Indeed, the entire contents of the memory of a computer is a single gigantic integer.

So Gödel did what programmers always do: He represented his domain in terms of integers. He assigned each symbol within *Principia* a prime number. For each variable, he assigned another prime raised to a power.

The details don't matter much to us here except to say that by making those assignments, Gödel could describe every statement within the symbology of *Principia* as a single integer.

---

10. *On Formally Undecidable Propositions of Principia Mathematica and Related Systems.*

Gödel also came up with a reversible way to combine sequences of those numbers into yet larger numbers. Thus, the statements of a proof could be turned into a sequence of numbers, and then those numbers could be combined into another number that represented the entirety of the proof.

Since his combination method was reversible, he could then decompose the number of any proof back into its original statements.

The statements at the beginning of every valid proof are the axioms of the system. Thus, by recursively applying Gödel's decomposition method, it became a matter of simple algorithmic manipulation to determine whether any particular number represented a valid proof based upon the axioms.

All that was needed was to continue the decomposition until nothing but axioms were left. If such a decomposition failed to result in axioms, the original statement was not provable.

Finally, he constructed the number for "Statement g is not provable." Call that number p. He then showed that the number for statement g could be p.

I'll leave you to think through that outcome. It hurt my brain. I read parts of Gödel's proof, and my brain hurt some more. I can safely say that if I understand some small portion of that proof, it is the kind of understanding my pet Chihuahuas have of the rising of the sun in the morning.

Having shown that mathematical formalisms were incomplete, Gödel went on to take down Hilbert's second challenge. He proved that mathematical formalisms cannot be proven to be consistent—that is, you cannot prove, within the formalism, that there are no statements that can be simultaneously shown to be both true and false.

The last of Hilbert's challenges, decidability, would fall five years later at the hands of Alonzo Church and Alan Turing. We'll look into that event a bit later.

For now, and for our purposes, it is important to reflect upon the nature of Hilbert's grand failure. The proofs by Gödel, Church, and Turing that destroyed Hilbert's dream were *algorithmic* in nature. They all depended upon repetitive mechanisms that transformed one chunk of data into another through a series of well-defined steps. In some abstract sense, they were all computer programs. Gödel, Church, and Turing were programmers—and David Hilbert, and the first-order logic that he espoused, was their inspiration.

STORM CLOUDS

But the ill winds of fascism and antisemitism that were blowing in the 1920s rose to a gale force as the 1930s wore on. Jews in Europe, who correctly read those winds, sought safety elsewhere, often in the US. Von Neumann had already moved to Princeton by the time Gödel published his proofs. Gödel, accused of traveling in Jewish circles, followed in 1938. Most of Hilbert's Jewish students and associates were expelled from the Göttingen institution in 1933 and fled to the US, Canada, or Zurich.

Hilbert himself remained in Göttingen. In 1934 he found himself at a banquet seated next to the Nazi minister of education,[11] who asked him how mathematics at Göttingen fared now that the Jewish influence had been removed. Hilbert answered: "Mathematics at Göttingen? There really is none anymore."

Since 1925, Hilbert had suffered from pernicious anemia—a vitamin B_{12} deficiency—which was untreatable at the time. The condition was debilitating and caused enormous fatigue. He died in 1943. So many of his associates and friends had been Jewish, or were married to Jews, or had otherwise traveled in "Jewish circles," that there were fewer than a dozen people left to attend his funeral. Indeed, news of his death was not widely known for many months.

---

11. Bernhard Rust.

On his tombstone is inscribed his failed dream: *Wir müssen wissen. Wir werden wissen.* Yet in the wake of that dream's demise came one of the greatest technological revolutions and societal transformations that humankind has ever experienced. Hilbert led the way, but he never set foot into the promised land.

JOHN VON NEUMANN

Neumann János Lajos (John Louis Neumann) was born into luxury in Budapest on December 28, 1903. His father, Max,[12] was a rich Jewish banker, and his mother's father was the owner of a successful heavy equipment and hardware provider. The Neumanns lived in an 18-room apartment in the heart of one of the most thriving cities in Europe at the time.

---

12. Neumann Miksa (1867–1929).

The Neumann family was Jewish. Jews were tolerated in Budapest, but the Neumanns understood that the political winds in Europe were not blowing in their favor. So, despite their current affluence and privilege, Max determined that his children would be well educated and well prepared for the bad times he saw on the horizon.

Their home life was intellectually and politically stimulating. Dinnertime conversations ranged from science to poetry to antisemitism. John and his brothers were tutored in French, English, ancient Greek, and Latin. In mathematics, John was something of a wunderkind who could multiply two 8-digit numbers in his head by the age of 6.

In 1919 there was a brief communist takeover in Hungary. Armed parties of leather-jacketed "Lenin Boys" roamed the streets and violently facilitated the confiscation of property based on the ideology of equity[13] ("equal facilities to all"). This period lasted only a few months, but the experience, and the violent deaths of 500 people, convinced John against Marxism in all its forms.

As bad as that period was, the rebound was worse. The communists had been largely Jewish, so antisemitic horror raged, and thousands of Jews were killed, and more were raped and tortured.[14] Fortunately, John survived this rampage, too.

John's mathematical prowess grew rapidly. His tutors were sometimes moved to tears by his innate abilities, and some even refused payment out of sheer joy. By age 17, he had published his first significant paper in mathematics. And as we learned in the last section, at age 19 his doctoral thesis, "The Axiomatization of Set Theory," attracted the attention and appreciation of David Hilbert.

While earning that Ph.D. in mathematics in Budapest, he was also earning a degree in chemical engineering in Berlin and, later, Zurich. After his Ph.D.,

---

13. Uncomfortable yet?

14. Ironically, I wrote that line before October 7, 2023.

he studied with Hilbert in Göttingen. His education involved continuously shuttling back and forth between these cities from 1923 on.

At his doctoral examination, Hilbert was one of John's examiners. He asked only one question of his now favorite student: "In all my years, I have never seen such beautiful evening clothes: Pray, who is the candidate's tailor?"

It was in 1928 that Hilbert presented his three big challenges to the mathematical community: to prove that mathematics is complete, consistent, and decidable. These challenges started a period of frenetic mathematical activity that was to culminate in the birth of modern computation.

In the meantime, the world of physics was in turmoil. Einstein's general relativity was barely a decade old. He had beaten Hilbert to that theory by a matter of days. Werner Heisenberg had just published a mathematical description of quantum mechanics based upon matrix manipulations.

Erwin Schrödinger had just described the same phenomenon using wave equations. These two approaches were mathematically incompatible and yet produced the same results.

It was von Neumann (he adopted the "von" in Germany) who settled the issue by showing that Schrödinger's equations were similar to some of Hilbert's work in pure mathematics from two decades before, and that Heisenberg's matrices could be cast into the same mathematical framework. The two theories were equivalent.

So, by 1927, von Neumann had made remarkable contributions in both pure mathematics and quantum mechanics. His name was getting around. He was the youngest *privatdocent* the University at Göttingen had ever appointed. He gave well-attended lectures; hung out with Edward Teller, Leo Szilard, Emmy Noether, and Eugene Wigner; and went for walks with Hilbert in Hilbert's garden. And, of course, as a young man in his 20s, he availed himself of the decadent nightlife of Weimar Berlin. What could go wrong?

For John von Neumann, things decidedly went right.

At the time, Europe was the epicenter of mathematics and science. The US was barely on the map. Princeton University sought to change that. Their strategy, conceived and driven by Oswald Veblen, was to convince some of the best European scientists and mathematicians to come to Princeton. Veblen raised millions from the Rockefeller Foundation, the Bamberger[15] family, and other private donors, and made generous offers to Europe's best. Given the rising antisemitism in Europe, and the rather large salaries being offered, this poaching strategy was very effective.

Von Neumann accepted Princeton's offer, and he arrived with his new wife in January of 1930. His friend Eugene Wigner arrived a day earlier. As Hitler rose to power, other well-known mathematicians and scientists followed von Neumann and Wigner to Princeton. Veblen founded the Institute for Advanced Studies (IAS) at Princeton and recruited luminaries such as Albert Einstein, Hermann Weyl, Paul Dirac, Wolfgang Pauli, Kurt Gödel, Emmy Noether, and many others.

While within this rarefied cohort of minds, von Neumann published his 1932 book, *Mathematical Foundations of Quantum Mechanics*. This rather ostentatious title was not an exaggeration. In this book, von Neumann proved,[16] with his typical mathematical precision, that there are no hidden variables guiding the fates of quantum particles, and that the bizarre superpositions of quantum states are not constrained to the realm of the ultrasmall, but rather extend to all ensembles of those particles, including human beings.

The mathematical arguments in von Neumann's book rocked the physics world and spurred the concepts of quantum entanglement, Schrödinger's questions about whether cats can be simultaneously dead and alive, and the many-worlds hypothesis. The debates over these issues rage on to this day.

---

15. The Bambergers had sold their department store chain to Macy's just before the stock market crash of '29.

16. Only to be disproven, but then re-proven, but then . . .

One young man of note read this book and was deeply impressed by it. His name was Alan Turing. He would join the IAS in Princeton a few years later.

ALAN TURING

"We shall need a great number of mathematicians of ability."

"One of our difficulties will be the maintenance of an appropriate discipline, so that we do not lose track of what we are doing."

—Alan Turing, 1946, Lecture to the London Mathematical Society

Alan Mathison Turing was born of noble blood in June of 1912, a time when nobility was no longer valued nearly so much as in previous decades. Alan's father was posted in India, where Alan was conceived. Alan's mother returned to England for the birth, but she departed to rejoin her husband just over a year later. Alan and his brother were brought up by the Wards, a kindly, if austere, retired military couple who lived in St. Leonards-on-Sea on the southwest coast of England, right on the English Channel.

His mother returned as World War I broke out, and stayed with the boys and the Wards during the war years but left again for India when the war ended.

At the age of 5, Alan found the 1861 book *Reading without Tears*. Three weeks later he had taught himself to read. He developed such an intense interest in numbers that, much to the annoyance of his elders, he would pause to inspect the serial numbers on each lamppost he walked past. He liked maps and charts, and studied them for hours. He enjoyed detailed formulas and recipes for herbal concoctions and remedies, and would make his own lists of ingredients. He valued structure, order, and rules, and became quite angry if they were breached.

The years from 1917 to 1921 were difficult for Alan. His parents were mostly away, and St. Leonards-on-Sea had little to offer his burgeoning genius. His schooling suffered, likely out of sheer boredom. He changed from a lively, jolly child to a taciturn adolescent.

Upon her return in 1921, Alan's mother was so alarmed at his demeanor and lack of progress (he had not yet learned long division) that she took him to London to educate him herself. The next year he was sent to Hazelhurst, a preparatory boarding school in Sussex.

Alan did not enjoy Hazelhurst. The schedule left him little time for his own interests—and those interests were starting to evolve. At one point in 1922, he found the book *Natural Wonders Every Child Should Know* by Edwin Tenney Brewster. He would later say that this book had opened his eyes to science.

He became quite inventive, creating such things as improved fountain pens, and tools for viewing picture stories. This kind of creative scientific thought was not encouraged at Hazelhurst, which was more interested in encouraging duty to the empire; but Alan could not be deterred.

Alan's interest in recipes and formulas graduated into a fascination with chemistry. He was given a chemistry set and found an encyclopedia to help, and he conducted many experiments.

In 1926, as Alan entered his teens, he was sent to Sherborne School in Dorset. On his first day at this new school, there was a general strike in the UK; no trains were running. So, out of sheer enthusiasm for school, Alan rode the 60 miles from Southampton on his bicycle.

Sherborne tried to focus Alan on a classical education, but Alan was having none of it. His interest was science and math, and that's all there was to it. By the time Alan was 16, he was able to solve complex math problems and had read, and understood, Einstein's popular[17] work on general relativity. One of his professors thought him a genius; but most, including those who taught science and math, were disappointed. Alan

---

17. An English translation of *Relativity: The Special and the General Theory*. This was a popularization, using basic math.

was not a good student, even in subjects he enjoyed. He simply could not be bothered with the basics.

Alan's attitude toward school led him to the edge of expulsion from Sherborne; but he was rescued by several weeks of isolation due to contracting the mumps, after which he passed his end-of-term examinations, showing improvement.

It was at Sherborne, in 1927, that Alan first met Christopher Morcom, for whom he felt a particular attraction. There has been speculation that Christopher was Alan's first love, possibly making Alan aware of his own homosexuality. If true, Christopher was likely ignorant of Alan's feelings. There's no evidence that the two had a physical relationship. They did, however, share similar interests in math and science, and would often huddle together in the library discussing relativity, or the calculation of π to many decimal places.

Alan arranged things so that he could sit next to Christopher in class, and the two became lab partners in chemistry and astronomy. When separated, the two would exchange frequent letters about chemistry, astronomy, relativity, and quantum mechanics.

Christopher had contracted tuberculosis as a child and was thereafter always at risk. He died just as the third year of his and Alan's friendship passed. Alan exchanged many letters with Christopher's mother for years afterward, especially on Christopher's birthday and on anniversaries of his death.

Turing studied applied mathematics at King's College in Cambridge and studied under Eddington and G. H. Hardy. Outside of his studies, he became a runner and a rower, reveling in the physical endurance required for such activities.

Inspired by one of Eddington's lectures, Turing worked out an independent proof of the central limit theorem.[18] He submitted this for his undergraduate

---

18. An important theorem in probability and statistics.

dissertation in November of 1934. He was awarded a fellowship at Cambridge, which included a stipend of £300 per year, room, board, and a seat to dine at the High Table.

He studied the works of Hilbert, Heisenberg, Schrödinger, von Neumann, and Gödel, and became fascinated by Hilbert's three challenges. In a lecture on that topic given by M. H. A. Newman, Turing heard the words "by a mechanical process." This got him thinking about machines and mechanisms. It was after one of his customary long-distance runs, while relaxing in a meadow, that he saw how to use a mechanism to meet Hilbert's third challenge.

THE TURING-VON NEUMANN ARCHITECTURE

Prior to Turing and von Neumann, all computing machines kept data separate from instructions. Babbage's Analytical Engine, for example, stored decimal numbers in cylindrical stacks of mechanical counters, while instructions were encoded on trains of punched cards. As we shall see in a future chapter, the Harvard Mark I and IBM's SSEC used a similar strategy. Numbers were stored within the mechanism itself, whereas instructions were stored on some kind of punched paper, or sometimes magnetic tape.

The reason for this separation was obvious at the time. Programs consisted of many instructions, and punched cards were cheap. Most programs did not manipulate vast quantities of numbers back then, and the means to store those numbers was expensive. And, in general, nobody had thought very hard about the idea that there would be any advantage to putting instructions and data into the same memory device.

Alan Turing and John von Neumann came up with the stored-program computer by very different means, and for very different reasons. Turing's machine is extraordinarily simple. Von Neumann's architecture makes no such pretense toward simplicity. Yet the two are related by the remarkable fact that they both keep their programs and data in the same memory. This was a revolution in computer architecture, and it changed everything.

TURING'S MACHINE

Alan Turing described his machine in his 1936 paper, "On Computable Numbers, with an Application to the Entscheidugnsproblem." The purpose of this paper was to answer Hilbert's third challenge, and answer it in the negative: There is no way to decide whether or not any arbitrary mathematical proposition is provable.

We are not going to analyze all the details of that proof here. There are many good resources for that. I recommend Charles Petzold's wonderful book *The Annotated Turing*.

As part of his proof, Turing needed a way to turn any program into a number. To do that, he wrote a program for his machine that simulated his machine—but I'm getting ahead of myself.

A Turing machine is a very simple mechanism consisting of an infinitely long paper tape divided into frames, rather like an old-style movie film. The tape sits on a platform that allows the tape to be moved only left or right. Think of a piece of wood with a long horizontal slot that the tape fits within and that is free to slide. On that platform there is a window that the tape slides under. The window is just a square the size of one frame.

That's it. There's nothing more to the device than that. It's a device with an infinite amount of memory, and a way to position that memory into a reading window. So all we need now is a central processor—and that is the human being who acts as the operator.

The human operator has a marker and an eraser. The human can make or erase an arbitrary mark on the frame of the tape under the window. The human can also move the tape left or right one frame at a time.

So we've got memory and a processor. Now all we need is a program. So let's write a program that doubles the length of a string of X's. We start with a tape that looks like this:

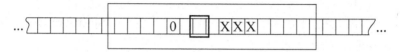

And we want it to end up looking like this:

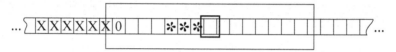

In short, the program will count the number of Xs to the right of the reading window, will change them all to *, and will write double the number of Xs to the left of the O. Here's that program:

Current	Mark	Next	Action
Start	blank, O	Start	Left
	X	FindO	*,Right
FindO	blank,*	FindO	Right
	O	FindB	Right
FindB	X	FindB	Right
	blank	Find*	X,Right,X
Find*	X,O,blank	Find*	Left
	*	FindX	X,Right,X
FindX	*	FindX	Left
	X	FindO	*,Right
	blank	HALT	

I'm sure you recognize this; it's just a state transition table. The human operator is told to begin at the Start state and just follow the instructions.

Each row is one of the transitions. So, if we are in the Start state and we see either a blank or an O in the window, we stay in the Start state and move the tape to the left. If we are in the Start state and we see an X in the window, we change the frame under the window to a *, move the tape to the right, and then go to the FindO state.

Any human would find this procedure remarkably boring. But if that human followed the instructions to the letter, the program would reliably double the number of Xs to the left of the O.

Why would I want to double the number of Xs? Other than a simple demonstration of the machine, it also shows that the machine can *calculate*. The multiplication by 2 that I show here is, of course, very primitive. But it is entirely possible to create programs that perform all manner of calculations, whether in binary, decimal, hexadecimal, or Egyptian hieroglyphics.

Of course, such state transition tables would be enormous. Turing solves this problem by introducing subroutines[19] from which he proceeds to build ever more complex machines without spewing massive state transition tables. The level of compression he achieved is—astonishing.

Once he has these tools in place, Turing does the Gödel trick: He turns everything into numbers. It's not hard to see that every state, every mark, every action could be represented by a number. Each row of the table could therefore be turned into a single number simply by concatenating the numbers for the states, marks, and actions. And if you concatenate all those row numbers, you get a single number for the entire program. Turing called this number the *standard description*. I'll use the term *SD*.

Since an SD is a number, it can be encoded on the tape of a Turing machine. You might encode it in binary, or in decimal, or in some other way. Turing chose a sequence of the digits 1, 2, 3, 5, and 7, for his own reasons.

---

19. They were more like macros. They were simple text replacement mechanisms that he used to avoid repeating the same state transition tables over and over.

Then, Turing wrote a program that would execute an SD on the tape. Let's call that program U for *Universal Computing Machine*. A human executing U on a machine with some SD encoded on the tape would execute the program encoded by that SD, placing the output of that program in a blank area of the tape.

If you have ever written a program that executed a state transition table, that's the kind of program U is. U simply searches through the SD for the transition row matching the current state and the mark, and then executes the actions specified in that row. Easy peasy.

Turing goes on to use his notion of SD to prove that no program D exists that can determine, in finite time, whether any arbitrary SD will have a particular behavior. Again, that proof is beyond our scope.

For our purposes, however, what Turing has invented is a stored-program computer. The SD is the program stored on the tape, and U is the program that executes that SD. Thus, if U could be mechanized—turned into an automatic machine instead of being driven by a human—that automatic machine would be, for all intents and purposes, a stored-program computer.

It is therefore likely that in 1943, when John von Neumann chanced to visit England, Alan Turing had a lot to say about computing machinery and the vision for what a computer could be.

Much has been written about Turing's subsequent work at Bletchley Park breaking the German Enigma codes, and his designs of the computing machinery that achieved that goal. Suffice it to say that those efforts were profoundly useful to the Allied cause.

After the war, Turing went on to work on several other computer projects. He designed the Automatic Computing Engine (ACE), and wrote many insightful reports about his endeavors. He also participated in the computer projects at Manchester.

Much has also been written about his tragic end, and the cruel circumstances that led up to it. I shall not replay that story here. Suffice it to say that

Alan Turing was as human as any of us and that, at the time, his homosexuality was not well tolerated by the country he helped to save.

Nevertheless, despite the indignity to which he was subjected, he kept his interests, and his sexuality, alive—though the latter required trips abroad. His end, however, is in some dispute.

Though officially a suicide, it was uncharacteristic. There was no foreshadowing, no note, nor any other behavior to suggest he was contemplating such an act. According to Hodges:[20]

> "There was no simple connection in the minds of those who had seen him in the previous two years. On the contrary, his reaction had been so different from the wilting, disgraced, fearful, hopeless figure expected by fiction and drama that those who had seen it could hardly believe that he was dead. He was simply 'not the type' for suicide."

I prefer his mother's theory that his poisoning was an accident—a case of using cyanide in his home chemistry experiments, and inadvertently contaminating his fingers.

VON NEUMANN'S JOURNEY

John von Neumann probably met Turing in 1935, the year before Turing's "On Computable Numbers" paper was published. Von Neumann had taken a break from Princeton to lecture at Cambridge, and Turing attended some of those lectures. We don't know if the two sat down to discuss Turing's work, but it seems likely. If so, nothing much came of it at the time.

In any case, Turing later wrote to von Neumann and asked him for a letter of recommendation to become a visiting fellow at Princeton. Turing arrived there in September of 1936, and the proofs of his paper arrived there five days later. Von Neumann was impressed by the paper and by Turing himself. The two worked in adjacent offices for several months.

---

20. Hodges, p. 487.

Eventually, von Neumann offered Turing a job as his assistant, but Turing declined, saying he had work to do in England.

And indeed he did! He returned home in July of 1938. A matter of months later, he would be at Bletchley Park. There, he played a (if not *the*) pivotal role in the design of the machines that broke the German Enigma code, and thereby hastened the victorious end of the war in Europe.

The Ballistics Research Lab

With war brewing in Europe, von Neumann turned his focus to the problems of ballistics. In previous wars, the path of an artillery shell was relatively easy to calculate. It was mostly a matter of gravity and air resistance. But the guns of the late 1930s were so powerful that the shells they fired could reach altitudes where the air was substantially thinner. The trajectories of those shells could only be approximated, and the approximations required massive amounts of calculation.

Ballistics wasn't the only problem that required such effort in calculation. Calculating the blast effects of the shock waves produced by high-explosive bombs and shells was a similar task.

The Ballistics Research Lab (BRL) was created to address these issues. At first, they used the same approach that Babbage was familiar with: rooms full of mostly women "computers" armed with desk calculators, endlessly doing sums and products.

Seeing the problems that they faced, and looking into the future, von Neumann foresaw that "there was going to be an advance in computing machines that would have to work partly as the brain did. Such machines would become attached to all large systems such as telecommunications systems, electricity grids and big factories."[21] This was a dream, a germ of an idea. Exciting, but incomplete: it was too early for that germ to begin to grow.

---

21. Bhattacharya, p. 103.

In September of 1940, von Neumann was appointed to the advisory board of the BRL. By December, he was also made chief ballistics consultant of the War Preparedness Committee of the American Mathematical Society. In short, he was in high demand.

Over the next two years, von Neumann became an expert on the shock waves created by munitions, including shaped charges. At the end of 1942, he was sent to England on a "secret mission." Not much is known about this, even today, though it is clear that he was learning even more about explosive shock waves.

The NCR Machine

It was during this trip that von Neumann saw the NCR Accounting Machine in action at the Naval Almanac Office in Bath. This device was a mechanical calculator with a keyboard, a printer, and six registers. It was capable of ~200 additions per hour. It was not programmable, but because of the registers and some clever tab-stop mechanisms, an operator could run through a sequence of repetitive operations relatively quickly. Von Neumann was so intrigued that on the train back to London he wrote down an improved approximation "program" for the machine.

A few months before his precipitous return to Princeton, von Neumann wrote that he had "developed an obscene interest in computation techniques." Whether this interest was stimulated by the NCR machine or a possible visit with Turing remains a matter of debate.

The evidence is sparse, but there is a reasonable chance that Turing and von Neumann met during this time and discussed computing machinery.

Perhaps it was the joining of the ideas of these two men that fertilized the germ in von Neumann's mind to begin to wiggle and grow.

Los Alamos: The Manhattan Project

It was in July of 1943, while he was still in England, that von Neumann received an urgent letter that said: "We are in what can only be described as a desperate need of your help." The letter was signed by J. Robert Oppenheimer.

Von Neumann had unknowingly already contributed to the Manhattan Project based on his research into explosive shock waves. He showed that airbursts are more destructive than explosions on the ground, and showed how to calculate the optimal altitude.

He arrived at Los Alamos in September, and hit the ground running. Oppenheimer's "desperate need" had to do with the theoretical design of the plutonium implosion weapon. Von Neumann's expertise with shaped charges led him to suggest surrounding the plutonium core with wedge-shaped charges that would focus the shock waves spherically inward.

Vital as his work on the bomb was, the Army and Navy said his work on shock waves and ballistics was just as vital. So von Neumann had the unique privilege of traveling to and from Los Alamos pretty much as he pleased. And this gave him a unique view of the American computing environment that no one else had.

The implosion device had to be modeled, and the calculation burden was enormous. So ten punched card calculators[22] were purchased from IBM. These devices were programmed with plugboards that would specify the fields on the cards, the operations to perform on those fields, and where to punch the results.

Imagine a deck of a thousand cards, each with the initial position of a particle within the implosion. Imagine running that deck through one machine to produce a deck of a thousand cards with the results, and then running that deck through the next machine, and then the next, and then the next. And then continuing that operation 24 hours a day, six days a week, for week after week.

---

22. "Picture a looming black monster, filling a six-foot cube when closed. The front part was a much modified 512 reproducer—two hundred-a-minute card feeds and two stackers. There were two double-panel plugboards dripping with wires, on the front, and a panel of numerical switches on the right end. Hinged to the back of the punch was a dour box of thousands of Lake relays, and hinged to that a second box."—Herb Grosch (www.columbia.edu/cu/computinghistory/aberdeen.html)

Von Neumann learned how to operate and program these machines, but he didn't trust the complicated manual dance of the card batches going from one machine to the next. One misplaced card, or one batch placed in the wrong machine, or one plug misplaced on the plugboard, and days of work could be lost. His germinating dream of computing machines began to take root.

Von Neumann began to spread this dream around Los Alamos. He mentioned it to the scientists and managers there. He wrote to Warren Weaver, the head of the Office of Scientific Research and Development (OSRD), asking him to help him find faster computing devices. Weaver referred him to Howard Aiken, who was the director of the Harvard Mark I electromechanical computer, which we will discuss in the next chapter.

The Mark I and the ENIAC

On one of his many visits home from Los Alamos in the summer of 1944, von Neumann decided to visit Aiken and the Mark I as well as visit his Navy clients. While on a train platform near the Aberdeen Proving Grounds, he had a chance encounter. Herman Goldstine was on the platform and recognized von Neumann from a lecture he had attended. The two chatted while waiting for the train. Goldstine mentioned that he was working on a computing device that used vacuum tubes rather than electromechanical relays and could perform more than 300 multiplications per second.[23]

You can imagine von Neumann's reaction. The whole tenor of the conversation changed from polite banter to a sudden intense interrogation. When the two parted, Goldstine had an action item: to arrange a visit.

On August 7, 1944, von Neumann visited Aiken, who agreed to give him a limited amount of Mark I machine time. Over the next several weeks, he worked with Grace Hopper and the Mark I team to design, program, and run one of the implosion problems.[24] The machine was more reliable than the punched card machines von Neumann was so concerned about, but

---

23. Bhattacharya, p. 105.

24. The problem was disguised, and no one on the Mark I team knew the purpose.

ironically it was considerably slower. So slow, in fact, that von Neumann considered further use impractical. In any case, the machine was already committed to a large backlog of problems for the Navy.

This was the first truly automatic computer that von Neumann had seen. He saw how it worked, and he even assisted in the programming and operation. He saw how the massive machine was automatically driven by instructions on paper tape. The germ was digging its roots deeper into his mind.

The same day he began his visit to the Mark I, he received an invitation from Herman Goldstine to visit the project he'd been so interested in back on the railway platform. So, in the following days, von Neumann traveled to the Moore School of Electrical Engineering at the University of Pennsylvania. What he saw there was a giant electronic machine composed of wiring banks, switches, gauges, and racks of circuitry containing 18,000 vacuum tubes. It filled a room 30 feet wide and 56 feet long, and it stood 8 feet tall. It was the ENIAC, and it changed his life forever. This clearly was the direction that computers needed to pursue. But not in this form.

The programming by plugboards and cords had to go. The roots of the germ had just found water.

Von Neumann's experience with the Mark I and ENIAC spurred a wide search, all across the US, for better and faster computing machines. But the work at Los Alamos could not wait.

Despite von Neumann's concerns about the punched card machines, and partly due to the organizational skill of the young Richard Feynman who worked on those machines, the computations were eventually completed and verified by several non-nuclear implosion tests.

Trinity

With the completion of those tests, the true nuclear test of the implosion of the plutonium bomb was scheduled. It was codenamed Trinity. At 5:29 a.m. on July 16, 1945, John von Neumann witnessed the explosion of the device his calculations and theories had helped create. As he watched the nuclear fireball, he said, "That was at least 5,000 tons and probably a lot more." It was a lot more. The yield was at least 20,000 tons of TNT.

Prior to Trinity, von Neumann sat on the committee that chose the short list of Japanese targets. His vote, and the eventual recommendation of the committee, was Kyoto, Hiroshima, Yokohama, and Kokura.

The emotional toll of choosing these targets must have been grueling. At one point, he left Los Alamos for his home on the East Coast. He arrived in the morning and slept 12 hours straight. Upon his awakening, late at night, he began a very uncharacteristic and manic rant about the future.

His frightened wife, Klári,[25] recalls his words this way:[26]

> "What we are creating now is a monster whose influence is going to change history, provided there is any history left, yet it would be impossible not to see it through, not only for the military reasons, but it would also be unethical from the point of view of the scientists not to do what they know is feasible, no matter what terrible consequences it may have. And this is only the beginning! The energy source which is now being made available will make scientists the most hated and also the most wanted citizens of any country."

And then, he suddenly shifted to a different topic, continuing his manic prophesy:

> "[Computing machines are] going to become not only more important [than atomic energy] but indispensable. We will be able to go into space way beyond the moon if only people [can] keep pace with what they create, [and if they do not] those same machines could become more dangerous than the bombs."

And so his dream had germinated and taken root, and the petals on the flower were unfurling.

---

25. Klára Dán von Neumann (1911–1963).

26. Bhattacharya, p. 102.

The Super

After Trinity and Hiroshima and Nagasaki, von Neumann continued to work on atomic weapons. His brief experience with communism in Hungary as a boy convinced him that the Soviet Union was the next enemy, and that bigger and better bombs were needed to resist them. So he began working with Edward Teller on the hydrogen bomb, the so-called "Super."

Modeling the fission-to-fusion chain of events in a thermonuclear detonation was well beyond the calculating abilities of the punched card calculators that had been so indispensable for the first atomic bombs. The machines that von Neumann had seen in the summer of 1944 whet his appetite for what was truly needed.

The speed of the ENIAC was astonishing. It could calculate a thousand times faster than the Mark I. However, the power to program it was severely limited by the plugboard approach. The machine could only perform a few steps in any procedure before stopping. Then, the next steps would have to be tediously encoded by rearranging the cables on the plugboard. Thus, the high speed of the computer was wasted by the long programming periods between runs.

On the other hand, the long paper-tape procedures that could be created for the Harvard Mark I were a huge advantage. It was easy to imagine applying a paper-tape approach to the ENIAC, but then the speed of the machine would be no faster than the speed of the paper tape.

The conclusion was obvious. The only way to get true computational power and speed was to put the instructions and the data into a medium that was as fast or faster than the processor itself. The program had to be stored with the data. The program had to *be* data.

The inventors of the ENIAC, John Mauchly and J. Presper Eckert,[27] proposed the building of a new computer named EDVAC (Electronic

---

27. John Adam Presper Eckert Jr. (1919–1995).

Discrete Variable Automatic Computer) in August of 1944—just about the same time that von Neumann visited the yet-to-be-completed ENIAC.

Eckert had recently invented a clever mercury delay line that was used to record and then subtract out the background noise in radar systems. He realized, while building the ENIAC, that the same approach could be used for storing rather large amounts of binary data. Since the vast majority of ENIAC's temperamental vacuum tubes were for memory, a mercury delay line memory would vastly reduce the number of vacuum tubes, and therefore reduce the cost and increase the reliability and capacity of the EDVAC.

This was likely discussed with von Neumann at the time. And indeed, von Neumann was added to the EDVAC project as a consultant.

The EDVAC Draft

Just under a year later, von Neumann wrote a curious document titled "The First Draft of a Report on the EDVAC." In it he described a machine composed of five primary units: input, output, arithmetic, control, and memory. The control unit read instructions from memory, interpreted them, and directed values from memory into the arithmetic unit and then back into memory. It was, of course, the model of a stored-program computer that we continue to use to this day.

This document was unfinished, and relatively informal. It was not meant for wide distribution. But Goldstine was beside himself with joy. He called it the first complete logical framework for the machine. And then, without telling von Neumann, Mauchly, or Eckert, he sent copies to dozens of scientists around the world.

The flower had bloomed, and its seeds were scattered far and wide. The von Neumann architecture was in the wild and free to roam. And roam it did. And wherever it landed, it took root and grew.

Turing saw the report and began planning the ACE (Automatic Computing Engine) in Manchester. The ENIAC itself was converted, at von Neumann's urging, and began operation in its new form in 1947.

The very first person ever hired solely to program a computer was Jean Bartik (born Betty Jean Jennings), one of the original programmer/operators of the ENIAC.

Von Neumann's wife, Klári, became a programmer and shuttled between Los Alamos and the East Coast writing and running programs for Teller's modeling of the Super using von Neumann's and Stanislaw Ulam's invention of Monte Carlo analysis.[28]

At this point, von Neumann leaves our story. I would, however, be severely remiss if I did not point out that the events I have related herein describe but the barest minimum of his achievements and accomplishments. The man was a genius and a marvel. He made such significant contributions in mathematics, physics, quantum mechanics, game theory, fluid dynamics, general relativity, dynamics, topology, group theory, and so much more that a single book, let alone a single chapter, would be woefully inadequate to cover them all.

John von Neumann died of cancer at the age of 53 on February 8, 1957. There is a reasonable chance that the cancer that killed him was a result of radiation exposure while at Los Alamos. He was terrified of death, and he refused to accept his circumstances up to the end.

There is a plaque on the wall of his birthplace that reads, in part: ". . . one of the most outstanding mathematicians of the 20th century." Like this chapter, I think that says far too little.

But we must return to our story and the legacy of the three great men this chapter is named for. The von Neumann architecture was tearing through the computational landscape. One machine after another became functional in the waning decade of the '40s. With the end of the war came the beginning of the information age.

---

28. See *Monte Carlo analysis* in the Glossary of Terms.

The Manchester Baby became functional in 1948 using Williams tube[29] memory. The EDSAC at Cambridge became operational in 1949 using mercury delay line memory. Mauchly and Eckert left the university to start UNIVAC. And the commercial computer industry was off to the races.

And—as we shall see—it has been a wild race indeed.

REFERENCES

Atomic Heritage Foundation. 2014. "Computing and the Manhattan Project." Posted by the Atomic Heritage Foundation July 18, 2014. https://ahf .nuclearmuseum.org/ahf/history/computing-and-manhattan-project.

Beyer, Kurt W. 2009. *Grace Hopper and the Invention of the Information Age.* MIT Press.

Bhattacharya, Ananyo. 2021. *The Man from the Future.* W. W. Norton & Co.

Brewster, Edwin Tenney. *Natural Wonders Every Child Should Know.* 1912. Doubleday, Doran & Co.

Gilpin, Donald. n.d. "The Extraordinary Legacy of Oswald Veblen." Posted by *Princeton Magazine.* www.princetonmagazine.com/the-extraordinary-legacy -of-oswald-veblen.

Gödel, Kurt. 1931. *On Formally Undecidable Propositions of Principia Mathematica and Related Systems.* Dover Publications, Inc. https://monoskop .org/images/9/93/Kurt_G%C3%B6del_On_Formally_Undecidable _Propositions_of_Principia_Mathematica_and_Related_Systems_1992.pdf.

Hodges, Andrew. 2000. *Alan Turing: The Enigma.* Walker Publishing.

Kennefick, Daniel. 2020. "Was Einstein the First to Discover General Relativity?" Posted by Princeton University Press March 9, 2020. https://press.princeton .edu/ideas/was-einstein-the-first-to-discover-general-relativity.

Lee Mortimer, Favell. *Reading without Tears. Or, a Pleasant Mode of Learning to Read.* 1857. Harper & Brothers.

---

29. A special kind of cathode ray tube that could write and read areas of charge using an electron beam.

Lewis, N. 2021. "Trinity by the Numbers: The Computing Effort That Made Trinity Possible." *Nuclear Technology* 207, no. sup1: S176–S189. www .tandfonline.com/doi/full/10.1080/00295450.2021.1938487.

Petzold, Charles. 2008. *The Annotated Turing*. Wiley.

Todd, John. n.d. "John von Neumann and the National Accounting Machine." California Institute of Technology. https://archive.computerhistory.org /resources/access/text/2016/06/102724632-05-01-acc.pdf.

Turing, A. M. 1936. "On Computable Numbers, with an Application to the Entscheidugnsproblem." https://www.cs.virginia.edu/~robins/Turing _Paper_1936.pdf.

Wikipedia. "Alan Turing." https://en.wikipedia.org/wiki/Alan_Turing.

Wikipedia. "David Hilbert." https://en.wikipedia.org/wiki/David_Hilbert.

Wikipedia. "EDVAC." https://en.wikipedia.org/wiki/EDVAC.

Wikipedia. "John von Neumann." https://en.wikipedia.org/wiki/John_von _Neumann.

GRACE HOPPER: THE FIRST SOFTWARE ENGINEER

Grace Hopper entered our field at a time when programmers literally punched holes in paper tape—holes that corresponded to the numeric instructions that drove the computer to execute a procedure. She became quite skilled at this task, and gradually became aware that there was a better way.

That better way, which she called *automatic* programming, involved having a computer program determine the numeric instructions from a more abstract language that was more comfortable for the programmer. She wrote the first such program and called it a *compiler*.

It is not an exaggeration to say that Grace Hopper was the first "real" programmer. A few others had written programs before her, but it was Hopper who first worked out the *discipline*[1] of programming. Perhaps, therefore, it would be better to say that Grace Hopper was the first true software *engineer*.

---

1. Harkening back to Turing's plea for mathematicians of ability to maintain the appropriate *discipline*.

She was the first programmer to face down obdurate and ignorant managers—not just because she was a woman, but because she was a *programmer*.

She also endured a period of debilitating alcoholism so severe that she considered, and sometimes attempted, suicide. Fortunately for all of us, this was a demon that, with the help of her coworkers and friends, she was able to wrestle to the ground.

We can credit her with either inventing or contributing to the invention of comments, subroutines, multiprocessing, disciplined methodologies, debugging, compilers, open source, user groups, management information systems, and much, much more.

It was through her efforts that we use standard terms such as *address, binary, bit, assembler, compiler, breakpoint, character, code, debug, edit, field, file, floating-point, flowchart, input, output, jump, key, loop, normalize, operand, overflow, parameter, patch, program,* and *subroutine*.

Her story is utterly fascinating, and her accomplishments, at the very start of the software industry, laid a massive foundation upon which the rest of us barely realize we are standing. She was the Atlas who bore the software industry upon her shoulders—and too few programmers know of her true contributions. It may also be fair to say that at some point, Atlas shrugged.

WAR, AND THE SUMMER OF 1944

Grace Brewster Murray was born in New York City on December 9, 1906. At age 7, she started disassembling alarm clocks to see how they worked. She was admitted to Vassar when she was 17 and graduated with high honors,[2] earning a bachelor's degree in mathematics and physics. She earned her master's at Yale two years later, in 1930. She was not yet 20.

---

2. Phi Beta Kappa.

She married Vincent Foster Hopper that same year.

She continued at Yale and in 1934 became the first woman to earn a doctorate in mathematics from that august institution. While earning that Ph.D., she returned to Vassar to teach mathematics. She was eventually tenured as an associate professor of mathematics in 1941.

Her innovative approach to teaching non-Euclidean geometry and general relativity to undergrads ruffled quite a few stodgy old feathers at Vassar. Those rankled superiors sought to reign her in, but they were thwarted by the students who flocked to her courses and were effusive in their praise. They considered her to be inspirational.

She loved being an educator. And to education she would eventually return. But fate stepped in and changed the course of her life.

It was the bombing of Pearl Harbor and the US entry into World War II that spurred the 36-year-old Grace Murray Hopper to leave her tenured mathematics professorship at Vassar, and her husband of 12 years, to join the Navy. It was that decision that, quite by accident, pushed her on the path to becoming the first true software engineer.

Upon joining the Navy, she finished first in her Midshipmen's School class and gained the rank of lieutenant junior grade. Because of her deep background in mathematics, she had expected to be ordered to work in communications on breaking codes. However, her orders sent her to Harvard to be the second in command of, and the third[3] programmer of, the Automatic Sequence Controlled Calculator (ASCC): the first computer in the US and, perhaps, the second computer in the world.

The ASCC was also known as the Harvard Mark I. It was the brainchild of Howard Aiken, who had duped[4] the Harvard faculty and wrangled the Navy into allowing him to build a giant calculating machine. Aiken

---

3. The other two were Robert Campbell and Richard Bloch. More on them later.

4. Beyer, p. 78.

proposed the project to IBM, and Thomas J. Watson[5] himself agreed to fund the design and construction. After five years, IBM delivered a 9,445-pound, 8-foot-high, 3-foot-wide, 51-foot-long assemblage of 750,000 relays, and a plethora of gears, cams, motors, and counters connected by 540 miles of wire. It was installed in the basement of Harvard's Cruft[6] Laboratory. This monstrosity[7] had a memory of 72 registers composed of 23 decimal digits. Each digit was an electromechanical counter with ten positions, 0 to 9. The registers were also adders that used an electromechanical delayed carry mechanism reminiscent of Babbage's spiral carry arms.

The Mark I was driven by a 200-rpm motor, allowing it to add one register to another in 300 ms. It also had a separate arithmetic engine that could multiply in 10 seconds, divide in 16 seconds, and take a logarithm in 90 seconds. The entire contraption was controlled, like Jacquard's loom, by instructions punched into a long, 3-inch-wide paper tape.

Aiken had not yet heard of Babbage's Analytical Engine, but Babbage would have looked upon this machine and felt intimately connected to it.

This was the Navy. The Mark I was a ship, and Howard Aiken was the captain. And that's just how he ran that operation. Everyone showed up in uniform and followed military protocol and etiquette. There was a war on, and they were all soldiers in that war.

Aiken was not an easy man to deal with, and not everyone appreciated his military style. One such person was Rex Seeber.[8] Seeber joined the

---

5. Thomas J. Watson Sr., a convicted white-collar felon and someone who sold equipment to Nazi Germany to help the trains run on time. He was the God King (chairman and CEO) of IBM in those days.

6. Think about that for a minute.

7. To see some wonderful pictures of this machine, see "Aiken's Secret Computing Machines" in this chapter's References section.

8. Robert Rex Seeber (1910–1969).

team in 1944 but asked Aiken if he could delay starting in order to take some earned vacation time. Aiken both denied and resented that request.

Thereafter, no matter how hard Seeber worked, Aiken ignored his suggestions and ideas. When the war ended, Seeber quit and took a position at IBM to design and build the machine that would overshadow Aiken and the Mark I.

Aiken was disappointed that the Navy had placed Grace Hopper, a female officer, as second in command of his ship.[9] When she reported for duty on July 2, 1944, the first words Commander Aiken spoke to Lieutenant Junior Grade Hopper were: "Where have you been?"[10] He then ordered her to use the Mark I to compute the interpolation coefficients for computing arctangents to an accuracy of 23 decimal places. He gave her a week.

In one week, Hopper, a woman who once said that she didn't know a computer from a tomato basket, would have to program a machine the likes of which few had ever before even imagined. A machine with no YouTube tutorial, nor even a paper instruction manual. All Aiken's team gave her was a hastily thrown together notebook that described the instruction codes.

The Mark I was programmed by punching codes onto a paper tape. The paper tape was composed of horizontal rows with 24 positions. Each position could have a hole punched in it or not. This, of course, corresponded to 24 bits—although that's not quite the way they thought of it.

The 24 bits were separated into three groups of eight. The first two such groups were the binary addresses of the input and output memory registers. The third was the operation to be performed. Operation 0 was "add," so `0x131400` was the instruction to add the number in register `0x13` to the number in register `0x14`.

---

9. Beyer, p. 39.

10. Beyer, p. 39.

But that's not how they wrote it. They wrote it like this: | 521| 53| |.
Look carefully at this and you'll probably figure it out.

Go it? No? This will probably help. The holes in the paper tape would be:

```
| | | |o| | |o|o| | | |o| |o| | | | | | | | | | | |
  8 7 6 5 4 3 2 1 8 7 6 5 4 3 2 1 8 7 6 5 4 3 2 1
      1       3       1       4       0       0
```

Now you see it, don't you? Are you screaming yet?

So Hopper's task was to punch a tape with the holes properly positioned
to compute all those arctangent interpolations. She had at her disposal
instructions to add, subtract, multiply, divide, and print. She had no way
to loop[11] and no way to branch. The tape had to be a long, linear list of
instructions that would compute all the coefficients in turn: a single
repetitive stream of instructions punched by hand into a long paper tape.

And every hole had to be correct.

---

11. Other than manually repositioning the tape or gluing the ends of the tape together into a loop.

Why did they use a code like | 521| 53| |? Because the machine that punched the tape had a keyboard with three rows of eight buttons labeled 87654321, and they depressed the corresponding keys one at a time and then advanced the tape to the next row.[12]

Are you tearing your hair out yet? Well, just wait!

The Mark I was not a machine sitting idle. The armed forces had lots of jobs for Aiken's team to do. They had to print out firing tables for various artillery pieces and naval guns. They had to print out navigation tables and analyses on various alloys of steel. There was a huge backlog, and Commander Aiken brooked no delay. There was a war on, and the job would get done.

So somehow, in the week she was given, she managed to get brief snippets of time with the other two programmers to help her learn some of the ropes. She also managed to sneak a few runs of her program in between the more important runs.

And she succeeded in that first task. It was not to be her last success—by a long shot.

DISCIPLINE: 1944–1945

Hopper and her crew of Richard Bloch and Robert Campbell buckled down and *learned* the inner workings of that machine. This led to some embarrassing realizations. For example, Aiken had spent a lot of money and effort in building automatic logarithm and trigonometry hardware. However, the crew rapidly realized that the 200 machine cycles that the hardware required to crunch those functions took more time than doing some simple interpolations with additions and multiplications. So these expensive facilities were seldom used.

---

12. Actually, the keyboard had two such arrays of 24 buttons because the machine punched two rows on the tape at the same time. See page 45.ff of *A Manual of Operation for the Automatic Sequence Controlled Calculator* (1946), https://chsi.harvard.edu/harvard-ibm-mark-1-manual.

Another quirk of the machine was that the result of a multiplication would be shifted right by a certain number of decimal digits based upon a plugboard setting. This was done to automatically keep track of the decimal point that was *assumed* in any particular program. Think about this for a few minutes and you'll understand why it was necessary.

Yet another was the fact that subtraction was accomplished by automatically taking the nine's complement of the subtrahend and adding the minuend. Nine's complement addition allows for two representations of zero. The first is all zeros, which is "positive" zero. The other is all nines, which is "negative" zero.

Then there were the troubles with round-off and truncation errors that might take place during long mathematical runs.

Dealing with such optimizations, tricks, and foibles became part of a repertoire of *disciplines* that Hopper and her crew began to create and propagate. These were the "rules on the shed wall" that everyone followed.

Meanwhile, the Navy added more and more computational problems to the backlog. The three programmers needed a way to crunch through those problems quickly and efficiently. To drive that point home, Commander Aiken's office was right next to the machine, and he'd raise holy hell if he ever heard the machine stop running or make an unexpected noise.

The task of programming and operating the machine was overwhelming, so they adopted a division-of-labor scheme. Enlisted sailors were added to the team to take over the day-to-day operation of the machine, while the three programmers wrote the code and produced the operating instructions for a given problem.

Those operating instructions were the real program—and they were intense. They represented a symbiosis of human and machine that together executed an algorithm. It worked like this:

Bit 7 of most instructions was the "continue" bit. If set, the machine would continue to the next instruction. If not, the machine would stop.

Instruction 64, however, would only stop the machine if the last computation involving register 72 did not overflow. The team used these stopping mechanisms to break a program up into a series of batches to guide the operation. Notes were written, sometimes on the tape itself but more often on paper, telling the operators what to do when the machine stopped.

If the program had a loop,[13] the machine would stop at the end of each iteration and the operators would be instructed to check the exit condition, and if not met, to back the tape up to the start of the loop, which was generally marked on the tape. The exit condition was determined by the operator's inspection of one or more of the memory registers.

If the program called for a conditional operation, the machine would stop when the condition was ready for the operator to assess, and the operating instructions would tell the operator how to reposition the tape, or perhaps to load an entirely new tape.

Thus, it was the operators who executed the loops and conditionals of the program, while the machine only executed the sequential mathematical instructions.

The operators kept that machine running 24/7, and the programmers were on call 24/7. It was a grueling workload—but there was a war on.

How'd you like to be one of those operators loading tapes, waiting for them to stop, reading the instructions, running up and down the 51-foot length of the machine, inspecting registers, and deciding how to move the tape?

Even worse, how'd you like to be on Hopper's programming crew, turning complex mathematical problems into sequences of holes on paper tapes and complex operating instructions that you hoped were clear enough for bleary-eyed operators to flawlessly interpret?

---

13. Occasionally, the ends of the tape would be connected to form a loop, but this was rare.

Well, don't answer yet, because what if you were working on a problem for which the 72 cells of 23 digits were insufficient? What if you needed to read many batches of data in from punched cards, operate upon each batch, and then punch batches of intermediate results out to other punched cards to be read in at the next stage of the computation?

The sequences of instructions that would eventually be punched on tapes were first written with pencil onto coding sheets. The codes written on those sheets were numeric. The idea of symbolic representation was still years away. To make that endless three-column list of numbers more intelligible, Hopper instituted a commenting discipline and put a column on the coding sheets for those comments.

Once coded and checked, and then rechecked by another programmer, those coding sheets were punched onto tape.

The punching of the tapes was horrifically arduous. Every hole had to be correct. Every hole had to be checked. And so the process was time-consuming to the extreme.

Of course, the programmers did not have time to manually punch the instruction tape themselves, so assistants were appointed to use the punching devices to translate the coding sheets into tapes.

Hopper managed this process, assigning one team to punch a tape and another to check that the punching was correct. Data tapes and cards were managed in a similar way.

Once the tapes were punched and the operating instructions were written, it was time to "test" the program. Small runs with sample inputs were used. This often did not go well. The machine might halt, or jam, or print garbage, or crash. The word *crash* was adopted due to the sound produced by certain failure modes that Hopper said was like an airplane crashing into the building.

At the start of a test, the operators would pull out an Islamic prayer rug, face it east, and pray for success. Then they'd run the test. If anything went wrong, they would write down all the values of the 72 registers, note the failing position of the tape, and send that "dump" back to the programmers to diagnose and propose repairs.

The machine itself was subject to mechanical failures. These were often very subtle. Contacts would corrode; brushes would bend; sometimes even literal bugs would get caught in the machine. One of their better diagnostic tools was Hopper's makeup mirror, which was used to inspect hard-to-see contacts and mechanisms.

Both software and hardware problems were frequently diagnosed by simply listening to the machine as it worked. It was possible to hear when counters incremented or clutches engaged. An operator or programmer intimate with the inner workings of the machine could detect when the machine made the wrong sound at the right time or the right sound at the wrong time.

If test output was produced, the results had to be checked by hand with desk calculators. This could be a lengthy and error-prone process. So Hopper instituted a discipline to use the machine to check itself.[14] They'd write instruction sequences that would check the output more quickly than humans could.

Once the program was working, the final output was typically just a long list of numbers printed on a teleprinter. Humans would then take that printout and interpret it and turn it into reports and documents for other humans to consume. Hopper learned how to use the machine to count page numbers and columns and add spaces and line ends in order to format the output and make the jobs of the humans easier and less prone to error. Commander Aiken was furious that she wasted time on formatting issues, but in the end, she convinced him that formatting saved time and prevented rework.

The machine was impossibly slow. Programs could run for days or weeks. So Hopper and her crew invented pipelining and multiprocessing. For example, the multiplier would take 10 seconds to produce a result. In

---

14. A foreshadowing of TDD (test-driven development).

that time, the machine could execute 30 instructions. So they found ways to use those intervening cycles to prepare the next stage of the problem while the slow operation was running.

This, of course, made the programs much more complicated. Now they had multiple processes running and had to be very careful to count cycles and ensure that the instructions did not interfere with each other.

To make matters worse, some long-running operations would use the bus at particular times in their processing. So the programmers had to carefully time the intervening instructions to avoid bus collisions.

Despite the complexity, and the associated risk, these efforts resulted in throughput improvements of up to 36%. When a program runs for three weeks, that's a pretty significant improvement.

Meanwhile, the flow of jobs never ceased, and they all had to be done yesterday. There was even a special phone connected directly to the Bureau of Ordnance in Washington, D.C. When that phone rang, it usually meant that schedules had to be moved up and deadlines shortened.

The work was so demanding that the crew often missed mess and had to scrounge for food late at night. So Hopper maintained a stockpile of food in the office, which she had one of the enlisted sailors replenish each week.

This was the world that Hopper and her crew worked in. And it was a hellish 24/7 wartime world. Fortunately, they developed and maintained an appropriate discipline so that they did "not lose track of what they were doing."[15] They were able to keep that machine doing productive work with an uptime of 95%.

As a result of the way she organized the team and maintained appropriate disciplines, Commander Aiken eventually put her in charge of the entire Mark I operation.

---

15. Turing's quote in the previous chapter.

SUBROUTINES: 1944–1946

The kinds of jobs that were given to the Mark I were mathematical in nature, and very high in data density. They were asked to create firing tables for ship and land artillery, navigation tables for dates and locations at sea, and a plethora of other such tasks. Of course, this meant that there were many subtasks that these problems had in common.

At first, they simply set aside snippets of code as reference material for future problems. They kept these snippets, also called *routines*, in their individual engineering notebooks. But as time when by, they realized that they could reuse these routines almost verbatim, and so they assembled them into a library.

Of course, these routines operated upon the registers in the Mark I, and in each program, they likely operated on different registers. For example, if there was a snippet that computed *2sin(x)*, that snippet needed to know what register *x* was stored in. In one program it might be register 31, and in another it might be register 42. So the team adopted the convention of basing the registers in their library routines at zero. Thus, when they copied the routines into a program, they simply had to add the "relocatable" addresses in the routine to the actual register base used in the program. They called this "relative coding."

Of course, all this copying and adding was done by hand on coding sheets. Nevertheless, it saved an enormous amount of time. Hopper began to see programs as assemblages of these routines bound together by extra code that we would nowadays call "glue code."

Despite the vast subroutine library they created, the operational limitations were dismaying. Loops were accomplished either by halting and repositioning, or by simply repeating the same segment of code over and over on the tape. Loops and conditionals created an operational workload that was almost unbearable. It came to a head during the war when John von Neumann asked the team to compute the results of the differential equations that described the implosion of the plutonium core of an atomic bomb.

This problem required hundreds of operator interventions and manipulations simply to deal with the loops and conditionals of the problem. In the end, the calculation was successful. But everyone involved, including von Neumann, realized that there had to be a better way.

So, in the summer of 1946, Richard Bloch, Hopper's #2, began work on hardware that would allow the Mark I to read from up to ten different paper tape readers. Instructions were added that would switch from one reader to another and allow the routine in the new reader to execute. The tapes in these extra readers were "relative," and the Mark I took care of relocating the register addresses. Thus, they implemented an online relocatable subroutine library.

But Hopper saw something else. She saw each of the routines as new commands that could be specified by a programmer without worrying about the actual code within those commands. The idea of a "compiler" was starting to germinate in her mind.

The Symposium: 1947

The enforced security and secrecy required by wartime prevented the various teams researching and operating computers from communicating. The ENIAC folks and the Mark I folks had not known of each other during the war. The only point of contact between them was John von Neumann, and he was under strict orders to keep his cards to himself.

But after the war, the veil of secrecy was lifted and the small groups of people involved with computers began to talk to one another.

Aiken now shifted his focus from wartime operation to promotion and public relations. He saw himself as the logical descendant of Charles Babbage, and he saw Hopper as his Ada. Hopper was always eager to please Aiken, and so she took on the role of giving lecture tours to the visiting VIPs. She was good at it. She was a natural educator and an inspiring lecturer. So these tours were very popular.

Aiken saw an opportunity for his Harvard team to lead the way in computing. So he invited researchers and interested parties from academia, business, and the military to a symposium titled "Large Scale Digital Calculating Machinery." In attendance were folks from MIT, Princeton, GE, NCR, IBM, and the Navy. Aiken even invited the grandson of Charles Babbage to give a talk—thus adding weight to his association with Babbage.

Aiken enjoyed being thought of as the "intellectual successor" to Babbage, who had held the Lucasian Chair in Mathematics at Cambridge—the same chair held by Isaac Newton. In later years, however, Hopper would say that Aiken learned of Babbage long after the Mark I was in operation, and thus his invention was not inspired by Babbage.

Aiken introduced the Mark I to the attendees and claimed credit for the design and implementation. He failed to acknowledge IBM in any way. Thomas J. Watson, who was in attendance, was livid—after all, it was IBM that had designed, built, and funded this project. So Watson plotted his revenge.[16]

Despite this faux pas, the symposium was a roaring success. The Mark I was demonstrated. Bloch spoke about the hardware that allowed multiple subroutines and branching. But the real topic of the symposium was—memory.

The ENIAC folks had shown that an electronic computer using vacuum tubes could be kept running, and was at least 5,000 times faster than the Mark I. The problem with the ENIAC, which was pointed out by von Neumann, was that the setup time for the ENIAC took longer than the programming and execution time on the Mark I.

The ENIAC was not programmed in the way that the Mark I was. It was not given a stream of instructions to execute. The ENIAC was programmed the way the analog computers of the day were programmed—with wires and plugboards. This seriously limited what the ENIAC could do in any given run, and it imposed very long reconfiguration times between runs.

16. See Chapter 5. Lorenzo, p. 30.

A problem of the size of von Neumann's implosion calculations would have taken longer on the ENIAC than on the Mark I.

If the ENIAC had been given a paper tape reader of the kind used by the Mark I, the calculation speed of the machine would far outstrip the ability of the paper tape reader to read the instructions. The machine would simply sit and wait for 100 ms or more between instructions, making it only marginally faster than the Mark I.

The solution was clear. Von Neumann had described that solution in June of 1945 in his "First Draft of a Report on EDVAC." The program had to be stored in a memory that was as fast as the computer itself. Since the computer had to have memory to store values, that same memory might as well store the program, too.

But what kind of memory to use? Some folks thought bits could be stored in sound waves of mercury; others thought magnetic drums or electrostatic drums would be best. Even cathode ray tubes and photographic memory were discussed.

But despite all this high-level discussion and deliberation, the "real" conference took place at the bar late at night. Of those alcohol-driven exchanges, Hopper said: "I don't think any [of us] ever stopped talking the whole time. Everybody stayed up all night talking about things. It was just a steady run of conversation."[17]

Much of this unofficial conversation concerned the potential uses for computers. They talked about automated command and control, aeronautics, medicine, insurance, and all manner of business and social applications. They were also concerned about where they were going to find all the programmers they would need.

Aiken didn't buy the memory versus speed argument. He felt the speed of electronics was superfluous and that the future of computing was electromechanical. And so one by one, the people under his command

---

17. Beyer, p. 154.

during the war, and then under his direction after the war, left to find better opportunities elsewhere.

Hopper's loyalty to Aiken was such that she stayed behind for another year or so. But the writing was clearly on the wall. There were several companies building stored-program computers, and many of them started offering her high-paying jobs. She was also getting offers from high-profile users like the Office of Naval Research.

In the summer of 1949, she took a job at a startup named The Eckert and Mauchly Computer Corporation (EMCC), founded by the two inventors of the ENIAC. Their goal was to build the UNIVersal Automatic Computer (UNIVAC).

THE UNIVAC: 1949–1951

When Hopper joined EMCC, there was no UNIVAC yet. The UNIVAC was more than a year away. But they did have a smaller version of the UNIVAC running, called the BINAC. EMCC was making the BINAC for Northrup Aviation. The BINAC was a binary machine. The UNIVAC was to be a *decimal* machine.

The UNIVAC I was built from over 6,000 vacuum tubes, weighed over 7 tons, and consumed 125kW of electricity.

It had 1,000 72-bit words[18] stored in mercury delay lines that had to be kept at a constant temperature of 104°F (40°C). Each word held either two instructions or one 12-character value. Each character was 6 bits and was alphanumeric. A word held a numeric value if all 12 characters were number characters.

The thousands of hot vacuum tubes and the tanks of 104°F mercury filled the unair-conditioned assembly floor with so much heat that the

---

18. Keep your eye out for that number: 72. You may be surprised how often, and in what context, you find it.

workers on the UNIVAC stripped down to shorts and undershirts and frequently had to douse themselves with bottles of water.

Mercury delay lines store bits in the sound waves propagating through a tube of mercury. A speaker deposits bits at one end, and a microphone collects them at the other. Thus, the memory is a rotating sequence of bits, and the fetch time was the average of the rotational latency. This allowed the UNIVAC to execute as many as 1,905 instructions per second.

The arithmetic unit had four registers: rA, rX, rL, and rF. Each could hold a single word, and they were used to hold the operands and results of arithmetic operations. The machine could add two 12-digit numbers in 525 µs, and it could multiply them in 2,150 µs.

The alphanumeric code for decimal digits was encoded in XS-3, which is BCD (binary-encoded decimal) plus 3. Yes, you read that correctly. So 0 = 0011_2, 1 = 0100_2, 5 = 1000_2, and so on. Why XS-3, do you ask? Well, it turns out that the UNIVAC I subtracted by adding the nine's complement, and you can very easily take the nine's complement of XS-3 by simply inverting the bits. Try it and you'll see.

This leaves the minor complication that every addition results in a number that is three too large, so the UNIVAC had to have circuitry to subtract three after every addition. (Don't ask any more questions about this; you'll lose your mind.)

You may think that 1,000 words is not enough to do much, and you'd be right. So the UNIVAC I also had an array of magnetic tape drives that they called UNISERVOs. These drives held tapes with a capacity of 2 million characters (characters were 6 bits—they didn't know about bytes back then). The transfer rate was 1,200 characters per second in blocks of 60 words.

Hopper was hired for her programming and management experience. Of course, this was a startup, and at a startup, everybody does everything. She quickly teamed up with Betty Snyder,[19] one of the original ENIAC

---

19. Frances Elizabeth Snyder Holberton (1917–2001).

programmers. Snyder introduced Hopper to the use of flowcharts to map out program control.

Flowcharts were used because in a stored-program computer, the flow of a program can become very complicated. This is especially true when programs modify their own instructions. Such self-modification was necessary when programming the UNIVAC because the machine did not have indirect addressing.[20]

Without indirect addressing, the only way a program can read through a sequential array of words is to increment the address within the instruction that reads the words. Thus, much of the programmers' efforts were in managing these modified instructions.

The code for the UNIVAC I was written on coding sheets in a semi-mnemonic form. Instructions were six characters (36 bits) wide. The first two characters were the operation, and the last three were a memory address and were interpreted as decimal digits. The third character was not used and was conventionally set to the character 0. In most instructions, the second instruction character was also 0.

Thus, an instruction had the form II0AAA (I for instruction and A for address). The fact that the words held *characters* meant that the operations could have mnemonic significance. Thus, the instruction B00324 caused the processor to Bring the contents of address 324 into both *rA* and *rX*. The instruction H00926 caused the processor to Hold (store) the value of the *rA* in location 926. The C00123 instruction stored the value of the *rA* register in location 123 and Cleared *rA*.

A stood for Add, S for Subtract, M for Multiply, D for Divide, and U for Unconditional Jump. Of course, as every good Emacs user knows, you run out of meaningful letters after a while. So J stood for storing *rX*, X stood for adding *rX* to *rA* (the address was ignored), 5 would print the

---

20. In other words, there was no way to dereference a pointer. You had to modify the address within an instruction.

12 characters in the referenced word, and 9 would halt the machine. And, of course, there were many other instructions.

The programmers would write the instructions on a coding form, but they would write them in pairs because, as you might remember from above, each word held two instructions.

So a program to add the contents of 882, 883, 884, and 885 and store the sum in 886 might look like this:

```
B00882      Bring 882 into rA
    A00883 Add 883 to rA
A00884      Add 884 to rA
    A00885 Add 885 to rA
H00886      Hold rA in 886
    900000 Halt
```

There were quite a few complications that had to do with the internal cycles of the machine. For example, certain instructions had to be executed from position one of a word. So instruction 0 was called *skip*. Today we'd call it nop. It did nothing, and it allowed the programmers to align instructions if need be. Jump instructions always transferred control to the first instruction of the referenced word, so aligning loops and conditionals using *skip* was pretty important.

Here, for example, is an excerpt from the programming manual. See if you can follow it. The ~ is the conventional notation for *skip*.

```
000    500003  ⌣
001    B00000
               A00005
002    C00000
               U00000
003    ΔΔELEC
               TRONIC  ⎫
004    ΔCOMPU          ⎬ Constants
               TER.ΔΔ  ⎭
005    000001
               900000
```

The execution of this coding will print:

ELECTRONIC COMPUTER.

and stop the computer.

OK, I'll help you. The 500003 prints the contents of location 3, which is the string " ELECTRONIC"[21]. Then, ~ skips. The B00000 brings the contents of location 0, which is the 500003 instruction, into *rA*. Then, A00005 adds the contents of location 5, which is 000001900000, to *rA*, causing it to now have the value 500004900000. This value is then stored by the C00000 instruction back into location 0. And finally, the U00000 instruction jumps unconditionally to location 0. But now location 0 has a 500004 as its first instruction, which prints the string " COMPUTER. ", and then the 900000 in the second half of location 0 is executed, which halts the machine.

Got it? Do you understand why that *skip* was necessary? Are you scared yet? You should be.[22]

Anyway, *this* is what Hopper and Snyder were facing, and *this* is why they absolutely needed the help of flowcharts. Of Snyder's help, Hopper said: "She [. . .] got me thinking in another dimension because you see the Mark [I] programs had all been linear."[23]

The UNIVAC I language I just showed you above was affectionately known as C-10. The instruction words were typed on a console that wrote to a magnetic tape. That tape could then be read into the UNIVAC I and executed. Today we would say that the C-10 language was a kind of very primitive assembly language, even though there was no assembler program that converted source to binary. The source and the binary were the same because of the UNIVAC I's convention of storing 12 alphanumeric characters per word.

The use of the mnemonic codes and decimal addresses had a profound effect upon Hopper. Writing A for Add instead of remembering and writing the numeric codes used by the Mark I made programming so

---

21. There was no lowercase in those days.

22. I'm channeling Yoda.

23. Beyer, p. 193.

much easier. She said: "I felt as if I'd acquired all of the freedom and all of the pleasures of the world; the instruction code was beautiful."[24]

I don't know if you think the above code is beautiful. If you do, I think medical attention might be necessary. But it's not hard to see why Hopper, coming from the extreme austerity of the Mark I, thought so.

After learning flowcharting and C-10, Hopper's role was to manage a team of programmers to write a library of useful subroutines and applications for the UNIVAC I—a machine that did not yet exist. This is where her experience with the subroutine library of the Mark I, and the strategy of using relative addressing, paid off in spades. Now it wasn't just the addresses of 72 registers that had to be managed; it was the 1,000 words that included the addresses of the instructions themselves. Keeping all the subroutines relative was utterly essential to maintaining sanity.

Remember, these subroutines were manually copied into the code by the programmers. All that relative addressing had to be resolved by hand.

The BINAC machine was available to test some of these subroutines, but it was a very different machine. It had 512 words of 30 bits, and did all its math in binary. The 30-bit words were not organized into 6-bit alphanumeric characters, so the instructions were numeric codes rather than alphanumeric mnemonics.

Nevertheless, Hopper's team would write the C-10 subroutines and then translate them to the BINAC, and test them there.

Of course, the BINAC machine was still in production. I doubt they had it at their immediate disposal, and likely had to negotiate "time on the machine" with everyone else who was trying to get the machine ready to ship to Northrup. Shipping the machine probably took priority over the testing of a subroutine library whose application was a year away.

---

24. Beyer, p. 194.

Nevertheless, the sheer workload of preparing this library for the UNIVAC I convinced Hopper that she had a significant labor shortage. There just weren't enough good programmers[25] out there. So she decided she was going to have to *create* them.

Hopper and Mauchly worked together to create *aptitude tests*. They agreed upon 12 desirable and three essential characteristics that might make a good programmer. These included rather obvious traits such as creativity and careful reasoning. Slowly they began to train and add programmers to their team.

SORTING, AND THE BEGINNING OF COMPILERS

Meanwhile, Betty Snyder had a breakthrough. The IBM salespeople at this time were telling the industry that computers could not sort records on magnetic tape, because you can't move things around on magnetic tape the way you can move cards. So Snyder wrote the first merge sort program that sorted records on magnetic tape.

She worked this algorithm out by sorting cards on the floor and mapping them to the management of the several UNISERVO tape units connected to the UNIVAC I.[26]

Then, she hit on an idea that had deeply profound implications. Sorting is parameter driven. If you are going to sort a bunch of records, you need to know the location and size of the fields that contain the sort keys, and the direction of the sort. So Snyder wrote a program that would take these parameters and then (wait for it . . . wait for it . . .) *generate* a program that would sort those records.

That's right, boys and girls, she wrote the first program that wrote another program based on parameters. In some sense, this was the

---

25. Mathematicians of ability, as Turing had said.

26. She actually got this working on the BINAC first.

first ever compiler. It compiled sorting parameters into a sorting program.

This got Hopper thinking.

ALCOHOL: CIRCA 1949

The years around 1949 were tough ones for Hopper. She was a middle-aged woman who had left everything behind, including a career and a husband, to enter a new and volatile field at a risky startup. That startup, EMCC, was not doing well. Finances were sketchy at best, and bankruptcy was never far away. Contracts were late and vastly underfunded. EMCC underestimated the cost of building a UNIVAC by a factor of three or more.

In the end, the company was bought at an extreme discount by Remington Rand, whose director of advanced research, Leslie Groves,[27] thought that the entire concept was unproven and unreliable.

The stress took its toll on Hopper, who badly relapsed into alcoholism. The first woman to graduate from Yale with a doctorate in math, one of the first female naval officers, and a gifted pioneer and senior executive in the field of computer programming was reduced to hiding bottles of booze around the office.

Her addiction was impossible to hide. Whispers about her "hitting the bottle" circulated around the office and between friends and acquaintances. Indeed, sometimes her drinking episodes were so severe and left her so debilitated that she had to beg friends to stay with her until she recovered.

As the cold weather of '49 closed in, she was arrested for public intoxication and disorderly conduct. She was committed to Philadelphia General Hospital, and was eventually released into the custody of a friend. She contemplated suicide.

---

27. Yeah, THAT Leslie Groves. You know: the general who oversaw the Manhattan Project.

Edmund Berkeley, the friend who took custody, wrote an open intervention letter to Hopper. He sent it to some of her friends, and also to her boss, John Mauchly. In that letter, he states:

> "I and many other people know full well what a wonderful intellectual and emotional endowment you have. Even when you function properly only 70 percent of the time. . .I can see in my minds eye the marvelous things you could accomplish with the 30 percent of the rest of your time (now wasted). . ."[28]

COMPILERS: 1951–1952

How do you sell a computer to someone who hasn't got a clue what a computer is? How do you convince them to pay millions of dollars for something that will then require them to spend millions more on the programmers who just might get the thing to work? And where are they supposed to find those egghead programmers in the first place?

If you followed my discussion of the C-10 language in the last section, you likely see the problem. Programming in that language would require "a great number of mathematicians of ability," and such people don't grow on trees.

Despite that, there were customers galore. By 1950, everyone could see the power and benefit of these machines, but nobody had the slightest idea how to use them. And this included the salespeople at Remington Rand, who had just purchased EMCC. Those salesmen had no clue about these machines, and were very reluctant to even mention them to their customers.

One customer said that the only way to get a UNIVAC salesperson to talk to him was to take him out and buy him a drink.[29]

---

28. Beyer, p. 207.

29. Beyer, p. 217.

To make matters worse, when a sale was made, Hopper's team was raided in order to help the new customer write the programs that they needed.

Nobody had understood the amount of labor required to support the customers of these machines. Hopper herself was frequently called upon to spend time with the customers, instructing them on the disciplines required to create functioning software.

In what little spare time she could find, Betty Snyder's sort generator tickled at the back of her mind. If a program could generate another program from a set of parameters, is there a more general-purpose set of parameters from which a program could generate another? Could a computer be *taught* to automatically generate programs?

In May of 1952, she presented a paper[30] to the ACM.[31] The paper was titled "The Education of a Computer," and it coined the term *automatic programming*. Automatic programming is the use of a computer to translate higher-level languages into executable code. Or, in other words, it's what we all do today. We are all automatic programmers.

In this paper, Hopper outlined the idea. She wrote: "It is the current aim to replace, as far as possible, the human brain by an electronic digital computer." This statement was not surprising to the audience, nor should it be to us. We all use computers to replace human brains—though perhaps *replace* is not the right word. A better word might be *relieve*.

We all use computers to relieve us from the drudgery of using our brains for mundane and repetitive work. Who wants to multiply two 6-digit numbers without the aid of a calculator?

But in the paper, Hopper takes this idea to a deeper level. She says that the computer removes the *arithmetic* chore from the mathematician,

---

30. See this chapter's References section.

31. Association for Computing Machinery, an organization she had helped to form and lead just a few years before.

replacing it with the chore of writing the program. While this can be stimulating at first, the "novelty wears off and degenerates into the dull labor of writing and checking programs."

She then says "common sense dictates [that] the programmer return to being a mathematician." She says this will be possible by providing the mathematician with a "catalogue of subroutines" that the mathematician can simply weave together to solve the problem at hand. (Months later she would call that woven specification *pseudocode*.) She says that the computer could then execute a "compiling routine" that would take the subroutines specified by the mathematician and produce the program that the mathematician desired. She called this a "compiling routine of type A."

And then she blew everyone's mind by saying that there could obviously be compiling routines of type B that would take even higher-level specifications and compile them down to type A. And then there could be type C compilers that would produce type B code.

She was on a roll.

In that one paper, in 1952, she described the entire future of computer languages.

Now, if you read her paper, you'll see that she had set her sights for a type A compiler pretty low. The "mathematician" would specify the subroutines using numeric codes, and would have to properly arrange the arguments and outputs. You and I would still consider that to be programming drudgery. But to her, and to the programmers of the day, it was revolutionary. She talked about how programs could be constructed in hours instead of weeks.

THE TYPE A COMPILERS

And thus, Hopper and her team began work on version 0 of the type A compiler: A-0. A few months later it was running.

So she ran a timing comparison between one programmer using A-0 and a team of experienced programmers just writing raw C-10 code. The problem was to produce a table of results for the simple mathematical function $y=exp(-x)*sin(x/2)$.

Using raw C-10 required three programmers working for a little over 14.5 hours (~44 man-hours). Using A-0, a single programmer got the job done in 48.5 minutes. That's a factor of over 50!

You'd think that a comparison like this would have everybody clamoring to throw money at Hopper and get a copy of A-0. Not so. Not nearly so. And for two reasons.

First, the programs produced by A-0 were slower than raw C-10 programs by a factor of 30% or so. This may not seem like a lot, but when computer time rents for hundreds of dollars per hour, everybody wants very fast execution times. Keep in mind that, back then, computer time cost at least ten times more than programmer time.

When the cost analysis considered the lifetime of a program, it turned out that hiring a programming team to code raw C-10 was cheaper than using one programmer to write A-0.

Second, programmers feared that compilers like A-0 might put them out of work. If you only need 1/50th the number of programmers, there are going to be a lot of hungry programmers out on the streets.

But Hopper wasn't done. Over the next few months, she and her team created A-1, and then A-2. These were refinements that made the pseudocode (the source code) easier and less cumbersome—although to us it would still look impossibly primitive. The language used alphanumeric "call numbers" for the subroutines and still followed the 12-character C-10 word format. It was as though she thought of the type A compiler as just a machine executing instructions—a kind of better UNIVAC-I rather than an actual language.

For example, APN000006012 raises the value in location 0 to the power in location 6, and stores the result in location 12. What does APN stand for? I think it stands for Arithmetic-Power-N. Similarly, AA0 is Arithmetic-Add, AS0 is Arithmetic-Subtract, and I guess you can figure out what AM0 and AD0 are for. All of these are three address instructions of the form IIIAAABBBCCC. The III is the instruction code, whereas the AAA, BBB, and CCC are memory addresses.[32] Generally, the operation would involve AAA and BBB and would produce the result in CCC.

There were lots of instructions like this. The TS0, TC0, TT0, and TAT were trigonometric functions corresponding to sine, cosine, tangent, and arctangent. The HS0, HC0, and HT0 were the hyperbolic trig functions. The SQR was square root, the LAU was log, and so on.

From Hopper's point of view, this was a breakthrough development. It was cutting-edge stuff. She was compiling the calls to subroutines, which had taken her months and years to create, into short and effective programs in a fraction of the time.

Look at the code you write, and notice that it is, for the most part, just an assemblage of calls to functions that call other functions that call yet other functions. What we think of as the function call tree had not, at the time, been conceived; but it was not to be long in coming.

LANGUAGES: 1953–1956

It was at this point that Hopper began to see a new possibility. She realized that pseudocode did not need to be related to the computer hardware.

There was no need to keep being enslaved by the UNIVAC-I's 12-character word. She also realized that different contexts required different symbology. While *sin* and *cos* made sense to mathematicians, different

---

32. No one had yet thought of naming variables—or if they did, they didn't think they could afford the storage.

symbols might make sense to accountants or businesses. She was beginning to see that programming could be a *language—a human language.*

Hopper was not working alone on this. She had built up a network of experts in many different companies and disciplines, and she encouraged active debate and conversation. Innovation flourished in this environment.

Remington Rand management was not interested in the innovation of languages. From their point of view, computers did math, not language, so the whole idea was ridiculous.

Meanwhile, the labor shortage problems continued to worsen. Programmers were hard to find and even harder to train. The cost of writing and maintaining C-10 programs continued to skyrocket with each new computer installation.

In 1953 a very frustrated Grace Hopper wrote a report[33] for the executives of Remington Rand, demanding a budget for compiler development as a way to get ahead of the labor issues and to create an environment in which computers could be used to give managers information.

This latter point was revolutionary. It had not occurred to most executives in the early 1950s that a computer could be used to gather and collate data so quickly that they could use it to make timely market, sales, and operations decisions. But Hopper drove home the point that this revolution in management information would be impossible without compilers.

She concluded her report with a demand for a large budget and 100% dedication of her staff to continue working on A-3. And the executives bowed to that demand. She became the director of the Automatic Programming Department at Remington Rand.

Hopper's management style was collaborative and encouraging. She valued creativity and innovation. She supported playfulness in solutions.

---

33. Beyer, p. 243.ff.

She delegated responsibility and allowed subordinates to be self-directed. And over it all, she maintained the vision of what computing would be.

In May of 1954, Hopper organized a Symposium on Automatic Programming. There, she saw two young men from MIT, Neil Zierler and J. Halcombe Laning Jr., talk about their *algebraic compiler*. This was a program that translated mathematical formulae into executable code. John Backus was there for this presentation, and ironically discounted it— equating the work with insanity. But the scales fell from Hopper's eyes.[34]

The demonstration of the simple translation of algebraic formula to code convinced Hopper that much, much more was possible. She was convinced that the right language could open computing to a much wider audience.

As a result, she directed her team to start using algebraic formulae and English words instead of the 12-character UNIVAC I format. This new language, named MATH-MATIC, was a type B compiler that compiled down into A-3. Hopper also appeased the lower-level programmers by allowing it to accept direct A-3 statements as well as C-10.

As you might imagine, once you are working in a language like that, 1,000 words of memory can start to seem like a pretty small place to live. So Hopper's team invented an overlay scheme that shuttled parts of the program on and off magnetic tape. This was not speedy, but it mitigated the memory constraints.

Fortunately, the Navy had recently revealed the work they had done on core memory,[35] and the industry very rapidly shifted.

Compared to mercury delay lines, CRT memory, and drum memory, core memory is *fast*. The access time is measured in microseconds, and the access is entirely random. Core was not cheap back then, but the speed

---

34. Acts 9:18.

35. See *core memory* in the Glossary of Terms.

and access method made computers 100 times more powerful than they were before. What's more, core memory was relatively small, and low power. A lot of memory could fit into a small space.

Even with faster computers, computer time was still very expensive. Compilers like MATH-MATIC, while making programs much easier to write, also made programs a lot slower. The advantage was still to the raw machine language programmers.

In 1954 a properly chastened John Backus, along with Harlan Herrick and Irving Ziller, set out to create a new language. They invited the young MIT duo, Lanning and Zierler, to demonstrate their algebraic compiler. The demo was terrifying because the generated code was *ten times* slower than code produced by a machine language programmer.

But Backus was no longer deterred. In November of 1954, he submitted his proposal for FORTRAN to his boss at IBM. As we shall learn in a later chapter, it took a team of 12 programmers 30 months to create a working compiler.

FORTRAN rose in popularity above MATH-MATIC, mostly due to the weight of IBM. Sales of IBM's 704 computers had vastly surpassed Remington Rand's UNIVAC computers. The wind was at IBM's back, and it would stay there for at least three decades.

But Hopper was already a step ahead. Her sights were set on something very different from FORTRAN. For her, the target was *business*, and the language should be one that businesspeople would be comfortable with.

COBOL: 1955–1960

The number of companies manufacturing computers proliferated rapidly. Hopper realized that languages like FORTRAN and MATH-MATIC allowed programs to be portable. A payroll system written for one machine could be made to execute on another with no, or minimal, alteration.

But Hopper felt that the algebraic form of MATH-MATIC and FORTRAN had been created by people like her: mathematicians and scientists. She feared that the algebraic syntax of those languages was a barrier to a much larger market: business. She did not believe that businesspeople spoke the language of higher mathematics, and she felt they were unaccustomed to the symbology that mathematicians used. So she set her sights on the language of business. And that language was . . . English.

This decision was not made lightly. She and her team studied the way the business departments of UNIVAC users wrote about their problems. They discovered that different departments used different shortcuts and abbreviations, and that the only common denominator was simple straightforward English. They also realized that long names, as opposed to algebraic variables like x and y, would allow business programmers to more directly say what they mean.

In a 1955 management report to Remington Rand titled "The Preliminary Definition of a Data Processing Compiler," she wrote that businesspeople would rather see:

```
MULTIPLY BASE-PRICE AND DISCOUNT-PERCENT GIVING DISCOUNT-PRICE
```

than:

```
A x B = C
```

Hopper and her team then began work on B-0, a language based upon English. As she worked with the language, it became clear that an abstract language that hides the details of the machine from the programmers allows the programmers to collaborate much more freely. The compiler takes on the burden of managing the details, vastly reducing the communication burden between programmers and even between teams.

Customers of the UNIVAC started using B-0 in early 1958. It spread to customers like US Steel, Westinghouse, and the Navy, and was renamed FLOW-MATIC by the marketing department of Sperry Rand.[36]

Selling this language was not easy. Businesses liked it well enough, but programmers remained skeptical.

However, Hopper had spent the better part of a decade nurturing and expanding her network of connections with programmers and users. Hopper also apparently understood that the way to programmers' hearts was to give them code. So she freely distributed the code for the compiler, and wrote manuals and papers in support. Many programmers responded by sending her fixes and extensions to the language.

To facilitate the communications within her network and in other networks of programmers, she worked with the newly formed ACM to create the first Glossary of Terms for the computer industry. This Glossary includes terms that we still use today. It even defines *bit*.[37]

FLOW-MATIC saw success with UNIVAC customers, but IBM was working on a competitor that it named COMTRAN, and the military was working on a language called AIMACO. There was a significant fear that a Tower of Babel was being built and that the industry needed a common language.[38]

By 1959, businesses were really starting to feel how quickly the cost of programming was growing. And the consensus was that a common language would greatly reduce both the cost of initial development and the cost of migrating systems to the rapidly changing and advancing hardware.

Hopper led the charge on this effort. Her first target was the military. At the time, the DoD was operating over 200 computers from various manufacturers

---

36. Sperry Gyroscope merged with Remington Rand in 1955.

37. But not *byte*. That was yet to come.

38. And perhaps we still do.

and had nearly that many more on order. The sheer cost of software development had exceeded $200 million. She convinced Charles Phillips, the DoD's director of Data Systems Research, that a portable business language that was hardware agnostic was his solution. With his backing, she formed the Conference on Data Systems and Languages (CODASYL), the first meeting of which was held in the spring of 1959 at the DoD.

This meeting was attended by 40 representatives from government agencies, corporations, and computer manufacturers. The names included Sperry Rand, IBM, RCA, GE, NCR, and Honeywell, to mention just a few.

Of this meeting, Hopper said: "I don't think ever before or ever since have I seen in one room so much power to commit men and monies."[39]

This group decided on a set of constraints for the new language. They included the following:

- Maximum use of English
- Ease of use above programming power
- Machine independent and portable
- Easy to train new programmers

It would not be hard to find some fault with this list, but we'll leave that for another section. Meanwhile, the group vehemently disagreed about algebraic notation. One faction thought that mathematical symbols were natural, even for businesses. The other was adamant that even basic operators like multiplication and addition should be spelled out in English.

Hopper was in the latter group, and when this issue came to a head some weeks later, she threatened to back out of the group altogether if mathematical symbols were accepted into the language.

---

39. Beyer, p. 285.

Hopper was usually someone who worked to find compromise and collegiality. This power play seems very out of character for her. It must have been something that she felt very strongly about. Looking back, it's not at all clear she should have.

Hopper won that battle—at least in the short term. And the language committee hammered out the Common Business Oriented Language (COBOL).

COBOL was a hybrid of many different languages and ideas. FLOW-MATIC played a big role, but much was drawn from IBM's COMTRAN, and the Air Force's AIMACO, which had been derived from FLOW-MATIC.

The first successful compilation of a COBOL program took place on August 17, 1960.

My COBOL Rant

I have used many computer languages. I've written in a dozen different assemblers. I've used FORTRAN, PL/1, SNOBOL, BASIC, FOCAL, ALCOM, C, C++, Java, C#, F#, Smalltalk, Lua, Forth, Prolog, Clojure, and many dozens of others. I have never hated[40] a language more than COBOL. It is a *horrible* language. It is wordy to the point of being mind-numbing. It is ponderous to write and even worse to read. It makes a program look like a military report. It separates things that should be together and puts together things that should be separated. In every way, the language is an abomination.

I believe the rampant success of the language was driven by corporate politics rather than technical excellence. Indeed, Hopper consciously and specifically kept programmers from significantly influencing the language and gave preference to users and managers. And it shows.

---

40. . . . unless it was XSLT.

I find this astounding, since Hopper was a programmer par excellence. I can only assume that she thought that the industry would never be able to find, or create, enough programmers who approached her level of intelligence. So she had to dumb down the language to a nearly moronic common denominator.

AN UNMITIGATED SUCCESS

Despite my hatred for the language, it succeeded. And it succeeded beyond all expectations. By the year 2000, it was estimated that 80% of all code written to that date was COBOL.

Hopper went on to have a successful and colorful career. She remained the director of Automatic Programming Development of the UNIVAC division of Sperry Rand until 1965. She continued on as a senior staff scientist, and she became a visiting associate professor at the University of Pennsylvania. She spent another 20 years working as director of the Navy Programming Languages Group.

In 1973 she was promoted to captain. From 1977 to 1983, she was assigned to the Naval Data Automation Headquarters in Washington, D.C., to monitor the state of the art in computing. At the urging of the House of Representatives, President Ronald Reagan promoted her to the rank of commodore—a rank that was later renamed to rear admiral.

In 1986 Rear Admiral Grace Hopper retired from the Navy as the oldest active officer in that service. Digital Equipment Corporation then hired her as a senior consultant. She held that position until her death, at age 85, in 1992.

Over her life, she received many awards, including the Defense Distinguished Service Medal, Legion of Merit, Meritorious Service Medal, and Presidential Medal of Freedom (posthumously).

In 1969 the Data Processing Management Association named her the first ever Computer Sciences "Man of the Year."

REFERENCES

Association for Computing Machinery. 1954. *First Glossary of Programming Terminology*. Committee on Nomenclature, ACM.

Beyer, Kurt W. 2009. *Grace Hopper and the Invention of the Information Age*. MIT Press.

Computer History Archives Project ("CHAP"). "Harvard Secret Computer Lab - Grace Hopper, Howard Aiken, Harvard Mark 1, 2 , 3 rare IBM Calculators," 13:55. Posted on YouTube on June 2, 2024. (Available at the time of writing.)

Eckert-Mauchly Computer Corp. 1949. "The BINAC." http://archive .computerhistory.org/resources/text/Eckert_Mauchly/EckertMauchly .BINAC.1949.102646200.pdf.

Harvard College. 1946. *A Manual of Operation for the Automatic Sequence Controlled Calculator*. Staff of the Computation Laboratory. Harvard University Press. https://chsi.harvard.edu/harvard-ibm-mark-1-manual.

Hopper, Grace Murray. 1952. *The Education of a Computer*. Remington Rand Corp.

Lorenzo, Mark Jones. 2019. *The History of the Fortran Programming Language*. SE Books.

Remington Rand. 1957. *Preliminary Manual for MATH-MATIC and ARITH-MATIC Systems for Algebraic Translation and Compilation for Univac I and II*. http://archive.computerhistory.org/resources/access/text/2016/06 /102724614-05-01-acc.pdf.

Remington Rand, Eckert-Mauchly Division, Programming Research Section. 1955. "Automatic Programming: The A 2 Compiler System, Part 2." *Computers and Automation* 4, no. 110: 15–28. https://archive.org/details /sim_computers-and-people_1955-10_4_10/page/16/mode/2up.

Ridgway, Richard K. n.d. "Compiling Routines." Remington Rand, Eckert-Mauchly Division. https://dl.acm.org/doi/pdf/10.1145/800259.808980.

Sperry Rand Corporation. 1959. "Basic Programming, UNIVAC I Data Automation System." www.bitsavers.org/pdf/univac/univac1/UNIVAC1 _Programming_1959.pdf.

Wikipedia. "UNIVAC I." https://en.wikipedia.org/wiki/UNIVAC_I.

Wilkes, Maurice V., David J. Wheeler, and Stanely Gill. 1957. *The Preparation of Programs for an Electronic Digital Computer*, 2nd ed. Addison-Wesley.

John Backus:
The First High-
Level Language

Most of us have known someone who is very smart but is devoid of ambition and direction. They live, day to day, gliding through life by breaking the rules through guile and feigned innocence. They aren't bad people; they just don't seem to care where they are going or how they will get there. The future is just not their concern.

And then one day a switch gets thrown and they suddenly become directed, productive, and motivated. They start to shine like a crazy diamond.

That was John Backus.

John Backus, the Man

John Warner Backus was born December 3, 1924. He grew up well-off as the son of Cecil F. Backus: a self-taught, self-made chemist who managed a group of nitroglycerine factories for Atlas Powder Company and eventually determined that the reason the factories kept blowing up was the faulty thermometers the company had been buying from Germany.

John's family life was less than satisfactory.[1] His father was unpleasant and aloof. His mother, who died before he turned 9, may have sexually

---

1. Lorenzo, p. 23.

abused[2] him. His stepmother was a neurotic alcoholic who sometimes yelled at passersby from her window.

As an adolescent, John was a bully who enjoyed mistreating his peers. He was eventually sent to a boarding school,[3] where he proceeded to goof around and break as many rules as he could. He repeatedly flunked out and was therefore kept in summer school, where he spent his time sailing and having a nice time. He seldom returned home.

Despite his low grades, he managed to graduate, and he enrolled at the University of Virginia. He took chemistry at his father's urging, but he didn't complete the lab work and seldom went to his classes, preferring to go to parties instead. He was eventually expelled.

It was 1943, and so he was drafted into the Army and stationed at Fort Stewart in Georgia. It was an Army aptitude test that began to change everything. He aced it. So the Army sent him to learn engineering at the University of Pittsburgh.

---

2. An LSD-induced suspicion that grew when he was in his 60s.

3. The Hill School in Pottstown, PA.

He breezed through the pre-engineering courses, spending much of his time at bars—but not to the exclusion of his studies, which he had begun to enjoy.

Yet another aptitude test convinced the Army that he was doctor material, and he was sent to study medicine at Haverford College, where he did very well indeed.

As part of the medical training, he interned for 12 hours a day at a hospital in Atlantic City. But after some months, a bump on his head was diagnosed as a slow-growing tumor—the removal of which left a hole in his skull covered by badly fitting metal plates. This relieved him of his internship duties and led to an honorable medical discharge from the Army in 1946.

After his discharge, in order to put some distance between himself and his family, he enrolled in a medical school in New York City. While there, he helped design a better-fitting replacement for the plate in his head. But he found medical school disappointing. He detested all the rote, brute-force memorization, and eventually he bailed out.

And so he was once again directionless—or nearly so. His one remaining interest was in building a hi-fi.[4] So he used the GI Bill to wrangle a slot in a radio technology school. And there he met "the first good teacher" he had ever had.[5]

With that teacher's help, Backus realized that he really liked math—and was pretty good at it too. So he enrolled in the graduate program for mathematics at Columbia University.

COLORED LIGHTS THAT HYPNOTIZE

In the spring of 1949, while studying for his master's at Columbia, he chanced upon "an interesting thing." A friend of his had told him to

4. A high-fidelity, often stereo, music system. Typically based on a record player and perhaps a radio.

5. Lorenzo, p. 24.

check out the IBM Selective Sequence Electronic Calculator (SSEC) situated in the IBM showroom on Madison Avenue.

This machine, with its flashing lights and clickety-clacking relays, set the standard for what a computer should look and sound like for decades thereafter. Think of the computer on *Star Trek*, or *Forbidden Planet*'s Robby.

The SSEC was Thomas J. Watson's revenge for being slighted by Howard Aiken at the symposium that presented the Harvard Mark I to the world. The SSEC was Watson's way of stealing Aiken's thunder.[6]

It was a massive conglomeration of 21,000 relays and 12,500 vacuum tubes. It was a Frankenstein's monster of a machine composed of electronic registers, relay registers, and memory punched on paper tape. Instructions were generally executed from paper tape, but could also be executed from either the electronic or relay memory registers. The registers were 76 bits wide, encoding 19 BCD (binary-encoded decimal) digits. The add time was 285 μs and the multiply time was 20 ms. From paper tape, it could execute ~50 instructions per second.

Although some instructions could be stored in and executed from its registers, it was not really a stored-program computer.

The machine was not meant to be sold, nor even reproduced. For the most part, it was just Watson's thumb in Aiken's eye. It was used in much the same way the Mark I was used and in the way Babbage had envisioned his machines to be used: for calculating tables.

Over the four years of its life, it calculated lunar ephemeris tables and did calculations for GE and for the Atomic Energy Commission. The latter used it for the NEPA[7] project—powering aircraft with nuclear engines. It was also used for studies in laminar flow and for Monte Carlo[8] modeling.

---

6. Lorenzo, p. 30.

7. Nuclear Energy for the Propulsion of Aircraft.

8. See *Monte Carlo analysis* in the Glossary of Terms.

In the end, however, it seems to me that IBM derived the most benefit from that ground-floor showroom on Madison Avenue displaying the impressive machine with its massive spools of paper tape, huge cabinets of vacuum tubes, futuristic console with all the blinking lights, and incessant chattering of its relays.

Backus was impressed by the flashing lights, the clacking relays, and the obvious power of the machine. So, upon graduating from Columbia with a master's in mathematics, he walked into the IBM office and asked for a job—and miraculously, they gave him one. He was to be one of the programmers of the SSEC—a job that he would later describe as "hand-to-hand combat."

The man who hired him was Robert Rex Seeber, Jr. Remember that Seeber had been hired by Howard Aiken to work on the Mark I. But the two did not get along well, probably because Seeber had requested some well-earned vacation time before starting. Aiken denied that request. Seeber worked long, hard hours for Aiken, but the mood between the two never healed, and became so sour that Seeber quit as soon as the war was over and took a job at IBM to design the SSEC. It seems that he and Watson both had the same goal when it came to getting even with Howard Aiken.

On the day Backus was hired, he had not yet begun job hunting and was just being shown around the IBM facility by a services representative. He offhandedly asked her if IBM was hiring, and she set up an immediate interview with Seeber. So Backus, unprepared and unkempt, sat down with the inventor of the SSEC. Seeber had Backus solve some mathematical puzzles, and he hired him on the spot as an SSEC programmer. Backus had no idea what that meant.

Programming the SSEC was much like programming the Mark I. The minutiae were different, of course, but the two machines were of a kind: mammoth decimal calculators driven by sequential instructions meticulously punched on paper tape.[9] It was hard, complicated, laborious, and intellectually strenuous work, but for two years, Backus loved it. The hook was set. Backus was a programmer.

SPEEDCODING AND THE 701

With the onset of the Korean War, IBM targeted the computing needs of the military/industrial complex. In 1952 the company announced "The Defense Calculator," aka the IBM 701, its first mass-produced[10] large computer. This was the machine that John Backus faced next.

The 701 was entirely electronic, employing ~4,000 vacuum tubes. It was also a stored-program machine, using 72 electrostatic Williams tubes[11] holding 1,024 bits each. The word size was 36 bits, so the machine could store 2,048 words. This was expandable to 4,096 by adding a second bank of 72 Williams tubes. These tubes could read and write memory in cycles of 12 μs, giving the machine an add time of ~60 μs and a multiply time of ~456 μs. Overall, the machine could execute ~14,000 instructions per second.

---

9. Similar to how the Mark I iteration could be created by gluing the two ends of the paper tape together into a loop. Backus described one incident when a half-twist was inadvertently added, turning the loop into a Möbius strip. Debugging *that* was a challenge!

10. They built 20 to 30 of these machines.

11. See *Williams tube (CRT) memory* in the Glossary of Terms.

Peripherals included drum and tape memory, a printer, and a card reader/punch. The machine rented for $15,000 per month.

The machine had a single 36-bit accumulator register, and another 36-bit multiplier/quotient register. Instructions were 18 bits wide with a sign bit, a 5-bit opcode, and a 12-bit address.

Why would an instruction have a sign? I'm glad you asked that question. You see, the machine was half-word addressable. That is, every 18-bit half-word in electrostatic memory was addressable. However, every full word was also addressable. An even negative address referred to a full word.

An even positive address referred to the left half-word at that address, and the adjacent odd address referred to the right half-word.

If the second bank of Williams tubes were installed, a special "trigger" bit had to be set under program control to specify that bank. Simple, huh?

The machine used binary math, but the data were stored as sign/magnitude rather than two's complement or one's complement. Thus, the lower 35 bits of a word was the absolute value of the number. This, of course, meant that there were both positive and negative zeros.

The 701 had no index registers and no means of indirect addressing. If you wanted to index through memory, you had to write programs that modified the instructions that accessed memory.

Data were entered into the 701 either through the front panel switches or from the first 72[12] columns of punched cards. Each of the 12 rows on a punched card contains 72 bits, so a card could contain twenty-four 36-bit words.

The 701 was designed for the kind of scientific and mathematical work needed by the military. Its job was to calculate ballistics, firing solutions,

---

12. Did you ever wonder why the last eight columns of an 80-column card were unused? It's because the 701 could read two 36-bit words from the first 72 columns.

navigation tables, and the like. Therefore, much of the work that Backus had to do was numerical, and necessarily involved fractions. But the 701 used fixed-point math. Keeping track of the decimal point was the programmer's job.

There was no compiler, and only the most primitive of assemblers for the 701. So Backus had to punch cards that corresponded to the numeric instructions that a simple loader program could properly read.

The sheer dreadful tedium of this task eventually drove Backus[13] to write a new kind of program. He called it *Speedcoding*, and gave the following justification:

> "It was pure laziness. Writing programs was a big drag—you had to have enormous detail and deal with things that you shouldn't have to. So I wanted to make it easier."[14]

Speedcoding was a floating-point interpreter that consumed 310 words of memory. It divided the remaining memory into about seven hundred 72-bit words. Each could contain either a 72-bit floating-point number or a 72-bit instruction. Each instruction was split into two operations: one mathematical and one logical. The mathematical operations used three addresses and the logical operation used another. The latter was often a jump or conditional jump, but it could also increment or decrement *index registers*.

Yes, index registers! Backus's virtual machine had real indirect addressing controlled by index registers. Walking through a list of numbers did not require the programmer to modify instructions!

There were a number of IO operations that drastically increased the convenience of printing, reading and writing cards, and storing data on drum or tape.

---

13. Under the direction of John Sheldon, Backus supervised the team that built Speedcoding.

14. Lorenzo, p. 49.

Backus even implemented a simple logging/tracing system with three different levels of tracing. This drastically reduced debug time.

On the down side, the syntax was still very strongly related to an assembler and tied to punched cards. The cards had fixed fields for the decimal addresses, flags, and symbolic operation codes.

PROGRAM LABEL	CONTROL	LOCA-TION	ALPHA-BETIC OP$_2$	R CODE	A AD-DRESS	B AD-DRESS	C AD-DRESS	ALPHA-BETIC OP$_2$	D AD-DRESS	L CODE	NU-BETIC OP$_1$	NU-BETIC OP$_1$	REMARKS	IBM 701 SPEEDCODING SYSTEM INSTRUCTION CARD
00000000	0	0000	00000	0	00000	0000	0000	00000	0000	00	000	000	0000	0000000000000000000000000000
11111111	1	1111	11111	1	11111	1111	1111	11111	1111	11	111	111	1111	1111111111111111111111111111
22222222	2	2222	22222	2	22222	2222	2222	22222	2222	22	222	222	2222	2222222222222222222222222222
33333333	3	3333	33333	3	33333	3333	3333	33333	3333	33	333	333	3333	3333333333333333333333333333
44444444	4	4444	44444	4	44444	4444	4444	44444	4444	44	444	444	4444	4444444444444444444444444444
55555555	5	5555	55555	5	55555	5555	5555	55555	5555	55	555	555	5555	5555555555555555555555555555
66666666	6	6666	66666	6	66666	6666	6666	66666	6666	66	666	666	6666	6666666666666666666666666666
77777777	7	7777	77777	7	77777	7777	7777	77777	7777	77	777	777	7777	7777777777777777777777777777
88888888	8	8888	88888	8	88888	8888	8888	88888	8888	88	888	888	8888	8888888888888888888888888888
99999999	9	9999	99999	9	99999	9999	9999	99999	9999	99	999	999	9999	9999999999999999999999999999

IBM 830521

Worse still, the interpreter was slow. Addition required 4 ms. Even a simple jump required 700 µs. Speedcoding applications ran *much* more slowly than efficiently coded 701 programs.

Still, the advantages were clear. Programming time was drastically reduced from weeks to *hours*.

For many applications, the programming time versus execution time trade-off made sense. But for many others, it did not. The 701 was an expensive machine, and computer time was often much costlier than programmer time.

But things were moving quickly. Core memory was the obvious replacement for Williams tubes, and it was growing ever more obvious, due in part to Backus's achievements with Speedcoding, that machines needed bigger address spaces, index registers, and floating-point processors. And so the IBM 704 was announced in 1954, and the solid-state transistor-based 7090 was just four years in the future.

THE NEED FOR SPEED

During 1953, Backus grew ever more concerned about the cost of programming. Machines, while still huge and expensive, were obviously getting cheaper. Transistors were on the horizon, and core memory was faster, denser, and more reliable than Williams tubes. So the cost of renting or owning a computer was beginning to decline, while the cost of programming was definitely on the rise.

Backus was also well aware of Grace Hopper's ideas of Automatic Programming, and though he had disparaged[15] her A-0 compiler, he was beginning to warm to the overall concept. His experience with Speedcoding showed him that a relatively small change in programming abstraction could lead to a massive change in programmer productivity.

So, late that year, Backus wrote a memo to his boss, Cuthbert Hurd, suggesting that IBM produce a compiler for the soon-to-be-announced 704. He suggested that it might take six months to create. Remarkably, Hurd approved. And so John Backus began to assemble a team.

Backus understood that execution time was going to be a critical factor. The programmers of the day were not going to tolerate the 10x slowness of an interpreter like Speedcoding. Indeed, they would likely not tolerate the slowness of a factor of 2 or even 1.5. In those days, programmers prided[16] themselves on the clever ways they could squeeze a few microseconds out of a sequence of instructions.

So the first rule of this new Automatic Programming effort was to create a compiler that generated *efficient* code. Indeed, language design was secondary to this goal. Efficiency of execution was the goal above all others.

---

15. He said it was "clumsy and ran slowly and was difficult to use," and later, "her ideas were just [such] cockamamie stuff."

16. Ask me how I know.

Given this goal, their task was to create a way for programmers to focus on the problem instead of on the machine. In essence, they were trying to abstract the details of the machine away from the programmer without compromising execution time. But, as the team would discover, the details of the 704 were not that easy to erase.

Backus's team included Irving Ziller, Harlan Herrick, and Bob Nelson. This was something of a ragtag team. IBM was a straightlaced "white shirt and tie" kind of place—pretty much by edict. But Backus and his team, tucked into the annex on the top of the nineteenth floor, were not quite so formal. Even the elevator operator made a joke about their dress.[17]

They worked together in a single room without dividers. Their desks were simply shoved up against each other. They were "in each other's pockets."[18]

Backus later said: "We had a great deal of fun. It was a very nice group of people. My main job was to break up chess games at lunchtime because they would go on and on." Meanwhile, IBM management left them alone. They considered the project to be open-ended research and were not really expecting a result.

Every so often, someone would ask how they were doing, and the team would reply: "Come back in six months."

The syntax they were considering was very simple, and it was not planned in any sense. Backus once said: "We simply made up the language as we went along."[19] Since efficiency was the overriding goal, and since the target machine was the 704, the language developed in a manner that allowed it to be efficient *on* the 704, without any thought of other machines.

---

17. Lorenzo, p. 75.

18. Ibid.

19. Lorenzo, p. 76.

Nearly a year after Backus had estimated six months for the whole project, the team was ready to publish its "preliminary report." Not a compiler, mind you. Not even a language specification. A *preliminary* report. But before it could be published, it needed a name. It was Backus who chose FORmula TRANslation. Herrick's reply was that it sounded like something spelled backward.

The report outlined the basic idea behind the language, but it was by no means a language specification. The team had decided to allow both fixed- and floating-point math and that variables could have names with one or two characters. The type of a variable was dictated by the first character of the name. Thus, names beginning with I through N were integers, and the rest were floating-point "real" numbers.

Backus and the team wanted to implement arrays of one and two dimensions, and were quite concerned about matrix manipulations. They wanted to have complex expressions with operators, subscripts, and parentheses.

They chose line numbers to label lines because that was often the way it was done in mathematical proofs. Their "if" statement included logical comparison operators such as =, <, and > and called out line numbers for the true and false branches. They came up with an arcane looping structure involving as many as seven arguments.

They gave no thought to IO.

That might not seem like much of a result for nearly a year of work for a team of four or five people, but it's important to remember that nothing like this had ever before been done, or even contemplated. They were in very new territory.

But then they got down to business, and the team began to grow, eventually to include Roy Nutt, Sheldon Best, Peter Sheridan, David Sayre, Lois Haibt, Dick Goldberg, Bob Hughes, Charles DeCarlo, and John McPherson.

They were the Program Research Group, and they considered themselves to be a small family of very unusual people who came together as a matter of fate. And they were all led by the "quiet leadership" of John Backus, who created "a little pool of silence" in which the team would invent the first ever efficient high-level language.

One of their early tasks was to decide how to represent the input to the compiler. You and I are used to thinking of source code as text files. Those files have names and reside in directories within our file systems. But Backus and his crew had no text files, no directories, and no file systems.

From their point of view, a program was a punched paper tape or a deck of punched cards. The 704 used punched cards as its primary input device, so it seemed clear that FORTRAN source statements would be punched into cards. But what format should they take?

In those days, we viewed the 72 usable columns[20] of a punched card as a set of fields with fixed positions. If there were five data elements on a card, they would be punched into five fields on that card, each field beginning and ending at a specific column number.

So, for example, if I wanted to represent my first name, last name, and date of birth on a card, I might arrange it as follows:

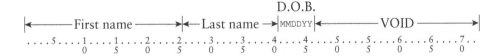

---

20. The 704 could only read the first 72 columns of an 80-column card, because each row of holes was read into a two-word (72-bit) register. And now you know that the last eight columns on a card were not really for sequence numbers. They just couldn't be read.

Given that mindset, it is not surprising that they decided to lay out FORTRAN statements in the same way, and make the compiler dependent upon that layout.

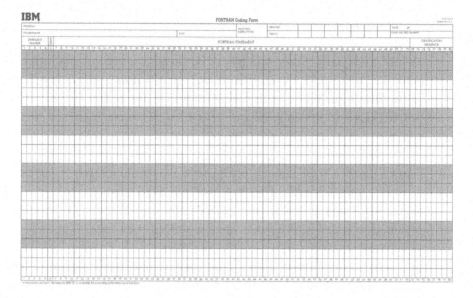

As shown in the figure above, the first five columns of each FORTRAN card were for the statement number. Column 6 was the "continuation" column. And columns 7 to 72 were for a FORTRAN statement.

Statement numbers were optional and not ordinal. They were used when the programmer wanted to refer to a statement. For example, the statement GO TO 23 would transfer control to statement number 23.

The continuation column was generally blank. However, if a single FORTRAN statement was longer than the 66 columns allocated on the card, the next card could hold the continuation of that statement. To denote this, the numbers 1 to 9 were typically placed in the continuation column.

The FORTRAN statement itself was free-form, and spaces were utterly ignored. So, for example, the statement GO TO 23 could be written as:

GOTO23

THE DIVISION OF LABOR

Early on, the team decided that the compiler would make a single pass over the source code to generate an executable program for the 704.

They wanted to avoid the headache of having the programmer feed the program deck and/or intermediate decks of cards into subsequent passes. Thus, the compiler had to reduce the source code into a set of intermediate data structures that they called tables.

Backus split the team up into six working groups, each responsible for a particular section of the compiler. Each section would produce "tables" for the other sections. Those sections were as follows.[21]

1. **The parser** — Written by Herrick, Nutt, and Sheridan. It read the source code, and separated it into statements that could be compiled immediately and those that would have to wait until a later time. This is the section in which the arithmetic expressions were parsed, parentheses and precedence were determined, and operations were converted into ordered tables. This section also dealt with subscripted variables.

2. **The code generator** — Written by Nelson and Ziller. It generated optimal machine code from the created tables. Loops were analyzed and reorganized to expel statements that did not require repetitive execution. This section began the process of tagging index register usage. At this stage, they assumed that the 704 had an infinite number of index registers.

3. **Un-named** — Authors unknown. This section integrated the outputs of sections 1 and 2 and was something of an afterthought. It was cobbled together to provide a consistent input to section 4.

4. **Program structure** — Written by Haibt. This section took the input from sections 1 and 2 (as integrated by section 3) and chopped the executable code into blocks with a single entry and a single exit.[22]

---

21. Lorenzo, p. 135.ff.

22. Shades of Edsger Dijkstra, though the team knew nothing of structured programming at the time.

These blocks were run through a Monte Carlo[23] simulation to determine which index register tags were used most frequently.

5. **Tag analysis** — Written by Best. It applied the results from section 4 to optimally reduce the number of index registers to the three that the 704 had to offer. Then, it created a relocatable assembly version of the program.

6. **Back end** — Written by Nutt. It assembled the relocatable program from section 5 and emitted the final binary onto punched cards.

It's important to remember that these programmers were working in the most primitive of assembly languages. The assembler was named SAP and was written by Nutt several years before.

The six sections took a lot of time to write. A lot more than six months. The first FORTRAN I program was not compiled and executed until early 1957.

But the result was worth the wait. The FORTRAN I language was easy to write, and the generated code for the 704 was extraordinarily efficient.

And the rest, as they say, is history.

My FORTRAN Rant

My exposure to FORTRAN was minimal. I dabbled around with it from time to time, but never used it in anger. Here, for example, is a little FORTRAN IV program I wrote back in 1974—just for fun. It calculates the first 1,000 factorials.

```
      INTEGER*2 DIGIT(3000)
      DATA DIGIT/3000*0/
      DIGIT(1)=1
      NDIG=1
      DO 10 I=1,1000
      ICARRY=0
      DO 11 J=1,NDIG
      DIGIT(J)=DIGIT(J)*I+ICARRY
      ICARRY=0
      IS=DIGIT(J)
```

---

23. See *Monte Carlo analysis* in the Glossary of Terms.

```
         IF (IS.LE·9) GO TO 11
         DIGIT (J)=IS-IS/10*10
         ICARRY= IS/10
11       CONTINUE
9        IF (ICARRY.EQ.0) GO TO 7
         NDIG=NDIG+1
         DIGIT(NDIG)=ICARRY-ICARRY/10*10
         ICARRY= ICARRY/10
         GO TO 9
7        WRITE (6,1) I,NDIG,(DIGIT(NDIG+1-K),K=1,NDIG)
1        FORMAT (1HO, 30('*'),1X,I4,' FACTORIAL CONTAINS ', I4,' DIGITS ',
         -30('*'),30(/1X,130I1))
10       CONTINUE
         STOP
         END
```

This program took 15 minutes of CPU time on a honking big IBM 370 back then. The equivalent Clojure program running on my laptop took 253 ms.

FORTRAN was not a pretty language back then. It's not particularly pretty even now. There's too much baggage from the past to allow FORTRAN to be a truly modern language. Even now, the old saying about FORTRAN remains true: "a collection of warts held together by syntax."[24]

The language served its purpose. It showed that a high-level language saved a lot of programmer time with a very minimal increase in execution time. But it is not a language that I want to use for any significant work. For all intents and purposes, it is a dead, or nearly dead, language.

Yes, I know some folks at NASA still use it because of existing libraries or existing space probes. But I don't think the language has a future.

ALGOL AND EVERYTHING ELSE

Backus worked on FORTRAN for a while longer, adding features like subroutines that could be independently compiled and linked for FORTRAN II. Those features made the language usable for much larger projects than FORTRAN I.

---

24. A quote written on a souvenir card from Pioneer Day at the 1982 National Computer Conference in Houston.

But after that, he and most of the rest of the team moved on to other adventures. Backus floated from one project to another, but he found that his advice was not sought, and was not particularly well received when given. For a while, he became somewhat obsessed with trying to prove the four-color map theorem.

FORTRAN was a success, but Backus found it unsatisfying as a language. He had designed it as a language for efficient execution on the 704 and had his doubts about its use as a more general abstract language. So when the ACM decided to form a committee to explore the possibility of a *Universal Programming Language*, he joined but later said that he hadn't really contributed much. As we'll see, that's not quite true.

This is the committee that eventually created the specification for ALGOL 60, but in the early days, the members called their goal the *International Algebraic Language* (IAL).

The specifications that the IAL committee produced were all in English. Backus found this frustrating and dangerously ambiguous: "an inconsistent mess."[25] He feared "it is likely that many man-years may be invested in producing a number of translating programs which will not reliably produce equivalent machine programs."

So Backus set about to invent a formalism with which to describe the language. This formalism was a symbolic metalanguage consisting of a set of recursively linked *production rules*. Each rule specified a construction that would be used in other rules. In this way, a complex syntax could be built up from simple beginnings. Using this language, which became known as Backus Normal Form (BNF), he published a formal specification of the IAL in 1959.

This publication landed like a lead balloon. The committee took no interest in it at all. They continued on with their English specifications.

---

25. Lorenzo, p. 230.

But one member did take note. He was Peter Naur, a Danish mathematician. He shared Backus's fears about English, took it upon himself to modify Backus's notation somewhat, and produced the specification for ALGOL 60 in time for the January 1960 meeting of the committee in Paris. This time, the notation stuck.

Four years later, Donald Knuth recommended changing the name of BNF to Backus–Naur Form. BNF has since become the standard notation for describing language syntax, and it is roughly the input format used by parser programs like yacc.

In the 1970s Backus fell into the same ideological trap that Dijkstra had fallen into decades before. He sought to turn programming into a mathematical formalism that could construct a hierarchy of proofs and theorems. But, whereas Dijkstra used structured programming as the basis for his formalism, Backus chose functional programming for his. However, the trap closed just as effectively on Backus as we shall see that it closed on Dijkstra.

Backus continued working in the research department of IBM and was eventually awarded the National Medal of Science, the Turing Award, and the Charles Stark Draper Prize.

He passed away in 2007. That year, an asteroid was named after him: Asteroid 6830 Johnbackus.

REFERENCES

Backus, John W. 1954. "The IBM 701 Speedcoding System." *Association for Computing Machinery.* https://dl.acm.org/doi/10.1145/320764.320766.

Backus, John. 1978. "Can Programming Be Liberated from the von Neumann Style? A Functional Style and Its Algebra of Programs." IBM Research Laboratory, San Jose, CA. *Communications of the ACM 21*, no. 8: 613–641.

Beyer, Kurt W. 2009. *Grace Hopper and the Invention of the Information Age.* MIT Press.

Computer History Archives Project ("CHAP"). "Computer History IBM Rare film 1948 SSEC Selective Sequence Electronic Calculator Original Dedicated," 10:36. Posted on YouTube on May 1, 2024. (Available at the time of writing.)

DeCaire, Frank. 2017. "Vintage Hardware—The IBM 701." *Frank DeCaire*, May 27. https://blog.frankdecaire.com/2017/05/27/vintage-hardware-the-ibm-701.

International Business Machines Corporation. 1953. *Principles of Operation: Type 701 and Associated Equipment*. International Business Machines, 1953. Available at https://archive.org/details/type-701-and-associated-equipment.

International Business Machines Corporation. 1953. *Speedcoding System for the Type 701 Electronic Data Processing Machines*. Available at https://archive.computerhistory.org/resources/access/text/2018/02/102678975-05-01-acc.pdf.

Lorenzo, Mark Jones. 2019. *The History of the Fortran Programming Language*. SE Books.

Office of Naval Research, Mathematical Sciences Division. 1953. *Digital Computer Newsletter 5*, no. 4: 1–18. www.bitsavers.org/pdf/onr/Digital_Computer_Newsletter/Digital_Computer_Newsletter_V05N04_Oct53.pdf.

Wikipedia. "IBM 701." https://en.wikipedia.org/wiki/IBM_701.

Wikipedia. "IBM SSEC." https://en.wikipedia.org/wiki/IBM_SSEC.

Wikipedia. "John Backus." https://en.wikipedia.org/wiki/John_Backus.

Edsger Dijkstra: The First Computer Scientist

Edsger Dijkstra is one of the most famous names in software. He is the father of structured programming and the guy who told us not to use GOTO. He invented the semaphore construct and was the author of many useful algorithms. He cowrote the first working version of the ALGOL 60 compiler and participated in the design of early multiprogramming operating systems.

But these accomplishments are mere mile markers along a battle-torn path. The true legacy of Edsger Dijkstra is the ascendance of the abstract over the physical, a battle he fought with himself, with his peers, and with the profession at large, and eventually won.

He was a pioneer and a legend and a programmer, and perhaps not particularly humble. Alan Kay once affectionately said of him: "Arrogance in computer science is measured in nano-Dijkstras." He went on to explain that "Dijkstra was much more funny than annoying for anyone who had any sense of self." In any case, the story of Edsger Dijkstra is fascinating.

THE MAN

Edsger Wybe Dijkstra was born in Rotterdam on May 11, 1930. His father was a chemistry teacher and president of the Dutch Chemical

Society. His mother was a mathematician. So the boy was surrounded by math and technology.

During the German occupation of the Netherlands, his parents sent him away to the countryside until things calmed down. After the war, a lot was broken, but there was also a lot of hope.

Dijkstra graduated high school in 1948 with the highest possible marks in math and science.

Like all young people, I suppose, he rejected his parents' technical calling at first, and thought he'd be better suited to study law and represent the Netherlands at the UN. But the technical bug caught him at Leiden University, and his interests quickly changed to theoretical physics.

Those interests changed again in 1951 when his father arranged for him to go to Cambridge, in the UK, to attend a three-week course introducing programming on the EDSAC. His father thought that learning about the new tools of the day would enhance his career in theoretical physics. But the result was quite different.

Although he struggled with English, he very much enjoyed the class; and he learned a great deal. He said that those three weeks changed his life. While there, he met the director of the Mathematical Centre (MC) in Amsterdam, Adriaan van Wijngaarden, who offered him a part-time job as a programmer.

Dijkstra accepted that job in March of 1952. He was the first programmer in the Netherlands. He was hooked by how unforgiving computers were.

The MC did not have a computer at the time. They were trying to build the ARRA, an electromechanical machine. He helped design the instruction set and wrote programs that would have to wait until the machine was built.

It was here that he met Gerrit Blaauw, who had studied under Howard Aiken at Harvard in '52 and would go on to help design the IBM 360 with Fred Brooks and Gene Amdahl. Blaauw imported both material and many decent techniques into the MC from Aiken's laboratory.

Dijkstra and Blaauw worked together on the ARRA[1] and other projects. Of Blaauw, Dijkstra once told the following story:[2]

> "He was a very punctual man, and that was a good thing because for a couple of months [he] and I debugged the FERTA[3] that was installed at Schiphol Aircraft.[4] The place was a little hard to reach and, thank goodness, he had a car. So early in the morning, at 7:00, I would jump on my bicycle, go to the highway, hide my bicycle, and wait on the side until Gerrit came and picked me up. It was a grim winter, and it could only be done thanks to an old Canadian army code and due to the fact that, as I said, Gerrit was a very punctual man. I remember one horrible occasion that we had been debugging the FERTA all day long and it was 10:00 in the evening and his [car] was the last car in the [...] parking lot, and it was beginning to snow, and the thing wouldn't start. I don't exactly remember how we got home, my guess is that Gerrit Blaauw fixed [...] another bug that day."

Dijkstra loved the challenge of "being ingenious and being accurate." But the deeper he got into the efforts of the MC, the more he feared that programming was not an appropriate field for him. He was, after all, being groomed as a first-class theoretical physicist, and programming computers was not first-class anything at the time.

This personal dilemma came to a head in 1955 when he expressed his fears to Wijngaarden. Dijkstra said:

> "When I left his office a number of hours later, I was another man. [Wijngaarden explained] quietly that automatic computers were here to stay, that

1. An early electromechanical computer.

2. "A Programmer's Early Memories" by Edsger Dijkstra.

3. An early electronic computer derived from the ARRA.

4. An informal reference to Royal Dutch Aircraft Factory Fokker (in English). Also known as the Nederlandse Vliegtuigenfabriek (Dutch Aircraft Factory) in the Dutch area of Schiphol.

we were just at the beginning and [I could] be one of the persons called to make programming a respectable discipline in the years to come. This was a turning point in my life...."[5]

In 1957 Dijkstra married Maria (Ria) Debets, one of the girls working as a "computer" in the MC. The officials in Amsterdam refused to recognize the profession of "programmer" that Dijkstra had written upon his marriage license. Of this, he says:

"Believe it or not, but under the heading of 'profession' my marriage act shows the ridiculous entry 'theoretical physicist'!"

THE ARRA: 1952–1955

Wijngaarden hired Dijkstra to program the MC's new ARRA computer. The problem was that the ARRA didn't work. Five years before, Wijngaarden had traveled to Harvard and had seen Aiken's Mark I and its successors. Impressed, Wijngaarden hired some young engineers to build a similar but much smaller machine: the ARRA.

The ARRA was designed to be a stored-program *electromechanical* beast. It had a drum memory, 1,200 relays, and some vacuum tube flip-flops for registers. The relays had to be cleaned regularly, but the contacts degraded so rapidly that the switching time was undependable, making the machine unreliable. After four years of development and constant repair, the poor machine was apparently only good for generating random numbers.

That was not a joke. They had written a demonstration program that simulated the rolling of a 13-dimensional cubic die.[6] At one point, a minister of government came in to see this demo. They fearfully turned the machine on and, for once, it started printing proper random numbers. It worked!—for a moment. Then it unexpectedly halted. Wijngaarden,

---

5. "The Humble Programmer." *Communications of the ACM* 15, no.10 (Oct. 1972), 859–866.

6. Only a bunch of mathematical geeks could come up with *that* as a demo.

thinking on his feet, explained to the minister: "This is a highly remarkable situation: The cube is balancing on one of its corners and does not know which way to fall. If you push this button, you will give the cube a little push and the ARRA will continue its computation." The minister pushed the button, and the machine once again started printing random numbers. The minister replied: "That is very interesting," and left shortly thereafter.

The machine never worked again.

A frustrated Wijngaarden recruited Gerrit Blaauw, who had just gotten his Ph.D. at Harvard while working with Aiken on the Harvard Mark IV. Blaauw joined the team and in very short order convinced them that their machine had no hope of success, and that they needed to start from scratch with electronics and not electromechanical relays.

So the team started in on the design of the ARRA. Well, actually, it was the ARRA 2, but they didn't want to advertise that there had ever been an ARRA 1.

So they just called the new machine the ARRA.

Being the "programmer," Dijkstra would propose an instruction set to the hardware guys. They, in turn, would assess whether that instruction set was practical to build. They'd make amendments and toss them back to Dijkstra. This iteration continued until they were all ready to "sign in blood." And then the hardware guys built the hardware, and Dijkstra started working on the programming manual and writing the IO primitives.

This division of labor established the idea that the hardware was a black box that executed the software, and the software was independent of the design of the hardware. This was an important step in computer architecture and a very early example of dependency inversion. The hardware depended on the needs of the software, rather than the software being subordinate to the dictates of the hardware.

They managed to complete the new machine 13 months later, in 1953. What's more, it worked—and they put it to work 24 hours a day calculating things like wind patterns, water movements, and the behavior of airplane wings. The machine completely replaced the team of women "computers" who had previously been doing these calculations on desk calculators. Those women became the programmers of the new machine.

At some point, they hooked a loudspeaker up to one of the registers and could listen to the rhythmic sounds as it operated. This was a good debugging tool because you could *hear* when it was executing properly and when it got caught in a loop.

The ARRA was designed as a binary machine at a time when most computers were using decimal (BCD). The electronics were vacuum tubes. It had two working registers, had 1,024 30-bit words of drum memory, and could execute ~40 instructions per second. The drum spun at 50 revs per second. The primary input device was five-channel paper tape. Output was typically sent to an automatic typewriter.

The instruction set that Dijkstra designed for the ARRA 2 should provide some insight into what he and his contemporaries thought a computer should be able to do: It was quite sparse, and focused much more on arithmetic than data manipulation. Later computers would reverse that decision!

Instructions in the ARRA 2 were 15 bits wide, so two instructions would fit into a 30-bit word. Those two instructions were referred to as *a* and *b*. So the machine could hold 2,048 instructions. The first five bits in an instruction were the operation code, and the last ten were the memory address (or an immediate value).

The two registers were named A and S. They were independently manipulated, but could also be used as a double-precision 60-bit number.

There were 24 instructions. Notice the lack of IO and indirect addressing. Notice also that Dijkstra used decimal to denote the operation codes. At the time, there was no thought of octal or hexadecimal:

```
0/n replace (A) with (A)+(n)
1/n replace (A) with (A)-(n)
2/n replace (A) with (n)
3/n replace (A) with -(n)
4/n replace (n) with (A)
5/n replace (n) by -(A)
6/n conditional control move to na
7/n control move to after na
8/n replace (S) with (s)+(n)
9/n replace (S) with (S)-(n)
10/n replace (S) with (n)
11/n replace (S) with -(n)
12/n replace (n) with (S)
13/n replace (n) with -(S)
14/n conditional control move to nb
15/n control move to nb
16/n replace [AS] with [n].[s]+[A]
17/n replace [AS] with -[n].[S]+[A]
18/n replace [AS] with [n].[S]
19/n replace [AS] with - [n].[s]
20/n divide [AS] by [n]:, place quotient in S, remainder in A
21/n divide [AS] by -[n]:, place quotient in S, remainder in A
22/n shift A->S, i.e. replace [AS] with [A].2^(29-n)
23/n shift S->A, i.e. replace [SA] with [S].2^(30-n)
24/n communication assignment
```

The two conditional control moves (jumps) executed only if the result of the last arithmetic operation was positive. The ARRA was a one's complement machine, which means there were two representations of zero, one positive and the other negative. So testing for zero by subtracting was perilous.

Notice that if you want to jump to instruction *a* or *b*, you have to use a *different* jump instruction. That must have been hellish to deal with when you inserted an instruction into your program.

The drum memory was arranged into 64 channels containing 16 words each. I infer that each channel corresponded to a track on the drum. I also infer that there were 64 read heads, and that each read head was routed to the electronics through relays. Those relays took from 20 ms to 40 ms to open or close. So the efficiency-minded programmer had to take care not to jump around between tracks.

What's more, it appears that the electronics for reading and writing the drum were able to read from two tracks at a time: one for instructions and another for data. This allowed the programmer to aggregate instructions on one track and data on another without having to change the state of the relays.

Just to add one extra complication, it appears that the actual tracks on the drum could only hold eight words around the drum circumference, but that each read/write head was actually a dual head that could read and write one or the other of two adjacent tracks. Thus, reading an entire 16-word channel required at least two revolutions of the drum.

Imagine having all that to think about while you are trying to write an interesting mathematical program.

Notice that the instruction set does not allow for indirect addressing. Either Dijkstra had not yet realized the importance of pointers, or the hardware designers could not easily implement indirection. So any indirect or indexed access had to be accomplished by modifying the addresses within existing instructions.

This was also the strategy for subroutines. The instruction set had no "call" instruction, nor any way to remember return addresses. So it was the programmers' job to store the appropriate jump instruction in the last instruction of a subroutine, before jumping to that subroutine.

The primitive nature of these machines and instruction sets likely had a dual effect upon Dijkstra. First, being so swamped by all the hideous detail and the deeply constrained environment likely precluded any serious consideration of computer science. But second, it also likely instilled within him the strong desire to shed all such detail and drive toward abstraction. As we shall see, that's exactly the path that Dijkstra took.

Indeed, there are hints of this battle between detail and abstract thinking in Dijkstra's "Functionele Beschrijving Van De Arra" ("Functional Description of the ARRA") from 1953. In that write-up, Dijkstra goes to great lengths to justify and explain the benefits of callable subroutines as opposed to the kind of "open subroutines" (code duplication) that Hopper had been using in the Mark I.

In his description of how to do a subroutine call, he says that "it would be nice to have control run through the same series of commands" instead of duplicating those commands over and over within the program, which "is quite bad [and] is wasteful of memory space." But then he turns around and complains that jumping to a subroutine in that fashion will cause a great deal of drum-switching time, adding a full revolution of the drum to each call and each return.

Coming to terms with this dichotomy is the story, and the legacy, of Edsger Dijkstra.

THE ARMAC: 1955–1958

The MC continued to make improvements to the design, and they built new machines based upon the ARRA.

The FERTA was built two years later (1955) and was installed at the Fokker factory next to Schiphol Airport. It was used to calculate matrices used for the design of the wings of the F27 Friendship. The architecture was similar to the ARRA, but memory was expanded to 4,096 34-bit words and speed was doubled to ~100 instructions per second, probably because the density of each track on the drum had doubled.

The ARMAC was another ARRA derivative that followed one year later (1956). It could execute 1,000 instructions per second because a small bank of core memory was used to buffer tracks on the drum. This machine had 1,200 tubes and consumed 10 kilowatts.

This was a period of intense hardware experimentation and improvement, but not much improvement in the software architecture—particularly the instruction set. However, the increase in memory and speed allowed Dijkstra to consider a previously untenable problem.

DIJKSTRA'S ALGORITHM: THE MINIMUM PATH

"What is the shortest way to travel from Rotterdam to Groningen, in general: from given city to given city. It is the algorithm for the shortest path, which I designed in about twenty minutes. One morning [in 1956] I was shopping in Amsterdam with my young fiancée, and tired, we sat down on the café terrace to drink a cup of coffee and I was just thinking about whether I could do this, and I then designed the algorithm for the shortest path. As I said, it was a twenty-minute invention. In fact, it was published in '59, three years later. The publication is still readable, it is, in fact, quite nice. One of the reasons that it is so nice was that I designed it without pencil and paper. I learned later that one of the advantages of designing without pencil and paper is that you are almost forced to avoid all avoidable complexities. Eventually, that algorithm became to my great amazement, one of the cornerstones of my fame."

—Edsger Dijkstra, 2001

Dijkstra chose the problem because he wanted to demonstrate the power of the ARMAC with a non-numerical problem that normal people could understand. He wrote the demonstration code to find the shortest path from one city to another through a simplified traffic network between 64[7] cities in the Netherlands.

The algorithm is not a difficult one to understand. It's a matter of a few nested loops, a bit of sorting, and a fair bit of data manipulation. But imagine writing this code without pointers. Without recursion. Without a call instruction for your subroutines. Imagine having to access your data by modifying the addresses within individual instructions. Further, consider the problems of optimizing this program to keep track of data from being flushed in and off the drum from the core buffer. My mind rebels at the thought!

Having dispensed with the demonstration, Dijkstra then created a similar algorithm to solve a more practical problem. The backplane of the next computer, the X1, had a vast number of interconnections, and copper is a precious metal. So he wrote the minimum spanning tree algorithm to minimize the amount of copper wire used on that backplane.

Solving these kinds of graph algorithms was a step toward the computer science that we recognize today. Dijkstra used the computer to solve problems that were not strictly numerical in nature.

ALGOL AND THE XI: 1958–1962

Dijkstra's efforts at the MC were taking place at a formative time in computing. Hopper's 1954 symposium on Automatic Programming[8] had generated a lot of buzz. At that symposium, J. H. Brown[9] and J. W.

---

7. Yes, he represented each city with a 6-bit integer.

8. See Compilers: 1951–1952, in Chapter 4.

9. From Willow Run Research Center.

Carr III[10] presented a paper on their efforts to create a universal programming language that was machine independent. Saul Gorn[11] presented a similar paper. Both papers advocated for divorcing the structure of the language from the physical structure of the hardware.

This was a revolutionary concept that flew in the face of the thinking of the day. Languages like FORTRAN, MATH-MATIC, and eventually even COBOL were strongly wed to the physical architecture of the machines of the day. This strong binding was thought to be necessary to achieve efficiency of execution. Brown and Carr acknowledged that universal languages might be slower, but they argued that they would reduce programming time and programmer error.

As an example of the wedding between language and physical architecture, consider the type int in the C language. Depending upon the machine, it is either a 16-, 32-, or 64-bit integer. I once worked on a machine in which it was an 18-bit integer. In C, an int is wedded to the machine word. Many languages of the day simply assumed that the data format of the language was the data format of the machine, including memory layout. Subroutine arguments were assigned fixed locations, precluding any kind of recursion or reentrancy.

In May of 1958, Carr and several others met in Zurich to begin the definition of a universal machine-independent programming language. They named it ALGOL.[12] The stated goal was to create a language based upon mathematical notation that could be used for the publishing of algorithms and mechanically translated into machine programs.

John Backus created a formal notation to describe an early (1958) version of the language. Peter Naur recognized the genius of the notation

---

10. John Weber Carr III (1923–1997).

11. From Ballistics Research Lab.

12. International ALGOrithmic Language.

and named it Backus Normal Form (BNF[13]). He then used it to specify the 1960 version of ALGOL.

Meanwhile, Dijkstra and the MC were busy building the X1 computer. This was a fully transistorized machine, with up to 32K of 27-bit words. The first 8K of the address space was read-only memory and contained boot programs and a primitive assembler. The X1 was one of the first machines to have a hardware interrupt—something that Dijkstra would make strategic use of. The machine also had an index register! At last, real pointers! Otherwise, it was similar in many ways to the ARRA and ARMAC machines.

The memory cycle time was 32 μs and the add time was 64 μs. It could therefore execute over 10,000 instructions per second.

In 1959 Wijngaarden and Dijkstra joined in the effort to define the ALGOL language. In 1960, with the BNF specification complete, Dijkstra and his close colleague Jaap Zonneveld surprised the computing world by quickly writing a compiler for the X1.

---

13. In 1964 Donald Knuth recommended that the name be changed to Backus–Naur Form.

"Surprised" might be an understatement. Naur wrote: "The first news of the success of the Dutch project, in June 1960, fell like a bomb in our group."[14] That bomb might explain some of the tension that arose later. I imagine Dijkstra & Co were viewed as upstarts who scooped everybody else.

Of their success, Dijkstra wrote:[15] "The combination of no prior experience in compiler writing and a new machine [the X1] without established ways of use greatly assisted us in approaching the problem of implementing ALGOL 60 with a fresh mind."

One of the techniques Dijkstra and Zonneveld used was "dual programming." Each would independently implement a feature and then they would compare the results. Dijkstra called this an "engineering approach." It has been suggested[16] that this approach so significantly reduced their debugging time that it led to a net reduction in their development time.

This was at a time when most teams implementing the language were debating which features to leave in or out. Dijkstra and Zonneveld left nothing out. They implemented the full specification—*in six weeks.*

Indeed, they even implemented the part of the specification that virtually everyone had planned on omitting: recursion.

This is ironic because recursion had been *voted out* of the language. Dijkstra and John McCarthy had strenuously advocated for recursion, but the rest of the committee thought that recursion was too inefficient and was otherwise useless. However, the wording of the resolution was ambiguous enough that Dijkstra sneaked the feature in anyway.

---

14. Daylight, p. 46.

15. Daylight, p. 57.

16. Private correspondence with Tom Gilb.

This got him into some trouble with the other members of the ALGOL team. Indeed, the issue of recursion versus efficiency generated quite a bit of tension. In a meeting in 1962, one of the members[17] got up and directed a nasty comment toward Dijkstra, Naur, and other proponents of recursion[18]—a comment that was greeted with loud applause and laughter:

> "And the question is—to state it once more—that we want to work with this language, really to work and not to play with it, and I hope we don't become a kind of ALGOL play-boys."

One reason that Dijkstra and Zonneveld were successful when so many other teams were still struggling was because Dijkstra created an abstraction boundary between the language and the machine. The compiler converted ALGOL source code into a p-code,[19] and an associated runtime system interpreted that p-code. Nowadays, we would call that runtime system a VM.[20]

This division allowed the language compiler to ignore the machine itself—which was one of the goals originally sought by Carr, Brown, Gorn, and the ALGOL team. Ignoring the machine made the compiler much easier to write. In short, Dijkstra invented a machine that was perfect for ALGOL, and then he made up the difference in his runtime system.

Of course, this caused certain inefficiencies. Simulating a p-code is always slower[21] than raw machine language. But Dijkstra justified this by stalwartly refusing to worry about efficiency in the short term. His focus

---

17. Gerhard Seegmüller.

18. Daylight, p. 44.

19. Portable code. A typically numeric code representing the instructions of a virtual machine.

20. A virtual machine like the JVM or the CLR.

21. Especially since just-in-time compilers were decades in the future.

was more upon the long-term direction of language and computer architecture. Thus, he said:[22]

> "In order to get as clear a picture as possible of the real needs of the programmer, I intend to pay, for a while, no attention to the well-known criteria 'space and time'. "

He went on to say:

> "I am convinced that [the] problems [of program correctness] will prove to be much more urgent than, for example, the exhaustive exploitation of specific machine features...."

And just to cap things off:

> "...Recursion] is such a neat and elegant concept that I can hardly imagine that it will not have a marked influence on the design of new machines in the near future."

And, of course, he was right. The PDP-11, with all its lovely index registers, one of which was a dedicated stack pointer, was only a decade away.

At the very start of the ALGOL project, Dijkstra and Zonneveld were concerned that Wijngaarden would (as was his wont) take undue credit. So the two clean-shaven programmers conspired to remain unshaven until the compiler worked. Only those with a beard could take credit for the compiler. Six weeks later, with the compiler working, Zonneveld shaved, but Dijkstra remained bearded from that point on.

THE GATHERING GLOOM: 1962

With the success of ALGOL 60 under his belt, Dijkstra looked to the future in a 1962 paper titled "Some Meditations on Advanced

---

22. Daylight, p. 59.

Programming." His first assertion is that software is an art that must become a science:

> "Therefore I would like to draw your attention in particular to those efforts and considerations which try to improve 'the state of the Art' of programming, maybe to such an extent that at some time in the future we may speak of 'the state of the Science of Programming'."

He then goes on to paint a rather gloomy picture of "the state of the art." He says that this change from an art to a science is "very urgent" because:

> "... The programmer's world is a very dark one with only just the first patches of a brighter sky appearing at the horizon."

He explains this by describing what it had, up to then, been like to be a programmer given "nearly impossible jobs" using machines that have capabilities "exhausted to slightly beyond their utmost limits." He explains that programmers under such circumstances fall back on "curious and tricky ways" to cajole their systems into working.

He calls the discipline of programming "extremely crude and primitive" and "unhygienic," and complains that the creativity and shrewdness of the programmers encourage the hardware designers to "include all kinds of curious facilities of doubtful usability." In other words, bad machines make bad programmers who encourage even worse machines.

What machines was he railing against? Rumor has it that it was the machines made by IBM.

As you read on in this paper, you realize that his specific complaint is that the machine architecture of the day makes recursion difficult and inefficient, and this tempts the compiler writers to constrain the language to prevent recursion.

He concludes the piece with an appeal to "elegance" and "beauty" and claims that unless programmers are given languages that are "charming" and "worthy or our love," they will likely not create systems of "superior quality."

This paper came at a time when the concerns of the industry were focused on quite a different problem. Those were the early days of "the software crisis." It was becoming ever more obvious that projects, if they were delivered at all, were breaking budgets and schedules; were inefficient, buggy, and did not meet requirements; and were unmanageable and unmaintainable.

I presume that sounds familiar to you. The software crisis never really ended. We've just kind of learned to accept and live with it.

Dijkstra's solution was science, elegance, and beauty. And as we shall see, he wasn't wrong.

THE RISE OF SCIENCE: 1963–1967

With a working ALGOL compiler, and thereby freed from the confines of the physical hardware, Dijkstra was able to experiment with all manner of computer science issues. One of those early issues was multiprogramming. Dijkstra captained a team of five other researchers at the Eindhoven University of Technology who embarked on a project to build a multiprogramming system named the THE[23] Multiprogramming System.

Dijkstra described this system in a famous paper[24] that he submitted to the *Communications of the ACM* in 1968. The structure of that system was unique at the time, and showed just how far Dijkstra had come from his ARRA days.

This system ran on the X8 computer, which was a much faster and more capable derivative of the X1. The X8 had a minimum of 16K 27-bit

23. Technische Hogeschool Eindhoven.

24. "The Structure of the "THE"-Multiprogramming System." See this chapter's References section.

words, expandable to 256K. It had a 2.5 µs core memory cycle time, allowing it to execute *hundreds of thousands* of instructions per second. It had indirect addressing and hardware interrupts[25] that included IO and a real-time clock. For the day, it was an ideal platform for experimenting with multiprocessing.

SCIENCE

The architecture of the THE system was quite modern. Dijkstra was very careful to separate it into black box layers. He did not want high-level layers knowing about the intricacies of the layers at lower levels.

At the lowest layer (Layer 0) was processor allocation—this layer decided which processor would be allocated to a particular process. Above this layer, the executing program had no idea which processor it was running on.

The next layer up (Layer 1) was memory control. The system had a primitive virtual memory capability. Pages in the core could be swapped to and from the drum. Above this layer, the program simply assumes that all program and data elements are accessible in memory.

The next level (Layer 2) controlled the system console.[26] It was responsible for ensuring that individual processes could communicate with their users with the keyboard and printer. Above this level, each process simply assumed that it had undivided access to the console.

Layer 3 controlled IO and the buffering of IO devices. Above this level, user programs simply assumed that data going in and out of various devices was a continuous stream requiring no management.

---

25. He called it "an interrupt system to fall in love with." I imagine that's the last time anyone said that about interrupts.

26. It may seem strange that an entire layer was dedicated to a single IO device. But the system console was the only device that was shared among all the processes, and it therefore deserved special attention. Nowadays, we would likely handle this differently, but back then a better solution wasn't clear. I remember working on systems at the time that faced the same issue.

Layer 4 was where user programs executed.

In the mid-1960s, the discipline required in order to design an operating system with a carefully layered structure was brand new. The idea of creating layers of abstraction that isolated high-level policy from low-level detail was revolutionary. This was computer science at its best.

SEMAPHORES

As part of this development, the team faced the issue of concurrent update and race conditions. To address this, Dijkstra came up with the semaphore abstraction that we have all come to know and love.

A semaphore is simply an integer upon which two operations[27] are allowed. The *P* operation blocks the calling process if the semaphore is less than or equal to zero; otherwise, it decrements the semaphore and continues. The *V* operation increments the semaphore, and if the result is positive, it simply continues on. Otherwise, one of the blocked processes is released before continuing on.

As part of his write-up on semaphores, Dijkstra invents the terms *critical section* and *indivisible action*. A critical section is any portion of the program that is manipulating a shared resource in a way that must not be interrupted by another. That is, it does not allow concurrent update. An indivisible action is an action that must fully complete before a hardware interrupt is allowed. In particular, the increment and decrement operations upon semaphores must be indivisible.

Of course, nowadays we programmers know these concepts well. They were taught to us in our earliest years of coding. But Dijkstra and his team had to derive these concepts from first principles and formalize them into the abstractions that we now take for granted.

---

27. Named *P* and *V* for historical reasons.

STRUCTURE

Another radically scientific concept adopted by Dijkstra was the notion that programs were structures of sequential procedures. Each such procedure had a single entry and a single exit. All adjacent procedures viewed it as a black box. Such procedures could be sequential in that one executed after the other, or they could be iterative in that a procedure executed many times in a loop.

This black box structure of sequential and iterative procedures allowed Dijkstra's team to test the individual procedures in isolation and to create reasoned *proofs* that the procedures were correct.

The testing enabled by this structured approach was so successful that he proudly asserted:

> "The only errors that showed up during testing were trivial coding errors (occurring with a density of one error per 500 instructions), each of them located within 10 minutes [of] (classical) inspection by the machine and each of them correspondingly easy to remedy."

Dijkstra was convinced that this kind of structured programming was an essential part of good system design and was responsible for the significant success of the THE system. To dissuade detractors who claimed that its success was due to its relatively small size, Dijkstra wrote:

> "... I should like to venture the opinion that the larger the project, the more essential the structuring!"

PROOF

And this is where things start to get a little strange. In his write-up of the THE system, Dijkstra makes a remarkable claim:

> "... The resulting system is guaranteed to be flawless. When the system is delivered, we shall not live in the perpetual fear that a system derailment may still occur in an unlikely situation."

Dijkstra made this claim because he believed that he and his team had proven, *mathematically*, that the system was correct. This is a view that Dijkstra would hold, promote, and evangelize for the rest of his career. It is also the source of what I consider to be his greatest mistake. In his view, programming was mathematics.

Indeed, in *On the Reliability of Programs*,[28] Dijkstra asserts that "programming will become more and more an activity of mathematical nature." And in this, Edsger Wybe Dijkstra was, in my view, dead wrong.

MATHEMATICS: 1968

The idea of software as a form of mathematics is a seductive one. There are, after all, many adjacencies. The early programs written by Hopper and her crew at Harvard were all numerical, and deeply mathematical in nature. The use of the Harvard Mark I to compute the solutions of systems of partial differential equations describing the implosion of the plutonium core of the Fat Man bomb required a very deep mathematical ability indeed.

It was, after all, Turing who claimed that programmers were "mathematicians of ability." And it was Babbage who was driven by the need to ease the burden of the creation of mathematical tables.

So when Dijkstra wrote that software would become more and more a matter of mathematics, he was standing on pretty firm historical ground. He therefore focused his endeavors on mathematically *proving* software programs correct.

We can plainly see this in his *Notes on Structured Programming*,[29] as he shows us the basic mathematical mechanisms for proving a simple algorithm correct. He outlines those mechanisms as enumeration, induction, and abstraction.

28. Dahl, Dijkstra, and Hoare, p. 3.

29. Dahl, Dijkstra, and Hoare, p. 12.

He uses enumeration to prove that two or more program statements in sequence achieve their desired goals while maintaining stated invariants. He uses induction to prove the same things about a loop. He uses abstraction as his primary motivation for black box structure.

And then, using all three of those mechanisms, he presents a proof of the following algorithm for computing the integer remainder of a/d:

$$a \geqslant 0 \text{ and } d > 0.$$

"**integer** r, dd;

$r := a$; $dd := d$;

while $dd \leqslant r$ **do** $dd := 2*dd$;

while $dd \neq d$ **do**

    begin $dd := dd/2$;

        if $dd \leqslant r$ **do** $r := r - dd$

end".

This is a lovely little algorithm that runs in logarithmic time using a shift-and-subtract approach. Any PDP-8 programmer would be proud.

The proof that Dijkstra presented was two pages long, followed by another page of notes. My own proof, based upon Dijkstra's, is a bit shorter but no less imposing (see next page).

It ought to be very clear that no programmer[30] would accept this as part of a viable process for writing software. As Dijkstra himself said:

> "The pomp and length of the above proof infuriate me [...] I would not dare to suggest (at least at present!) that it is the programmer's duty to supply such a proof whenever he writes a simple [...] program. If so, he could never write a program of any size at all!"

---

30. Other than, perhaps, those in an academic environment doing research on formal proofs of algorithms.

Expand:

Given $2^x D > N \mid x=0$
Then $dd = D$
And while is not entered $\Rightarrow dd = D \times 2^0$

Given $2^x D > N \geq 2^{x-1} D \mid x=1$
Then $dd = D$
The while is entered: $N \geq dd$
$dd = 2^1 D$
The while exits: $2^1 D > N \Rightarrow dd = 2^1 D$

Assume $dd \Rightarrow 2^x \mid 2^x D > N \geq 2^{x-1} D \mid x > 0$

IF $2^{x+1} D > N \geq 2^x D$
Then after the xth loop $dd = 2^x D$ (assumed)
The while is entered: $dd \leq N$
$dd = 2^{x+1} D$
The while exits: $dd > N$

Single Reduction
Given $dd = 2^{x+1} D \mid x \geq 0$
$0 \leq r < 2^{x+1} D$

$dd = 2^x D$
If $dd > r$ Then $0 \leq r < 2^x D$ $r = r - qD$ q int $= 0$

If $dd \leq r$
$r = r - dd$ and $0 \leq r < 2^{x+1} D - 2^x D$
$0 \leq r < 2^x D$ $r = r - qD$ q int > 0

Reduce:
Given $dd = D \Rightarrow D > N$ by Expand
$r = N \Rightarrow r \mid r = N - qD$ $q = 0$
$0 \leq r < D$ $r = N$

Given $dd = 2D \Rightarrow 2D > N \geq D$ by Expand
The loop is entered
$\Rightarrow 0 \leq r < D$ $r = N - qD$ q int

Assume $dd = 2^x D \Rightarrow 2^x D > N \geq 2^{x-1} D \mid x > 0$
$\Rightarrow dd = 2^{x-1} D$
$0 \leq r < 2^{x-1} D$ $r = N - qD$ $q \geq 0$ int

IF $dd = 2^{x+1} D \Rightarrow 2^{x+1} D > N \geq 2^x D \mid x > 0$
The loop is entered: $r > 0$
$\Rightarrow dd = 2^x D$
$0 \leq r < 2^x D$ $r = N - qD$ q int

$2D > N$

$D > N$
OR
$2^x D > N \geq 2^x D$

But then he goes on to say that he felt the same kind of "fury" when examining the early theorems of Euclid's plane geometry. And this is where Dijkstra's dream shows up.

Dijkstra dreamed that, one day, there would be a body of theorems and corollaries and lemmas that programmers could draw from. That they would not be relegated to proving their code in such horrid detail, but rather would restrict themselves to techniques that were already proven, and could create new proofs based upon the old ones without all the "pomp and length."

In short, he thought software was going to be like Euclid's *Elements*, a mathematical superstructure of theorems, a vast hierarchy of proofs, and that programmers would have little to do other than assemble their own proofs from the resources in that vast hierarchy.

But here I sit, in the waning months of 2023, and I do not see that hierarchy. There is no superstructure of theorems. The *Elements* of software has not been written. Nor do I believe it ever will.

There is an odd parallel between Hilbert and Dijkstra in this regard. Both were seeking a grand edifice of truth that simply cannot exist.

Dijkstra's dream has not been achieved. In all likelihood, it cannot be achieved. And the reason for that is that software is not a form of mathematics.

Mathematics is a positive discipline—we prove things correct using formal logic. Software, as it turns out, is a negative discipline—we prove things incorrect by observation. If that sounds familiar, it should. Software is a science.

In science, we cannot prove our theories correct; we can only observe them to be incorrect. We perform these observations with well-designed and well-controlled experiments. Likewise, in software, we almost never try to prove our programs correct. Instead, we detect their incorrectness by conducting observations in the form of well-designed tests.

Testing was something that Dijkstra complained about by saying: "Testing shows the presence, not the absence, of bugs." And, of course, he was correct. What he missed, in my opinion, is that his statement proved that software is not mathematics, but rather a science.

STRUCTURED PROGRAMMING: 1968

In 1967, after all the successes he had enjoyed, the MC disbanded Dijkstra's group because they saw no future in computer science. Dijkstra, for that reason among others, descended into a six-month severe depression for which he was hospitalized.

Upon recovery, Dijkstra started to really stir things up.

In an ironic twist, it was Dijkstra's dream of mathematics that led him to what is perhaps his most valuable contribution to computer science and the software craft: structured programming. In hindsight, we appreciate that value, but at the time, it stirred up quite a controversy.

In 1967 Dijkstra gave a talk at the ACM Conference on Operating System Principles in Gatlinburg, TN. He had lunch with some of the attendees, and the discussion turned to Dijkstra's view on the GOTO statement. Dijkstra explained to them why GOTO introduced complexity into programs. The group was so impressed by this discussion that they encouraged him to write an article for *The Communications of the ACM* on the topic.

So Dijkstra wrote a short article describing his views. He titled it "A Case Against the Go To Statement." He submitted it the editor, Niklaus Wirth,[31] who was so excited to publish it that in March of 1968 he

---

31. Yeah, THAT Niklaus Wirth. You know: the inventor of Pascal.

rushed it through as a letter to the editor rather than a fully reviewed article. Wirth also changed the title to "Go To Statement Considered Harmful."

That title has echoed down through the decades.

The title also raised the ire of an entire cohort of programmers, who were horrified at the very idea. It's not clear to me whether those programmers actually read the article before declaring their angst. Whatever the case may be, the programming journals lit up like a Christmas tree.

I was a very young programmer at the time, and I remember quite well the fracas that ensued. There was no Facebook or Twitter (X) at the time, so the flame wars were conducted in letters to the editors all around the industry.

It took five to ten years or so for things to settle down. In the end, Dijkstra won that war. As a rule, we programmers do not use GOTO.

DIJKSTRA'S ARGUMENT

In 1966 Corrado Böhm and Giuseppe Jacopini wrote a paper titled "Flow Diagrams, Turing Machines, and Language with Only Two Formation Rules." In this paper, they proved that "every Turing machine is reducible to, or in a determined sense is equivalent to, a program written in a language which admits as formation rules only composition and iteration." In other words, every program can be reduced to statements in sequence or statements in loops. Period.

This was a remarkable finding. It was generally ignored because it was deeply academic. But Dijkstra took it very seriously, and the argument he laid down in his article is hard to refute.

In short, if you want to understand a program—if you want to prove the program correct—you need to be able to visualize and examine the execution of that program. That means you need to turn the program into a sequence of events in time. These events need to be identifiable with some kind of label[32] that ties them back to the source code.

In the case of simple sequential statements, that label is nothing more than the line number of the source code statement. In the case of loops, that label is the line number adorned with the state of the loop; for example, the *n*th execution of line *l*. For function calls, it is the stack of line numbers that represent the calling sequence. But how do you construct a reasonable label if any statement can jump to any other statement using a GOTO?

Yes, it's possible to construct those labels, but they would have to consist of a long list of line numbers, each adorned with the state of the system.

Constructing proofs using such unmanageable labels is simply unreasonable. It's too much to ask.

So Dijkstra recommended maintaining provability by eliminating unconstrained GOTOs and replacing them with the three structures we've come to know and love: *sequence*, *selection*, and *iteration*. Each of those structures is a black box with a single entry and a single exit, and each is likely composed of the same structures in a recursive descent.

As a simple example, consider this payroll algorithm:

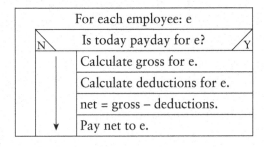

---

32. He used the term *coordinate*. Consider this alongside Babbage's notation for dynamics.

Nassi–Shneiderman diagrams like this constrain the algorithm to the three structures. You can see the *iteration* around the outside, the *selection* as the first element of the iteration, and the four *sequences* along the Y path of the selection. Each of those four sequences are subsequences that are themselves composed of sequences, selections, and iterations.

Why, if we are not going to follow Dijkstra's dream of creating proofs, is this strategy valuable? Because even though we don't write proofs for our code, we want our code to be *provable*. Provable code is code that we can analyze and reason about. Indeed, if we keep our functions small, simple, and provable, then we needn't even create Dijkstra's labels.

In any case, Dijkstra won the argument rather decisively; the GOTO statement has been all but completely driven out of our modern menagerie of languages.

It would be a mistake, however, to think that Dijkstra's view of structured programming was simply the absence of GOTO. That's the part that most of us remember, but his intention was far more involved than that. It went as far as layers of architecture and the directions of dependencies. But I'll leave you, gentle reader, to discover this for yourself within his wonderful writings.

REFERENCES

Apt, Krzysztof R., and Tony Hoare (Eds.). 2002. *Edsger Wybe Dijkstra: His Life, Work, and Legacy*. ACM.

Belgraver Thissen, W. P. C., W. J. Haffmans, M. M. H. P. van den Heuvel, and M. J. M. Roeloffzen. 2007. "Unsung Heroes in Dutch Computing History." https://web.archive.org/web/20131113022238/http://www-set.win.tue.nl /UnsungHeroes/home.html.

Computer History Museum. "A Programmer's Early Memories by Edsger W. Dijkstra." Lecture presented at the First International Research Conference on the History of Computing, Los Alamos, New Mexico, summer of 1976. Posted June 10, 2022. 24:23. Posted on YouTube on June 10, 2022. (Available at the time of writing.)

computingheritage. "Remembering ARRA: A Pioneer in Dutch Computing," 9:13. Posted on YouTube on June 4, 2015. (Available at the time of writing.)

Dahl, O.-J., E. W. Dijkstra, and C. A. R. Hoare. 1972. *Structured Programming*. Academic Press.

Daylight, Edgar G. 2012. *The Dawn of Software Engineering: From Turing to Dijkstra*. Lonely Scholar Scientific Books.

Dijkstra, E. W. 1953. "Functionele Beschrijving Van De Arra." Mathematisch Centrum, Amsterdam. https://ir.cwi.nl/pub/9277.

Dijkstra, Edsger. 1968. "The Structure of the 'THE'-Multiprogramming System." *Communications of the ACM*. www.cs.utexas.edu/~EWD/ewd01xx /EWD196.PDF.

Dijkstra, Edsger W. "Edsger Dijkstra - Oral Interview for the Charles Babbage Institute - 2001," 2:09:32. Posted on YouTube on Jan. 3, 2023.

Markoff, John. 2002. "Edsger Dijkstra, 72, Physicist Who Shaped Computer Era." *New York Times*, August 10, 2002. www.nytimes.com/2002/08/10 /us/edsger-dijkstra-72-physicist-who-shaped-computer-era.html.

University of Cambridge, Computer Laboratory. 1999. "EDSAC99, EDSAC 1 and After: A Compilation of Personal Reminiscences." www.cl.cam.ac.uk /events/EDSAC99/reminiscences.

Van den Hove, Gauthier. 2009. "Edsger Wybe Dijkstra, First Years in the Computing Science (1951-1968)." MsCS Thesis, Université de Namur. https:// pure.unamur.be/ws/portalfiles/portal/36772985/2009_VanDenHoveG _memoire.pdf.

Van Emden, Maarten. n.d. "Dijkstra, Blaauw, and the Origin of Computer Architecture." *A Programmer's Place*. https://vanemden.wordpress.com/2014 /06/14/dijkstra-blaauw-and-the-origin-of-computer-architecture.

Van Emden, Maarten. n.d. "I Remember Edsger Dijkstra (1930-2001)." *A Programmer's Place*. https://vanemden.wordpress.com/2008/05/06/i-remember -edsger-dijkstra-1930-2002.

Wikipedia. "Dijkstra's algorithm." https://en.wikipedia.org/wiki/Dijkstra's _algorithm.

Wikipedia. "Edsger Dijkstra." https://en.wikipedia.org/wiki/Edsger_W._Dijkstra.

Nygaard and Dahl:
The First OOPL

Object-oriented programming, one of the most significant revolutions in our industry, was the result of the efforts of two remarkably different people: the shy and bookish Ole-Johan Dahl and the larger-than-life, bull-in-a-china-shop Kristen Nygaard. Together, through a series of happy accidents, political manipulations, and deep insights, this odd couple revealed the software paradigm that drove language design into the twenty-first century.

Their story is fascinating, and is an example of how two wildly disparate talents can acquire the synergy to change the world.

Kristen Nygaard

Kristen Nygaard was born in Oslo, Norway, in 1926. He was the son of William Martin Nygaard, who taught high school, worked as programme secretary for Norwegian National Broadcasting, and consulted on literature for the National Theatre in Bergen.

Kristen was a bright child who was interested in many things, including science and math. In grade school, he was listening to university-level lectures, and won a national mathematics award.

He attended high school under the Nazi occupation, and endured the bombings of Oslo and the Nazi takeover of the education system.

When the war ended, Nygaard enrolled in the University of Oslo and studied science, and he earned a bachelor's degree in astronomy and physics.

In 1948 he took a full-time position at the Norwegian Defence Research Establishment (NDRE), where he met Ole-Johan Dahl. In his first years there, he focused on numerical analysis and computer programming.

In 1952 he joined the Operations Research (OR) group, and was soon its director. He led several defense-oriented studies there. As an example, with the war still vivid in everyone's minds, he was asked to study the combat efficiency of soldiers to determine how far they could march over challenging terrain and how much food and water they should carry and still be able to face the enemy after a certain number of days. To ensure the validity of the results, Nygaard and his group joined the actual soldiers, marching where they marched and eating what they ate.

Nygaard's stated ambition was "to build up OR as an experimental and theoretical science in Norway [...] to be reckoned as being among the top groups in the world in three to five years." In that effort, he became one of Norway's leading experts in OR. Later he helped to found the Norwegian OR Society, and acted as its chair from 1959 to 1964.

In 1956 he earned his master's degree in mathematics from the University of Oslo. His thesis was titled "Theoretical Aspects of Monte Carlo Methods." That topic is important for our discussion for reasons that you'll soon discover.

Nygaard was a political animal in every sense of the word. He was ambitious, entrepreneurial, and politically astute. In his later years, he would run for office in the Norwegian Labour Party, use his expertise to support the Norwegian Trade Unions, and become the national leader of the "No to EU" organization, dedicated to keeping Norway from joining the European Union.

He enjoyed taking controversial stands. He once wrote: "Has anyone resented the content of your work recently? If not, what is your excuse?"

Kristen Nygaard was described by Alan Kay as "a guy who is larger than life in almost any possible dimension."

OLE-JOHAN DAHL

In October of 1931, Ole-Johan Dahl was born in the seafaring town of Mandal into a seafaring family. His father, Finn Dahl, was a ship's captain, as were virtually all his male relatives. The family's seafaring tradition went back generations.

Finn wanted his son Ole to grow into a true seafaring man, but circumstances often thwart such desires. Ole was a quiet, bookish misfit of a lad who preferred playing the piano and reading books on mathematics.

He had little interest in the sea, or sports, or his father's dreams.

Mandal was the southernmost town in Norway, and the folks there had their own way of speaking. When Ole was 7 years old, the family moved 200 miles to the north to Drammen, just outside Oslo. The dialect there was quite different, and Ole never mastered it. For the rest of his life, he struggled with his speech and was self-conscious about it.

Ole was good at school. The other students nicknamed him "the professor" because he sometimes helped the teachers explain mathematical concepts. He was also an exceptional pianist.

Then came the Nazis.

When Ole was 13, his cousin was shot dead by a German solider, and the whole family fled to Sweden. There, he entered high school a year early, and excelled.

After the war, in 1949, Ole enrolled at the University of Oslo. He studied mathematics and was exposed to a computer there—which, given the date, he programmed in machine language. In 1952, as part of his compulsory military service, he began working part-time at the NDRE while at university, and then full-time after graduation.

His supervisor at the NDRE was Kristen Nygaard. The two of them were destined for greatness.

For all his life, Ole-Johan Dahl was professorial, socially awkward, and shy. He envied Nygaard's skill with people, but he was confident enough in his own abilities to hold strong opinions and not back down when pressed.

This made his professional relationship with Nygaard quite effective—if sometimes, perhaps, a bit loud.

Dahl retained and refined his skill in music, but he seldom played solo in public. He preferred to play chamber music along with others. Indeed, he was a member of an international amateur club that toured Europe.

Music was Dahl's preferred social outlet. He could communicate in music without the self-consciousness of his speech. He would often bring sheet music along with him to conferences and try to find someone to play duets with him. It was in the musical environment that he met his wife and made many of his lifelong friends.

SIMULA AND OO

SIMULA 67 was the first object-oriented programming language. It influenced both Bjarne Stroustrup in the creation of C++ and Alan Kay in the creation of Smalltalk. The story of how Nygaard and Dahl created this language is quite a tale. Get ready to take some notes to keep track of dates and acronyms, because this is a whirlwind adventure through the twisty little mazes of Scandinavian bureaucracies, American capitalism, and the raw ambition of Kristen Nygaard.

By the early 1950s, the political leaders of most countries realized that they needed to acquire expertise in computation lest they be left behind in the computational arms race. In Norway, this need was addressed by two organizations: the NDRE and the newly created Norwegian Computing Center (NCC).

Ole-Johan Dahl had come to the NDRE as a soldier in 1952 and worked as a programmer for the NDRE's Ferranti Mercury computer. The Mercury was a core memory machine with 2,000 vacuum tubes and a floating-point processor.

The core memory was 1,024 words of 40 bits, and was backed up by four drum memory units containing 4K words each.

Over the next several years, Dahl wrote an assembler for the Mercury. Then, inspired by early reports of ALGOL, he wrote a high-level compiler named Mercury Automatic Coding (MAC). By the end of that decade, Dahl had become one of Norway's foremost experts in computer programming.

Nygaard had come to the NDRE, also as a soldier, in 1948. He employed manual Monte Carlo[162] methods to help with the operation and research of Norway's first nuclear reactor. His success with this led to him being placed in charge of operations research at the NDRE, and he became an expert in that field in Norway.

Monte Carlo methods depend upon simulating the system being studied. Manual simulation is labor intensive and error prone. Nygaard realized that computers could be utilized to do the brute-force simulation work. So Nygaard led his team to create several different simulations for the Mercury. This experience caused him to consider whether he could formalize the concept of simulation into a mathematical language that would be easy for a computer to understand and easier for analysts to write. By 1961, he had compiled a set of notes that he called the *Monte Carlo Compiler*.

Nygaard's ideas were based on two kinds of data structures: one he called *customers*, which were passive repositories of attributes; the other he called *stations*. Customers were inserted into queues within the stations. The stations operated upon those customers and then inserted them into the queues of different stations. Every insertion of a customer into a station queue was driven by an *event*. The network of stations and customers driven by events was called a *discrete event network*.

Nygaard was not an expert in programming. Writing a compiler was not something he was prepared to do. So he enlisted the help of the best programmer he knew: Dahl. The two collaborated on creating the formal definition of a language that they called SIMULA, which they finished in May of 1962.

Early on, they decided to base their work on ALGOL 60. Their plan was for SIMULA to be a preprocessor that took the description of the discrete event network as input and produced ALGOL 60 code to execute the simulation.

The envisioned syntax involved keywords like station, customer, and system arranged in such a way as to define the simulation network. As an example, here are some fragments offered by Nygaard and Dahl from their 1981 paper.[1] The influence of ALGOL is evident in this syntax:

```
system Airport Departure := arrivals, counter, fee collector,
    control lobby;
customer passenger (fee paid) [500]; Boolean fee paid;
…more customers…
station counter;
    begin accept (passenger) select:
    (first) if none: (exit);
    hold (normal (2, 0.2));
    (if fee paid then control else fee
    collector) end;
station fee collector …
```

---

1. See *Monte Carlo analysis* in the Glossary of Terms.

In the meantime, Nygaard found himself in a worsening professional environment. He strongly opposed the management direction of the NDRE. This led to significant personal animosity with the director of the NDRE. So, in May of 1960, he accepted a position at the NCC to build up a civilian operation research department.

Nygaard raided his previous staff at the NDRE and convinced six of them to join his new effort. Dahl stayed behind for a few more years, but eventually joined the NCC in 1963.

The NCC had acquired a British machine called the Digital Electronic Universal Computing Engine (DEUCE)[2] in 1958. It used mercury delay lines to store 384 32-bit words, and a drum that held 8K words. The machine was slow. Operations were measured in hundreds of microseconds or milliseconds. This was not the machine that Nygaard needed for SIMULA.

In February of 1962, the NCC made a deal with the Danish Computing Centre (DCC) in Copenhagen for a new computer called the GIER (Geodætisk Instituts Elektroniske Regnemaskine). Nygaard wasn't happy about this deal, because the computer was not much better than the DEUCE. But the deal had been made for financial reasons.

The NCC simply could not afford the kind of multimillion-dollar machine that Nygaard wanted.

To make matters worse, the NCC was not particularly thrilled with Nygaard's and Dahl's ideas for SIMULA. Their objections were

- There would be no use for such a language.
- If there was a use, it must already have been done before.
- Dahl and Nygaard were not competent to engage in such a project.

Work like this was for larger countries with more resources. Or, to put it another way, the bureaucrats and bean counters weren't for it.

---

2. "The Development of the SIMULA Languages." See this chapter's References section.

But history has a way of coming up with happy accidents. Sperry Rand had just begun marketing its new UNIVAC 1107, and the company wanted to attract European customers. So, in May of 1962, just as Nygaard had gotten rebuked by the NCC for SIMULA, he found himself invited to the US to see the new machine.

Nygaard accepted the invitation, but his goal was not so much to buy a machine as it was to sell SIMULA. When he arrived, he started promoting SIMULA as a language for the UNIVAC machines. Bob Bemer was there in those meetings and heard Nygaard's sales pitch.

Bemer had worked for John Backus during the FORTRAN years and had worked with Grace Hopper during the COBOL years. He was also instrumental in the creation of ASCII and nearly got fired from IBM for proposing the concept of time-sharing.

But in May of 1962, Bemer had become an ALGOL enthusiast and was looking for ways to promote ALGOL over FORTRAN—and SIMULA looked to be a good strategy.

The Sperry Rand folks were so impressed by Nygaard's presentation that they invited him to present SIMULA at the next IFIP[3] 1962 World Congress in Munich. And so the concept of SIMULA gained almost instant global credibility.

Meanwhile, the Sperry Rand folks thought that SIMULA would give them an edge over their competition. So they came up with a scheme that they presented to Nygaard one evening at a Greek nightclub "while listening to bouzouki music, watching a beautiful belly dancer."[4] They needed a site to demonstrate the 1107 in Europe, so they proposed a 50% discount to the NCC—contingent on the NCC creating SIMULA.

---

3. International Federation for Information Processing.

4. Simula Session IX, Section 2.5.

The 1107 was a solid-state computer with 16K to 64K of 36-bit core memory. It had a drum that could hold 300K words. It used thin-film memory for internal registers, and had a 4-µs core memory cycle time. This was an ideal machine for Nygaard and SIMULA.

As you might imagine, this made Nygaard and Sperry Rand coconspirators in an attempt to get the NCC to break the deal it had made with the DCC for the GEIR. If they succeeded, Sperry Rand would get its demonstration site *and* get the SIMULA language that it could use to attract a whole range of customers interested in Monte Carlo simulations (e.g., nuclear research labs). Nygaard would get the machine he wanted for SIMULA, *and* SIMULA would be promulgated to Sperry Rand's global customers, with Nygaard's name all over it. The prestige value was enormous.

Opportunities like this do not come along every day, and Nygaard was *not* going to let it pass him by. So Nygaard started canvasing the folks at the NCC to seed the idea of the UNIVAC deal. Most of them thought he had lost his mind, and dismissed the idea.

Then, Sperry Rand send a contingent to the NCC in the summer of 1962 to formally present the deal; but the NCC remained reluctant. The 50% discount was enticing, but even then it was more money than the GEIR. What's more, they'd be on the hook for financing SIMULA. So Bob Bemer sweetened the deal by offering to pay for the development of SIMULA under a contracting arrangement.

This decision was too big for the NCC, so they sent it upstairs to the Royal Norwegian Council for Industrial and Scientific Research (NTNF).

Nygaard had already been promoting the idea to the folks at the NTNF, so they turned right around and told Nygaard to write up a report to help the NTNF make this decision.

Guess what Nygaard recommended. He couched it in all the right words, of course. His argument was that the needs for computing power in many different areas were growing rapidly, and a machine like the 1107 would last well into the future. Et cetera, et cetera.

The NTNF decided to cancel the GEIR order and agreed to accept the UNIVAC 1107. Sperry Rand was so eager to close this deal that they made very aggressive delivery promises, and backed up those promises with contractual penalties.

Those delivery promises were not kept. The machine that was promised for March of 1963 was not delivered until August. The operating system software that was promised was not acceptable until June of 1964. The penalties were significant, and so Sperry Rand agreed to upgrade the hardware rather than deliver cash.

Thus, Nygaard got a lot more machine than he bargained for. Quite a coup.

But frustration loomed. The conditions that had motivated Nygaard to leave the NDRE were now impeding his work at the NCC. Those conditions were simply that the NCC needed revenue, and research did not generate revenue. Moreover, even though the development of SIMULA was being funded by Sperry Rand, that development did not bring in *new* revenue. Worse still, the NCC had no experience with contract software and did not view itself as a software contractor, so the NCC had no idea how to deal with the Sperry Rand contract for SIMULA.

This situation festered for nearly a year. And, as before, Nygaard's professional frustrations led to personal animosities that eventually led to firings and resignations at high levels. But this time it wasn't Nygaard who left. Rather, when the dust settled, the board of the NCC had created a new Department for Special Projects and made Nygaard the director of research.

SIMULA I

While Nygaard was wrapped up in all those political machinations, Dahl was working on the SIMULA compiler, and things were not going well. The problems that were vexing him had to do with stacks.

ALGOL 60 was a block-structured language. This means that functions could have local variables that were stored on a stack.

You and I understand this at a deep level. Look at the following Java program:

```
public static int driveTillEqual(Driver... drivers)
{
  int time;
  for (time = 0; notAllRumors(drivers) && time < 480; time++)
    driveAndGossip(drivers);
  return time;
}
```

Where is that `time` variable stored? You and I both know that it's on the stack. Most of us have grown up with the common knowledge that local variables are stored on the stack.

But in the late 1950s, this was a *radical* concept. The computers of the day did not have stacks. They did not have index registers that could be used as stack pointers. Many did not even have indirect addressing.

I remember this well. Even in the late '70s, when I was working on Intel 8085 microprocessors and PDP-8–like computers, the idea of storing variables on a stack was both foreign and repugnant. It was repugnant because the number of cycles I'd have to burn in order to manage a stack was beyond my means to afford. The idea that I'd have to access every variable through an offset to a stack pointer was terrifying.

So I find it quite remarkable that the folks who designed ALGOL 60 made the stack the primary storage medium.

But it was the stack that was vexing Dahl—and for a very interesting reason.

Block-structured languages allow the declaration of local variables, *and local functions.*

The following is a program written in a mythical Java-like language that allows for local functions:

```
public int sum_n(int n) {
  int i = 1;
  int sum = 0;

  public int next() {
    return i++;
  }

  while (n-- > 0)
    sum += next();
  return sum;
  }
}
```

The function next is local to the function sum_n. Moreover, next has access to the local variables of sum_n. Only sum_n can call next.

Dahl saw the block of a function like sum_n as a data structure that had functions that could manipulate it. This was very similar to the notion of *stations* in the definition of SIMULA. Stations were data structures that contained queues of customers and could operate on the customers in those queues.

So Dahl's plan was to write a preprocessor that created ALGOL 60 blocks that would act as the stations and customers of his and Nygaard's simulation model.

The problem, however, was the queues. Queues don't behave like stacks. The lifetime of an object on a stack is strictly longer than the lifetime of the object above it on the stack. This is the first-in, last-out nature of a stack.

However, the lifetime of an object on a queue is the opposite. The first object in the queue is the first one out.

Dahl could not make the lifetimes of the objects in the queue match the lifetimes of ALGOL 60's blocks. So he was forced to consider a different strategy: garbage collection.

His idea was to allocate the ALGOL 60 blocks on a heap instead of a stack. In effect, he wanted to change ALGOL 60 to work something like the following Java program:

```java
class Sumer {
  int n;
  int i = 1;
  int sum = 0;

  public Sumer(int n) {
    this.n = n;
  }

  public int next() {
    return i++;
  }

  public int do_sum() {
    while (n-- > 0)
      sum += next();
    return sum;
  }

  public static int sum_n(int n) {
    Sumer s = new Sumer(n);
    return s.do_sum();
  }
}
```

Dahl was still thinking in terms of ALGOL 60 blocks, but now he planned to put those blocks into a garbage-collected heap instead of on the stack.

Dahl's garbage collector was not the general solution that you and I are used to. Rather, it was a compromise between a stack and a heap. It consisted of several groups of memory blocks. A group held many contiguous blocks of the same size. The groups themselves were noncontiguous, and each contained blocks of a different size.

The individual blocks had bits at the beginning and end that marked them as used or free. Thus, it was very easy to reclaim storage within a group.

And it was also easy to treat any particular group as a stack. Lastly, a storage allocator like this cannot fragment the way a traditional heap can.

Reclamation of blocks was achieved through reference counting and a last-resort garbage collector.

Once the storage allocator was designed, it was clear that SIMULA could not be a preprocessor that generated ALGOL 60. What Dahl needed to do instead was to modify ALGOL 60 to use the new storage allocator and to implement the SIMULA features within that compiler.

That decision had massive repercussions on SIMULA itself. Once you've got blocks on a heap with lifetimes that are free from the restrictions of a stack, all manner of possibilities arise. For example, why should customers be passive data structures? Why should all the activity be in the stations? Indeed, the activity between customers and stations could be considered quasi-parallel processing.

With that generalization came another realization. Stations and customers were all just instances of a broader class of quasi-parallel *processes* within a simulation. It was becoming clear to both Dahl and Nygaard that SIMULA might grow to be a general-purpose language, not just a language for Monte Carlo simulations.

Now, I want you to stop and consider how remarkable it is that the mere act of breaking the lifetime constraint imposed by the ALGOL 60 stack started this cascade of generalizations and revelations. I imagine that Dahl and Nygaard were electrified by the possibilities that suddenly confronted them. Indeed, they said of these years that they were a combination of "semi-madness [...] very hard work, frustration, and euphoria."

The envisioned syntax of SIMULA had changed enormously. Instead of *customers* and *stations*, they opted for the generalization of *activities*:

```
SIMULA begin comment airport departure;
set q counter, q fee, q control, lobby (passenger);
  counter office (clerk);…
activity passenger; Boolean fee paid; begin
  fee paid := random (0, 1) < 0.5…
    wait (q counter) end; activity clerk;

begin
counter: extract passenger select
  first (q counter) do begin
  hold (normal (2, 0.3));
    if fee paid then
    begin include (passenger) into: (q control);
         incite⁵ (control office) end
    else
    begin include (passenger into: (q fee); incite
         (fee office) end;
  end
  if none wait (counter office);
  goto counter
end…
end of SIMULA;
```

Note the wait, hold, and incite verbs. These were control statements for the process scheduling part of SIMULA. In essence, the activities in a SIMULA program were independent processes managed by a non-preemptive task switcher.

It was March of 1964, and up to this point the design of SIMULA was still all on paper. Remember, in those days, programming was not a

---

5. Later changed to activate, but I love the word incite.

matter of typing code on a screen and running a bunch of unit tests every few minutes. Compiles and tests took hours, if not days—and computer time was terribly expensive. So, big up-front design was the only economically viable solution.

The software was written solely by Dahl—though he got some ALGOL help from Ken Jones and Joseph Speroni at Sperry Rand. By December of 1964, the first prototype of SIMULA I was ready.

For the next two years, Dahl and Nygaard went on the road teaching SIMULA I to UNIVAC customers all over Europe. Other computer companies took note and started making plans for SIMULA compilers on their machines.

At this point, SIMULA I was still a simulation language, and as more and more programmers used it for simulations, it became clear that some significant changes needed to be made. Some of those changes would enhance the creation of simulations, but others would push the language toward general purpose.

One of their observations is of special interest to us. They noted that in the many simulations they had written, there were processes that shared many attributes and operations but differed in other ways. And so the idea of classes and subclasses was conceived.

The storage allocator was also reconsidered, because the use of fixed-size blocks wasted a lot of space. This was becoming more and more problematic as the sizes of the simulations grew. So they adopted the compacting garbage collector pioneered by John McCarthy in Lisp.

In May of 1967, Dahl and Nygaard presented a paper on *class* and *subclass* declarations to the IFIP Working Conference on Simulation. This paper outlined the first formal definition of SIMULA 67 and used the term *object* in reference to instances of classes and subclasses. It also introduced the concept of virtual (polymorphic) procedures. Their presentation was well received. A few weeks later, in yet another conference, Dahl and

Nygaard proposed that the notions of *type* and *class* were identical. By February of 1968, the SIMULA 67 spec was frozen.

The syntax for SIMULA 67 is remarkably similar to languages like C++, Java, and C#. In the following example, you should be able to see that similarity:

```
Begin
   Class Glyph;
      Virtual: Procedure print Is Procedure print;;
   Begin
   End;

   Glyph Class Char (c);
      Character c;
   Begin
      Procedure print;
        OutChar(c);
   End;

   Glyph Class Line (elements); Ref
      (Glyph) Array elements;
   Begin
      Procedure print;
      Begin
         Integer i;
         For i:= 1 Step 1 Until UpperBound (elements, 1) Do elements
            (i).print;
         OutImage;
      End;
   End;

   Ref (Glyph) rg;
   Ref (Glyph) Array rgs (1 : 4);

   ! Main program;
   rgs (1):- New Char ('A');
   rgs (2):- New Char ('b');
```

```
  rgs (3):- New Char ('b');
  rgs (4):- New Char ('a');
  rg:- New Line (rgs);
  rg.print;
End;
```

Despite that similarity, SIMULA 67 was still a simulation language, and it still maintained many of the artifacts of SIMULA I, such as keywords like hold and activate to manage the task switcher. In the end, this would be its undoing as a general-purpose language.

Sperry Rand wanted this new language for the 1107, and the company commissioned its own programmers, Ron Kerr and Sigurd Kubosch, to get to work on modifying the existing ALGOL 60 compiler. This effort was going well until, in September of 1969, they were told to abandon the 1107 in favor of the new UNIVAC 1108.[6]

The 1108 was a much better machine. It had integrated circuits, wire-wrapped backplanes, faster core memory, memory protection, multiprocessor ability, 256K capability, and much better mass storage. And it had a time-sharing operating system. In many ways, the 1108 sat at the transition between the old and the new.

The first commercial version of SIMULA 67 was finally released in March of 1971, and it enjoyed substantial success. It was implemented on many other machines, like the IBM 360, the Control Data 3000 and 6000, and the PDP-10. Many universities, especially in Europe, adopted it as a good language for teaching computer science.

It was only a few years after its initial release that Bjarne Stroustrup used the language at the University of Aarhus, Denmark, and later in Edinburgh. He was greatly impressed by the way classes could be used to create

---

6. This is a machine that I used in high school. The machine was located on the South Side of Chicago at the Illinois Institute of Technology. My high school was in the far-north suburbs and dialed in through a 300-baud modem. We wrote IITRAN programs using teletypes and paper tape. I had a blast.

nicely partitioned modular programs. He was also severely disappointed in the actual performance of SIMULA 67 programs and the SIMULA 67 compiler itself. Indeed, he feared that a major project of his nearly failed because of these problems.

So, in 1979, Bjarne Stroustrup decided to write a preprocessor for C that gave it "SIMULA-like" qualities. That preprocessor became C++.

References

Berntsen, Drude, Knut Elgsaas, and Håvard Hegna. 2010. "The Many Dimensions of Kristen Nygaard, Creator of Object-Oriented Programming and the Scandinavian School of System Development." International Federation for Information Processing. https://dl.ifip.org/db/conf/ifip9/hc2010/BerntsenEH10.pdf.

Dahl, O.-J., E. W. Dijkstra, and C. A. R. Hoare. 1972. *Structured Programming*. Academic Press.

Holmevik, Jan Rune. 1994. "Compiling SIMULA: A Historical Study of Technological Genesis." *IEEE Annals of the History of Computing* 16, no. 4: 25–37.

Lorenzo, Mark Jones. 2019. *The History of the Fortran Programming Language*. SE Books.

Nygaard, Kristen. 2002. Curriculum Vitae for Kristen Nygaard. http://kristennygaard.org/PRIVATDOK_MAPPE/PR_CV_KN.html.

Nygaard, Kristen and Ole-Johan Dahl. 1981. "SIMULA Session IX: The Development of the SIMULA Languages." ACM. www.cs.tufts.edu/~nr/cs257/archive/kristen-nygaard/hopl-simula.pdf.

O'Connor, J. J., and E. F. Robertson. 2008. Biography of Kristin Nygaard. School of Mathematics and Statistics, University of St. Andrews, Scotland. https://mathshistory.st-andrews.ac.uk/Biographies/Nygaard.

Owe, Olaf, Stein Krogdahl, and Tom Lyche (Eds.). 1998. *From Object-Orientation to Formal Methods: Essays in Memory of Ole-Johan Dahl*. Springer.

Stroustrup, Bjarne. 1994. *The Design and Evolution of C++*. Addison-Wesley.

University of Oslo. 2013. Biography of Ole-Johan Dahl. University of Oslo Department of Informatics. Published October 10, 2013. www.mn.uio.no /ifi/english/about/ole-johan-dahl/biography.

Wikipedia. "Bob Bemer." https://en.wikipedia.org/wiki/Bob_Bemer.

Wikipedia. "English Electric DEUCE." https://en.wikipedia.org/wiki/English _Electric_DEUCE.

Wikipedia. "Monte Carlo method." https://en.wikipedia.org/wiki/Monte_Carlo _method.

Wikipedia. "Ole-Johan Dahl." https://en.wikipedia.org/wiki/Ole-Johan_Dahl.

Wikipedia. "Simula." https://en.wikipedia.org/wiki/Simula.

Wikipedia. "UNIVAC 1100/2200 series." https://en.wikipedia.org/wiki/UNIVAC _1100/2200_series.

John Kemeny: The First "Everyone's" Language—BASIC

The story of BASIC is the story of programmers who thought programming should be available to everyone. It is the story of an impossible dream, and of genius that was, in the end, rendered blind by its own brilliance.

The Man, John Kemeny

Like John von Neumann, János György (John George) Kemeny was born a Jew in Budapest, Hungary. In 1926, the year of his birth, the winds of antisemitism and fascism were already strong. When Hitler invaded Austria in 1938, János was just 11 years old. His father, Tibor, realized that Hungary was next. Tibor was in the import/export business and had contacts in the US. So he bundled up the family and took them to New York. They left in the nick of time, leaving everything behind—including some family members who were neither seen nor heard from again.

John was precocious. At age 13, knowing no English, he was enrolled as a sophomore in a New York high school. Three years later he graduated valedictorian. He became a US citizen, and studied mathematics at Princeton. In 1945, at the age of 19, he took a job at Los Alamos, on the Manhattan Project, working for Richard Feynman and alongside John von Neumann.

At one point during that time, Feynman recalled[1] that Kemeny was awakened at midnight and interrogated, under lights, as to whether his father was a communist.

Kemeny worked in the computation center, where there were 17 of the previously mentioned[2] IBM punched card calculating machines run by a staff of 20. They kept those machines working 24 hours a day, six days a week, solving partial differential equations related to the implosion of the plutonium core of the first atomic bombs. Finding the solution to a single equation required that the 20 staff members and 17 machines work for three full weeks.

The machines took punched cards as input, performed a simple mathematical function upon the data in those cards, and then produced punched cards as output. A typical problem required tracking something on the order of 50 points in three dimensions. Each point was represented by a card.

Each machine was programmed with plugboards, and the cards had to be shuttled from machine to machine to machine, with the right setup in each machine and the right card decks going to the right machines for over 400 hours.

As we learned earlier, John von Neumann was deeply involved with these calculations and frequently consulted with the computation center. He was frustrated by the time and effort these calculations required. That frustration, along with his associations with the Harvard Mark I and the ENIAC teams, caused him to develop a radical new idea, which he informally wrote up in June of 1945. His paper, "First Draft of a Report on the EDVAC," shook the computing world.

In 1946, while still working at Los Alamos, Kemeny attended a lecture[3] by von Neumann in which he discussed the ideas in that paper. Von

---

1. See "Richard Feynman Lecture — Los Alamos from Below" in this chapter's References section.

2. In Chapter 3.

3. Kemeny, p. 5.

Neumann's vision, as described in that lecture, was for computers that had the following characteristics:

- Were fully electronic
- Represented numbers in binary
- Had a large internal memory
- Executed programs stored in memory alongside data
- Were general purpose

This was a lecture to which Babbage would have been vigorously nodding in agreement. The lecture also sparked something in Kemeny. He felt it was a utopian dream and wondered if he would live long enough to see such a thing.[4] It would only be seven years before that dream came true for him.

Not long after attending that lecture, Kemeny returned to Princeton to pursue his degrees. His doctoral thesis, titled "Type-Theory vs. Set-Theory," was supervised by Alonzo Church. As a doctoral student, he was appointed as Albert Einstein's mathematical assistant.

In 1953, while consulting for the RAND Corporation, his utopian dream was fulfilled by being able to play with von Neumann's JOHNNIAC, and later an early IBM 700 series computer. And *play* is the right word. Of this time, he said: "I had great fun learning to program a computer, even though the language used at that time was designed for machines and not for human beings."[5]

That sentiment on language design would end up driving one of Kemeny's main missions: providing computer access to everyone.

After his long and storied career, he received the New York Academy of Sciences Award in 1984, the Institute of Electrical Engineers Computer

---

4. Ibid.

5. Kemeny, p. 7.

Medal in 1986, and the Louis Robinson Award in 1990. He also received 20 honorary degrees.

It has been reported that he anonymously paid for the tuitions of disadvantaged students.

THE MAN, THOMAS KURTZ

If Kemeny was Batman, Tom Kurtz was Robin. Kurtz was born in 1928 in Oak Park, IL. As a boy he was very interested in science, and took physics and mathematics at Knox College, in Galesburg, IL.

In 1950, while attending a summer session at UCLA, he encountered the SWAC,[6] one of the earliest electronic computers in the US. This machine was built by the National Bureau of Standards. It used 2,300 vacuum tubes and had 256 37-bit words. It was for this machine that Kurtz wrote his first program—and he was hooked.

He received his Ph.D. in mathematics from Princeton and was recruited to Dartmouth by Kemeny to help promote computing at the university. The association between the two of them was long-lived and is at the very heart of the story of BASIC.

THE REVOLUTIONARY IDEA

In 1953 (the year after I was born), Kemeny was hired to rebuild the math department at Dartmouth, nestled in the Upper Valley of New Hampshire.

That department was aging out quickly and needed youthful energy and perspective to reboot it. The young Kemeny was recommended for the post by both Einstein and von Neumann.

---

6. Standards Western Automatic Computer.

Kemeny was eager to get Dartmouth into computing, so when MIT procured an IBM 704, Kemeny requested access to it. He recruited Tom Kurtz to haul steel boxes full of punched cards back and forth between Cambridge, MA, and Hannover, NH, once every two weeks.

Can you imagine waiting two weeks for a compile?

Within a couple of years, it was clear that they needed something better than a two-week turnaround time. So, using $37,000 from the furniture budget, Kemeny purchased an LGP-30[7] "desktop" computer.

This machine had 4,096 words, 31 bits each, stored on a magnetic drum. There were 113 vacuum tubes and 1,450 solid-state diodes.[8] It was a single-address machine with built-in multiply and divide. It had a clock rate of 120KHz and a memory access time of between 2 ms and 17 ms. The IO devices were a teleprinter and a paper tape reader/punch. You programmed it using a very simple machine language, or a truly bizarre language named ACT-III that delimited everything with apostrophes.[9]

The few students who were granted access to this machine loved it. One even wrote an ALGOL-like compiler for it. Another wrote a program to successfully predict the outcome of the 1960 New Hampshire presidential primary election. That prediction was newsworthy and gave the university some good media exposure.

But since only one student could use the computer at a time, access was severely limited. So they also continued using the 704 at MIT. On one of Kurtz's trips schlepping punched cards and listings between Hannover and Cambridge, he met John McCarthy[10] and bemoaned the fact that

---

7. Librascope General Purpose 30. This machine reminds me a lot of the ECP-18. See Chapter 9.

8. Diode logic is a power-hungry and finicky way to make AND and OR gates.

9. See https://en.wikipedia.org/wiki/File:ACT_III_program.agr.jpg.

10. Yeah, THAT John McCarthy. You know: the inventor of Lisp, among many other things.

access to the LGP-30 was so limited. McCarthy responded that Dartmouth should start thinking about time-sharing.

So one day, Kurtz decided to conduct an experiment. He *physically* "time-shared" the LGP-30 between batches of five students. Each batch of five would have 15 minutes to run as many compiles and tests as they could, sharing as they went. Each student would have access for a minute or so to load, compile, and print. Then the next, then the next, and so on.

Strangely enough, this strategy worked. Given sufficient coordination, the machine could be shared. This gave Kurtz the idea that a machine with many terminals and appropriate software could be massively shared among many students—perhaps the entire student body. Kurtz imagined that computing could be opened for everyone.

IMPOSSIBLE

Kurtz said to Kemeny: "Don't you think the time is approaching when every student should learn how to use a computer?"[11] Kemeny loved this idea. So, in ~1963, he commissioned Kurtz and Tony Knapp to fly out to Phoenix to talk with GE about donating a computer. That didn't go all that well, so they made similar requests to IBM, NCR, and Burroughs. GE then came back with a relatively inexpensive ($300,000) proposal for two machines: a DATANET-30 and a DATANET-235.

The DN-30 was the front-end communications processor for 128 terminals. It had 8K of 18-bit words. The DN-235 was the batch[12] machine that would actually execute programs. It had 8K of 20-bit words. The system also included two magnetic tape drives and a hard disk with a capacity on the order of 5MB to 10MB.

---

11. Kemeny and Kurtz, p. 3.

12. A batch machine executes one job at a time, from beginning to end. A job consisted of a batch of programs executed in sequence with instructions to the operators to mount and dismount magnetic tapes and the like.

The 1957 Sputnik scare opened up new government financing for STEM (science, technology, engineering, and mathematics). So Kurtz wrote to the National Science Foundation (NSF) for a grant. The proposal said they would use a dozen undergraduate students as programmers to write a time-sharing system from scratch. The NSF folks were of the opinion that writing such a system was a job for experts, not undergrads, and were therefore very skeptical of the plan. But Kemeny was persistent, and he talked them into it anyway.

The machines were ordered in the summer of 1963. They arrived in February of '64, and the Dartmouth Time Sharing System and the BASIC Compiler came to life on May 1 of that year.

This miracle of timing was accomplished by having the undergraduate students, along with Kemeny, who wrote the BASIC compiler, code everything up in the months before the machines arrived. Kemeny was able to debug parts of his compiler by borrowing a bit of time on a computer at the GE office in Boston. However, the vast majority of the code was written by the undergrads with pencil and paper, and sat waiting for a machine.

Now, let's go back over this. Kemeny, Kurtz, and a gaggle of geeky undergrads wrote a front-end terminal management system that communicated with a back-end time-sharing system and a compiler, from scratch, in assembly language, on two primitive and quirky GE computers, in less than one year; and they only had access to the machine for the last three months of that year. They did what the experts said was impossible. They did what much larger and more experienced teams had failed to do. And they did it in their "spare" time.

Don't tell me that the age of miracles has ended, because *that* was one freaking miracle.

A Personal Memory

I have a very tiny bit of experience with a DATANET-30. The machine was huge, enormous, and room filling. It made a hell of a racket. The disk was composed of a half-dozen or so 36-inch platters that were half an inch thick. It shook the floor and sounded like a jet engine as it spun up. The DN-30's serial communications facilities allowed it to talk to 128 terminals at once.

But as I recall, the assembly language code that handled the communications ports was driven by interrupts for each bit coming in from the serial lines.

The software had to assemble those bits into characters because there was no way GE could pack 128 UARTs[13] into that old behemoth of a contraption.

BASIC

Kurtz had wanted the language to be FORTRAN, but Kemeny was insistent that existing languages were not consistent with the idea that "every student" should learn computing. So Kemeny set about designing a new, simpler, more inclusive language. I suspect that he chose the name and *then* figured out the acronym: BASIC stands for Beginners All-purpose Symbolic Instruction Code.

BASIC is Kemeny's brainchild. He'd never seen a compiler before and knew nothing of compiler theory. Still, he wrote the compiler in the months between the purchase and delivery of the machines.

And it was a compiler. It ran on the DN-235 and compiled BASIC programs down into machine language.

BASIC was designed to be easy, general purpose, interactive, fast, and abstract—always keeping in mind that it was meant for "every student."

The line numbering scheme allowed for easy editing on a teletype. The fact that every statement began with a keyword kept the grammar, and

---

13. A UART (universal asynchronous receiver/transmitter) converts a serial stream of bits into a parallel stream of bytes. In the early '60s, devices like that would fill a large printed circuit board and cost a tidy sum. By the '70s, you could get them on a single chip for a few dollars.

therefore the compiler, simple. The fact that students could key in a program and see it execute in seconds made it the first wide-access interactive language ever devised.

Of course, this was 1964, and compromises with the hardware had to be made. Memory was frightfully expensive in those days, so variable names were restricted to one letter and one optional digit. There were no named functions or named lines. There was no file IO. There was an IF, but no ELSE. There was a DO, but no WHILE. All these things would come later; but in 1964, even this was a miracle.

TIME-SHARING

But the bigger miracle was that the system could support dozens and dozens of terminals. Twenty, or thirty, or forty students could be entering BASIC programs at the same time and seeing results within seconds. This was true time-sharing—and it was a game changer.

Everyone took notice! More and more people wanted terminals in their offices, in their classrooms, in their high schools, in their homes. Terminals were popping up everywhere.

Of course, students wrote games. Other students played those games. There were football games and tic-tac-toe games. I mean, when you turn the student body of a university loose to write code, they will write *games*.

GE was thunderstruck. They had thought this to be impossible, or at least to require many human-decades of work. They licensed the time-sharing and BASIC software from Dartmouth in exchange for more hardware, and they opened up time-sharing service centers around the country and around the world.

Government, business, science, finance, you name it: Everyone wanted a time-sharing terminal.

A Personal Memory

In 1966 my father, a science teacher, took his summer school students on a tour of International Minerals and Chemicals—the folks who gave us Accent, one of the first consumer MSG[14] seasonings. One of the researchers was working on a teletype. I sidled up to this man, and he showed me how the time-sharing system and BASIC worked. I was hooked. I went home and pretended I had a computer. I would write the commands down on paper, and then write what I expected the computer to do. I played that game with my friends. They would write commands, and I would pretend to be the computer and write the answers.

In those early, crazy years before the minicomputer, the number of time-sharing services in the US offering BASIC grew to around 80. Perhaps 5 million people had learned BASIC by that time.

COMPUTER KIDS

More and more high schools got time-sharing terminals, and more and more kids got hooked on computers. This was the age of the computer kids.

In the late '60s, my high school got a time-sharing connection to a UNIVAC 1108 at the IIT in Chicago. The language we used was IITRAN, which was more like ALGOL than BASIC.

My buddies and I took over the operation of the single terminal—an ASR-33 with a modem wired into a traditional telephone. The telephone had a dial lock, but any good geek knows that you can dial a locked phone by tapping out the phone number on the hook switch.

The math teachers were thrilled that we took things over. They certainly didn't want to load dozens of paper tapes into the machine at ten characters per second. They certainly didn't want to tear off listing after listing and put them in the output basket. But *we* did! *We* were the

---

14. Monosodium glutamate.

operators! And when we were done with all that loading and tearing, we *played*. We had at our disposal a time-sharing terminal and carte blanche to use it. And boy oh boy, did we take advantage of that!

And our experience was just one of thousands. In high school after high school across the nation, the computer kids were taking over time-sharing terminals and drinking from the firehose.

Is it any wonder that the whole industry changed as all those computer kids entered the workforce?

ESCAPE

But the computer revolution had just begun. Minicomputers were cropping up all over the place, and their users wanted BASIC, or something like BASIC, to write quick little interactive programs. And so as quickly as it had arisen, time-sharing died away.

The massive machines in huge machine rooms that cast terminal connections hither and yon across the countryside were replaced by little machines the size of a small refrigerator or a microwave oven; and then eventually by personal computers.

But compilers are hard to write. Interpreters are easier. And so BASIC interpreters spread like wildfire.

This only accelerated when personal computers entered the fray. In the end, although interpreted BASIC vernaculars were everywhere, the BASIC *compiler* from Dartmouth shrank back to Dartmouth and stayed there in its own little cul-de-sac.

THE BLIND PROPHET

The vast expansion of BASIC into the minicomputer, and then the personal computer, world was, at first, ignored by the Dartmouth team.

They simply kept on modernizing their version of BASIC to keep up with industry norms. They added features for structured programming, for plotting, for file manipulation, named functions, modules, and many, many others. By the mid-'80s, the Dartmouth BASIC was a very capable language that might have rivaled Pascal.

But it was still BASIC. The authors never abandoned the keyword nature of the language. Every new feature added a new set of keywords. The authors never embraced the C notion that everything was a function, and that all IO ought to be mediated by functions.

When the Dartmouth team finally looked around the industry and saw all the BASIC interpreters and all the hacks and warts that various vendors had added to the language, they were horrified. Their solution was to invent yet another version of BASIC that they called "True BASIC." This they offered to the world, and the world answered with silence. Nobody cared.

It is remarkable to me that programmers possessing the clear genius of Kemeny and Kurtz, who started the time-sharing revolution and who brought computing to the masses, got caught in the age-old trap of NIH.[15] How could they continue to promote a keyword-based language in the face of the success of C? Indeed, in their argument[16] for True BASIC, they compared it to FORTRAN, COBOL, and Pascal, but never even mentioned C. Yet, by 1984, not only was C the language of choice around the industry,[17] but C++ and Smalltalk were already on the horizon.

SYMBIOSIS?

In 1972 Kemeny wrote a book titled *Man and the Computer*. The central thesis of this work was that computers were a new species of life that was symbiotic with humankind. This may sound silly, but look around you.

---

15. Not Invented Here.

16. Kemeny and Kurtz, p. 89.ff.

17. Except for Apple, which held out for Pascal for another year or so.

How many computers are within arm's reach? How many times per day do you interact with some computer? Is your watch a computer? Is your phone a computer? Are your earphones computers? Are your car keys computers? Are you not completely surrounded by computers that you interact with moment by moment? And is that trend not dramatically increasing?

Perhaps computers are not alive by our strict definition of life. But no one can deny that they have evolved into an ever-deepening synergy, if not symbiosis,[18] with us.

Throughout the book, Kemeny falls back on time-sharing as his solution to providing computer access to everyone. Instead of talking about home computers, he talks about home terminals to large data centers scattered around the world. He cannot seem to foresee (and who can blame him?) that within 50 years, computers of vastly more power than he could imagine would number in the trillions and be a part of our moment-by-moment lives.

PROPHESIES

In the book, Kemeny makes several predictions. Here are just a few:

Artificial Intelligence

"The decade of the 1960s showed that this task is vastly more difficult than some of the proponents of artificial intelligence had guessed.

"Although there have been a number of notable successes, in many cases the human effort to teach the computer has turned out to be horrendous, and the amount of labor required for a computer to simulate human intelligence is discouragingly great. Often it reaches a point at which the effort is simply not worthwhile."[19]

---

18. Symcybrosis?

19. Kemeny, p. 49.

I find it fascinating that this statement from 1972 is as true today as it was then. And I say this while editing this paragraph with a machine that is continuously checking my spelling and grammar and offering me alternatives to both.

I also find it fascinating that Kemeny was speaking in direct opposition to the much more common notion that computers would become intelligent in a matter of years or decades. Consider, for example, the popular filmography of the day: HAL 9000 from Kubrick's *2001: A Space Odyssey*, or Colossus from *The Forbin Project*, or Johnny #5 from *Short Circuit*.

In these days of large language models like ChatGPT & Co, we still see these vastly impressive tools *as* tools and not as intelligent beings. One of the greatest put-downs of the year 2023 was when Chris Christie, during the first GOP primary debate, accused Vivek Ramaswamy of sounding like ChatGPT.

Phones

". . . on a push button telephone, it should be entirely possible to 'type in' a party's name and rough address and have the telephone company computer find his phone number and dial it. Of course this will mean extra use of a computer, and therefore an extra charge should be made for the service . . ."[20]

If only he could see what today we consider a "telephone" to be. Not only can we type in our party's name, we can simply speak it. Our phones contain lists of all our contacts. None of us bother to remember telephone numbers anymore—even though telephone numbers still exist!

And anyways, nowadays we choose to text, or chat, or post on X or Instagram, or . . .

Privacy and Big Brother

"If governments and big businesses are allowed to invade our privacy, it is our own fault for allowing them to do so. They are perfectly capable

---

20. Kemeny, p. 55.

of doing this without computers, although computers make it much easier to keep track of millions of people. Computers have lowered the price tag for Big Brother but have not brought about a change in principle."[21]

Here I sit, in 2023 . . .

. . . with the fear of government censorship and domestic intelligence gathering through social media.

. . . with many platforms that we rely on for domestic and world news only providing their own viewpoints as truth, and with some bending to government pressure to suppress vital information.

. . . with data breaches as common as tomorrow's weather report because nobody could (or would) see the obvious vulnerabilities in technologies like SQL.

. . . with the constant risk of our private data being gathered and transmitted, while at the same time making it impossible to protect our children from disinformation and propaganda.

And Kemeny's words hit home. Our fault. Our own fault.

The End of Moore's Law

"It sounds plausible to say that since computing speed has increased by a factor of a million in twenty-five years a similar increase in speed can be expected in the next twenty-five. However, this brings us up against one of the absolute limitations in nature—namely, the speed of light."[22]

---

21. Ibid.

22. Kemeny, p. 63.

He was right, of course. The 1-μs cycle times of the early '70s have only increased by a factor of a few thousand, not a million. And there is not much hope that our clock rates will increase much more than they have. For the last 20 years, we've been stuck at ~3GHz, and there is nothing[23] on the horizon that seems likely to change that.

> *"I fully expect that within the next generation we will see computer memories capable of holding the contents of the largest library in the world."*[24]

Hell, I think I could hold the entire 1972 Library of Congress on my phone. Kemeny expected memory to increase in volume and speed—but he had no idea that we would now be looking at terabytes for pennies.

Terminals/Consoles/Screens

"The one area that is lagging behind the rest in cost improvement is the very important one of computer terminals. A cost of $100 per month is quite typical for the rental and servicing of a computer terminal. And these terminals are fairly primitive. [...] I see absolutely no reason why a very reliable computer terminal could not be manufactured to sell for the price of a black-and-white television set. This will be necessary if computers are to be brought into the home."[25]

This prediction was more than fulfilled half a decade later. The Sinclair ZX-81 was a little computer with a membrane keyboard that hooked up to your B&W TV. It was released (as the name implies) in 1981. I had one of these little beasts. It was fun, but not very reliable.

Of course, Kemeny was not thinking about an actual computer in the home. He was thinking of a terminal that would sit on your kitchen counter and connect by phone to a data center.

---

23. Quantum computing can create efficiencies in certain, very constrained, applications, but not generally.

24. Kemeny, p. 64.

25. Kemeny, p. 66.

Networks

"The next decade is likely to see the development of huge computer networks. Indeed several modest networks are in existence today [. . .] The full impact of modern computers will be felt by most people only when large multiprocessor computer centers are built all over the United States and tied efficiently to the existing communications network."[26]

He called this one pretty well. The late '70s and early '80s were the era of the Bulletin Board Services. People with modems and terminals (e.g., the Silent 700 printer by Texas Instruments) could dial in to these tiny little "data centers" and share software. These were replaced starting in 1980 with dial-up services like CompuServe. This eventually provided people with access to email. In 1998 the email rage was so pervasive that the rom-com *You've Got Mail* with Tom Hanks and Meg Ryan was a hit.

But "the full impact?" Kemeny could hardly imagine what that full impact has been. Our phones, watches, refrigerators, thermostats, security cameras, and cars are tied into a globe-spanning high-speed wireless network.

Education

". . . by 1990 every home can become a mini-university."[27]

The COVID-19 pandemic certainly proved that one—though whether true or false is a matter of some debate and concern. In any case, it is certainly true that a university-quality education is available to anyone who has access to the internet and has the will to study.

THROUGH A GLASS DARKLY

John Kemeny was a programmer. He became a programmer in 1946 when he dreamed of von Neumann's utopia of a stored-program computer. He

---

26. Kemeny, p. 67.

27. Kemeny, p. 84.

proved his mastery of the craft when he wrote the BASIC compiler and guided a group of undergraduates to build the first practical time-sharing system with little more than "stone knives and bearskins." His goal was the democratization of computers—the bringing of computation to the masses. He believed that *everyone* could and should use computers. He provided free computer access at Dartmouth and recommended that all educational institutions should do likewise. He even proposed free computer access as a condition for accreditation.

Kemeny saw the future through a glass darkly—but he saw it. And he devoted his life to that vision.

John Kemeny was a programmer.

REFERENCES

Dartmouth. "Birth of BASIC." Posted on YouTube on Aug. 5, 2014. (Available at the time of writing.)

IEEE Computer Society. n.d. "Thomas E. Kurtz: Award Recipient." www .computer.org/profiles/thomas-kurtz.

Kemeny, John G. 1972. *Man and the Computer.* Charles Scribner's Sons.

Kemeny, John G., and Thomas E. Kurtz. 1985. *Back to BASIC.* Addison-Wesley.

Lorenzo, Mark Jones. 2017. *Endless Loop: The History of the BASIC Programming Language.* SE Books.

O'Connor, J. J., and E. F. Robertson. n.d. "John Kemeny: Biography." School of Mathematics and Statistics, University of St. Andrews, Scotland. https:// mathshistory.st-andrews.ac.uk/Biographies/Kemeny.

The Quagmire. "Richard Feynman Lecture — 'Los Alamos from Below'," 1:18:00. Posted on YouTube on July 12, 2016. (Available at the time of writing.)

Von Neumann, John. 1945. "First Draft of a Report on the EDVAC." Moore School of Electrical Engineering, the University of Pennsylvania.

Wikipedia. "John G. Kemeny." https://en.wikipedia.org/wiki/John_G._Kemeny.

Wikipedia. "LGP-30." https://en.wikipedia.org/wiki/LGP-30.

Wikipedia. "Thomas E. Kurtz." https://en.wikipedia.org/wiki/Thomas_E._Kurtz.

JUDITH ALLEN

This story hits very close to home for me. It is the story of the first binary electronic computer that I ever laid my eyes and fingers upon. It is also the fascinating, uplifting, and sometimes disturbing story of Judy Allen, a young feminist who became a programmer in the late '50s.

Of her feminism, she writes:

> "[We] did the work *for our daughters and granddaughters*, and all of womankind. We showed up, wearing our lipstick, our power suits and high-heeled shoes, with all our superior skills, knowledge, and experience, and the added qualification of insight and intuition—which we honored—and respect for human relationships over profit. We demanded equal pay, and dignity, and demanded laws be passed. We demonstrated in the streets and testified in court and Congress.

> "We pissed off our male colleagues when we wouldn't 'just shut up and take notes.' We took advantage of every opportunity for advancement, often at the expense of our free time and sometimes, family time. We *never* asked for special dispensation because we were pregnant, premenstrual, a single mother, or exhausted. We were constantly dissed: disrespected, dismissed, disregarded. We had to fight for every promotion, be better educated, better qualified, and harder working than our male 'equals.' And still we had

to fight for equal pay in order to get even small adjustments. We fought battles that were not won for many years. After decades of persistently demanding, we lost the big one: The Equal Rights Amendment."

If you think that statement is a bit exaggerated, her story may convince you otherwise.

THE ECP-18

The machine was called the ECP-18. It was a very simple single-address machine, with 1,024 15-bit words on a drum memory. It had a Star Trek front panel with buttons that lit up when you pushed them. There was a set of 15 buttons for the accumulator, another for the address register, and another for the program counter. These buttons were arranged on a console that sat above a desk upon which rested an ASR 33 Teletype.

In 1967 one of these machines was rolled into my high school lunch room during my freshman year. The company that was marketing these to high schools was going to do a demo.

I was already a computer nerd by this time, and the machine transfixed me. Even though it was powered down, it took all my willpower to leave it and go to class.

During study hall, I would get a bathroom pass and return to look at it. At one point, the sales engineer was putting the machine through its paces. I hovered, like an annoying mosquito. I watched as the engineer punched buttons on the machine.

I'll describe the details of my interactions with this little machine in part 2. For now, suffice it to say that through my observations of the sales engineer, I inferred the architecture of the machine and how to write simple programs for it. I even got one such simple program to work by sneaking ten minutes on the machine while no one else was looking. The effect upon me was profound, even though I was never able to touch that machine again.

A week or so later, that ECP-18 was wheeled out of my high school, never to return. That was a tough day for me. It is only recently, more than five decades after that glorious event, that I discovered the story you are about to read.

JUDITH SCHULTZ

What follows I've pieced together from Judith's memoir, which was written in the spring of 2012 as she was being treated for her fifth recurrence of breast cancer. It's not clear to me that she survived past the end of that year. As the memoir proceeds, it transitions from an account of her life to a fictional tale that abruptly ends.

Judith B. Schultz was born in 1940, in Oregon, near the mouth of the Columbia River. Her father, Travis, was a daffodil bulb farmer, and she was raised on the farm doing farm chores. But her mother had different dreams for her.

She was precocious. She had a knack for writing and was good at math. So she got a scholarship to Oregon State College.

Her father abjectly refused to allow her to attend.

"You don't need this," he said. "You're not going to college. Just a waste of time and money we don't have. You're only 16, you'd lose your innocence. They'd give you highfalutin' notions, make you question everything you believe. You'd come home with your head full of ideas, probably be an atheist. Or a commie. You don't need college to be a wife and mother. Get that uppity idea out of your head."[1]

But her mother took her aside and said, "I'll take care of Dad." And so, in the fall of 1956, Judith went to college.

She majored in home economics, and took electives in math and writing.

Her first writing course was taught by a published novelist, and he took an "interest" in her. At first, she thought that interest was solely academic. He praised her writing, which excited her. But as time went on, his baser interest became clear, and she had to escape his office after rejecting his advances. After that, his academic interest in her waned.

Her math teacher, Arvid Lonseth, on the other hand, was a gentleman who noticed her talent for the topic and urged her to change her major. So, at age 17, she became a math major.

In the fall of '57, the math department acquired its first computer. It was an ALWAC III-E. This was a 32-bit machine with a 4K drum memory. The internal registers were kept on a special area of the drum, as were other working storage registers. The machine had ~200 vacuum tubes and

---

1. Memoir, Chapter 4, Corruption of Innocence.

~5,000 silicon diodes. It had a 5-ms add time and a 21-ms multiply/divide time. IO was a TTY and paper tape. Programming it was accomplished by flipping the rows of toggle switches on the front panel. It was very likely a deep technical challenge.

Judith was the only girl in the first computer programming class ever offered at OSC. The boys pressed around the machine and would not allow her access. She learned by watching and listening, but never by actually touching. She got an A anyway, and then took the course a second time.

This time, she knew the answers before the boys, and "wiggled" her way to the console and flipped the switches before the boys had any clue what was going on.

She loved it. She was hooked.

At 18, she married Don Edwards, another of the math students. She left school and bore three children in quick succession. At 22, in 1962, she returned to school to finish her degree.

One of her classes was Computer Programming. It was in this class that she encountered the computer invented by the professor, Dr. Allen Fulmer.

It was the ECP-18.[2]

Again, she was hooked. She loved working with the machine. She loved programming—in binary machine language.

But life intruded. She finished her degree and began a teaching career. But as her children grew, she decided to "have a crack at being a full-time mother,"[3] so she left teaching and stayed home with the house and the kids.

But after five months, she was desperate for something else. Being a housewife was not what she wanted. And that's when the phone rang.

It was Dr. Fulmer, with a plan. He was going to market the ECP-18 to high schools and colleges, but he needed someone to write a symbolic assembler. Would she like to do that?

OK, now stop. We are talking about a machine with 1,024 words of drum memory. A machine that can only be programmed by toggling programs in binary through the front panel. A machine whose only IO device is an ASR 33 Teletype with a paper tape reader/punch that operates at ten characters per second.

He was asking her to write a symbolic assembler—in binary—and without indirect addressing. This is no mean feat.

Of course she agreed. It was something she could do from home with only occasional trips to the lab to run tests.

Of course he could not pay her; but she settled for 40% of the company.

Her husband was not pleased, but he acquiesced: "Fine with me, as long as nothing slips at home. I don't like coming home to a dirty house."[4]

---

2. Fulmer had built the machine in his mother's garage using transistors donated by Tektronics.

3. Memoir, Chapter 6, Metamorphosis.

4. Ibid.

Two months later she had that assembler working. It was a two-pass affair. I imagine that it was similar in ways to the PAL-III assembler that Ed Yourdon wrote for the PDP-8, except that Yourdon had 4K of core, indirect addressing, and auto-index registers to work with.

She learned to solder, and she helped Dr. Fulmer build the garage prototype that would be used as a sales demonstrator.

And then, in 1965, with only stipends for clothing and travel and still no income, Judy went on the road. From Seattle to San Francisco, she took that garage-built machine to colleges and high schools and teacher's conventions. She even took it to a trade show in New York City, where she ran afoul of the unions, who destroyed the machine because she dared to unpack and plug it in herself.

By 1966, she and Dr. Fulmer had sold eight of the machines for $8,000 apiece. And they sold the company to GAMCO industries out of Texas. Of the 40% she took from that sale, she simply said: "It was worth it."

By this time, she was the country's foremost authority on teaching high school and college kids about computers. She was in demand, and able to command salaries that just two years before she could not even dream of.

Her career exploded, and she went on to earn a Ph.D., and be a significant voice in computer education from the '70s through the '90s.

A STELLAR CAREER

I'd like to end this with some kind of "happily ever after" coda. And, in some ways, that would probably be an apt report. She had a stellar career and led a full and rich life.

Unfortunately, she had not had her last encounter with "interested" men. One of those encounters ended in violence, which was then covered up by her male associates. Her battle with cancer had yet to begin. And was she never done fighting for her feminist goals.

This book is not the place for the more sordid and disturbing of her stories; I refer you to her memoirs, which are replete with them. Some of them are quite scary.

For my part, I am simply filled with gratitude that I was able to touch that little machine that she had put so much of her energies into. That mere touch had a profound impact upon my life and future career.

I never met Judy Allen, but because of that ECP-18, her effect upon me was profound.[5]

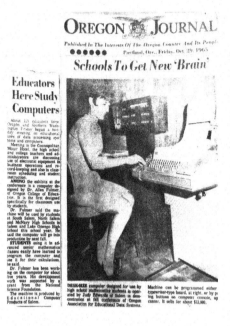

OREGON JOURNAL

Published In The Interests Of The Oregon Country And Its People

Portland, Ore., Friday, Oct. 29, 1965

Schools To Get New 'Brain'

Educators Here Study Computers

DESK-SIZE computer designed for use by high school mathematics students is operated by Judy Edwards of Salem in demonstration at fall conference of Oregon Association for Educational Data Systems. Machine can be programmed either typewriter-type board, at right, or by pushing buttons on computer console, upper center. It sells for about $13,900.

REFERENCES

Allen, Judy. 2012. "New Writing: A Memoir of a Life and a Career in the Sixties and Seventies." https://lookingthroughwater.wordpress.com/2012/05/25/foreword-a-memoir.

Edwards, Judith B. *Computer Instruction: Planning and Practice*. Northwest Regional Educational Laboratory. https://files.eric.ed.gov/fulltext/ED041455.pdf.

A few ancillary documents and brochures about the ECP-18.

Personal correspondence with Allen Fulmer.

---

5. Picture of *Oregon Journal* article courtesy of Allen Fulmer.

Thompson, Ritchie, and Kernighan

The creation of Unix and C occurred between 1968 and 1976 and was perhaps the most profound event in the history of our industry. Unix derivatives run everything from server farms to thermostats, and the software within them is almost certainly written in some kind of C derivative.

C and Unix are coupled inventions that took place in some kind of bizarre recursive loop. Unix forced the invention of C, and C forced the reinvention of Unix. That coupling was inevitable and persists to this day. It is, in some sense, like the worm Ouroboros, the snake that eats its own tail. However, rather than consuming itself, that virtuous cycle of creation spews forth a breathtaking panoply of massively useful ideas and inventions.

The story of that cycle involves many more people than I can account for here, so I will focus upon the three who had the greatest impact of all: Ken Thompson, Dennis Ritchie, and Brian Kernighan.

Ken Thompson

Kenneth Lane Thompson was born in New Orleans in early 1943. He was a Navy brat and spent the first two decades of his life traveling the country and the world. He never lived in one place for more than a year or two at a time.

As a youngster, he loved mathematical and logical problems. He must have been attracted to computers even then, because he sometimes worked math problems in binary. He was also interested in electronics, which was his hobby throughout his teens.

He joined the chess team in sixth grade while in Texas. He read lots of chess books. He once quipped: "I guess nobody in 6th grade ever read a chess book before because as soon as you read a chess book you're better than everybody else."[1] And then he stopped and never played personally again, because although he liked winning, he disliked making others lose.

He graduated high school in Chula Vista, CA, and studied electrical engineering at the University of California, Berkeley. While at UCB, he discovered computers and was completely and thoroughly hooked. "I consumed computers, I loved them,"[2] he said.

There was no computer science (CS) curriculum at the time, so he continued in electrical engineering (EE) and got his BS in 1965, and his MS a year later.

He had no ambitions outside of school. Indeed, his graduation was a surprise to him; he wasn't paying any attention to minor details like that. He didn't apply to grad school himself; one of his advisors did it for him. He was accepted without knowing the application had been submitted.

His plan was simply to continue ignoring the details and stay at UCB. "I owned [the place], my fingers were in absolutely everything. [. . .] I almost ran the school as far as computers go. [. . .] The main monster computer[3]

---

1. From Computer History Museum. "Oral History of Ken Thompson," Posted on YouTube on Jan. 20, 2023. (Available at the time of writing.)

2. From Vintage Computer Federation. "Ken Thompson Interviewed by Brian Kernighan at VCF East 2019," Posted on YouTube on May 6, 2019. (Available at the time of writing.)

3. An IBM 7094, a $3 million transistor-based computer with a 2-μs cycle time, floating- and fixed-point multiply and divide, and 32K 36-bit words. This was the first computer to sing a song. The song was "Daisy Bell," the song sung by HAL 9000 as it was being disconnected in the movie *2001: A Space Odyssey*. The 7094 played a significant role in NASA's Gemini and Apollo programs, as well as missile defense systems in the '60s.

at the university shut down at midnight and I'd come in with my key and I'd open it up and it would be my personal computer until 8 a.m. I was happy. No ambition. I was a workaholic, but for no goal."

After receiving his MS, his teachers conspired, without his knowledge, to get him a job at Bell Labs. At their recommendation, Bell Labs repeatedly tried, and repeatedly failed, to recruit him—he skipped out on the recruiting appointments. "Again, no ambition." Finally, a recruiter came to his door. Ken let him in and offered him gingersnaps and beer. [4]

The recruiter offered to fly him to Bell Labs and cover his expenses. He agreed because there were some high school friends on the East Coast he wanted to visit. He told the recruiter, in no uncertain terms, that he was not taking a job.

His stroll through the corridors of Bell's computer science research lab impressed him. Office door after office door had a name he recognized. "It was just shocking." But then he left to drive down the coast and see his friends, who were scattered at different places along the way.

---

4. IBM 7094 at Columbia, for reference.

Somewhere around his third stop there was an offer letter waiting for him. Somehow Bell Labs had tracked him down.[5]

He accepted a position at the Labs and began work on the Multics project in 1966.

Thompson is an avid pilot who convinced many of his coworkers to learn to fly and get their pilot licenses. He would organize flying events to restaurants and other venues. At one point, in the winter of 1999, he and Fred Grampp paid a Russian outfit to teach him to fly a MiG-29.

DENNIS RITCHIE

Dennis MacAlistair Ritchie was born in Bronxville, NY, on September 9, 1941. He was the son of a scientist named Alistair Ritchie who worked on switching systems at Bell Labs.

Despite the fact that his sixth grade teacher once remarked that his work in math was "spasmodic," he graduated from Summit High School in Summit, NJ, in 1959, and from Harvard in 1963 with a BS in physics. While at Harvard, he took a course titled Programming for the Univac I. This piqued his interest in computers and set the stage for his graduate school efforts.

After graduation, Ritchie was accepted into the Applied Mathematics graduate program at Harvard. His field of study was the theory and use of computing equipment.

In 1967 Ritchie followed his father to Bell Labs, and began to work on the Multics project and was involved with the creation of the BCPL compiler for the GE 635 computers that drove Multics. He was still

---

5. This version of the story was from 2019. In a 2005 version of this story, he says the letter was waiting for him when he returned home. This is more likely, but less colorful. The two tales, told at two different times, provide an interesting insight into Thompson's psyche and memory.

working on his Ph.D. at the time, and was living and working in his parents' attic and basement.[6]

Ritchie *almost* earned that Ph.D. I say "almost" because, although his thesis was written and approved, he never submitted a bound copy—which was a requirement. Why not? There is some debate over this. Some think it was the nontrivial binding fee that Ritchie was determined not to pay. Others believe that Ritchie simply couldn't be bothered. His brother John said that Ritchie already had a coveted job as a researcher at Bell Labs, and "never really loved taking care of the details of living."

Albert Meyer, one of Ritchie's collaborators during his graduate studies, said of him: "[Dennis] was a sweet, easy going, unpretentious guy. Clearly smart but also kind of taciturn. [...] I would have loved to [continue to] collaborate with him [...] but yeah, you know, he was already doing other things. *He was staying up all night playing* Space War!"[7]

A year later, Bell Labs became concerned about Ritchie's Ph.D. status, and so in February of 1968 they wrote to Harvard:[8]

"Gentlemen:

"...Would you please verify for our information that Dennis M. Ritchie will receive his Doctor of Philosophy degree in Mathematics in February 1968.

Thank you very much."

To which Harvard replied two weeks later:

"With reference to your inquiry of February 7, 1968, this is to inform you that Mr. Dennis M. Ritchie is not a candidate for his Doctor of Philosophy degree in February 1968."

---

6. His bedroom was in the attic and his office was in the basement.

7. From "Discovering Dennis Ritchie's Lost Dissertation." This statement gave me the chills, because: me too ...

8. "Dennis Ritchie Thesis And the Typewriting Devices in the 1960s".

Whoops!

Bill Ritchie suspects that there may have been some kind of traumatic event that caused his brother to block out the thesis. He said:[9]

> "[…] something happened . . . from that point forward, February 1968, all mention of that thesis or anything having to do with it was buried, never talked about until after he died. This includes that Dennis never contradicted the Turing Prize committee or the Japan Prize committee when they formally stated that he held a PhD. This isn't just something that happened 50 years ago, it is lifelong behavior. And is very different from how Dennis ran his life for the most part, it is hard to imagine why he kept the PhD story so hidden but he did. "

On the other hand, Ritchie's brother John says:[10]

> "[H]e certainly was in many ways a mysterious guy, and the lack of a PhD is a perfect representation of the mystery. No one knows what the real story is […]. I don't attribute this to some traumatic event, as Bill speculates, though maybe it was. Maybe it was the binding fee. Maybe he panicked at the idea of defending the thesis to the panel. We'll never know."

Anyway, it never really mattered. Dennis Ritchie simply joined the ranks of those of us programmers who have been called[11] "doctor" without actually having the certificate.

Ritchie's thesis was lost for nearly half a century. After his death, through the efforts of his sister, Lynn, a copy was found and is now available online.[12] It's worth a look, if only to see the extraordinary care with which all the mathematical symbolism was typewritten. According to his

---

9. Private correspondence.

10. Private correspondence.

11. Ask me how I know.

12. See https://www.computerhistory.org/collections/catalog/102784979.

brothers, he convinced Bell Labs to give him an IBM 2741 Selectric typewriter terminal, and a leased WATS[13] data line into his office in the basement of the Ritchie family home, so that he could continue working until 4 a.m.—"which he did." Apparently, he also used that terminal to prepare his thesis. God only knows what software he might have used, *or written*, since mathematically competent word processors were still many years in the future.

Of those years, Ritchie wrote:[14] "My undergraduate experience convinced me that I was not smart enough to be a physicist, and that computers were quite neat. My graduate school experience convinced me that I was not smart enough to be an expert in the theory of algorithms and also that I liked procedural languages better than functional ones."

At another time, he said: "By the time I finished school it was fairly clear that [...] I didn't want to stay in theoretical. I was just more interested in real computers and what they could do. And particularly struck by [...] how much more pleasant it was to have interactive computing as opposed to decks of cards and so forth."

Thompson once said of Ritchie: "He was sharp. He was much more mathematical than I. Once he got an idea, he was almost bulldog. He'd just work on it until it happened."

Kernighan once said: "I saw lots of different facets [of Ritchie], but all fundamentally centered around work as opposed to social life. He was not a party kind of guy, but he definitely was incredibly good to work with. He had a wonderful dry sense of humor that showed up very frequently. He was private, kind, and extremely funny. [...] I would describe [him] as an exceptionally nice guy who sort of may come across shy, but inside he was one of the kindest, most giving people I have met in a long time."

---

13. Wide Area Telephone Service, a flat-rate long-distance telephone connection.

14. "Dennis M. Ritchie," Bell Labs Biography.

He must indeed have been quite private. In those rare instances when he wrote about himself, it was only in the briefest and most self-effacing ways. His siblings referred to his introverted need for privacy as his "force field" that blocked any kind of intimate discussion.

To drive this point home, his brother John related a story from the early 2000s. Ritchie's three siblings were worried about him and conspired to get their introverted brother to talk about his feelings. One morning, as the four sat together on their porch in the Pocono Mountains, John executed their plan[15] by suggesting that they all take turns describing, on a scale from 1 to 10, how they were feeling about their life and how happy they were. Lynn said around 7. Bill said around 8. John made something like that up too. Then they turned to Ritchie, who sat silent for a long while, looking agonized, and then said: "Well, up until about four minutes ago I would have said 8."

John also wrote a song about Ritchie. He performed it at the Dennis Appreciation Day at the Labs in 2012:

> He was the living epitome of self-effacement
>
> Worked till the wee hours down in the basement
>
> Mom sorta wondered what she did beget
>
> She remained puzzled by the internet
>
> Being his siblings made us lucky kids
>
> Don't ask us to explain what the [heck] he did
>
> His prose revealed him as an elegant styler
>
> I have a vague sense that it dealt with compilers
>
> [Chorus]
>
> Dennis our brother,
>
> Unlike any other
>
> The solar system's most unlikely star
>
> Dear old DMR.

---

15. John describes it as "the most stupid contrived gimmick you can imagine."

Dennis Ritchie passed away in October of 2011. Brother Bill eulogized him as follows:

> "He had an incredible intellect, he was deeply creative, he was a natural visionary, he had an extraordinary ability to listen to absorb, he had a deep well of compassion and kindness, and pretty much from birth he was at the right place, at the right time, with the right people."

Oh, and by the way, according to his brother Bill, Ritchie's favorite things to listen to, that "fit Dennis to a T," were the Apple Gunkies[16] and Nocturnal Aviation broadcasts that played on MIT student radio.

BRIAN KERNIGHAN

Brian Wilson Kernighan was born in Toronto in 1942.

His father was a chemical engineer who ran his own small business making "a variety of poisonous substances for farmers." Running that small business was "hard work," and Kernighan was not tempted to take it over.

As a youth, Kernighan was intrigued by amateur radio. So, during his high school years, he built a small Morse code ham radio setup from "Heathkits of one sort or another."

He was adept at building Heathkit electronics. Among his projects, in later days, were an audio system, a color TV, and an oscilloscope.[17]

He was good enough at high school math that his math teacher suggested the Engineering Physics program at the University of Toronto. In typical self-deprecating style, he described that program as a "catch-all program for those who didn't really know what they wanted to focus on."

---

16. See www.dpbsmith.com/applegunkies/?%7Cag.

17. I bet it was just like mine.

The first computer he saw was an IBM 7094 in 1963. He said it was in a big air-conditioned room populated by professional-looking people. "Ordinary people (and especially students) did not get anywhere near it."

He tried to learn FORTRAN in school. He studied the FORTRAN II manual[18] and understood the syntax, but he couldn't figure out how to get started.

He took an internship at Imperial Oil (now Exxon) in 1963 and tried to write a COBOL program, but he couldn't get it working.[19] He described it as an "endless series of IF statements."

In 1966 he spent a summer internship at MIT using the CTSS[20] to build tools for Multics in MAD[21] (Michigan Algorithm Decoder).

The next year, he landed an internship at Bell Labs and wrote "really tight" GE 635 assembly code to implement a list processing library for FORTRAN. It was this experience that finally hooked him on programming.

He was permanently hired at Bell Labs in 1969 and began working on several projects unrelated to Multics and Unix. But Thompson and Ritchie had offices nearby. So did Richard Hamming,[22] who impressed upon Kernighan the importance of writing and the importance of *style*.

Hamming was fond of saying: "We give them a dictionary and grammar rules, and we say, 'Kid, you're now a great programmer.'" Hamming felt

---

18. By Daniel D. McCracken, a name that echoes down the long hallways of my mind.

19. I'd like to welcome him to the club. In 1970 I too wrote one big COBOL program that I never got working. I very nearly got fired from that job, but was rescued by one of the older hands who convinced my boss that I was better at assembler than COBOL.

20. Compatible Time Sharing System.

21. If a MAD program had more than a critical number of compile errors, the compiler would print out a full-page ASCII image of Alfred E. Neumann. What? Me worry?

22. Yeah, THAT Hamming.

that there ought to be the notion of *style* in writing programs in the same manner as there is in writing prose.

It was from Hamming that Kernighan caught the writing bug and the style bug. This would become very important later on.

MULTICS

"They had a very nice time-sharing system at MIT and they decided they were going to do the next one better—kiss of death."

—Ken Thompson[23]

The Multiplexed Information and Computing Service (Multics) was a second-generation time-sharing system involving GE, Bell Labs, and MIT. Multics was meant to succeed the Compatible Time-Sharing System (CTSS) at MIT.

In 1954 John Backus described the idea of time-sharing. He said that "a big computer could be used as several small ones [if there was] a reading station for each user." The computers of the day were not powerful enough to handle that kind of operation. Memory and vacuum tube processors were just too constraining.

But the idea continued to percolate. In 1959 Christopher Strachey published a paper, "Time Sharing in Large Fast Computers," in which he described a system where one programmer could debug a program on his terminal while another programmer on another terminal was running a different program. John McCarthy, at MIT, was taken with this idea and wrote a memo that spurred[24] MIT to develop a true time-sharing system.

---

23. Vintage Computer Federation, 2019.

24. As he would later spur Kurtz and Kemeny at Dartmouth.

In 1961 the Experimental Time-Sharing System began working. At first it used an IBM 709,[25] but that was replaced by a 7090[26] and then a 7094.

This became CTSS, and was likely the first operational time-sharing system. It went into routine service in 1963.

CTSS was one of those prototypes that got shipped. It became the real system. But the designers had stars in their eyes. They wanted a bigger and grander system. They wanted Multics.

Initial planning for Multics began in 1964. GE was to build a machine that was bigger and better than the IBM 7094. Bell Labs and MIT would collaborate on the software, with MIT doing most of the design and Bell Labs in more of an implementation role.

The Multics concept was grand. Perhaps, for the day, grandiose. It included memory mapping. Dynamic linking. Files mapped into memory, and memory mapped into files. It could dynamically reconfigure itself as new hardware was added or removed without stopping the system.

According to Ken Thompson, it was a gargantuan project to produce: "The time-sharing system that was going to end all time-sharing systems. It was hugely overdesigned and wildly uneconomical." Kernighan said it was an example of The Second System Effect.[27]

The primary language that was intended for Multics was PL/1. But the difficulty in writing the compiler, and in writing PL/1 programs, spurred Martin Richards, with the help of Dennis Ritchie, to develop a much simpler language called the Basic Combined Programming Language (BCPL).

---

25. A vacuum tube computer with 32K 36-bit words of core. It executed 42,000 additions per second and 5,000 multiplications per second. This is the machine that FORTRAN was developed on.

26. The transistorized version of the 709.

27. Brooks Jr., Frederick P. 1975. "The Second-System Effect." *The Mythical Man-Month: Essays on Software Engineering*. Addison-Wesley.

In the end, after three years of effort between 1966 and 1969, Bell Labs decided to end its involvement with the project. This left Thompson, Ritchie, and many others with a bit less to do—although at Bell Labs in the late '60s, that was not necessarily a bad thing.

PDP-7 AND SPACE TRAVEL

"Unix was built for me. I didn't build it as an operating system for other people. I built it to do games and to do my stuff."[28]

—Ken Thompson

At Bell Labs, you weren't assigned to work on a project so much as you found projects to work on. So when Multics ended, Ken Thompson found other things to do.

What would you do? Would you write a space-travel game? Among many other things, like positional astronomy and music generation, that's what Ritchie[29] and Thompson did.[30] They had those big Multics machines lying around for a while, so they played with them.

They wrote the space-travel game for Multics, and then again for the standard GE operating system GECOS. But they didn't like the way it worked. First, the display was "jerky," and second, a game session would cost $75 in computer time.[31]

There was, however, a little-used PDP-7[32] from 1965 that had a nice DEC 340 vector graphics display. The machine served as the remote job entry terminal

---

28. Vintage Computer Federation, 2019.

29. My sense is that it was Thompson who wrote the games and Ritchie who lent support with infrastructure and utility subroutines.

30. Me too. Except mine was not space travel so much as space war. See https://github.com/unclebob /spacewar.

31. In those days, you paid by the CPU second.

32. DEC sold about 120 of these machines back then. They went for about $72,000 in 1964. This particular PDP-7 was serial number 34.

for a circuit analysis system. Engineers would use light pens to draw[33] circuits on the display and then send them off to a bigger machine for analysis.

So Thompson and Ritchie, coding in PDP-7 assembler, wrote their own floating-point math routines, their own fonts and character display subroutines, and their own debugger in order to get the space-travel game working on the PDP-7.

Ritchie described the game this way: "It was nothing less than a simulation of the movement of the major bodies of the solar system, with the player guiding a ship here and there, observing the scenery, and attempting to land on the various planets and moons."

Kernighan says: "It was mildly addictive and I spent hours playing it."

Ritchie's brother Bill, who once played the game in his teens, said: "I remember [Ritchie] let me play once. What stays with me is that the distances were so [v]ast you needed to really accelerate; then, it became impossible to slow down again fast enough."

Thompson also wrote a three-dimensional multiplayer space war game. The DEC 340 display had a binocular hood that you could attach to it.

Thompson's game used that hood to give the users depth perception as they flew around space and shot at each other. There were several of these PDP-7 remote job entry stations around the Labs, so Thompson used the 2000-bps dataset (modem) to connect two machines together in order to have two-player space battles.

Ritchie's brother Bill tells the story: "Of course, *Space War* was more fun [than *Space Travel*]. Dennis would occasionally let me bring friends to the Labs at night to get a tour and play *Space War*."

---

33. Yes, even way back in 1969, there were graphics terminals with pointers. I imagine the pointer was a photosensitive light pen.

Thompson and Ritchie did the development for the PDP-7 on the GECOS machine, which had a cross assembler[34] for the PDP-7. I presume they punched the source code on Hollerith cards. The GE would compile down to PDP-7 binary and would punch a paper tape. They would carry that tape across to the PDP-7 and load it.

The PDP-7 had an 18-bit word and shipped standard with 4K of core. The machine that Thompson and Ritchie used had an extra 4K and a big disk.[35] The disk was big in the physical sense because the enclosure was 6 feet tall, and the platter itself spun vertically like an airplane propeller. They were advised not to stand in front of it in case the disk "let go."

The disk was also big in terms of capacity, at least for the day. It stored a million 18-bit words.

The PDP-7 instruction set was very simple.[36] There were 4 bits for the instruction code (16 instructions), an indirect addressing bit, and 13 bits to reference a memory address. So it could directly address all 8K:

```
== Op ==  I  ========address=========
[][][][] [] [][][][][][][][][][][][][]
```

There was a single register (the accumulator), and an overflow bit (called the link) that held the carry of any addition.

There was no subtract instruction. To subtract, you negated the subtrahend and then added the minuend. The PDP-7 was a two's complement machine, so negating the accumulator was a matter of inverting each bit with the CMA instruction and then adding 1.

---

34. Ritchie, in *The Development of the C Language*, described this as a set of macros for the GEMAP assembler on the GE-635, and a post-processor that punched the PDP-7 compatible paper tape.

35. The DEC RB09, the same as the RD10, based on Burroughs hardware.

36. Essentially, an 18-bit PDP-8.

The disk transfer was very fast for the day. It could transfer one word every 2 µs. It used DMA[37] hardware to transfer the words into memory. The PDP-7 had a 1-µs core memory cycle time and required 2 µs to execute most instructions. This worked because the DMA would jump in and steal a cycle *between* instructions.

However, instructions that used the indirect addressing bit for manipulating pointers required three cycles. If an indirect instruction executed while the DMA was trying to read from or write to the disk, the DMA would be forced to wait too long and would issue an overrun error.

This gave Thompson a challenge. Could he write a disk scheduling algorithm that would work in general, and in particular with this finicky beast? So he set about to prove that he could.

Unix

"... and at some point I realized, without knowing it before that point, that I was three weeks from an operating system."

—Ken Thompson

Thompson was deeply influenced by his experience with Multics, which had a tree-structured file system, an architecture of independent processes, simple text files, and a command shell that ran as an independent process. Thompson thought of the file system as a problem of scheduling and throughput. He wanted to get the maximum amount of data on and off the disk in the shortest amount of time.

The challenge, of course, is to translate the structure of the data on the physical disk into files and directories, and to manipulate that translation as efficiently as possible.

---

37. Direct memory access. The hardware would shove words from the disk into the memory without requiring any intervention from the computer. However, the DMA "stole" cycles from the computer, so during transfer, the computer and the disk would compete for the core memory.

A disk is a spinning platter coated with a magnetic film. Read/write heads move radially across the surface of the disk. When writing data, those heads lay down streams of magnetized dots in circular tracks. Those tracks are typically subdivided into sectors, which are simply arcs within the circular track. The in and out "seeking" of the read/write heads causes the tracks to be concentric circles on the platters. Some disks had many platters stacked up like plates. Each platter had its own read/write head.

So to access some data on the disk, you had to know four things: which head to select, which track to seek to, which sector to read, and where, within that sector, the data resided.

Thompson wanted to translate that horror scene of a mechanism into the abstraction of a file, which was just a nice linear array of 18-bit words (the PDP-7 did not use bytes). Thus, a file may be composed of many sectors, which might live on many different tracks and on many different platters. Somehow they had to be linked together, and somehow they had to be indexed so that they could be found.

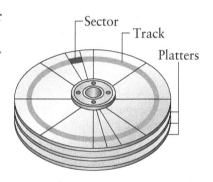

Thus was born the inode structure that has persisted in Unix ever since.

The idea was simple. Each sector (block) on the disk was assigned a relative integer[38] (a block pointer) from which the head, track, and sector parameters could be calculated. A fixed number of specific blocks were set aside for index nodes (inodes), each of which was given its own number.

Each inode contained some metadata,[39] followed by a list of n[40] pointers to blocks that contained the data of a file. The last element of the inode

---

38. Been there. Done that.

39. Describing the permissions and ownership of the file.

40. Probably 11 in the PDP-7.

was a pointer to a block that contained more block pointers if the file required more than n blocks. A directory was a file that contained a list of names and associated inode numbers.

That's it. Easy peasy. And all in PDP-7 assembly language.

Having gotten this working, he needed some programs to test it. His goal was to create several competing programs to access the disk and put a load on his "scheduling" algorithm. This, of course, requires a bit of task switching.

And that brings us to the quotation at the top of this section. Because it was at this point that he realized that he was three weeks away from an operating system.

Why three weeks? Because he needed three programs: a text editor, an assembler, and a shell/kernel. He reckoned each would take a week—especially because his wife and infant son were about to take a three-week vacation to visit her parents in California.

Three weeks later, there was Unix—the bastard child of Multics, born of a disk scheduling challenge and a three-week vacation.

The Unix of those days was not byte based. The 18-bit word length of the PDP-7 dominated it. And so files were sequences of 18-bit words—but that was soon to change.

The PDP-7 was not a fast machine by the standards of the day, and it was severely limited in memory. The OS took 4K, and that left 4K for the users. Both Multics and the GECOS system were built on machines that were ten times faster and had much more capacity. Yet this simple little OS on the PDP-7, with nothing but an ASR 33 Teletype as a terminal, was somehow more convenient, and more fun, to use.

Thompson wrote a program he called scribble-text, which allowed the DEC 340 display to act as a second terminal, allowing the PDP-7 to handle two users at the same time.

"I started picking up really impressive users," said Thompson of that period. These included Brian Kernighan, Dennis Ritchie, Doug McIlroy, and Robert Morris.

The name "Unix" was apparently a collaboration between Kernighan and Peter Neumann, who both have different memories about the event.

Kernighan thought of reducing Multics to Unics as a play on multi- versus uni-. Neumann came up with the acronym: UNiplexed Information and Computing Service. Rumor has it that the lawyers at the Labs thought Unics was too close to eunuchs, and so Unix became the accepted name.

As fun and productive as the PDP-7 system was, it was still quite constraining. So the small gaggle of users began to lobby Bell Labs for a bigger and better machine.

Bell Labs, in those days, was (to say this gently) *rolling in dough.*[41] The philosophy was that any individual at the Labs ought to be able to spend their loaded salary on stuff. So you could get four or five folks together and buy some pretty significant equipment. But you *did* have to get buy-in from your supervisors.

At first, the gaggle just outright asked for a PDP-10 in order to research operating systems. This would have been a behemoth of a machine, with a 36-bit word. It would also have cost half a million dollars. They were told, in no uncertain terms, that there would be no money for operating system research. Multics had been such a fiasco and waste of resources that nobody wanted a repeat of that.

So the gaggle schemed and plotted and, with the help of Joe Ossanna, came up with a very creative proposal.[42]

---

41. Actually, it was AT&T that was rolling in dough. They had a monopoly. To keep the feds off their backs, they dumped a small fraction of that dough into Bell Labs.

42. Or, to put it more succinctly, and to quote Ken Thompson, a "lie."

The patent office at Bell Labs had a problem. Writing patent applications with typewriters was incredibly labor intensive. The applications had to be formatted "just so," complete with line numbers. Wouldn't it be nice if there were a computerized word processor that understood the "just so" format of a patent application, including all the line numbering requirements?

Indeed, the patent office was looking seriously at a vendor who was promising to provide that for them. The vendor's product didn't do it yet, but they promised that with time . . .

So the growing gaggle of Unix users, led by the wily Ossanna, proposed the purchase of a PDP-11 and the creation of software that would allow the patent office to edit, store, and print properly formatted patent applications.

This was perfect. As Thompson said: "The second proposal was to *save* money rather than to spend it. No operating systems, *honest*! And it was for somebody *else*. It was a three-way win."

PDP-11

"The excuse was text processing, but the real reason was to play."

—Ken Thompson

And so, in 1970, the PDP-11(/20)[43] was purchased. The CPU arrived in the summer, and the other peripherals trickled in over the next few months.

They got a rudimentary version of a byte-oriented Unix running on it using a cross assembler[44] on the PDP-7. All using paper tape.

---

43. The /20 suffix was added later. This machine was so new that DEC hadn't really thought about different model numbers yet.

44. Written in B; see next section.

Then, the machine sat, waiting for the disk. It waited for three months, all the while enumerating the closed knight's tours on a 6 x 8 chessboard.

Memory in the PDP-11 was addressed by the byte, but the internal architecture was 16 bits wide. Two bytes made a word, and words were stored in memory in little-endian format (least significant byte first).

The computer had eight internal 16-bit registers. R0 through R5 were available for general-purpose use. R6[45] was the stack pointer, and R7 was the program counter (the address of the currently executing instruction).

The rich[46] instruction set could use the registers as values, pointers, or pointers to pointers. An instruction could also cause a register to be pre-decremented or post-incremented by either 1 or 2.[47] Later, this came in really handy for C's i++ and --i expressions.

Once the disk arrived, Unix came up very rapidly. The PDP-11 had 24K *bytes* of core, a half-megabyte disk, and enough terminal ports for ten patent clerks to enter patent applications.

Joe Ossanna wrote nroff, and later troff,[48] as the primitive text processing and typesetting tools, and they were off to the races. The patent office loved it.

Meanwhile, at night, the gaggle of boys and girls would continue their play. But they had to play carefully, because if they crashed the fragile file system, all the patent work would get lost.

The patent office was so enthralled with this system that they bought the team another PDP-11 to play with. According to Kernighan, the spending

---

45. Mostly by convention, but some instructions used it specifically.

46. The PDP-11 was a complex instruction set computer (CISC).

47. Useful for incrementing pointers to the next word.

48. There is much that could be said about these tools. They played a very important part in the whole early-Unix story. But that part of the story is out of scope here.

of money in those days at the Labs "wasn't a budget, it was a quota—a license to spend money in some sense—but for the good of everybody."[49]

One day, Thompson got an idea based on a paper written by Doug McIlroy in 1964. In the paper, McIlroy suggested that programs should be connectable like garden hoses.

In a matter of hours, Thompson implemented Unix pipes. He said it was a "trivial" change. Then, in the span of a single night, he and Ritchie modified all the existing Unix apps by pulling out any chatty console messages. They also invented stderr and routed error messages to that.

The end result was that the existing Unix apps could be connected by pipes and act as *filters*. The effect of pipes and filters on the Unix team was "mind blowing." Thompson referred to it as a "frenzy" of ideas and activity.

C

"I tried to rewrite the kernel in C and failed three times. And being an egotist, I blamed it on the language."

—Ken Thompson

The story of C begins with a language called TMG, which stands for *Transmogrifier*. TMG was the invention of Robert McLure, who was a friend of Doug McIlroy. TMG was a yacc-like language for generating parsers.

When McClure left the Labs, he took the source code for TMG with him. So McIlroy, using nothing but pencil and paper, wrote TMG in TMG. Then, he desk-executed this paper version of TMG and fed himself TMG, generating PDP-7 assembler code. In short order, he got TMG running on PDP-7 Unix.

---

49. Kernighan and Thompson at VCF East 2019.

Thompson thought that no computer was complete without FORTRAN, so he wrote FORTRAN in TMG. However, the generated compiler would not fit in the 4K user partition he had allocated for PDP-7 Unix. So he started removing bits from the language and recompiling it until the generated compiler fit in 4K.

The resultant language was not very similar to FORTRAN. Indeed, Thompson thought it looked more like the Multics language BCPL. So he called it B.[50]

He wanted to add more features, but every time he did, he'd blow the 4K limit. Fortunately, B was an interpreted language. It generated a P code that a small interpreter would execute. This made the language slow, but much easier to compile. It also meant that the executable code could be held in a file and executed *virtually*, without trying to fit it into memory.

Virtual execution was slow, but useful as a way to shrink the compiler back down to 4K. When a new B feature made the compiler too big, Thompson would execute the new compiler virtually, and modify it to generate smaller code so that the new compiler would fit back in 4K.

This is kind of like shaking a can of rocks to get the most efficient packing density.

One of those features that Thompson added was Stephen Johnson's brilliant idea of "semicolon" for[51] loops. This is where the C for loop came from.

Another of those features was the ++ and +=[52] style operators we know and love in C.

---

50. An alternative theory is that he liked naming languages for his wife, Bonnie. A few years earlier, he had written a language for Multics and named it Bon.

51. The for(init;test;inc) format is one of the most beautiful abstractions of the day. Prior to that, for loops were horrible constructions based upon integers and limits. Ugh.

52. Though in B, and in very early C, they were =+ and not +=.

The syntax of B is very much like C. Indeed, it is hard to imagine how Thompson derived B from FORTRAN. Of this, Ritchie wrote:

> "As I recall, the intent to handle Fortran lasted about a week. What he produced instead was a definition of and a compiler for the new language B. B was much influenced by the BCPL language; other influences were Thompson's taste for spartan syntax, and the very small space into which the compiler had to fit." —"The UNIX System: The Evolution of the UNIX Time-sharing System" *AT&T Bell Laboratories Technical Journal*, 63(8): 1577-1593.

Here's a sample of B from Thompson's 1972 user reference. You C, C++, Java, and C# programmers will find it very familiar.

```
/* The following program will calculate the constant e-2
to about 4000 decimal digits, and print it 50 characters
to the line in groups of 5 characters. The method is
simple output conversion of the expansion
```

$$\frac{1}{21} + \frac{1}{31} + \ldots = .111\ldots$$

```
where the bases of the digits are 2, 3, 4, ... */
main() {
    extrn putchar, n, v;
    auto i, c, col, a;

    i = col = 0;
    while(i<n)
        v[i++] = 1;

    while(col<2*n) {
        a = n+1;
        c = i = 0;
        while(i<n) {
            C =+ v[i]*10;
            v[i++] = c%a;
            c =/ a--;
        }
        putchar(c+'0');
        if(!(++col%5))
            putchar(col%50?' ':'*n');
    }
    putchar ('*n*n');
}
v[2000];
n 2000;
```

B was popular on the PDP-7, but it was slow and constrained by memory. So Ritchie decided to port it over to the GE-635[53] at the Murray Hill computer center.

When the PDP-11 came, and Unix was operational, Ritchie decided to port B to the PDP-11. However, the architecture of the PDP-11 posed a problem.

B was a language that had no explicit types. The implied type of everything was the word. On the PDP-7, that was an 18-bit integer. However, the PDP-11 was a byte-oriented machine, and a byte is too small to do decent arithmetic or even hold a pointer. So Ritchie needed to add types to the language. The first types he added were `char` and `int`. He also rewrote the B compiler to generate PDP-11 machine code. He called the language NB (for New B).

Ritchie unified array and pointer processing, and extended the `int` and `char` type system to include pointers to pointers. So `char **p;` declared a pointer to a pointer to a `char`, and could be dereferenced by `char c = **p;`. He also added an early version of the preprocessor that provided `#include` and `#define`.

The year was 1972, and at this point, Ritchie thought the language deserved a new name. He called it C.

Soon after, in 1973, Thompson and Ritchie decided that managing the Unix kernel in assembler was impractical, and that it was essential to port Unix to C. However, this turned out to be nontrivial.

Thompson tried, and failed, *three times*. Thompson would blame the language for the failures, and Ritchie would make adjustments and add features to "beef up" the language. However, it was not until Ritchie added `struct` to C that Thompson was finally able to successfully port Unix. Of this, Thompson says: "Before [struct] it was too complicated, I just couldn't keep it all together."[54]

---

53. Or possibly the slightly larger GE-645.

54. One wonders how he kept it all together in assembler.

K&R

In the waning years of the 1970s, I was working at Teradyne Central, a division of Teradyne Inc. that was producing test equipment for various telephone companies. On one particular occasion, a few of my associates and I flew out to Murray Hill to talk with some Bell Telephone engineers.

At some point in the discussion, I asked one of them what language they were using. The engineer glanced at me with something like surprise and disdain and said: "C."

I had never heard of "C." So I went home and started doing some research. Back in those days, bookstores had computer sections. In one such section, in a Kroch's and Brentano's, I found this book.[55]

The big blue C on the front reminded me of the "large friendly letters" that said "Don't Panic" on the cover of *The Hitchhiker's Guide to the Galaxy*.

Inside was a pleasant font, a casual-style, *lowercase code*, and most importantly of all, *Chapter 0*.[56] Clearly, these authors were my kind of people. I took it home and started to read.

I was an assembly language bigot in those days. I thought high-level languages were for weenies. If you wanted to get something done, real programmers used assembler.

But as I read K&R, I realized something. C was assembler. It just had a better syntax than most assemblers. But just like assemblers, it had everything I needed. It had pointers, shifts, ANDs, ORs, increments,

---

55. Yes, that is my original copy, with all the stains and marks and wear. I keep it in a Ziploc bag nowadays.

56. Which was foolishly elided from the second edition!

decrements . . . I mean, every operation I used on a daily basis in assembler was a first-class citizen of C.

I was in love. I completely reshaped my view of compiled languages. I devoured that book. I studied every page. I pored over the table of operator precedence on page 49. I spent several hours, out in my backyard by a campfire,[57] analyzing the storage allocator starting on page 173.

Back at work, I started evangelizing as hard as I could. It was a tough sell at first. But I managed to purchase a C compiler from Whitesmiths (a company founded by P. J. Plauger) that could generate assembler for the 8080 µprocessor.

I wrote gobs of utility functions. I wrote an operating system.[58] I wrote sample applications. I wrote several specific-purpose projects for customers, all in C, all running on our proprietary 8080 platform. I was in heaven.

It took a year or more, but Teradyne Central eventually converted their entire software operation to C.

That book changed my life, and the lives of many, many other software developers.

TWISTING ARMS

Kernighan had written a tutorial for B, which he was able to convert to C with relative ease. That tutorial grew in popularity, and Kernighan thought a book was in order.

Apparently, Ritchie was reluctant at first, but Kernighan "twisted his arm" enough to gain acquiescence. Kernighan wrote the first drafts of all the tutorial chapters, while Ritchie wrote the chapter on the Unix system calls and the C Reference Manual appendix.

---

57. My copy still carries the faint smell of smoke.

58. BOSS, which stood for Basic Operating System and Scheduler . . . or (as one associate put it) Bob's Only Successful Software.

Kernighan compared Ritchie's contributions to C itself: "precise, elegant, and compact." Bill Plauger added that the precision was "spine-tingling."

The two authors collaborated on refining the draft, and the book was published in 1978 by Prentice Hall under a Bell Labs copyright.

In the Preface, the authors wrote:

> "The [Unix] operating system, the C compiler, and essentially all UNIX applications programs (including all of the software used to prepare this book) are written in C. [...] For the most part, the examples are complete, real programs, rather than isolated fragments. All examples have been tested directly from the text, which is in machine-readable form."

Nowadays, when I write books about software, I get the code working in my IDE and then paste it directly into my word processor. But in the days before word processors and IDEs, these authors pioneered the process for ensuring that published code was working code.

Who knew, back in 1978, that K&R would be one of the best-selling, most-used, most-valued, most-cherished, and most-honored computer books of all time.

SOFTWARE TOOLS

So enamored was I with K&R that one day, while perusing the shelves at Kroch's, I spied another book with Kernighan's name on it. I bought it without a second's thought. The book was titled *Software Tools*.

This was another watershed book for me. Kernighan, knowing that FORTRAN IV was a very popular language in those days, had written a pre-processor that compiled a reasonable C-like language that he called ratfor (Rational FORTRAN), down to FORTRAN IV. Then, he and Bill

Plauger[59] proceeded, before my very eyes, to write the Unix suite of applications in ratfor.

I was not familiar with Unix at the time. I'd heard of it, of course, because it was mentioned in K&R, but I had no idea what it was. *Software Tools* drove the point home in no uncertain terms. The Unix mindset was simple, easy, and usable.

I found a transcription of their software on a DECUS[60] tape at some point and got it loaded up on the VAX-750 that we had at Teradyne. And everything changed again. Unix-style tools beat VMS (DEC's OS) hands down.

I never looked back. If ever I had to use a PC, I made sure the Unix tools and shell were loaded. I was very pleased when Apple decided to put Unix beneath the Macintosh. And, of course, I have since used lots and lots of Linux-based systems.

Unix forever!

CONCLUSION

The story I just told of the creation of Unix and C spans the years between 1969 and 1973—perhaps four years in all. Of course, the story continued after this and was just as rich and impressive. Still, what took place in that handful of months changed everything.

Nobody told Thompson and Ritchie to do what they did. They were primarily driven by their own playfulness, and by the needs of their enthusiastic and growing community. They were free-running, free-wheeling explorers working in a cash-rich and very relaxed environment. And, of course, they were brilliant.

What could go wrong? After all, they were just changing the world.

---

59. Phillip James (P. J. [Bill]) Plauger (1944–).

60. Digital Equipment Corporation User Society.

REFERENCES

Anasu, Laya. 2013. "Dennis Ritchie '63, The Man Behind Your Technology." *The Harvard Crimson.* www.thecrimson.com/article/2013/5/27/the_dennis _ritchie_1963.

Bell Labs. n.d. "Dennis M. Ritchie." Bell Labs Biography. www.bell-labs.com/usr /dmr/www/bigbio1st.html.

Brock, David C. 2020. "Discovering Dennis Ritchie's Lost Dissertation." Computer History Museum. June 19, 2020. computerhistory.org/blog/discovering -dennis-ritchies-lost-dissertation.

Computer History Museum. "Oral History of Ken Thompson," 1:42:55. Posted on YouTube on Jan. 20, 2023. (Available at the time of writing.)

Computerphile. "Recreating Dennis Ritchie's PhD Thesis - Computerphile," 18:32. Posted on YouTube on May 28, 2021. (Available at the time of writing.)

Dennis Ritchie Thesis and the Typewriting Devices in the 1960s. Website maintained by the Ritchie family. https://dmrthesis.net.

Kernighan, Brian. 2020. *UNIX: A History and a Memoir*. Kindle Direct Publishing.

Kernighan, Brian W., and Dennis M. Ritchie. 1988. *The C Programming Language*, 2nd ed. Pearson Software Series.

Kernighan, Brian W. and P. J. Plauger. 1976. *Software Tools*. Addison-Wesley.

Linux Information Project. 2005. "PDP-7 Definition." Updated September 27, 2007. www.linfo.org/pdp-7.html.

Losh, Warner. 2019. "The PDP-7 Where Unix Began." *Warner's Random Hacking Blog.* https://bsdimp.blogspot.com/2019/07/the-pdp-7-where-unix-began.html.

National Inventors Hall of Fame - NIHF. "Pushing the Limits of Technology: The Ken Thompson and Dennis Ritchie Story," 3:10. Posted on YouTube on Feb. 18, 2019. (Available at the time of writing.)

Nokia Bell Labs. "The Lasting Legacy of Dennis Ritchie: The Impact of Software on Society," 3:29:02. Posted on YouTube on Oct. 3, 2018. (Available at the time of writing.)

Poole, Gary Andrew. 1991. "Who Is the Real Dennis Ritchie?" *Unix World*, January 1991. https://dmrthesis.net/wp-content/uploads/2021/08/BLR-Article -UNIXWorld-Jan1991-A.pdf.

Richie McGee Family Channel. "DMR Early Influences," 11:57. Posted on YouTube on June 21, 2020. (Available at the time of writing.)

Ritchie, Dennis M. 1979. *The Evolution of the Unix Time-sharing System*. Bell Laboratories.

Ritchie, Dennis M. 2003. "The Development of the C Language." Bell Labs/ Lucent Technologies. www.bell-labs.com/usr/dmr/www/chist.html.

SHIELD. "The Greatest Programmers of All Time: Dennis Ritchie | Father of C Programming Language | Unix," 5:21. Posted on YouTube on Mar. 31, 2021. (Available at the time of writing.)

Supnik, Bob. 2006 (rev.). "Architectural Evolution in DEC's 18b Computers." Revised October 8, 2006. www.soemtron.org/downloads/decinfo /architecture18b08102006.pdf.

Thompson, K. 1972. "Users' Reference to B." Bell Labs Technical Memorandum. www.bell-labs.com/usr/dmr/www/kbman.pdf.

Thompson, Ken. n.d. "How I Spent My Winter Vacation." http://genius.cat-v.org /ken-thompson/mig.

Vintage Computer Federation. "Ken Thompson Interviewed by Brian Kernighan at VCF East 2019," 1:03:50. Posted on YouTube on May 6, 2019. (Available at the time of writing.)

Wikipedia. "B (programming language)." https://en.wikipedia.org/wiki/B _(programming_language).

Wikipedia. "Compatible Time Sharing System." https://en.wikipedia.org/wiki /Compatible_Time-Sharing_System.

Wikipedia. "Inode pointer structure." https://en.wikipedia.org/wiki/Inode _pointer_structure.

Wikipedia. "Ken Thompson." https://en.wikipedia.org/wiki/Ken_Thompson.

Private correspondence with Brian Kernighan, Bill Ritchie, and John Ritchie.

THE KNEE OF
THE CURVE
III

In this part of the book, we're going to look at the crazy growth of the programming industry, starting in the 1970s and continuing into the 2020s.

This is the story of *my* career. The events will be told from my personal point of view. As such, this part of the book is somewhat autobiographical. However, the focus is on the programming industry, and so I'm leaving out the vast majority of personal information.

This is the story of a young man (me) who, at the age of 12, was transfixed by computers in 1964, found employment in the early '70s, and continued to be employed as a programmer, and eventually as a consultant and trainer, for the next five decades and change.

More importantly, this is the story of an industry that grew from adolescence to maturity during the same period. I, and the software industry, followed similar paths.

As you read, try to keep track of the rapidly increasing pace of technological advancement. This story starts when software development was still quite primitive. It ends with IDEs, VMs, graphics processors, object-oriented programming, design patterns, design principles, functional programming, and more.

THE 11 SIXTIES

The sixties. What can I say? It was the era of the counterculture: "Turn on, tune in, drop out." The Vietnam War, the Cuban Missile Crisis, the assassinations of JFK, RFK, and MLK. Jimi Hendrix, Neil Young, campus riots, Kent State, sex, drugs, and rock and roll. And the ever-present threat of nuclear annihilation.

It was also the decade when humankind first ventured into space.

I became a programmer in 1964 at the age of 12. My mother gave me a birthday present that I still have today. It was a Digi-Comp I, made by E.S.R. Inc.

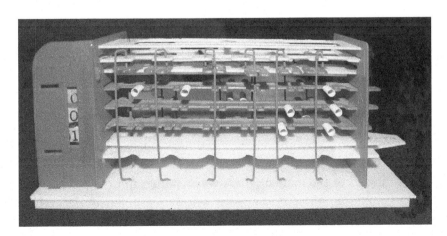

This little machine fascinated me. It has three red flip-flops that can slide back and forth and drive the 1-0 display on the left. The six metal rods are three input and-gates that sense the positions of the flip-flops by "feeling" the little white tubes that the programmer places on them. Tension is kept on those rods with springs or rubber bands at the very top (you can barely see them). If a rod is not blocked by one of those white tubes, then as the operator cycles the machine by moving the white lever at the far right in and out, the rod will slip into a groove and engage a mechanism on the back side of the device that can change the state of one or more of the flip-flops.

In essence, this is a 3-bit finite state machine with six and-gates that control the transitions.

I spent hours with this little device, trying all the experiments in the accompanying manual. Those experiments showed how to make the machine count in binary from 0 up to 7 and then back to 0. Another experiment counted down from 7 to 0 and then back to 7. There was an experiment that would add 2 bits, creating a sum and carry bit (you had to use a special piece of plastic called an or-gate to combine two of the and-gates to make that work!). Another experiment would play the game of Nim with seven stones.

I tried all of those experiments over and over, but—at the age of 12—I could not work out how to make the machine do what *I* wanted it to do.

You see, I had a program in mind for this machine. I named it *Mr. Patterson's Computerized Gate*. It was a simple program that simulated a waiting room for a wise man named Mr. Patterson who gave advice. The gate allowed the next person in the waiting room to enter once the previous advice seeker had exited.

I wanted to make my Digi-Comp execute this program, but I did not know what pattern of white tubes on the flip-flops would make this happen.

At the end of the manual, there was a paragraph that offered the *Advanced Programming Manual* to anyone who sent a dollar to the company. So I sent in my dollar and waited—for six weeks. (There was no Amazon in those days. Six weeks was pretty normal.)

I still have this little manual. I keep it in a Ziploc bag. It is perhaps the most cogent description of Boolean algebra, written for a 12-year-old, that I can imagine.

The manual was completely unapologetic. In its 24 pages, it covered logical operations, truth charts, Venn diagrams, Boolean variables, associative and distributive properties, logical AND, logical OR, and De Morgan's Theorem.

After that, it simply advised me to write down the sequence of bit changes I was seeking, encode them as Boolean expressions, and reduce those expressions to lowest terms using the Boolean algebra I had just learned.

This procedure resulted in a simple set of six or fewer AND statements, one for the "set" and "reset" operations of each flip-flop. The book then showed me how to encode those statements as white tubes on the flip-flops.

So I wrote down the bit transitions for *Mr. Patterson's Computerized Gate*. I converted them into Boolean equations. I reduced those equations to lowest terms, producing the six needed AND statements. I put the tubes on the flip-flops according to the encoding instructions, and then I cycled that machine.

And my program worked! And I was a programmer! The sheer euphoria caused by the feeling of unlimited power (that every programmer knows) put me on the course of my life. I was a programmer, and I would always be a programmer.

My neighbor, Mr. Hall, who lived across the street, showed up one day with a box full of 24 old relays. He worked at TeleType and scrounged these old devices at the request of my father.

A relay is a simple device. A coil of wire can be energized to become an electromagnet. An armature attracted by that magnet will push electrical contacts together or apart, either making or breaking a circuit. Such relays could have many such contacts and could therefore make or break many circuits.

At the age of 13, I held these devices in my hand, moving the armatures back and forth and watching the motion of the contacts. I could see the coil, and I knew what it implied. And so I fired up an old electric-train transformer (48V) and energized one of the coils and watched the contacts move.

I set about creating a circuit of several different relays that would play the game of Nim. I also designed a system of relays that would simulate a Digi-Comp I. I struggled to make these assemblages of relays work, but my knowledge of electronics was insufficient to the task. So I subscribed to *Popular Electronics* and devoured every issue.

I learned about transistors, resistors, capacitors, diodes, Ohm's law, Kirkoff's law, and much more. My high school buddy, Tim Conrad,[1] and I built many different machines. Some out of relays, some out of

---

1. As I write this, I am in a hospital waiting room waiting to see my tenth grandchild, who has just been born. His name is Conrad.

transistors, and some out of the new integrated circuits (ICs) that were showing up on the market.

In the end, by expending an immense amount of effort over a period of many months during 1967–68, using transistors, hex-inverter ICs, dual JK flop-flop ICs, and a plethora of resistors, capacitors, and diodes, we cobbled together an 18-bit binary calculator that would add, subtract, multiply, and divide. We won first prize at the Illinois state science fair that year.

  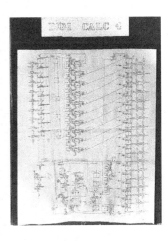

ECP-18

The year before was my freshman year of high school. The Math Department brought in an educational computer for a two-week trial. It was not intended for students; it was there so that the math teachers could evaluate whether it could be used in a computer science course.

This machine was an ECP-18.[2] As I described in Chapter 9, this machine was built by Judy Allen's company, and they hoped to put them in schools all over the country. It was a 15-bit machine with 1,024 words of memory stored on a magnetic drum. It looked like one of the consoles on the *Star Trek Enterprise*. I was in love.

---

2. See Chapter 9.

They set it up in the cafeteria, where I just happened to have a study hall. The technician plugged it in and checked it out. I attached myself to this person like a shadow. I saw every little thing he[3] did. I heard every little thing he muttered under his breath. I watched as he toggled a program into the machine to test it out.

My experience with the Digi-Comp I had taught me octal. So, as he toggled bits into the machine using lovely little push buttons that lit up when he pushed them, I noticed that they were grouped into threes. He would punch in 1 5 1 7 2 and say under his breath: "Store the accumulator in 1 7 2."

Then he would punch in 1 2 1 7 0 and say: "Add 1 7 0 to the accumulator."

The architecture of the machine just sprang into my mind. It became obvious to me what a memory address was, that each memory cell stored

---

3. Over the last few years, I have often wondered if this technician might have been Judith Allen. However, my memory of his voice insists that he was male.

15 bits, and that there was an accumulator that was used for all the manipulations of memory cells. It was clear to me that instructions were stored as 15-bit cells in memory, and that they were divided into operation code and addresses.

Watching and listening to this technician for 30 minutes opened the whole world of electronic computers to me. I suddenly knew what they were.

The next day the machine was still in the lunchroom. It was turned on, and no one was near it. So I ran over to it and punched in a little program. It was a dumb thing that computed *a+2b*. The program was something like this:

```
0000 10004
0001 12005
0002 12005
0003 12006
0004 00000
0005 00010
0006 00003
```

In location 0 was an instruction that loaded the contents of location 4 into the accumulator (AC). For some reason, I thought that it was important to clear the AC out. The next three instructions add the contents of location 5 twice, and the next adds the contents of location 6.

That was the program! (Do you see the flaw?) I started the execution at location 0, and the 0023 popped up into the AC. The program worked! YAY! I was a GOD!

I was never allowed to touch the machine again. The math teachers took it into their office and were the only ones allowed near it. I spent several days watching them from afar as they fiddled with the machine. But, alas, they would not entertain the idea of letting me close enough to push a button.

Two weeks later they wheeled the machine away, never to be seen again. It was a sad day.

So, what was the flaw in my little program?

Address 0003 was the last executable instruction. For some reason, I just figured the computer would know that the program was done and that it would just stop there. I did not know that 00000 was the halt instruction. I found that out later, when one of the manuals for the machine was left out on a table in the math office.

WHAT FATHERS DO

My despondence over the loss of the ECP-18 was short-lived, because my previously mentioned friend, Tim, found a Digital Equipment Corporation sales office 30 minutes from our homes. My father[4] would drive us up there every Saturday, and Tim and I would "play" with the PDP-8s that they had on display. The office staff felt it was good advertising or something. Also, my father could be quite convincing about such matters.

My father procured a rather large number of books for me to read. They included manuals on COBOL, FORTRAN, and PL/1, and books on Boolean algebra, operations research, and various other topics. I inhaled these books. I had no computers to execute programs on, but I gained a tenuous understanding of the languages and concepts.

By the time I was 16, I was ready.

---

4. Ludolph Martin.

THE SEVENTIES

12

The '70s are about to begin, but the '60s ended with a bang. Nixon is sworn in. Borman, Lovell, and Anders aboard *Apollo 8* have just returned after having read from Genesis on Christmas Eve as they orbited the moon. The Beatles' *Abbey Road* was soon to be released, and the band was on the verge of breaking up. Armstrong, Aldrin, and Collins will launch this year aboard *Apollo 11*, and a man will walk on the moon for the first time.

The '70s saw the birth of disco, yuppies, the first resignation of a US president, the Arab oil embargo, and the growing "malaise" within the children of "The Greatest Generation."

1969

I got my very first job as a programmer in 1969. I was an awkward 16-year-old with no concept of what it meant to be employed. My father, Ludolph Martin, had marched into A.S.C. Tabulating Corp. and told the managers there that they would give his son a job over the summer.

My father was like that. He was a tall, heavy, imposing man who spoke his mind, was not reluctant to tell people what he wanted, and did not take no for an answer. He was also a junior high school science teacher, which is likely where I got my scientific interests from. After his death, we received so many letters from past students telling us of all the quietly generous things my dad had done for them.

I was hired on a temporary part-time basis—meaning they had no intention of keeping me around. I imagine that since they could not say no to my father, they took the next best option.

A.S.C was just a few miles from my home, in Lake Bluff, IL, about 30 miles north of Chicago. I was able to get to my new job by riding my bike.

For the first week or so, they stuck me in a closet and told me to update IBM manuals. In those days, IBM would send out monthly updates to their technical manuals. These updates would be packets of pages with corrections and new information. My job was to pull down the three-ring binder of a manual and replace the changed pages. This was the first time I ever saw "This page intentionally left blank."

There were a lot of manuals, and a lot of updates. They were all kept in that closet, and while I was there, nobody took a manual to use it for reference, so I'm pretty sure this was just busywork to keep me out from underfoot.

I imagine that my father made them promise to show me something about programming. I already knew a fair bit, having read through COBOL, FORTRAN, and PL/1 manuals and having written simple PDP-8 assembly programs on my weekend jaunts to the DEC sales office with Tim Conrad. So Mr. Banna, my supervisor, gave me a book on EASYCODER and asked me to write a very simple program.

EASYCODER was the assembly language of the Honeywell H200 series computers. It was binary compatible with IBM's 1401 machines, but was faster and had a richer instruction set.

By today's standards, the instruction set was bizarre. The memory was byte addressable, but the bytes were not the bytes that you and I know and love. In fact, I don't even think they called them bytes. They called them characters.

Each character was 6 bits long and also had a word-mark bit and an item-mark bit. A word was any string of characters that ended with a word mark. An item was any string of characters that ended with an item mark.

A record was any string of characters that ended with both a word and item mark.

Arithmetic instructions generally worked with words. So you could add two 10-digit numbers together if each of those two numbers ended with word marks. You could move items around. And you could input and output records. At least that's the way I remember it.

Anyway, the program Mr. Banna asked me to write was for one of their clients: the Illinois State Scholarship Commission (ISSC). They had a magnetic tape with all the student records on it. My job was to read each student record, assign the student an ID number, and write the updated student record onto a new tape. The ID numbers were just six-character integers that were incremented by one for each successive record.

Mr. Banna took me to a cabinet that had a stack of punched cards in it. The stack was quite tall and was striped like a barber's pole. The stripes were batches of about 150 cards each. The cards in each batch were either red or blue, and the batches alternated: red, blue, red, blue . . .

Mr. Banna told me to take the top batch off the stack, and he gave me a printout of the contents. It was a small IO subroutine library for reading and writing magnetic tape, printing, and reading and punching cards. He told me that I should put this deck on the end of my program so that I could call those subroutines from my program.

I understood this concept pretty well, having done something similar with paper tape at the DEC sales office. So I studied the listing and the

EASYCODER manual and started to write my program on the coding forms he provided.

I still have a pad of those old coding forms. Here's what they looked like:

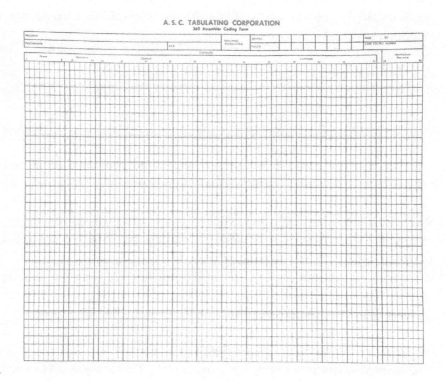

The program was pretty small. I think it fit on just one form. So when I had written it and checked it over, I handed it to Mr. Banna. A day later he sat me down and showed me all the mistakes I had made (e.g., I had used word marks when I should have used item marks, etc.). He made the corrections on the coding form and then told me to take it to the keypunch room and leave it for the keypunch operators to punch.

The next day the tiny deck of 20 or so punched cards was ready. Mr. Banna showed me how to check the deck against the coding forms, and how to use a keypunch machine to correct any errors.

Once the deck was ready, Mr. Banna walked me up to the computer room. The door was locked, but he knew the access code. So in we went.

The room had three big computers in it: two IBM 360s and the H200. The noise in the room was not quite deafening; those cooling fans were loud, but not as loud as the line printers and card reader/punches.

Mr. Banna waved to one of the operators, and the two walked me over to the H200. Mr. Banna handed the deck to the operator and told me to watch. I saw the operator mount the assembler tape, put my deck into the card reader, toggle an address into the front panel of the H200, and hit Run.

The magnetic tape spun, and then the card reader chattered as it read my cards. The machine blinked for a bit as the assembler processed my source code, and then two or three cards were punched. Those cards contained the binary executable.

Mr. Banna took the ISSC student tape down from the rack and handed it to the operator. The operator mounted that tape onto one of the big tape drives.

Then Mr. Banna pulled down a tape from a rack that was labeled "scratch." He showed me how to make sure that the tape had a write ring inserted into the back of the tape so that it could be written on.

Then he handed the scratch tape to the operator, who mounted it onto another tape drive.

The operator then took the tiny binary deck out of the punch hopper, put it into the reader, toggled a different address into the console, and hit Run.

The cards were read, and immediately the two tapes began to spin. The whole thing was over in a matter of minutes. The two tapes rewound, and the tape drives opened up.

The operator put a blank label on the scratch tape, pulled the write ring off the back, and handed the tape to Mr. Banna, who wrote the identity of the tape on the label with black magic marker.

Mr. Banna handed the newly labeled tape back to the operator and asked him to dump it. The operator remounted it, toggled yet another address into the front panel, and hit Run, and the tape began moving as the line printer chattered away.

When the printout was complete, the operator took the tape off the drive and handed it to Mr. Banna. The operator tore the listing off the printer and handed it to *me,* with a smile and a wink. And then Mr. Banna and I retired back downstairs to the programming room.

The two of us looked through the 50 or so pages of that listing. It was a simple character dump of all the records on that tape. We made sure that each student record had the new ID field inserted, and that the ID fields had the correct numbers in them.

When we were done, I said: "The program worked!" Mr. Banna replied: "Yes, Bob, it did. And now I have to let you go."

And that was the end of my first job as a programmer.

1970

When I was 18, I returned to A.S.C. and printed junk mail as a second-shift offline printer operator for a few months. Then they hired me as a "programmer analyst." I wrote a COBOL program or two, but quickly got involved with a large minicomputer project.

The H200 was gone, and in its place was a GE DATANET-30. It was a behemoth of a machine, with a couple of very primitive tape drives and a gigantic disk drive with several platters that were 36 inches in diameter and half an inch thick. When you first turned it on, that disk drive shook the floor and sounded like a jet engine revving up.

This machine ran the Local 705 Teamsters Union's real-time remote entry accounting system. It managed a dozen or so modem lines connected to the Local 705 headquarters in Chicago, where clerks would enter data about members, employers, and agents. I imagine that some of Kemeny's students' code was running in there somewhere.

Apparently, A.S.C. management were not thrilled with the cost and reliability of this big old clunker of a machine. So they decided to purchase a minicomputer and rewrite the whole accounting system from scratch. In assembly language, of course.

Minicomputers were the new big thing. Everybody and their brother were trying to get into the minicomputer market. DEC was certainly the leader, but there was no lack of other contenders. One of those contenders was a company named Varian.

The minicomputer A.S.C. chose for the rewrite of the Local 705 system was a Varian 620/F. I was able to locate a photograph of the L version, which was nearly identical to the F.

This machine had 64K 16-bit words of core memory. It had a 1μs cycle time. It came with a yukky little card reader, an even yukkier card punch, an ASR 33 TTY, two tape drives, and an IBM 2314-compatible disk drive. It also came with a batch of RS-232 ports that could plug into the modems.

The programmers of this system were me, two of my high school buddies (Tim Conrad and Richard Lloyd), a 23-year-old systems analyst, and two women in their 30s. We were a great team. God, we had fun! We also worked stupidly long hours. Sometimes we'd work through the night and into the next day. There were 60-, 70-, and 80-hour weeks.

A.S.C. was run by an old air force officer, and he ran the place like it was a battalion. Schedules were impossible, but would be met no matter what.

We still wrote our code on coding forms, but by then my buddies and I had taught ourselves to type on an IBM 026 keypunch. So I would punch my own decks of cards. The source code of our system was kept on magnetic tape, and we used a line editor that copied the input source tape to the output source tape while reading and executing our editing directives from cards. The assembler ran on the 620 and produced binary magnetic tapes that we could quickly load and run.

We wrote every part of that system. There was no code running in that computer that we didn't write. We wrote the operating system, the accounting system, the modem management system, the disk management system, and the overlay loader. We wrote every single bit that executed anywhere in that 64K machine. My buddies and I were 18; we dominated that project. We did the impossible. We were gods.

After a year of work and a successful delivery of the system, a bunch of us quit in a fit of pique. We did not feel that we had been properly compensated for our godlike heroism.

I repaired lawnmowers for about six months while looking for another programming job. Oddly, I found no one who wanted to hire a 19-year-old who could not produce a recommendation from their last employer. (Tip: Don't quit before you have another job!)

I was engaged to be married. And my mother took me aside and in the kindest words possible called me a blithering idiot (my words, not hers). I had to agree with her. Humbled, I crawled back to A.S.C. and begged for my job back.

A.S.C. took me back, but at a significantly reduced salary. I spent another year there, mending fences and getting married. After the fences were mended and my very young wife and I were situated in our tiny apartment in Waukegan, IL, I started looking for a new job. My buddy Tim Conrad had gotten a job at Teradyne Applied Systems (TAS) in Chicago a few months earlier, and it was through his recommendation that they offered me a position. I left A.S.C. on good terms and with a recommendation, and joined TAS in early 1973.

1973

TAS built computer-controlled laser trimming systems. These systems contained a honking big 50KW water-cooled CO_2 infrared LASER manipulated by X-Y mirrors driven by computer-controlled galvanometers. They burned lines into resistors that were silk-screened onto ceramic circuit modules. As the laser carefully carved lines into those resistors, their resistance was being continuously monitored by our measurement system. We could trim those resistors down to 0.01 percent tolerances. I mean, how much fun is that for a 20-year-old! Yikes!

I turned 21 in December of 1973. I woke up the morning of my birthday to a phone call. My mother told me that my father had died suddenly and in his sleep. He was 50 years old.

This was the era of miniaturization and precision. The TAS laser trim system would cycle miniaturized circuits into the trimming and measurement rig, and use high-power lasers to trim the electronic components to very precise values. Among the products that we trimmed were the crystals for the first digital watch: the Motorola Pulsar.

Teradyne built their own minicomputer, called an M365. It was based on a PDP-8, but with 18-bit words instead of 12. We wrote our code in assembler on *video terminals* that were also produced by Teradyne. No more punched cards!

The system used a master operating program (MOP) written by the parent company, Teradyne in Boston. We got the source code of the MOP and modified it heavily, adding our own application to it. It was one big monolithic program. That was the way of things back then. We shared and forked source code, but had no common binaries. Frameworks were not a concept. Source code control systems were nowhere on our radar.

Our source code was stored on magnetic tape cartridges that could only drive in one direction. The tapes in the cartridges were long continuous loops. You didn't rewind those tapes; you just kept on driving them forward until they got to the beginning again.

The drive speed was slow, so sending a 100-foot tape forward to its load point could take two or three minutes. Therefore, cartridges came in lengths of 10 feet, 25 feet, 50 feet, and 100 feet, and we chose which length to use quite judiciously. Too short, and your data wouldn't fit. Too long, and you waited forever for the tape to reach load point.

Editing on the video terminal was not like editing in a current IDE with a mouse. Nor was it like editing in vi with cursor control keys. Instead, the editor was a line editor similar in many ways to the punched card-driven editor we used on the 620/F. At least you could scroll the code on the screen; but to change the code, you had to enter editing commands on the keyboard. For example, to delete lines 23 through 25 you typed 23,25D.

The core memory of the M365, in those days, was on the order of 8K. So the editor could not load the entirety of the source code from tape into memory. Thus, to edit a source file, you loaded your source tape in one drive and a scratch tape in another. You'd read in a "page"[1] from the source tape, edit that page on the screen, and then write that page out on the scratch tape and read in the next page from the source tape.

And, remember, those tapes only went in one direction, so once you wrote out a page, there was no easy way to go back and look at the code you had just changed.

Therefore, we printed our code out into large listings. We used red pens to mark our planned changes on those listings, and then we walked page by page through those listings, editing each page in sequence.

If this sounds primitive, that's because it was. The magnetic tape was only a little better than high-speed paper tape. Indeed, the editor was derived from DEC's original paper tape editor for the PDP-8. It thought it was using paper tape.

---

1. A "page" did not correspond to a printed page; it was simply a block of data that contained lines of code. We tended to keep our pages small so that we did not run out of memory while editing.

Compiling was a similarly primitive chore. We'd load the source tape into a drive, and load the assembler. The assembler was derived from the PDP-8 PAL-D[2] assembler, and it required three passes through the source code. The first pass simply built up the symbol table. The second pass generated the binary code, which was written onto a scratch tape. The third pass generated the listing. For a reasonably large program, the process took 45 minutes or more.

The tapes were not particularly reliable. At least once per day, the tape drives would fail to properly read from a tape. The drives could not back up and reread, so if this happened during a compile, the compiler would abort. The bell on the video terminal would ring with a single "ding," and then we'd hear the printer start chirping out error messages.

We had an open lab with several M365 editing stations, and one larger machine for running compiles. So whenever we heard that "ding" and "chirp," we'd all groan and someone would go to the machine, wait for the tapes to return to load point, and then restart the compile. It was often very frustrating.

The video terminals were also rather susceptible to static electricity. In the wintertime, you might walk near a terminal, accidentally bump it, feel the shock, and then hear "ding" and "chirp," and you'd know you just wrecked someone's compile. We learned to ground ourselves before walking near a terminal.

TAS was even more fun than A.S.C. Oh, we still worked some long hours, but not nearly as frantically as at A.S.C. But something else happened at TAS. I very gradually began to understand some of the concepts of software design.

Tim Conrad and I would debate these concepts endlessly. We wrote all kinds of interesting programs that had little or nothing to do with laser

---

2. Written in the late '60s by Ed Yourdon.

trimming. At TAS, we often had *time*. Time to think, to plan, to explore, to . . . play.

Tim and I worked out sorting algorithms, searching algorithms, indexing schemes, and queuing schemes. We did not have Knuth's *Fundamental Algorithms* (1968), because we didn't know it existed. But we invented or discovered many of those algorithms together as we coded this or that or the other interesting project. Those were heady days.

I discovered that Teradyne's video terminal had a primitive kind of cursor addressing. It was also blazing fast, because it was connected directly to the computer's IO bus. So I found myself doing what nobody else had done at Teradyne up to that point: designing screen layouts and forms, and writing the code to provide real-time updates of those screens and forms. These weren't quite GUIs, but the awesome possibilities bounced around in my mind.

It was while working at TAS that I saw my first handheld calculator: the HP-35. I was thunderstruck by this device. It was small. It was fast. It did square roots and trig functions. It had an LED readout. One week the engineers in our office had slide rules on their belts. The next week they all had HP-35s. Change was in the air, and that change was coming fast.

Looking back, I should have stayed at TAS; it was an environment rife with possibilities. But 21-year-olds are not known for their wisdom. The commute was long and bothersome, and I longed for a change of scenery. And so I took a job at Outboard Marine Corporation (OMC) in my hometown of Waukegan, IL.

1974

I took the job because it was close to home—so close that I could ride my bike to work. I won't say that the job wasn't technically challenging; it was. But I was not a good cultural fit for that company. I realized this on my first day when my boss instructed me to wear a tie from then on.

OMC made things like Lawn Boy lawnmowers, and Johnson outboard motors for boats. To make the engines, they built a huge facility for aluminum die casting. Walking around that facility was pretty impressive. The die-cast machines were large, imposing devices, each operated by a single person. The mold would close, liquid aluminum would be injected, the mold would open, and the operator would pry the hot aluminum casting out of the mold and put it in a large metal basket.

Overhead was a rail system on which a vehicle carrying a huge bucket of molten aluminum alloy would shuttle between the furnace and the individual die-cast machines, filling their aluminum reservoirs. It was awe inspiring.

Our job was to program an IBM System/7 to monitor the progress of all the die-cast machines. We would count the number of pieces each machine made, time each mold, and report scrap. This was accomplished through a huge local area network that connected the die-cast machines and several reporting stations on the floor to the System/7, which was up in the control room, where the whole plant was visible from an observation window.

IBM was late to the minicomputer game. They had bet on mainframes. I think they thought that minicomputers were going to be a flash in the pan. If so, they were wrong. Eventually, they realized that DEC and the other minicomputer companies were dominating shop floor-control applications, and they wanted in. So they came up with the System/7.

One look at the control panel and you just knew that this was an IBM device. The System/7 had a 16-bit architecture. Memory was solid state instead of core. I believe ours was 8K. It had eight registers and a very simple register-based instruction set (RISC).[3] It had a cycle time on the order of a microsecond. I believe ours had a small internal disk drive.

It was also physically large for the day. A PDP-8 or an M365 could fit under a desk. The System/7 was the size of a restaurant freezer.

---

3. Reduced instruction set computer. This was a reversal from the trend to make computer instructions ever more complicated. The idea was that a RISC machine required less hardware and could, therefore, be cheaper and faster.

OMC sent a bunch of us off to the big IBM building in Chicago, next to the Marina Towers. There, for five days, we learned System/7 assembler. I recall the class being something of a joke. The instruction set was trivial to learn. Five days was just too long.

In any case, we came back with our certificates and were bona fide System/7 programmers.

After having spent a year editing code on video terminals, I was suddenly thrust back into the world of punched cards. The System/7 had no native compiler. Compilation was done on the big IBM 370 mainframe located in the IT building a half mile down the road from the plant. So it was back to coding forms and keypunching for me.

The source code was kept on disk files on the 370. We'd edit those files using the same old line-editing approach that I'd used back at A.S.C. We'd punch editing directives on cards, submit those cards to the 370, and then submit compile jobs to the 370.

The 370 was a great big mainframe computer that was in a computer room that I never saw. It was a batch-oriented machine that could do only one job at a time.[4] Our edit and compile jobs would wait in the batch queue, on disk, for hours. Once the machine found the time for our jobs, it would transmit the binary over a private network connection to the System/7, where it would be stored on the internal disk. The listing would be sent to a remote printer in the control room.

So we programmers shuttled back and forth from the plant to the computer facility. We'd punch cards and load our jobs in the IT building, and then drive over to the plant and wait for the compile to arrive. Depending on how busy the 370 was, that compile might take an hour or it might take a day. We never really knew for sure.

---

4. Well, sometimes it could do two, but not the way you and I would think of it today.

Once the binary file arrived and was safely stored on the internal disk of the System/7, we could run it and test it. The front panel was our debugger. It had single-step capability, and we could see the contents of the registers on the lights. We'd debug, mark up our listings, and then drive back to the IT building to start the process all over again.

I hated it. I hated the ties. I hated the bureaucracy. I hated the inefficiency.

I hated the culture. I hated it all so much that I could not bring myself to get to work on time, or to take schedules seriously. Eventually, they fired me—and I deserved it.

But before that fateful day, two good things happened to me while at OMC. My first child and daughter was born in June of 1975. And in early 1976, I got an inkling of my future fate as a consultant, author, and instructor.

Some of the programmers at OMC had subscriptions to trade journals. Up to that point, I hadn't even known that publications like that existed. I saw the magazines lying around in the cafeteria of the IT building—and I started to read them.

Most of the articles were boring, but one of the articles I read completely floored me. It was an article about something called *structured programming*. I devoured the article. I *understood* the article. It was as if the scales had fallen from my eyes. GOTO was harmful.

I couldn't let this idea go. I was writing code in System/7 assembler, but the concepts still applied. Subroutines were good. Wild jumps between modules were bad. I was so enamored of this concept that I started to write about it.

Who was I writing to? Nobody. Me. I don't know. I just wrote. A few weeks later I realized that I had written a one-day training class on structured programming. So I left it on the desk of the training manager in the IT building.

Much to the annoyance of my boss, who thought that I should have been spending my time on—you know—"the project I was hired for?", the training manager arranged for me to get on the OMC private plane and give that course to a programming team down in St. Louis.

That was my first time flying for business, my first time training a group of programmers, and my first time flying in a small airplane. I was on top of the world!

The trip was a success. The programmers I trained were very appreciative. And my boss told me to never do that again.

Like I said, it wasn't a good cultural fit for me.

I had known for several months that my job was in peril. I could tell by the looks my boss would give me and the tone of his voice whenever we interacted. So I started looking around for a new job.

I called my buddy Tim and asked him if there were any opportunities back at TAS. He told me they had a hiring freeze[5] at the moment but that a new division of the parent company was starting up in Northbrook, IL— much closer to my home.

I called that new division, which they had named Teradyne Central, and I got an interview. It went well. There were only a handful of folk there, and they were in deep startup mode. All engineers, all using equipment I was familiar with, and in desperate need of programmers.

They wanted to hire me; and I should have taken that offer right then and there. But wisdom is not known to be prevalent in 23-year-old men. I had decided that I needed to get at least one job right. I decided that I was going to make OMC work. Dumb. Dumb. Dumb.

So I stuck it out until, in the fall of 1976, they fired my ass.

---

5. Some of you might remember the 1973 oil embargo and the inflation and recessions of the '70s.

1976

So there I was. Out of a job. No letter of recommendation (again!). And my wife was seven months pregnant with our second child.

So I called up Teradyne Central (TC) and said that I had reconsidered (after several months). They asked me to come in, and things went well until they asked me why I had left OMC. There was no point in hiding what had happened, so I told them straight out.

The look on their faces dropped about 12 floors. They hadn't expected that. So I left without much hope.

They called me back a week later and said that they had spoken to my boss at OMC. I owe that man a beer. He told them the truth: that it was not a good cultural fit. He told them that I was smart and creative, but that I just hated working there and that, in the end, he'd had no choice. He told them that I would likely find a startup a lot more motivating.

Fortunately[6] for me, they took him at his word and hired me.

This was the job I got right. Boy, did I ever! This was TAS all over again. It was small, it was energetic, it was creative. There were tight schedules and impossible deadlines. But there was also time. Time to create. Time to read. Time to play. I can't imagine a better environment for a young software developer to grow in.

The product we sold was a distributed processing system for measuring the quality of the telephone system. We called it 4-TEL. Telephone companies were divided up into service areas. When you called 611 back in those days, you were connected to your service area headquarters. The service area would dispatch repair technicians to fix faults in the telephone system.

---

6. "God has a special providence for fools, drunkards, and the United States of America."—Otto von Bismarck

Each service area covered about 100,000 telephone lines, divided up into several central offices. Each central office could handle as many as 10,000 lines and had the switching equipment that connected to the individual subscribers. Copper wires originated at the central office and crossed the landscape to reach each individual home and business.

Our system placed a central M365 minicomputer in the service center. It was called the Service Area Computer (SAC). The SAC was connected by modem lines to M365 computers in each central office. That computer was called the Central Office Line Tester (COLT). The COLT was connected to an elaborate dialing and measurement system that we produced. The COLT could dial up a phone line, without ringing it; connect to that line; and test the electronic AC and DC characteristics of that line. By doing so, we could measure the length of the line, the condition of the telephone at the far end, and any faults that might exist along the span.

The SAC had up to 21 terminals that could be operated by testers. A tester could test any line in the service area within seconds and get a comprehensive report on the condition of that line, along with a recommendation for what kind of repair technician would be appropriate.

Every night the SAC directed each COLT to test every single line in its central office. The COLT would send back a report on the condition of those lines, and the SAC would print a morning report of failures. Thus, technicians could be dispatched to fix a problem before a customer ever discovered anything was wrong.

To properly program this system, I had to hang out with hardware engineers, field service engineers, installation engineers, and other software engineers. TC made little distinction between them. We were all just engineers. Hardware engineers wrote software. Software engineers built hardware. We all did field service and installation.

When a customer called with a problem, a big bell would ring in the lab. Any one of us would pick up the phone and take the field service call, talking directly to customers or to one of our field service engineers in the field.

In short, it was a startup; everybody did everything.

I learned how to troubleshoot and install elaborate systems. I crawled on the floors of central offices built in the 1900s. I flew hither and yon to installations in urban and rural settings alike.

But mostly what I did was write code. Lots and lots of M365 assembly code, in the same manner as when I was at TAS working with Tim. Except this time there was *a lot* more code. The M365 for the SAC had 128K 18-bit words of core. The COLT had 8K of core.

Controlling 21 terminals and one or two dozen COLTs simultaneously meant that the SAC needed some kind of multiprocessing task switcher. The folk in Boston had created a simple little thing called MPS,[7] and we made a lot more use of it than I think they ever expected.

MPS was a non-preemptive polling task switcher. The M365 had a primitive interrupt system, but we didn't use it. Instead, we arranged the software into processes that waited for events by calling event-check subroutines (ECSs). A process remained blocked until its ECS returned true. If the system had 50 processes running, 49 of them would be blocked and one would run. When the running process decided to wait for an event, its ECS would be added to the list of waiting processes, and then all the ECSs in the list would be polled in priority order until one returned true, and then that process would run.

Every keystroke on a terminal, every character sent or received on a modem, every character output to a screen was an event that some ECS was looking for. We had processes running all over that system. One for each terminal, for each modem, for timed events, and more. And even

---

7. I can only guess that stood for *multiprocessing system.*

though the M365 only ran at 1MHz, that system ran smooth as silk. No lag. No hiccups. No lost characters. It was a joy to behold—most of the time.

I was in heaven. This was a really complicated system with a lot of moving parts. Not only did I have to master all the software behind those moving parts, but I needed to learn a lot of electronic theory in order to understand it all.

We all had private or shared offices, but most of the time we worked in the open lab. In that lab, you'd see folk writing software, debugging software, soldering parts onto boards, probing electronics with oscilloscopes, breadboarding parts into prototype circuits, and doing a plethora of other engineering-related activities. Because so much of what I had to do involved hardware, I had to learn about the hardware engineering process and the associated disciplines. Disciplines that I would eventually carry over into software.

SOURCE CODE CONTROL

There were four or five of us who were primarily software engineers. We maintained the SAC and the COLT source code. Nobody specialized.

Everybody worked on everything.

There was a SAC master source tape and a COLT master source tape. Both of those tapes were subdivided into several dozen named modules. Think of those modules as source files, if you like.

Next to the rack with the source tapes there was a table upon which sat the master listings for the SAC and the COLT. These were in three-ring binders, and each was subdivided by module with tabs.

Next to the rack and table there was a corkboard. The corkboard was vertically divided into a column for the SAC and one for the COLT. In each column were the names of the corresponding modules. Also on the corkboard there were some colored thumbtacks. I was blue. Ken was white. CK[8] was red. Russ[9] was yellow.

When you wanted to make a change to a module, you put your colored thumbtack in that module's name on the corkboard. Then, you'd open the three-ring binder and remove the listing of that module. You'd mark that listing up as necessary with a red pen. Then, you'd get the master source tape and make a working copy of it. You'd edit just your module on that working copy, just the way we did at TAS. Then, you'd compile and test—again, just as we did at TAS. When you were satisfied that your changes worked, you'd go get the master source tape and copy it onto a new master source tape, replacing just your module. You'd scratch the old master and put the new master on the rack, replace the listing with the new listing for your module, and then pull your thumbtack off the corkboard.

And if you believed that's what we actually did, I've got a bridge to sell you. Oh, that was the theory all right. And we did follow it most/some of the time. But we all knew each other. We all knew what we were all working on. And we were all in the same lab together most of the time. So more often than not, we'd just shout that we were working on a particular module. Somehow it all worked out—most of the time.

1978

The M365 was a big machine that used core memory. It was the size of two microwave ovens. It took a lot of power. It had tape drives. It wasn't meant for the nitty-gritty industrial environment of a central office. The more of these that we shipped, the more the field service burden grew. We needed a better solution.

---

8. My buddy and associate. He asked us to call him CK because he told us his name was not pronounceable by Chicagoans. He often laughed at the way I pronounced my own name, with the midwestern hard O (like a doctor asking you to say AHHHH). He later changed his name to Kris Iyer.

9. Russ was the CEO. In those early days, he wrote a lot of code.

Single-chip microcomputers were brand new. Intel had created the 4-bit 4004 in 1971, the 8-bit 8008 in 1972, the much better 8-bit 8080 in 1974, and the even better 8085 in 1976. That's the one we chose.

The plan was to entirely replace the M365 COLT with an 8085 COLT. The hardware guys built the processor board, the solid-state RAM boards, and the ROM boards. CK and I got busy translating the M365 COLT code into 8085 assembler.

The assembler ran on the M365, so we were able to use the same edit/compile procedure that we used for regular M365 programming. We had a special jury-rigged circuit board that allowed us to transfer the 8085 binaries from the M365 to the RAM in our 8085 prototype.

Translating assembly language programs written for an 18-bit word-oriented single-accumulator computer to the assembly language of a byte-addressed 8-bit computer with several registers is an interesting challenge. Yet we made very quick work of it. I think the whole project was complete within six months. We even got the whole thing running in read-only memory.

In the end, we had 32K of ROM and 32K of RAM crammed into a tiny little box one-fifth the size of the original M365 COLT. No tape drive, minimal power, hermetically sealed in a bulletproof rack-mounted industrial enclosure. Perfect.

Except for one little thing. The program was a monolith. Any small change to any module caused all the addresses within the program to change, and forced us to re-burn and redeploy 32K of ROM. Since the ROM chips were 1K each, we had to burn 32 chips. That was a nightmare for the field service folk, and was wildly expensive in terms of parts.

My boss, Ken, had the solution. Vectors. We'd create vector tables in RAM that pointed to all the subroutines in ROM. We'd make sure that all calls to those subroutines went through those RAM vectors. Then, we'd write a little boot process that would load those subroutine addresses into RAM at startup. Easy peasy.

It took me three months to implement that. It was massively more complicated than any of us thought it would be. I had to break out all the subroutines, size them all, come up with a sorting that fit those subroutines into 1K ROM chips, and make sure all the subroutines were called correctly.

Oddly enough, what we implemented was a foreshadowing of objects. Each ROM chip now had its own vtable, and all the calls were indirect through those tables. This allowed us to modify, compile, and deploy each chip independently of all the others.

1979

By this time, we had many more programmers and a much larger installed base, and the customers were demanding ever more features. The bottleneck in all this was the M365 and the brain-numbingly inefficient edit/compile process we had to follow. It was time to get a bigger and better computer. It was time for a PDP-11.

We purchased a PDP-11/60 with two RK07 removable disk drives, a printer, two tape drives for backup and software distribution, and 16 RS-232 ports. The RK07s were 25MB removable disks, but we never removed them. We just used the 50MB as our primary storage.

That may not seem like a lot of space, but back then it was nearly infinite. I remember the day we ordered the system. I walked around the halls of Teradyne Central, cackling like the Wicked Witch of the West, shouting "FIFTY MEGABYTES! MUAHAHAHAHAHA!"

We also ordered a few VT100 terminals. I had the maintenance man build out a little room with six workstations, all nicely decorated with space pictures. We put the VT100s in there. Our CEO told us that "Programmers will *not* have VT100s on their desks." You can imagine how long *that* rule lasted.

The manuals arrived before the machine did, and I took them home and inhaled them over a long weekend. I learned about the RSX-11M operating system, the editor, the assembler, and the DCL command language. By the time the machine arrived, I was ready.

We built out a computer room for the machine, and I made sure it had a combination lock on the door. That machine was *mine*, and nobody was getting in that room without my say-so. Yeah, I was *that* guy. But believe me, nobody else wanted that job.

Getting the machine up and running was quite a chore. It came with a DECwriter terminal, which stayed in the computer room as the main console. It also came with a tape containing a minimal version of the RSX-11M operating system.

So I loaded the operating system from the tape and got the minimal system up and running. That system didn't know about the disks or the RS-232 ports. It only knew about the tapes. In order to configure the operating system for the RK07s and the RS-232 ports, it had to be recompiled, and some critical source files had to be changed.

I started this process on a Friday. The last compile finished, and my system came up with everything running properly sometime Saturday morning. That was one long session, but in the end, all the VT100s were up and running in our workstation room—and mine, on the desk in my office, was working nicely too.

Teradyne in Boston had some PDP-11s, too, and they sent us a cross assembler for the M365. We rigged up a special RS-232 line to a real M365 so that we could download binaries from the 11/60. So M365 development gradually transitioned over to the 11/60.

I found an 8085 assembler from Boston Systems Office (BSO). We used that to compile the code for the 8085 COLT. So 8085 development transitioned as well.

I got a magnetic tape from the DECUS user group. It had all kinds of nifty programs on it. One of them was a true screen editor named KED. It allowed us to edit source files on the VT100 screen without worrying about pages or typing nasty commands. It was a bit like vi.

The 11/60 was a robust machine. It had 256K bytes and a 1-μs instruction time. Fixed- and floating-point math were very fast. It easily supported all six workstations at once. (Seven if you counted my office, but I usually worked in the workstation room.)

However, the BSO compiler for the 8085 was a terrible memory hog. You could only get two of those running at any given time, and then all the other terminals would get very laggy. So I wrote a little script that would queue up requests for that compiler and run them in single file. This was frustrating because you might have to wait three to five minutes just to get your compile to start. But this was still *much* better than using M365s for compiling everything.

I found a simple email program for the PDP-11. It was only intra-office, since we had no outgoing network connection. However, it allowed all the programmers, and eventually everyone with an account on the PDP-11, to communicate by email. This was a brand-new experience for everyone—including me.

REFERENCES

Knuth, Donald. 1968. *The Art of Computer Programming, Vol. 1: Fundamental Algorithms.* Addison-Wesley.

THE EIGHTIES 13

The baby boomers are past 30 now and are approaching the peak of their power. The yuppies have matured. It is "Morning in America." And things are looking up pretty much across the board. It was as though nothing much could go wrong. Moore's law was in full force. The internet grew. By the end of the decade, the Web would be born at CERN, the Berlin Wall would fall, the Cold War would end, and the long-endured threat of a nuclear holocaust would fade like a barely remembered nightmare.

1980

Teradyne Central had been very successful selling the 4-TEL system to General Telephone and United Telephone. These were multimillion-dollar sales contracts, and they allowed our company to grow and expand. But we had made no inroads at all into the largest of all the telephone networks: Bell.

Bell Telephone had their own line test system that they called the Mechanized Line Tester (MLT). We wanted to sell our COLTS and/or SACs into Bell service areas. So we negotiated several engineering sessions with Bell.

You might wonder why Bell would give us the time of day, but they were in the midst of a big antitrust battle at the time, and so they had to give the appearance of not being too much of a monopoly.

Anyway, my boss and I took a trip to New Jersey to talk with the MLT engineers. The talk really didn't go very far, but there was one very special moment. At one point, I asked one of the engineers what language they used to program the MLT system. That engineer looked at me with the most condescending expression and said: "C."

I had never heard of C. My curiosity was piqued. So I found a copy of *The C Programming Language* by Kernighan and Ritchie (K&R) at a nearby Kroch's and Brentano's and began to read. Within a few days, I was completely sold. We *had* to get a C compiler for the PDP-11!

I found one sold by Whitesmith's, a company started by P. J. Plauger. It could compile down to the PDP-11, but also to the 8085! I got it running on the PDP-11 and started to write C programs just to play around. The C programs ran just fine on the 11. But getting them to run on the 8085 was a bit more of a challenge.

The C library expects IO devices, even if you are just going to run *helloworld.c*. So I had to write an IO subsystem for the 8085. It was very primitive, but it worked well enough. And with that I could get C programs running on our 8085 system.

I got a copy of *Software Tools* by Kernighan and Plauger. In this book, they showed you how to turn FORTRAN into a C-like language named *ratfor*. They also showed how to build many of the standard Unix tools in ratfor. Tools like `ls`, `cat`, `cp`, `tr`, `grep`, and `roff`.

I remembered seeing a software tools directory on one of the DECUS tapes. So I loaded it up and got the whole suite running. Now we had Unix-like commands running on the 11. I quickly became a roff fanatic and wrote all my documents using that lovely markup language for the next few years.

I loved the MPS system on the M365, and I thought we should have something like that for the 8085. So I wrote, in C (mostly), a clone of MPS and got it working on the 8085. I called it Basic Operating System and Scheduler (BOSS[1]). This set the stage for several important projects to come.

I had become a C advocate. I evangelized C everywhere I went in the company. But this was an assembly language shop, and the primary reaction to my encouragement was: "C is too slow." I was determined to counter this meme with some working projects—and I didn't have to wait long.

I got my first subscription to a software magazine in 1980: *Dr. Dobb's Journal of Computer Calisthenics & Orthodontia*. I read it religiously and was flabbergasted to see, in the May 1980 issue, the entire source code of Ron Cain's *Small-C* compiler.

SYS ADMIN

I remained the de facto system administrator for the PDP-11. I was the go-to guy if anything went wrong. I was the guy who made sure that incremental backups were made every night and full backups were made every week. I was the guy who defragmented the disks once each month. And I was the guy who made sure we had the right software and tools running on that system.

I set up some modem lines so that I could dial in to check on things. I brought a VT100 and an acoustic coupled modem home so that I could do system maintenance on the weekends. On those occasions when I had to travel to a customer site for more than a couple of days, I'd ship a VT100 and modem using air freight and set them up in my hotel room.

I just *had* to stay connected.

---

1. Around the office, it became known as "Bob's Only Successful Software."

THE pCCU

The telephone companies were going through a digital revolution. It was driven by the cost of copper. Copper is a precious metal, and the telephone companies had *a lot* of copper buried underground or hung on telephone poles. They wanted to reclaim that metal.

So they started replacing the old relay-operated switches in their central offices with *digital* switches. A digital switch digitally encodes a telephone conversation and multiplexes it onto a coaxial cable. That cable ran several miles out to a neighborhood where the receiving unit demultiplexed the conversations back out onto *much shorter* copper wires that led to the homes and business being served.

You can imagine that this threw a monkey wrench into our SAC/COLT architecture. Dialing still had to be done at the central office where the switch was, but measurement had to be done out at the receiving unit where the copper wires were. So we came up with the idea of the COLT Control Unit (CCU), which would talk to the switch in the central office, and the COLT Measurement Unit (CMU), which would be located out in each receiving unit. The CCU would talk to the CMUs using modems.

This was a major architectural change to the 4-TEL system, and one we had promised our customers we would make. But our customers were not keeping to their original schedule for deployment, and so we did not feel particularly pressured to spend our resources on it.

But then one small customer installed a digital switch and asked us to please deliver a CCU/CMU as soon as possible.

My boss told me this and I panicked. I said the CCU/CMU was *at least* a year away. But he smiled at me and did a double-eyebrow raise (as he so often did) and said: "Ah, but this is a special case."

The special case was that the customer only had two receivers, and we could determine which receiver to use based on one digit in the phone number. Better still, the receivers were actually satellite central offices that had switching equipment in them, so dialing would be done out at the receiver rather than at the main central office. Therefore, all we needed was a new device in the central office to receive commands from the SAC, and all we had to do was look at the phone number and then route those commands to the appropriate COLT in the satellite CO. Easy peasy.

We called this new device the pCCU. And I wrote the whole thing in C, with BOSS, and got it running in just a few days. We shipped it to the customer and . . . Bob's your uncle.

It was during the heady days of 1980 that I started reading lots of software books. That nearby Kroch's and Brentano's had a growing Computers section that I would peruse on a semiweekly basis. I read *Queuing Theory, Fundamental Algorithms, Structured Analysis and System Specification*, and many others. These books rocked my world.

1981

THE DLU/DRU

One of our customers in Texas had a single service area that was geographically very large. Texas; what can I say. It was so large that they had to have two repair centers, one in Baytown and the other in San Angelo. The SAC was in San Angelo, and they needed some way to get some of our SAC terminals into Baytown.

SAC terminals were custom made. They used a proprietary, very high-speed serial connection. There was no way to hook them up to modems. So our solution was to create two new devices that would be connected by a 9600-bps modem line. The Display Local Unit (DLU) would plug into the SAC in San Angelo. The Display Remote Unit (DRU) would plug into a rack in Baytown, and our terminals would be hung off its high-speed serial port. Both the DLU and DRU would be 8085s.

We had to create virtual terminals in the SAC—I did that. I knew that old M365 SAC code like the back of my hand. I also designed and wrote the DLU software using C and BOSS.

The design of the DLU was a typical data flow consumer–producer system. One process listened to the SAC and bundled up packets to send to the DRU. Another process pulled those packets out of the queue and transmitted them down the 9600-bps modem line. There were a few other processes running to handle various sundries.

The DRU was designed and written by my protégé, Mike Carew. Mike was brilliant, strong-willed, and stubborn as a mule. We used to play *Dungeons & Dragons* together, and he was always the big, brawny fighter.[2] His solution to the DRU design was to write the entire character flow from the modems to the terminals in a single process, and then to replicate that process for each terminal.

So, whereas I had several small and very different processes running in parallel and passing data to each other in queues, he had one big process replicated once for each terminal. The two of us debated these two approaches endlessly. On one occasion, we stood before a group of other developers, teaching them about the internal designs of the DLU and DRU, and continued the debate in front of the students. It was, of course, a joy.

And, of course, despite the ideological differences in the designs, the system worked very nicely. The customer and the company were happy.

The previous four years of projects were something of a revelation to me. I was beginning to understand what the principles of software design were. The initial vectoring of the 8085 ROM chips introduced me to the idea of independent developability and independent deployability. The pCCU and, later, the DLU/DRU got me thinking about the various modes of cooperating processes. And, of course, the C language was a significant lubricant for those ideas.

---

2. His character's name was Stilgar.

Those ideas were about to come together in a massive project that would consume me for several years.

The company was growing, and had grown out of the little offices we had in Northbrook. It was time to build our own building. Plans were laid, architects were hired, and construction began. In the meantime, we moved to a temporary facility on Wolf Road in Wheeling, just a few miles away. We were there for a year.

We took the opportunity of the move to trade in the PDP-11/60 for a VAX 750. The VAX was a much faster and much more powerful machine. It had a megabyte of RAM and a 320-ns cycle time. It was a beast!

We got it installed in the computer room and got it all connected up.

Running VMS was a lot better than running RSX 11-M. All our compilers and tools still ran in PDP-11 mode. Our difficulties with the BSO assembler faded away because we had plenty of memory and a faster machine. Life was good!

THE APPLE II

Meanwhile, something new appeared in our CFO's office. There, on his desk, sat an Apple II. He used it to run VisiCalc, the first spreadsheet application.

This was the first time I had seen a personal computer used in a business environment. It was also the first time I saw a computer on someone's desk. I was convinced that there would be a computer on my desk in the near future, though I wasn't sure how I was going to justify it.

As the next two years wore on, more and more Apple IIs showed up in the office, but they were always on the desks of the businesspeople.

Accountants, sales managers, marketing managers—they all needed to be able to do spreadsheets. They all had computers. I was jealous.

NEW PRODUCTS

Growing companies need new products. The CEO called a few of us together and challenged us to think about what new products we could produce and sell. There we were, right smack dab in the middle of the computer revolution and the telephony revolution. The opportunities were endless. My boss, Ken Finder, my colleague Jerry Fitzpatrick, and I were chosen to figure out a new direction.

First, we had to get smart about a whole bunch of technologies. So it was time to play. We spent about half a year prototyping voice technologies and playing around with the new ST-506 5MB 5.25-inch disk drives from Seagate.

At one point, we thought about using phoneme generators. Jerry breadboarded up a simple phoneme generator and telephone interface, and I cobbled together an 8085 C program that would take a sentence from the keyboard, break it into words, look up the phonemes for that word, and send them to the generator. It could also dial a phone.

The 8085 pulled the phoneme library from the VAX using a serial port and loaded it into a binary tree in RAM. This was the first time I had written a recursive binary tree walker, and it thrilled me.

Once it was ready, we used the system to call people around the office and ask them a series of questions, like: "Who was the first president of the United States?" The phoneme voice was very robotic, but based on our research, it was understandable. In the end, though, we opted for a very different technology.

Meanwhile, I was the system administrator for the VAX 750, and we were rapidly expanding beyond its capabilities, so I planned for a VAX 780 to be installed in the new building.

As we were preparing for the move, Ken, Jerry, and I firmed up our vision for the new product. In the fall of 1981, we proposed that new product: the Electronic Receptionist—E.R. The world's first digital voicemail and call management system.

1982

Have you noticed that when you call a company nowadays, a computer answers and reads off a whole bunch of annoying disclaimers and instructions, like: "Press 1 for doctors, press 2 for new appointments, press 3 for complaints . . ."? Don't blame me for those systems. That's not what I wanted E.R. to do. I wanted the E.R. to be a traditional old-time telephone operator who could connect you to your party, no matter where your party was.

When you called a company with an E.R., it simply asked you to spell[3] the name of the person you wanted using the buttons on your phone.[4] Then, it would connect you to that person. That person would have already told the E.R. what phone number they could be reached at, and the E.R. would transfer the caller to that number. If the callee did not answer, the E.R. would take a message and then deliver that message later.

Remember, this was long before cell phones, so finding people when they were away from their desk phone was often impossible. With the E.R., you simply told it what phone you could be reached on. Indeed, you could give it several options, and it would try them all.

We filed for a patent, and held the first patent application for voicemail in the US.

Now we had a lot to do. All the hardware had to be designed, debugged, and prepared for production. All the software had to be designed and written. And we needed a development environment.

One of our top engineers, Ernie, designed and built a new computer board based on the Intel 16-bit 80286 chip. It was a monster compared to the 8085. We called it "Deep Thought."[5] This was to be the main computer for the E.R.

---

3. Remember John Kemeny's prediction?

4. . . . much like Kemeny had envisioned.

5. Of course. We were all fans of *The Hitchhiker's Guide*.

We equipped it with 256K RAM and a 10MB Seagate ST-412 5.25-inch disk drive.

There weren't a lot of small operating systems available in those days. CP/M from Digital Research had been around for a few years, but we needed something with a bit more capability. Their MP/M-86 variant was very new, but we tried it out and it seemed to work.

We got an assembler and C compiler for the VAX 780 and rigged up a development environment using some off-the-shelf boards. And we started to write prototype code for the E.R.

The voice and telephony hardware was driven by an Intel 80186 that shared memory with Deep Thought. The 80186 had a special connection to several voice/telephony boards designed by Jerry Fitzpatrick. We called those boards "Deep Voice." The audio technology was single-bit CVSD.[6] This allowed us to hold five minutes of voice per megabyte.

For debugging purposes, I built a little Forth-like interpreter that would run on Deep Voice. We could use it to make the board play certain sounds, or voice files, and to respond to touch tones and other events. The Forth system wasn't used in production, but it was always there if we needed to troubleshoot something.

It took another year, and yet another office move, but eventually the whole thing fit into a chassis the size of a large microwave oven and had a couple of 5.25-inch floppy disk drives for initial loading and an RS-232 port for a console.

XEROX STAR

Meanwhile, our company started purchasing new word processing stations for our technical writers. The Xerox Star was a remarkable

---

6. Continuously variable slope delta modulation. A very efficient way to digitally encode voice for those days.

machine. It had a black-and-white bitmapped graphics display that could render an entire 8.5-by-11-inch page in a variety of fonts. The cursor was controlled by a trackpad called a "cat." The files were stored on 8.5-inch floppy disks, and were displayed on the screen using a "folder" metaphor, very much like what we see today.

This fascinated me, and I started researching the ideas behind that system. I learned about windows, icons, mouse devices, and more.

1983

Just as we were getting started on the nitty-gritty of the E.R., Apple announced the 128K Macintosh. I went to a nearby computer store (Apple Stores were far in the future) and saw one in operation. I was able to sit down and play with it for an hour or so, firing up MacPaint and MacWrite. I was sold! It was not long before we had one in the lab. Before the year was out, I had purchased[7] one for myself.

Meanwhile, we started working on the guts of the E.R. software.

God, we had fun! We built the whole thing from the ground up. We wrote all the voice processing software, all the voicemail software, all the file management software.

This was my first significant foray into structured analysis and structured design. We went through the whole discipline and found it to work pretty well. We did *not* use a waterfall process; it was more like a completely unregulated kanban. We just got stuff working in some semblance of a rational order.

I learned about regular expressions, the Unix philosophy, design principles, and many other things. And all these things I was learning, I was able to apply. It was electrifying.

---

7. $3,600. Ouch!

We had an E.R. running in our office, and we used it every day. It worked great. We installed a few E.R.s hither and yon as trials, and tried desperately to market the devices to various companies. There was plenty of interest, but nobody was buying. It was a new product in a new market, and we simply ran out of runway.

In the end, the company canceled the project *and the patent application.* The patent was awarded to VMX a year or so later. And now doggone E.R.-like machines are everywhere annoying everyone. Perhaps it's best, for the sake of my peace of mind, that they aren't actually E.R.s. So don't blame me.

INSIDE THE MACINTOSH

At home, I purchased the Aztec-C compiler for the Mac. I also got a copy of *Inside Macintosh*. This was my very first exposure to a big framework and a GUI. The size of the book was daunting. The amount of stuff to learn was terrifying. But learn it I did. I got pretty good at writing C programs at home on my little Mac.

BBS

Personal computers were showing up all over the place. So were bulletin board services. These were just little computers in people's basements that were connected to an auto-answer modem. If you had a modem, you could dial into a BBS, get news, share opinions, and download software.

Downloading required a protocol called XMODEM. It was just a dumb little ack/nak protocol with a simple checksum, but it worked tolerably well. The Mac had a terminal emulator, but it didn't use XMODEM for downloads. So I fired up my C compiler and wrote a little XMODEM plug-in so that I could upload and download binaries.

One of the first things I uploaded was my Wator[8] program, a graphical simulator of sharks and fish in a predator–prey relationship. I uploaded it

---

8. Wa-Tor (Water Torus), A. K. Dewdney, Computer Recreations, *Scientific American*, December 1984.

in binary, but it included the source code and a lot of documentation. It was a tutorial for how to build GUI programs on the Mac. Lots of people downloaded it. My name started to get around.

C AT TERADYNE

At about this time, the programmers at Teradyne decided that C was going to be the standard language. The assembler bias was long forgotten. So we hired a C expert to come in and teach a weeklong class to everyone.

1984–1986: VRS

Even though we dropped the E.R. product, we still had a new voice technology, *and* we had an existing market to sell it into: the telephone companies. So we came up with a new idea: the Voice Response System (VRS[9]).

If a squirrel bit through a telephone line, 4-TEL would detect it in the overnight scan of all the lines. A repair craftsman[10] would be dispatched in the morning. The repair technician would call a test engineer at the service center and ask them to test the line. The test results would show that the line was broken and, by measuring the capacitance of the line, would come up with an estimate for where the break was. That estimate was accurate to within a thousand feet or so.

The craftsman would drive to the approximate area, climb a pole, and call a test engineer again to request a "fault location." This was a procedure that 4-TEL provided. The test engineer would ask 4-TEL to run the procedure. 4-TEL would give instructions to the test engineer such as "Open the line" or "Short the line" or "Ground the line." The test

---

9. This name was chosen based on a contest among the engineers. Among the contestants was the Teradyne Interactive Test System and Sam Carp (still another manifestation of capitalist avarice repressing the proletariat).

10. The technicians were called "craftsmen" according to the nomenclature within the phone companies at the time.

engineer would relay these instructions to the craftsman on the pole. The craftsman would acknowledge when the instruction was complete, and the test engineer would proceed to the next step in the procedure. In the end, 4-TEL could quite accurately tell the craftsman the distance, in feet, to the fault.

As you can imagine, this was a great boon to the craftsman. Rather than walking along thousands of feet of line trying to see where the squirrel had bitten through, 4-TEL would tell them within 10 to 20 feet. On the other hand, this was no fun for the test engineer. They had to sit there on the phone with the craftsman, simply waiting to push the next button and relay instructions.

The VRS allowed the craftsman on the pole to interact with 4-TEL fault location using touch-tone commands and voice output. The test engineer never needed to get involved. Moreover, our voicemail technology was used to queue up dispatch orders for the repair technicians. Their day's work could be loaded into voicemail messages by the dispatcher, and the craftsman could reply with results using similar voicemail.

All that lovely E.R. software was simply reapplied to a product that we were already selling. It was a major value add.

CORE WAR

At home, my success with Wator led me to create a bigger and better upload. It was an implementation of A. K. Dewdney's *Core War*[11] game. It included a graphical depiction of warring programs, an assembler for the programs, and some pretty awesome visual and sound effects (for the day). I uploaded the binaries, source code, and massive documentation to CompuServe. Lots of people downloaded it. My name was spreading more.

---

11. He published it in his Computer Recreations column in the May 1984 issue of *Scientific American.*

1986

During a lull in product activity, I started reading Adele Goldberg and David Robson's *Smalltalk-80*. I was fascinated by this language.

It turned out that Apple had a version of Smalltalk[12] for the Macintosh. I managed to procure it and got it running on my Mac. I wrote several little programs in Smalltalk, and the wheels started turning in my mind.

THE CRAFT DISPATCH SYSTEM (CDS)

Our customers enjoyed the VRS so much that they asked us to tie it into their trouble-ticket systems. These systems were big, old, mainframe-driven databases from the seventies written in COBOL.

In those days, when a fault was detected on a phone line, whether through the 4-TEL nightly scan or through a complaint from a customer, a trouble ticket was created by the service center. In the early days, these tickets were routed to testers and repair dispatchers by little conveyor belts or pneumatic tubes. In the '70s and '80s, the routing became electronic, and the tickets were displayed on IBM 3270 green screen terminals.

When a repair craftsman was done with a repair, they'd call up the dispatcher, report the results of that repair, and then ask for the next trouble ticket. The dispatcher would bring the next trouble ticket up on their green screen and read it to the craftsman. Our customers wanted to eliminate that step and have the VRS read the trouble tickets to the craftsmen using our voice technology.

Thus was born the CDS.

Trouble tickets had a number of fixed fields with very predictable values. These might include the customer's name, address, phone number, and so on.

---

12. Kent Beck was on the development team for that Smalltalk system

However, the trouble ticket also contained a fair bit of quasi-free-form information that the craftsman needed.

This quasi-free-form information included a set of standard abbreviations and arguments separated by slashes. For example, the free-form field might include something like /IF clicks loud, meaning that there was interference on the line in the form of loud clicks.

There were literally hundreds of these kinds of free-form abbreviations. They would be typed in by the repair clerk while on the phone with the customer, and then interpreted and read to the craftsman by the dispatcher. Our customer wanted the CDS to be able to interpret and read this information.

However, there was no syntax check on these free-form fields. They could have typos or nonstandard formats. It all depended on who typed them in and how they felt that day. Dispatchers were usually smart enough to figure out what the repair clerk meant. Our system was going to have to be able to do the same—at least for the vast majority of trouble tickets.

FIELD-LABELED DATA

I needed some way to represent all the complex information in a trouble ticket within a data packet that could be interrogated and interpreted in order to convert it to voice. That data were complex and hierarchical. The free-form fields could have other fields within them. It was a horror scene.

I was on an airplane, flying to one of our customers' sites, when a thought occurred to me. Perhaps there was some way to encode all that hierarchical complexity into a long character string that could be decoded and interrogated by our system. And so field-labeled data (FLD) was born.

The syntax was arcane and very different, but otherwise, this was the rough equivalent of XML. The complex hierarchical data could be held in a treelike structure in memory, and dumped out to a string to be stored on disk or transmitted over a socket.

FINITE STATE MACHINES

The process of dispatching and closing trouble tickets was not standardized. Each telephone company and each service area had their own ideas about what the steps in those processes ought to be. So we had to come up with a scheme to allow each service center to easily configure the various processes.

Or rather, we had to come up with a scheme whereby that configuration could be specified in something other than code. *We* would still configure the system for the customer, but we didn't want that to be done by writing new code for each customer.

We needed to configure simple step-by-step procedures driven by events. At some point, I came up with the idea of specifying the procedures as state transition tables written in a text file. Each line in the text file was a transition of a state machine. Each such transition had four fields: [Current-State, Event, Next-State, Action]. You read a transition like this: "When you are in the Current-State and you detect this Event, then you go to the Next-State and perform the Action."

The states were simply names. They had no special significance. The events were things that our system could detect, like Digit-Pressed, Phone-Connected, Phone-Disconnected, Message-Spoken, and so on. The actions were commands that would be sent to the MP/M-86 shell and executed as though they were typed in from the keyboard. Those commands could speak messages, dial numbers, record a voicemail, and so on.

The action commands needed to communicate with one another. So we invented a disk-based data repository that we called the *3DBB*.[13] An action command could store information in the 3DBB under the key of the overall job. The next action command could go to the 3DBB and fetch that data to continue the job. (And if that sounds a lot like uservices to you, well—there's nothing new under the sun.)

---

13. Drizzle Drazzle Druzzle Drone.

With FLDs stored in the 3DBB, we suddenly had a very rich and flexible way for our action commands to operate. The complexity level of the jobs we could handle increased by an order of magnitude. The combination of FLDs, 3DBB, and finite state machine structure was a big step in solving the problems of interpreting the trouble tickets.

OO

At home, I needed a new project. My investigations of Smalltalk had led me to get serious about object-oriented programming. It seemed to me that this was the future.

I read Stroustrup's book *The C++ Programming Language* with rapt attention. I wanted a C++ compiler for the VAX, but there were none to be had for less than $12,000, and I couldn't talk my boss into spending that much money.

The Smalltalk system on the Mac was too slow to be useful for anything serious. So I decided to write my own OO framework in C.[14]

I made a lot of progress on this, but life got in the way, and my priorities got rerouted.

1987–1988: THE UK

For the previous several years, Teradyne had made inroads selling 4-TEL in Europe. Eventually, this caused us to create a software development team in the UK. In late 1987, I was asked to move to Bracknell to lead this team. My wife and I saw this as a once-in-a-lifetime opportunity for our family, and so we agreed.

I spent the first quarter of 1988 transitioning the CDS team to new leadership and handing off my remaining sysadmin responsibilities to others. By April, we were ready to go.

---

14. Shades of both Bjarne Stroustrup and Brad Cox.

Our time in Bracknell was wonderful. My wife, my children, and I were exposed to a new culture and a new environment, and we thrived.

Professionally, this was a management position with much less coding responsibility than I was used to.

Unwilling to completely back away from coding, I developed the discipline of riding my bicycle to work at 6 a.m., working on code until 8 a.m., and then going to meetings and working on team leadership and general management issues until 4 p.m.

By this time, we had a DECnet connection between the VAX 750 in Bracknell and the big VAX 780 at our headquarters in Illinois. That computer also had a DECnet connection to the computers in Boston. So files could be moved across the Atlantic (at 9.6 kbps), and email was interoffice.

One of the projects in the UK was the development and deployment of μVAXes to replace the M365s. There was a similar effort going on in the US as well. Indeed, the project to convert the M365 software to a disk-based system like a PDP-11 had been underway since 1983, and had not been going all that well. The μVAX was a brand-new product from DEC, and the customers in the UK were anxious to get 4-TEL running on them. I didn't do any coding for this. Mostly I just attended meetings and nodded a lot.

I continued writing home projects in C on the Mac and uploading them to various services like Compuserve. One of my favorites was the game *Pharaoh* for the Mac.

Overall, however, this part of my career was less focused on software technology and more on management. That was about to change upon my return to the US.

REFERENCES

Goldberg, Adele and David Robson. 1983. *Smalltalk-80: The Language and its Implementation*. Addison-Wesley.

Kernighan, Brian W. and P.J. Plauger. 1976. *Software Tools*. Addison-Wesley.

Kernighan, Brian W. and Dennis M. Ritchie. 1978. *The C Programming Language*. Prentice Hall.

Rose, Caroline, Bradley Hacker, and Apple Computer. 1985. *Apple Inside Macintosh*. Addison-Wesley.

Stroustrup, Bjarne. 1985. *The C++ Programming Language*. Addison-Wesley.

THE NINETIES 14

The era of optimism and growth continued. We were on top of our game. But cracks were already beginning to show. Iraq's invasion of Kuwait was fought back by the "shock and awe" of Operation Desert Storm. CNN broadcast the war, live, from Baghdad. But there were wars and rumors of wars in Congo, Chechnya, Yugoslavia, and Kosovo, among others.

Terrorism was on the rise—the first World Trade Center bombing, the Oklahoma City bombing, the US Embassy bombings, and the bombings in Manchester, England and Argentina.

The times were generally good, and they culminated with the dotcom bubble. But the unease was growing, and the times were about to turn a very ugly corner.

1989–1992: CLEAR COMMUNICATIONS

Upon my return from the UK, I found that some things had changed at Teradyne. Several of my previous associates (and good friends) had left to join a startup named Clear Communications. I followed shortly thereafter.

We were working on SPARCstations from Sun Microsystems with 19-inch color monitors! The OS was Unix, and the language was C. Our product, Clearview, was a T1 communications monitoring system. The plan was to have a big geographical map on the screen with the T1 network overlaid on top. The T1 lines would be drawn in green, yellow, or red, depending upon their status. Clicking on a line would bring up the error history in the form of pretty little bar charts or line graphs.

This was *real GUI stuff*, and I was in heaven—for the first year, anyway.

Startups don't often experience the exponential growth they all hope for. They also don't often fail rapidly. What most do is muddle through. And that's what Clear Communications did. They muddled through, diluting all the stock options with ever more rounds of funding. Yuck.

Technically, however, the first couple of years were grand. A friend of ours at a different company gave us a dial-in link to their computer, which had a hard link to—*the internet*! We dialed them up twice per day to send email and gather Usenet (Netnews) using UUCP. *We were online!*

Within a year or so, Sun released their C++ compiler. We had a lot of code written in C, but the C++ compiler could compile that without any trouble. So we started writing C++ code along with all the C code in our system.

We had a half dozen programmers, and so I put together a course to teach them C++.

USENET

Now that I had an internet connection, I started reading Netnews. I joined the comp.object and comp.lang.c++ newsgroups. I had read Stroustrup's books on C++, including *The Annotated C++ Reference Manual*, and my skill with the language was rapidly accelerating. So I started publishing articles on those newsgroups. More often than not, those articles were responses to questions that others had asked, or were part of the many long-winded debates we used to have. This was one of the first social networks. It was a blast.

In the midst of my interactions on these newsgroups, I came across references to articles published in a magazine named *The C++ Report*. I got a monthly subscription to that magazine and devoured every issue. The articles were published by people like Jim Coplien, Grady Booch, Stan Lippman, Doug Schmidt, Scott Meyers, and Andrew Koenig. The quality of the writing and editing was very high, and the content was invaluable. I learned a ton from them.

UNCLE BOB

Billy, one of the programmers in our office, gave nicknames to everyone. Mine was "Uncle Bob." Whenever Billy had a question, he would holler across the lab: "Uncle Bob! What do I do about this?" His use of the term was incessant, and I found it very annoying.

Meanwhile, I was reading as many books as I could find about object-oriented design. One of the best at the time was *Object Oriented Design with Applications* by Grady Booch. That book was a watershed. It used a spectacular diagramming convention to depict classes, relationships, and messages. The convention looked like this:

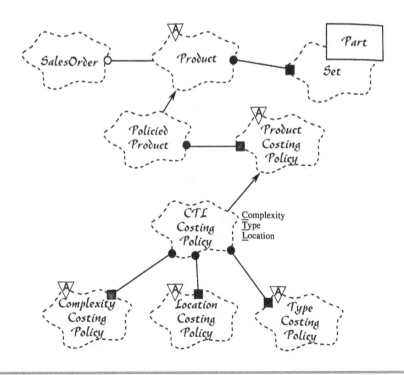

This was a radically new concept in representing software! I could see the utility immediately. And I just loved those clouds. I got really good at drawing those diagrams on whiteboards, and I used them to design much of the software we were working on at Clear.

My buddy, Jim Newkirk, and I went on a few business trips to talk to suppliers and vendors. On one such trip, we spoke to the software engineers who were using Objective-C. I had heard about this language, and so I sat down with them to inspect some of their code. I thought it was interesting, but I preferred C++.

Some of those business trips took us to Silicon Valley. Jim and I would take advantage of those trips to peruse the computer bookstores that were so common there. We often shipped home several hundred dollars' worth of books.

1992: THE C++ REPORT

I was still working at Clear, but my focus was changing. It was clear to me that the business was struggling, but my career was on the upswing. I continued to interact on the newsgroups and was attracting a significant following there.

I started submitting articles to *The C++ Report*, and to my surprise I found that they were always accepted. I got to know Stan Lippman, the editor, pretty well.

As technically stimulating as the work at Clear was, the business itself failed to thrive. The long hours and constant stress took their toll.

Eventually, I started thinking that I needed a change. And just then, I got the phone call that changed my life.

1993: RATIONAL INC.

The phone call was from a headhunter. They had an opportunity in Santa Clara, CA. I wasn't planning on moving all the way out to the West

Coast, so I didn't take the call seriously until they said that the project was a computer-aided software engineering (CASE) tool: a tool for *drawing software diagrams.*

There weren't a lot of software diagramming techniques out there at the time, and Santa Clara is where Rational was—and that was the company that Grady Booch worked for.

So I got *a lot* more interested. I probed the headhunter for more data. He wouldn't tell me who his client was, but the information he gave me was conclusive. By the time I had hung up the phone, I knew I had to jump on this one.

I set up an interview and, sure enough, the company was Rational, and the project, Rose, was a tool for drawing those lovely cloud diagrams in Booch's book. This was one of the best interviews I've ever had. I was very clearly a good fit for them, and they were a good fit for me. So they offered me a position—but I'd have to move out there. That would take some convincing at home.

My wife was willing to consider such a move, so Rational paid our way to do a little house hunting. Two days later we were convinced that we could never afford a house anywhere near Silicon Valley. The prices were three times higher than anywhere we had ever lived before.

So the answer was no. We were not going to move.

I was desperate. There had to be a way. And so my wife said, "Why don't you consult for them." I was 40 years old and had worked as an employee for over 20 years. The thought of going independent was terrifying. But I suggested that option to Rational, and they were amenable.

I spent three months in Santa Clara working with the Rational Rose team. I spent another six months back at home working remotely. It was a wonderful experience.

We were working in C++ using an *object-oriented database*. Our diagrams were drawn on SPARCstation screens and were stored in an object representation. It was heady stuff.

I met Grady two or three times during that period. He lived and worked near Denver, and flew out to Santa Clara from time to time. On one of those occasions, I pitched the idea of a book to him.

I wanted to write a book on object-oriented design that focused on C++ and used Booch's diagrams. Grady was amenable to guiding me through the publishing process, and he introduced me to Alan Apt, his publisher at Prentice Hall.

I started working on some sample chapters, and Alan sent them out for review. When I got the reviews back, I was thunderstruck that one of the reviewers was James O. Coplien. I had read his book *Advanced C++ Programming Styles and Idioms* in 1992 and considered him to be one of my heroes.

Unfortunately, his review was less than stellar. About the only thing I remember now was the phrase *"Flowcharts for the nineties!"* Ouch!

But I kept on writing and improving. Soon enough I had a book contract.

Meanwhile, I kept on posting on Usenet. One day I realized that nobody was calling me "Uncle Bob" anymore, and for some perverse reason I missed it. So I put the name in my email signature that was also used for my Usenet postings. The name started to spread. I was posting a lot.

1994: ETS

After nine months, the contract with Rational was over. The first release of Rose was on the stands, and it was time to move on.

Terror struck. Where was I going to get clients from? I checked in with Teradyne, and they had a few little odds and ends for me to do, but it wasn't going to pay the bills long term.

And then I got another one of those phone calls. It was Rational—but not the Rose team. Instead, it was their contract programming office. They had a client that they didn't have the capacity to serve and wondered if I would like a referral.

The client was the Educational Testing Service out in Princeton, NJ. I flew out there and started consulting with them on C++ and object-oriented design. I'd fly out for two or three days every couple of weeks. It was a great gig. Princeton is a great town!

ETS had contracted with NCARB, the National Council of Architectural Registration Boards. They wanted ETS to create an automated test for certifying architects. The idea was to create a GUI that architects could use to draw architectural diagrams. Those diagrams would be stored and forwarded to a scoring system that would interpret the diagrams and score them for architectural principles.

There were 18 different kinds of diagrams that the architects would have to draw. They included things like floor plans, roof plans, property lines, and structural engineering. The GUI programs and the scoring programs would run on IBM PCs.

The plan for the scoring programs was to use a kind of fuzzy-logic inference network to measure various features of the architects' designs and create a final pass–fail grade.

For every GUI program there was a corresponding scoring program. They called the pairings *vignettes*.

ETS had allocated four part-time programmers to this job. They had no experience with C++ or object-oriented design. I was there to coach them through the hard parts. They had just over three years to finish all 18 vignettes.

After a few months, it became clear to me that this team was never going to achieve that goal. They were too distracted with other projects. This project was going to require *focus*. So I convinced my buddy Jim to fly out to Princeton with me and pitch a different solution. He and I would build a team and get the project done for them.

It took a bit of negotiation, but a month later we had a long-term development contract.

The plan was for Jim and I to work for several months on the most complex of all the vignettes, called *Vignette Grande*. This was the vignette that focused on floor plans. Our goal was to both get elements of this vignette working *and* to create a reusable framework that would allow the other vignettes to be developed in short order. Then, we would recruit a larger team to work on the other 17 vignettes.

Reusable frameworks. Ah, how naive we were. All the books and articles on OO promised reusability. We thought that we were hotshot OO designers and that we could create a reusable framework par excellence.

Many months later we had Vignette Grande working, and we had what we thought was a reusable framework. So we reached out to the best people we knew and recruited them to work with us on a contract basis.

Everybody worked from their homes.

The trouble started right away. We found that the reusable framework we had produced was not reusable. The other vignettes did not fit with the decisions we had made while writing Vignette Grande. After a few weeks, it became clear that, if we didn't do something about it, the other 17 vignettes would not be delivered on time.

So we informed ETS that we were changing the plan. The team would focus on the next three vignettes and also on refitting the framework in such a way that all three vignettes found it useful. This took many more months, but in the end it paid off. We had three vignettes all using the framework, and Vignette Grande standing alone using the old framework.

We recruited a few more people and started producing vignettes like a sausage machine cranking out sausages. Each new vignette took a fraction of the time because the framework was, indeed, reusable. In 1997 we delivered all 18 vignettes on time. They were in use for nearly two decades.

It turns out that in order to make a reusable framework, you need to actually use it in more than one application. Who knew?

Meanwhile, I continued writing that book and delivered it to the publisher—a bit late, but in time for a 1995 copyright date.

THE C++ REPORT COLUMN

By this time, I had two articles published in *The C++ Report*. Stan Lippman wrote to me and asked me to write a monthly column. Grady Booch had decided to stop writing the Object-Oriented Design column, and Stan wondered if I wanted to take it up. Of course I agreed.

PATTERNS

I attended a C++ conference in 1994. Jim Coplien was there, and he was wearing a note pinned to his shirt that said "Ask me about patterns." I asked him, and he took my email. A few weeks later I got an email from him telling me about four authors who were writing a book and who were looking for online reviewers. The book was titled *Design Patterns*, and the authors were Erich Gamma, Richard Helm, John Vlissides, and Ralph Johnson. The email from Coplien directed me to an email mirror that contained the ongoing discussions about the book.

In the emails on that mirror, the four authors were affectionately referred to as the GOF (Gang of Four). Every few days one or another of the GOF would post an FTP address in an email on that mirror. The FTP address pointed to a PostScript file that contained one of the chapters they were working on. What would follow was a flurry of comments, corrections, debates, and further examples. Being involved with that was a heady affair.

Of course, this was all pre-Web. Tim Berners-Lee had created the first web server less than four years before, and Marc Andreessen had released Mosaic just the year before. Few of us knew anything about those efforts. So email, FTP, and Netnews were our primary means of internet communication.

One of the emails on the mirror was a call for papers for a new conference named PLoP (Pattern Language of Programming), to be held near the University of Illinois campus in Monticello, IL. This was being organized by The Hillside Group, which had been formed by Grady Booch and Kent Beck and included Jim Coplien, Ward Cunningham, and several others.

The conference was dedicated to the discussion and promotion of design patterns, and I dearly wanted to attend. So I submitted three different papers, at least one[1] of which got accepted: "Discovering Patterns in Existing Applications."

That paper outlined the many GOF patterns that we realized we had been using in the NCARB software. It also discussed some others that I suggested ought to be patterns. Finally, it gave some hints about the book I was writing that was to be published the following year.

1995–1996: First Book, Conferences, Classes, and Object Mentor Inc.

My first book talked about some design principles. I made specific references to the Open–Closed Principle and the Liskov Substitution Principle. I had read about both of these principles in the works of Bertrand Meyer and Jim Coplien. I also made mention of the concept of dependency inversion, though I did not name it as a principle. In addition, I talked about component coupling, cohesion, and stability, and I even talked about metrics of abstraction and instability, but I did not specifically describe them as principles. Those ideas were still in the future for me.

---

1. I don't remember if all of them were accepted or not. I rather think not. Only one appears in the proceedings.

I finished up that first book in a flurry of late-night activity, and I saw it published. That was quite an event for me. It also put my name out there in a much larger way. I started giving talks at conferences, and the more the book got around, the better attended those talks were. The more talks I gave, the more my name got around. Eventually, the conferences started inviting me as a featured speaker.

I was still interacting a lot on the newsgroups, and I changed my signature to indicate that I was available for consulting and training. The calls started coming in. I put together a five-day course on C++ and found myself teaching it to various companies across the US. I put together another five-day course on object-oriented design and found myself teaching *that* to various companies across the US. Even Teradyne asked me to teach a few—including one in Bracknell.

Principles

In May of 1995, I read a posting[2] on the comp.object newsgroup. The title was "The Ten Commandments of OO Programming." The advice offered was not bad; but after all our activity with the NCARB project, I considered it to be a bit naive. So I responded with my own 11 commandments, which enumerated and encapsulated a set of design principles. It was this response that was the true birth of the SOLID and Component Principles. Though they had not yet been named.

Within a year, I had refined, named, and begun teaching a set of nine design principles:

- OCP, the Open–Closed Principle
- LSP, the Liskov Substitution Principle
- DIP, the Dependency Inversion Principle
- REP, the Release-reuse Equivalence Principle
- CCP, the Common Closure Principle

---

2. See https://groups.google.com/g/comp.object/c/WICPDcXAMG8.

- CRP, the Common Reuse Principle
- ADP, the Abstract Dependencies Principle
- SDP, the Stable Dependencies Principle
- SAP, the Stable Abstractions Principle

Teaching, writing, and conferences were taking lots of my time. Jim Newkirk took up the load on the NCARB project while I danced around the country teaching and consulting. My client list was starting to look pretty impressive. I was teaching and consulting at Xerox, General Motors, Nortel, Stanford (SLAC), Lawrence Berkeley Labs, and many others.

Jim and I founded Object Mentor Inc. Jim picked up some of the consulting load along with all the NCARB stuff. Business kept on coming in, so we hired Bob Koss, an experienced C++ teacher, to help with the training.

1997–1999: THE C++ REPORT, UML, AND DOTCOM

We completed the NCARB project, on time, in 1997. It was successfully deployed, and we continued to maintain it for years thereafter.

In late 1997, Doug Schmidt, the current editor of *The C++ Report*, called me. He said he was leaving his position as editor and wondered if I wanted to take it on. Of course, I said I would.

This was the era of the dotcom boom. The Web had exploded all over the business community. Domain names were getting bought and sold for hundreds of millions of dollars. Companies without products or employees were being evaluated in the billions. Anybody who claimed to be doing anything on the internet was an immediate commodity. It was nuts.

Rational's response to this was to gather Grady Booch, Ivar Jacobson, and Jim Rumbaugh together and heavily promote them for *Software Best Practices*. The three were affectionately known as The Three Amigos, and they began to develop the Unified Modeling Language (UML) and the Rational Unified Process (RUP).

I got involved with the UML side of that because of my heavy use of Booch's earlier cloud notation that I had used in my book. I stayed away from the process side because I was not a big believer in *any* kind of software process.

Book 2: Design Principles

My ideas on design principles had solidified[3] quite a bit since that comp. object posting in May of 1995. I had finalized the separation of the component principles from the class principles and had added the Interface Segregation Principle.

I now saw my previous book as being both incomplete and too narrowly focused. It was time to start writing a more complete and more general treatise on object-oriented software design. I approached my publisher and was quickly under contract—the dates of which I would find rather challenging.

Overall, I was pretty busy. I had my hands in just about every part of the industry. Object Mentor Inc. was very profitable and growing. Life was good—and then it got better.

1999–2000: eXtreme Programming

All the consulting I was doing was technical. I was advising people on how to use C++ and object-oriented design. That consulting was well received, but several of my clients asked me to help them out with process. Ugh.

So I sat down and wrote out a software process that I called C.O.D.E. Don't ask me what that stands for. Don't ask me anything about it. It was awful. My goal was to create an extremely minimal process that would not impose the kind of nasty soul-killing bureaucracy that would suppress the creativity and ingenuity of the programmers.

---

3. Ha ha. But the name SOLID had not yet been chosen.

While writing this abomination, I stumbled around on the internet looking for other people who might have a better idea. There weren't a lot of search engines on the Web at that time, so *stumble* is the right word. I don't know how I got there; it was probably through a newsgroup posting. Anyhow, I finally wound up at c2.com, the first online wiki written in Perl by Ward Cunningham. On that wiki was a very active discussion on Kent Beck's eXtreme Programming (XP).

Wow! This was *exactly* what I was looking for. It was perfect—well, except for his nonsense about writing tests first—but otherwise, it was just what I needed to tell my clients. I was really excited.

But before I could do anything about it, I had a one-day course to teach at the February 1999 OOP conference in Munich. During a break, I stepped out of my classroom and there, before me, was Kent Beck. He had just stepped out of the room where he was also teaching a class. I had met Kent earlier at the PLoP conferences, so I recognized him immediately and asked him to tell me more about XP.

We sat together at lunch and he regaled me with tales of his projects using XP. I was thrilled—except for all the test-first nonsense. I was still the editor of *The C++ Report*, so I asked him to write an article about XP. He agreed, and we returned to our classrooms.

Kent wrote that article, and it was published in the next issue. It was very well received, and I was confident that I could refer my clients to that article. I scrapped my C.O.D.E. abomination and never thought of it again.

And then it occurred to me that training and consulting in XP could be a good business to get into. I conferred with my business partners, Jim Newkirk and Lowell Lindstrom, and we agreed. So I wrote to Kent and told him of our plans. I asked if he wanted to be involved and if we could get together for a planning session.

Kent invited me to his home near Medford, OR. He and I spent two days conspiring to create a business offering around XP. We sketched out the basic flow of a five-day course. We hashed out a bunch of other issues.

We took a drive up to Crater Lake—because I'd always wanted to see it.

We also did some pair programming, and he showed me about the test-first nonsense. In two hours, the two of us, writing code in the tiniest little test-first steps that I could imagine, got a cute little Java applet working.

I'd never seen anything like this before. I'd been a programmer for 30 years at this point, and I never thought I'd see an entirely new method of writing code. This floored me. I was also deeply impressed by the fact that we worked for two hours and never debugged anything. I was convinced. This was a technique I needed to get *good* at.

I flew home, and Kent, Jim, and I collaborated on the structure of our course offering. These were going to be *events*. Remember, this is the *dotcom* era, and there was money spilling out over everything related to software. So an event was exactly what was called for.

We rented a large facility. We hired several new instructors. We were going to ride the dotcom bubble for all it was worth.

We called the event XP Immersion. It was a five-day course going from 9 a.m. to 9 p.m. each day. The first eight hours were lecture and exercise. Then a catered dinner. Then a guest speaker. We recruited Martin Fowler, Ward Cunningham, and a host of other well-known software celebrities. And we held one of these events every three months while we also continued our training and consulting in C++, Java, and object-oriented design.

The XP Immersions were a massive success. We'd have 60 students in each. They were gala affairs that resulted in high praise and great reviews. We were on top of the world.

We started getting calls to help companies *transition* to XP. We created a very lucrative business offering around training and consulting. We'd go into those companies for a period of several months and teach their staff how to do this miraculous thing called XP.

REFERENCES

Booch, Grady. 1990. *Object Oriented Design with Applications*. Benjamin-Cummings Publishing C.

Coplien, James 0. 1991. *Advanced C++ Programming Styles and Idioms James O.* Addison-Wesley.

Ellis, Margaret A. and Bjarne Stroustrup. 1990. *The Annotated C++ Reference Manual*. Addison-Wesley.

Gamma, Erich, Richard Helm, Ralph Johnson, and John Vlissides. 1994. *Design Patterns: Elements of Reusable Object-Oriented Software*. Addison-Wesley.

Martin, Robert Cecil. 1995. *Designing Object Oriented C++ Applications Using the Booch Method*. Prentice Hall.

THE MILLENNIUM

All the king's horses and all the king's men . . .

The decade of the millennium started on a high, but overall it was a decade of uncertainty and decline. The September 11 attacks, the War on Terror, Al-Qaeda, ISIS, Hezbollah. The second Iraq war. The Afghan war. The London Underground bombing. The Madrid train bombing. A rise in social dissatisfaction and unrest. The rising fear of climate change. A political reshuffling. The financial crisis of '08. And an economy that never quite managed to find its legs.

2000: XP LEADERSHIP

XP Immersions were running like gangbusters. We held them every three months. Twice a year they were in different states, the other times in our office near Chicago. Meanwhile, the consulting and training business was raging. Life was good!

In the fall of 2000, Kent Beck called a meeting near his home in Medford, OR. He called it the *XP Leadership* meeting. He invited me, along with Martin Fowler, Ward Cunningham, and many other XP luminaries. The purpose of the meeting was to decide the future of XP.

We did the usual things one does at meetings like this. We went on hikes and boat rides, and we met in conference rooms to brainstorm and argue.

In one such meeting, the idea of forming a nonprofit organization to promote XP was proposed. Many of the folks in the room had been members of The Hillside Group and had not enjoyed that experience. So they recommended against the proposal. I disagreed, and said so rather forcefully.

When the meeting was over and we were all returning to our rooms, Martin Fowler came up to me and said he agreed with my position and suggested that we meet the following week when we were both in Chicago.

We met at a coffee shop and hashed out the idea of a meeting, not just for XP but for all the "lightweight" processes that had been popping up over the last few years. Our idea was to get proponents of XP, Scrum, DSDM, FDD, and several other experts together and see if we could reduce our ideas down to a core ideology. Our contention was that all these approaches had more in common than in difference, and that finding that commonality would be useful.

So we composed an email recommending a meeting in February 2001 on a Caribbean island (Anguilla), and sent it out to a wide audience. The subject line of that email read something like "The Lightweight Process Summit."

Within hours, Alistair Cockburn called me and said that he was just about to send a similar email, but he liked our invitation list better than his. He offered to do all the legwork to set up the summit if we would agree to have the meeting in Salt Lake City.

2001: AGILE AND THE CRASH(ES)

And so a group of 17 software experts met at the Snowbird resort and wrote the Agile Manifesto. Little did we know the impact that was going to have on the industry at large.

Shortly thereafter, the first meeting of the Agile Alliance was held at the Object Mentor office near Chicago. The organization was formed and began operations.

Agile had become the Next Big Thing™, and we knew we had a tiger by the tail.

But ill winds were beginning to blow. By the spring of 2001, it was becoming clear that the dotcom bubble was becoming unstable. Enrollment in *all* our classes was down a bit, and consulting opportunities were starting to wane. Business was still pretty good, so our outlook, though guarded, was still quite positive. But no guard could prepare us for what happened next.

The last XP Immersion began on Monday, September 10, 2001. There were 30 or so students who had flown in from all over the country. The course began well, and we were full of optimism.

On Tuesday, everything changed. Two 767s were deliberately crashed into the World Trade Center towers, and another into the Pentagon. We had been attacked, and we were at war. The class continued. The students put their heads down and continued to work. Air travel was mostly canceled, but a few special flights remained scheduled for that week so that people could return from business trips and vacations.

Some of our students and instructors (including Kent Beck) got home on those special flights. The rest rented cars and drove back to their homes in various parts of the country.

In the weeks that followed, the dotcom bubble burst with a vengeance. For the better part of two years, courses and consulting were dead. We had to cut our staff and our salaries to the bone. It was as though there was no software being done anywhere.

One silver lining, if you can call it that, was that I now had plenty of time to work on my second book—which was quite late by now. The book had grown from a treatise on object-oriented design to a compendium of principles, patterns, and practices. I had written hundreds upon hundreds of pages, and I was still writing more.

At last, in the middle of 2002, I took the 800 pages I had written; whittled, chopped, and hacked them down to just over 500; and submitted that as my final manuscript. The book, *Agile Software Development: Principles, Patterns, and Practices,* was published in 2003.

2002–2008: WANDERING IN THE WILDERNESS

The next several years were something of a desert in my career. Object Mentor Inc. was not growing; it was muddling. We had *some* business. There were months when we were even optimistic about the future. But those periods never lasted long. We kept the doors open through austerity, but business never returned to its pre-2001 state.

We tried this and that and a few other things, but nothing really panned out. By 2007, it was pretty clear to me that narrowly focused training and consulting businesses like ours were simply not going to succeed.

Worse, the coming of the Web and the subsequent dotcom crash had sucked all the oxygen out of the software environment and left everyone wary. There were few advances in software technology; few new ideas percolating up through the industry. It was as though we had hit some kind of plateau. Even the massive hardware improvements, like the iPhone and the iPad, were not indicative of new ideas in software. Software was in the doldrums, and I saw no way to escape with the company intact.

CLEAN CODE

In the midst of that desert, a bit of manna fell on me. I had, for some time, thought that someone should write a book on good coding technique. I had not thought myself worthy to write such a book. After all, telling programmers the difference between good and bad code requires a lot of chutzpah. Who was I to lay down a set of rules like that?

But then it occurred to me: I had been a programmer for nearly four decades. If not me, then who? I could at the very least write a book on the techniques that had worked for *me* over the years—and there were a lot of them. And so I began the book titled *Clean Code*.

The last straw for Object Mentor was the financial crisis of 2008. That was the executioner's axe. We had no reserves and no way to survive. The company was dead.

2009: SICP AND CHROMA-KEY

Closing down a business is not a fun task. But in the end, I was once again a lone consultant offering my services to companies around the world.

There was enough business to keep my family fed and happy while I paid off the (rather significant) debt I'd incurred trying to keep Object Mentor Inc. afloat. What's more, the sales of *Clean Code* were encouraging.

And then another bit of manna fell upon me. My communications on the internet had gradually transitioned from the newsgroups to Twitter.

Someone tweeted a suggestion to read the book *Structure and Interpretation of Computer Programs* (SICP). I found a used copy on Amazon or eBay and purchased it. It sat on my desk, unopened, for several months.

Then one day, I opened it and started to read. I was transfixed! Some kind of bizarre energy filled me, and I all but threw each page as I read. It was exciting and enthralling. I read, and read, and read.

The language was Scheme, a derivative of Lisp. I was a C/C++/Java/C# programmer and had always thought of Lisp as some kind of academic plaything. Boy, was I wrong. I couldn't put the book down.

And then, on page 217, the authors slammed on the brakes. They told me that everything was about to change. They warned me that the whole model of computation was going to be overthrown at significant risk. And they introduced—*assignment*.

I was floored. I had read 200 pages of mostly code. There were math programs, table manipulation programs, bitmap manipulation programs, encryption algorithms, and many others. And in not one of them had there been even a single assignment statement! I had to go back and check. I couldn't believe it.

How could something so intrinsically associated with computation be absent from their programs? How could they write such elaborate systems without ever changing the state of a variable? I had to learn more. I had to *write* this kind of code!

In another tweet, I had seen someone refer to the language Clojure as Lisp based on Java. I looked it up and found that it was the creation of Rich Hickey. I had encountered Rich in my debates on comp.object and comp.lang.c++ a decade before, and had thought highly of him at the time.

So I determined to learn this language and learn the techniques I found in SICP.

Thus began my foray into the fascinating world of *functional programming*.

VIDEO

In the meantime, I noticed that network speeds had increased to the point that video over the internet was feasible. Amazon Web Services was also alive and well, and hosting videos could be accomplished without having to purchase my own dedicated hardware and network connections.

My lectures at conferences had always been very successful, and I was still being invited to give keynote talks. So I thought that perhaps I should record myself giving talks and put them online. Maybe people would pay to watch.

YouTube was brand new in those days and was not a place to put videos for sale. Any video solution I came up with would have to be homegrown.

So I bought a digital home video camera and started recording myself giving talks in my office.

The recordings were awful. They were boring. Without an audience, there was no life. It was just me talking. Ick.

I showed the videos to some family and friends. They agreed. Boring.

Then, I showed them to my sister Holly, and she said: "You need to use chroma-key."

I had no idea what chroma-key was, so I looked it up.

This was just at the knee of Amazon's curve. Amazon started out selling only books. They added a few new products every once in a while. Then, suddenly, right around 2009, you could buy *everything*. I found a green screen and some lights on Amazon and had them delivered.

I set up the screen and the lights and filmed myself again. And this time I put myself on the moon. To do that, I needed to buy some video editing software. It took me a few days to get the hang of it, but then my moon videos started looking pretty good.

But they were still boring. Still just me talking.

So then I thought that perhaps I should write a script, and instead of shooting the whole lecture in one go, I could shoot individuals scenes. Perhaps those scenes could be from different vantage points and in different locations. And perhaps I could make things more interesting by changing my dress and my demeanor between scenes.

I scripted and shot a 15-minute pilot episode. Then, I edited it. That's when I learned that every minute of produced video represents an hour of scripting, shooting, and post-processing effort. That 15-minute video represented 15 hours of work! Yikes!

But it was worth it. That video was exciting. It was fun to watch, and it conveyed information to those who watched it. It was like magic.

CLEANCODERS.COM

So I approached my son Micah, who was running his own successful software business at the time. I asked him if he wanted to go halves on a new venture. I would produce several episodes, each an hour long. He would write the website and hosting facilities to sell and present those videos. He agreed, and Clean Coders Inc. was formed.

2010–2023: VIDEOS, CRAFTSMANSHIP, AND PROFESSIONALISM

I was still traveling around the world giving talks, training, and consulting. But in my time at home, I would produce episodes. A one-hour episode was worth 60 hours of work. That meant I could realistically produce one episode per month.

One by one, the episodes appeared. At some point, Micah got the website up and running, and we started to offer the videos online at cleancoders.com.

I had a substantial Twitter following, and I tweeted the web address. Lo and behold, people started buying the videos.

It's quite amazing how much information you can convey in a video. Not only can you lecture, but you can also demonstrate coding techniques. You can virtually pair-program with your viewers. I found the whole process electrifying. I could say more in an hourlong video than I could say in 20 to 30 pages of text, and convey more of the information more reliably.

My viewers seemed to agree, because they kept on buying the videos.

By the end of 2011, we had $100,000 in revenue, and we realized we were on to something.

I hired my daughter Angela Brooks to handle filming and editing, and we were off to the races—again.

Agile Off the Rails

In the meantime, the Agile movement had gone off the rails. What had started as a movement driven by programmers had changed to a movement driven by project managers. Programmers were gradually, but very effectively, pushed out of the movement.

I found this particularly galling because I had hoped, for the last decade, that the Agile movement would be the force that raised the bar for programmers. I thought it would drive programming to become a profession steeped in high standards, disciplines, and ethics. But it was not to be.

It occurred to me that this new video medium could be a better approach for conveying the disciplines, standards, and ethics that would raise the bar of software craftsmanship.

And so my mission ahead was clear.

For the next decade, with the help of my lovely daughter Angela and my brilliant son Micah, I would produce 79 videos, each an hour long.

Seventy-nine hours of lecture and demonstration. Seventy-nine hours of me teaching everything I knew about software—or at least everything I could cram into such a set of videos.

Each year I would say that I had perhaps a dozen more videos to create, and each year I would extend that by another half dozen or so. It never occurred to me that the videos would be a decade-long project.

MORE BOOKS

In that decade, I wrote several more books:

- *The Clean Coder* is all the nontechnical stuff that I left out of *Clean Code*. It was my first book on professional behavior.
- *Clean Craftsmanship* is a very detailed book on the technical and nontechnical disciplines, standards, and ethics of a software professional.
- *Clean Architecture* is a deeply technical book about software in the large. It reprises the design principles and describes the goals, problems, and solutions of software architecture.
- *Clean Agile* is a reprise of the origins of the Agile movement and a call to return to those origins.
- *Functional Design* is a very technical book about how to design systems in a functional programming environment.

THE COVID-19 PANDEMIC

The pandemic ended my career as a traveling trainer and consultant. Oh, I still visit customers from time to time, but it is no longer a significant part of my business. What training I do nowadays is mostly done through Zoom—and honestly, I try to keep those commitments to a minimum.

2023: THE PLATEAU

You've likely noticed that the last ten years of this history were rather sparse. The reason for that is probably due to the curve that most people undergo as they grow and age.

Early in your career you will be almost entirely in input mode. You are learning as much as you can and absorbing idea after idea without presenting very many new ideas. As you gain experience, you continue to absorb ideas but also begin to present your own ideas, synthesized from your experience and the ideas you had absorbed. This process continues, reaching a peak between your 30s and 50s. During that peak, the synergy of the ideas coming in and the ideas going out is at its greatest.

There's a tremendous amount of feedback and intellectual activity. But as time goes on, the output of ideas overtakes the input, and the synergy and feedback begin to slow. In the end, as you approach retirement, you are outputting the vast accumulation of your ideas without taking many new ideas in.

This may sound sad, and it may not apply to everyone, but it is not at all uncommon. And it may, indeed, be that process that is responsible for the sparsity of my comments on the last decade.

However, I think there may also be something else going on. That same process may be what's happening to our industry at large. Programming itself may not be generating many more new ideas.

This may strike you as an odd statement. After all, there have been several new and exciting languages created in the last decade or so: Golang, Swift, Dart, Elm, Kotlin, and many more. But I look at those languages and all I can see are a bunch of old ideas reshuffled into new packages. I don't see anything particularly innovative about any of them—at least not as innovative as C, or SIMULA, or even Java were in their days.

Let's look at this another way. The difference in programmer productivity jumped by a factor of 50[1] (or more) when we stopped writing code in binary and started writing in assembler. It jumped by a factor of around 3 to 5 when we transitioned to languages like C. The increase was perhaps a modest 1.3 when we moved to OO languages like C++ or Java. Perhaps we got another 1.1 out of languages like Ruby or Clojure.

Those factors may be off, but the trend certainly is not. The incremental advantages of each new language have diminished toward zero. It looks, to me, like we are approaching an asymptote.

---

1. See the section Compilers: 1951–1952 in Chapter 4.

And ours is not the only asymptote we are approaching. The hardware we ride upon has also stopped its crazy exponential growth. Moore's law died right around 2000. Clock rates have stopped getting faster. Memory capacities are no longer doubling every year. The increase in chip density has slowed as we approach the atomic limits.

In short, advances in both our hardware and our software may have reached a plateau.

And that may be the perfect segue into Part IV: The Future.

REFERENCES

Martin, Robert C. 2003. *Agile Software Development, Principles, Patterns, and Practices*. Pearson.

Martin, Robert C. 2019. *Clean Agile: Back to Basics*. Pearson.

Martin, Robert C. 2017. *Clean Architecture: A Craftsman's Guide to Software Structure and Design*. Pearson.

Martin, Robert C. 2008. *Clean Code: A Handbook of Agile Software Craftsmanship*. Pearson.

Martin, Robert C. 2021. *Clean Craftsmanship: Disciplines, Standards, and Ethics*. Addison-Wesley.

Martin, Robert C. 2023. *Functional Design: Principles, Patterns, and Practices*. Addison-Wesley.

Martin, Robert C. 2011. *The Clean Coder: A Code of Conduct for Professional Programmers*. Pearson.

Sussman, Gerald Jay, Hal Abelson, and Julie Sussman.1984. *Structure and Interpretation of Computer Programs*. MIT Press.

THE FUTURE IV

Predicting the future is hard.

LANGUAGES 16

How many languages are we currently working in? Let me see if I can enumerate them:

C, C++, Java, C#, JavaScript, Ruby, Python, Objective-C, Swift, Kotlin, Dart, Rust, Elm, Go, PHP, Elixr, Erlang, Scala, F#, Clojure, VB, FORTRAN, Lua, Zig, and probably several dozen others.

Why? Why are there so many different languages? Are there really that many different use cases for languages?

For example, Java and C# are virtually identical. Oh, they differ in certain ways, but if you stand back and look at them from a small distance, they are the same language. To a lesser extent, the same is true of Ruby and Python, or C and Go, or Kotlin and Swift.

There are commercial interests involved, of course. There is also a fair bit of historical baggage involved. And then there's the fact that we apparently hate every language we use so much that we are always searching for the holy grail of languages—the *one* language to rule them all and, in the darkness, bind them.

It seems to me that our industry is trapped on a hamster wheel pursuing the perfect language—but getting nowhere.

This wasn't always true. There was a time when each new language was different and innovative. Think of the differences between C, Forth, and Prolog, for example. Those were languages that had *ideas*. But as time has worn on, the differences between new languages have decreased to the point of nearing zero. Is Kotlin really so different from Swift? Is Go really so different from Zig? And is there anything truly new in any of those languages?

Yes, at the fringes you can point to a few differences and perhaps the hint of a new idea. But for the most part, these languages and all the newer languages are simply reshuffles of old ideas. It seems to me that we are approaching the Ecclesiastes of software languages: *"Vanity of vanities, all is vanity. What has been done, will be done again. There is nothing new under the sun."*

OK, that sounds like a downer. But there's another way to look at it. What is happening to us, right now, has happened before to different industries.

Consider, for example, chemistry. Chemists now have a standard way to represent chemicals. There are several standard notational styles for chemical formulae and the specifications of reactions. Every chemist understands $2O_2+CH_4 \rightarrow 2H_2O+CO_2$. But in the early days of alchemy, there was no standard nomenclature. Every alchemist did what was right in their own eyes, and wrote down their results in whatever arcane symbology suited them.

Or consider English. In the early days of written English, there were no standard spellings. Writers simply used whatever spelling matched their mood. Thus, in the fourteenth century, Chaucer wrote: "Whan that Aprille, with his shorures sote, The droghte of March hath perced to the rote, And bathed every veyne in swich licour, Of which vertu engenered is the flour."

Or consider electronics. In the early days, we had no standard symbols for capacitors, resistors, batteries, or even wires. The symbols we used were gradually standardized over time.

The point is that all new disciplines suffer through a chaotic but necessary explosion of ideas, notation, and representation. But then the dust settles, cooler heads forge a consensus, and a standard ideology and notation arises. And once that happens, the Tower of Babel is reversed, and communication between practitioners and disciplines increases. And that is when *real* progress is made.

So I expect this to happen to us. I expect that, at some point in the near[1] future, cooler heads will prevail, and we will all finally agree to adopt a very small set of languages, each of which has its own particular niche of use cases. It would not surprise me at all if we actually reduced that set down to a single language. It would surprise me even less if that single language were a derivative of Lisp.

Imagine the benefits of a single computer language! Employers would not have to hunt for programmers who know Calypso-lang. Books, articles, and research papers could be published with code, and every programmer would understand them. The number of frameworks and libraries would vastly shrink. The number of platforms you'd have to port your systems to would shrink as well.

A single language would be a remarkable boon to the software businesses, to programmers, to researchers, and to users.

At some point, we *will* get off the computer language hamster wheel.

TYPES

Should our compilers check and enforce the types of our data? Or should the types of our data be checked and enforced at runtime?

This tug-of-war has been going on for many decades—and without resolution.

---

1. For some definition of "near."

Types probably entered the programming world with FORTRAN. Variables that began with I through N were integers; the rest were floating point.

Expressions in FORTRAN were either integer or floating point. If you tried to use variables or constants of different types in an expression, the compiler would complain.

C was untyped. Oh, you could declare the type of a variable, but the compiler only used that declaration for memory layout, memory allocation, and arithmetic operations. It did *not* use the declared types to enforce any type restrictions. Thus, you could pass an integer to a function that was expecting a floating-point number. The compiler would happily generate that code. Running, that program had undefined behavior—which usually meant that it worked in the lab but crashed and burned in production.

Pascal and C++ were statically typed. The compiler checked every usage of a declared type to make sure it was appropriate. Such strictures vastly reduced[2] the incidence of undefined behavior.

Smalltalk, Lisp, and Logo were dynamically typed. Variables did not have declared types. The compilers did not apply any type restrictions. Types were checked at runtime, and if they were found to be inappropriate, the program was terminated in a defined manner. There was no undefined behavior, but you *could* be surprised by an abrupt termination at runtime.

Java and C# are statically typed. Ruby and Python are dynamically typed. Go, Rust, Swift, and Kotlin are statically typed. Clojure is dynamically typed.

And on and on it goes. Back and forth, the pendulum swings. Some decades we prefer statically typed languages. Other decades we prefer dynamically typed languages.

Why can't we decide? The answer is that statically typed languages are hard, and dynamically typed languages are easy. Statically typed languages

---

2. But they did not eliminate this behavior.

are like jigsaw puzzles. Every piece has to fit in just the right place, in just the right way. Dynamically typed languages are like LEGO bricks or Tinkertoy pieces. It is much easier to fit the pieces together, but you sometimes fit the wrong piece into the wrong place.

The solution to this, in my mind, is a compromise. Type checking should be formal and strict, but should be checked at runtime when and where the programmers decide. Writing comprehensive unit tests, by following a discipline like TDD, is a good strategy. There are also some excellent libraries[3] that allow for comprehensive dynamic type checking in various languages.

This will keep us from trying to fit the wrong piece into the wrong place, but will maintain the LEGO feel of the language.

LISP

Why do I think that Lisp is the likely end result of language consolidation?

First of all, Lisp is syntactically trivial. I can write down the syntax on a single side of a single index card. The syntax of Lisp is almost literally nothing more than (x y z. . .).

One of the hallmarks of our current suite of languages is that they are all syntax rich. There are lots of grammar tricks that must be learned. This makes the languages hard to learn, and vastly increases the potential for error.

Heavy syntax also impedes the progress of a language. New features have to be added to the syntax and grammar of the language, making the language even heavier and more unwieldy.

Consider how the syntax of Java has changed since the late '90s. Think about the bizarre syntax of generics and the bolted-on feel of lambdas. At

---

3. I like Clojure/spec.

some point, these languages simply collapse in on themselves in an implosion of arcane grammar and syntax that obscures the simple intentions of the programmers.

My second point about Lisp is that the sparseness of the syntax enables an extraordinarily rich expressiveness. The language seldom gets in the way of anything you want to say. This is something that has to be experienced to properly understand, but here is a simple example:

```
(take 25 (squares-of (integers)))
```

Third, Lisp is not a programming language; it is a data description language with an associated runtime that can interpret the described data as a program.[4] All Lisp programs exist in the data format of the language. The programs *are* data, and they can be manipulated *as* data. This means that you can write programs that write and execute other programs on the fly. You can also write programs that modify themselves on the fly.

This is a power that was used in the earliest days of computers, before we could afford index registers or indirect addressing. We kept that power so long as we were programming in assembler, but the risks, so close to the metal, were so high that we seldom used it. Once we moved into languages like C and Pascal, we abandoned that power without even really noticing.

It turns out, however, that the ability of a program to modify itself or write other programs on the fly is immensely powerful—as every Lisp macro programmer knows. That power vastly extends the expressive nature of the language. And when that power is used in an abstract environment like Lisp, which is *far* from the metal, it is also quite safe.

Finally, Lisp is the language that refuses to die. We've tried to kill it several times, but it just keeps coming back.

---

4. In other words, it is a von Neumann architecture.

17 AI

All the futurists are telling us that we are standing on the precipice of an AI revolution. They predict changes and disruptions and issue dire warnings about the loss of jobs, the loss of freedom, and the ultimate destruction of humanity. It's as if they all watched *Terminator* too much when they were young.

No, Skynet is not going to wake up and nuke us all. We are nowhere near producing a machine that will "wake up."

That's not to say that AI, large language models (LLMs), deep learning, and big data aren't interesting and fruitful technologies. They certainly are, and their effects upon us are likely to be significant. But there's nothing supernatural about them, nor are they going to approach anything even remotely similar to human intelligence and creativity.

THE HUMAN BRAIN

To the best of our knowledge, the cognitive activities of the human brain are the product of the interaction of approximately 16 billion neurons. Each of those neurons connects to many, many thousands of other neurons—some near, and some far away. Each neuron is, itself, a fantastically complex information processor that is mostly dedicated to the chemical processes that maintain the life and function of the neuron, but that must also play a role in the cognitive process.

Each neuron is a small analog computer that takes those thousands of input signals and converts them to an output signal that is then transmitted to hundreds, if not thousands, of other neurons. The signals are analog in nature because the information carried by the signals they read and produce is in the frequency of the pulses they create.

Thus, if you raise your finger slowly, your brain sends a sequence of low-frequency pulses to the various muscles that control that finger. The faster you wish to raise that finger, the higher the frequency of the pulses sent to those muscles.

By the same token, if you feel a light pressure on your skin, it is because the sensory neurons are sending a stream of low-frequency pulses to your brain. The heavier the pressure, the higher the frequency of those pulses.

The translation of the inputs of a neuron to its output is a complex and dynamically modified function. It is within that modification that much of our memory, and much of our perceptual and motor muscle skill, likely reside.

In short, your brain is a massively interconnected suite of 16 billion analog computers, all collaborating to make you, you.

It is hard to draw a comparison between such a complex organ and our current microchips, but I shall try.

Modern chips are a marvel of complexity. They can contain upward of 100 billion transistors. Most of those are engaged in peripheral activities such as dynamic caching, graphics processing, USB control, video codecs, short-term RAM, and a plethora of other things.

Let us guess that only 20 billion transistors are actually engaged in the CPU itself. This seems like a very generous guess considering that the venerable Motorola 68000 chip, from 1979, had (ironically) only 68,000 transistors in total.

Each of those transistors is a remarkably simple on/off switch with two inputs and one output. They communicate with each other over a bus that allows 64 transistors to communicate at any given time, and they can communicate 4 billion times per second. A little math suggests that the information rate is 256 billion bits per second. More or less. Not bad.

Yes, this is a gross simplification, but bear with me.

How many bits does a neuron carry? That's not really a fair question, because the signals that neurons process are analog. But still, there must be some limit to the resolution. I don't know what that limit is, but it seems to me that a reasonable guess would be 200 distinguishable frequencies. It could be more or less than that, but again, bear with me. If neurons can carry 200 distinguishable frequencies, that's about 8 bits.

Neurons are slow devices. They react to changes in approximately 10 ms. That's 100 changes per second.

So, what is the information rate of a brain? If each neuron receives signals from 5,000 others, each neuron is integrating $5000 \times 8 \times 100$ or 4 million bits per second. And since there are 16 billion neurons, that's about 128 quadrillion bits per second. That's a million times more throughput than the Apple M3 chip.

That number is probably very wrong. In fact, I think it falls far short of the actual information rate of the brain, because I doubt that the central processor of the M3 chip uses anything close to 20 billion transistors, and I didn't take into account the complex and dynamically modified transform function being controlled by the information processor within each neuron. So I'm tempted to give the brain another two or three orders of magnitude advantage.

But let's let the factor of 1 million stand. Could we approximate the processing power of a human brain if we coupled a million M3 chips over a 100Gb network? No, because the information rate of the network is only 100 billion bits per second. That's just 10,000 bits per second, per chip. And that means that those poor M3 chips would be starved for bits—they'd all be slowed down, more or less, by the bottlenecked ponderous rate of the network.

When it comes to information processors, it is the number of interconnections, not the clock rate, that matters most.

OK, enough of this. I think I've made my point. Our current technology is not close to the information processing power of a single human brain. Skynet is not going to wake up. AIs are not going to solve world hunger. LLMs are not going to take all our jobs away. But that doesn't mean they aren't useful.

NEURAL NETS

One of the foundation stones of AI is the idea of neural networks. They are called neural networks because they mimic some of the architecture and properties of the interconnections and functions of neurons in biological systems.

The basic idea is that there are layers of nodes, and that each node in layer 1 is connected to many nodes in layer 2, while each node in layer 2 is connected to many nodes in layer 3, and so on. In the cerebrums of human beings, there tend to be four layers connected more or less like that.

The interconnections have weights, and those weights are dynamically alterable based on whether the network is successful according to the desired function. Adjusting these weights is often called *training*.

In the simplest of cases, each node produces a numeric output that depends upon the sum of all the weighted numeric inputs. Information is entered at level N, which feeds level N-1, which feeds level N-2, and so forth, until the output arrives at level 1.

Simple networks like this can be trained to do some remarkable things. For example, you can train a four-layer neural network to recognize handwritten digits encoded into a bitmap of 24-by-24 pixels of 8 grayscale bits each.[1] Such a network could have 784 (28 × 28) input nodes; 512, 256, and 128 nodes in the intermediate layers; and 10 output nodes, one for each digit. Recognition accuracy of 92% is easily achievable.

Processing a 24-by-24 image requires a substantial amount of processor power. Even in the simplest case, it would need 1,780 multiplications and additions and 1,006 comparisons, not to mention the data manipulations for dealing with the nodes and edges of the graph. A modern computer, a GPU, or specially designed hardware can accomplish that kind of arithmetic in small fractions of a second.

Ninety-two percent accuracy is pretty good for some applications. To get better than that would require a larger and more complicated net. But that's OK, we've got the memory and computer power. So facial recognition, object recognition, and situational awareness are not outside the power of such networks.

On the other hand, neural nets can make mistakes. They make decisions based upon weights created by intense training, and those weights cannot be predicted in advance. There is no formula for determining what the weights should be. All we can really do is run a lot of data through the net and then *hope* that we've covered all the conditions.

So when a neural net makes a mistake, how do we know what went wrong? Can we reach into the net and tweak just one weight? Or do we have to tweak them all? The latter case seems most likely—and that makes the problem of debugging virtually intractable. About all you can do is retrain the network to be better, and return to the strategy of *hope*.

So, while the tool is very powerful, it has limits. There are many situations where *hope* is not a viable strategy.

---

1. The MNIST data set.

It seems clear that this technology is going to expand. New hardware will be created. New learning algorithms will be invented. Better weighting and transform schemes will be found. And that will be a good thing so long as we also remember the limitations.

BUILDING NEURAL NETS IS NOT PROGRAMMING

While neural networks run under the direction of software, the creation of neural networks is not programming. Designing and training appropriately scaled neural networks for various applications has about as much to do with programming as it has to do with designing a suspension bridge. It is not a programming activity. Neural networking is a very different kind of engineering.

Spreadsheet programs are built by programmers, but spreadsheets themselves are created by accountants. Neural network engines are built by programmers, but neural networks are created by neural network engineers. Neural networks cannot exist without software, but software can exist without neural networks.

Therefore, while the tooling behind neural networks will be something we programmers will be deeply involved with, neural networks themselves have little to do with the future of programming. They are just one application out of many that we'll be dealing with in the future.

When you hire a programmer to write a program, you do not expect to *hope*[2] that the program works. You hire a programmer to provide you with a program that delivers *certain* results. The stock in trade of a programmer is *determinism*. We, programmers, do not deal in hope;[3] we deal in binary truths. The systems we build are deterministic. Others may use the deterministic outputs of the systems that we produce as a proxy for hope, but those outputs are no less deterministic. We deal with black-and-white

---

2. There is a lot of hope that goes into the schedule and budget, but there is a single definition of a working program (um . . . hopefully).

3. I certainly hope so!

facts. We use those black-and-white facts to build the deterministic tools that help others in their struggles with the amorphous clouds of gray.

LARGE LANGUAGE MODELS

When you mix a little[4] bit of neural networking, a nice little Markov chain algorithm, the contents of the Library of Congress, every page on the Web, and all the research papers in every university library, you can get some pretty surprising results.

Surprising, but not necessarily very intelligent.

Or, perhaps I should say that the results are sometimes intelligent, but never creative or unique. And if the results are intelligent, it is not due to any innate intelligence within the LLM software. Rather, any intelligence you perceive will necessarily be the result of the intelligence of the writings that the LLM is based upon.

You see, an LLM is an excellent exemplar of GIGO—garbage in, garbage out. If, for example, you were to train LLM software using the writings of criminals, you'd get a lot of criminal output. Or, if you trained it with the writings of genocidal maniacs, you'd get a lot of genocidal mania out. And if you happen to train it with the writings of relatively intelligent people, you'll get relative intelligence out—sometimes.

But in no case will you get anything unique or creative.

For example, I asked one famous LLM to say something wise. Its response was:

    Life is a journey where the beauty lies not just in reaching the
    destination, but in savoring each step of the way. Embrace the
    lessons, cherish the moments, and find wisdom in the tapestry of
    experiences that shape your unique story.

---

4. By some definition of "little."

If your eyes aren't rolling, you are probably under 30. Life is a journey? Really? I mean, OK, sure, but that old saw has been around for a very, very long time and has pretty well worn a groove in all our minds—if we're over 30.

I asked that same LLM to say something unique, and it said:

```
In the symphony of existence, each individual is a note,
contributing a unique melody to the grand composition of the
universe. Embrace the rarity of your own tune, for it is in the
harmonious diversity of all notes that the true beauty of life's
music is revealed.
```

I know. I'm sorry about those eye muscles. They should be pretty sore after that. Anyway, just do a DuckDuckGo search for "In the symphony of existence" and see just how unique that statement was.

It's pretty easy to convince yourself that LLMs are not intelligent. The answers to the two questions above do not pass the Turing test. No intelligent human being over 30 would have responded that way to those questions—unless they were doing a comedy skit about large language models.

This is not to say LLMs aren't useful. They certainly are. They are often a better alternative to a search engine. For example, I asked it: *"Who wrote: In the symphony of existence, each individual is a note?"* And it replied:

```
Me.
```

No! Really? Imagine that! I never would have guessed. (Close your eyes and press on your temples for a few seconds. That should reduce the pain.)

So then I asked it: *"Who wrote about the symphony of life?"*

And it told me that this was a:

```
common metaphor used by various writers, philosophers, and
speakers over time.
```

Yeah, I know. Thanks.

But enough of this ridicule. Let's do something useful with it: *"Write a Java program to calculate 50!"*

Lo and behold, it replied:

Certainly! Calculating the factorial of 50 (50!) is a large number, and it may not fit into standard data types like int or long. Therefore, it's common to use a data type with arbitrary precision, such as BigInteger in Java. Here's a simple Java program to calculate 50! using BigInteger:

```java
import java.math.BigInteger;
public class FactorialCalculator {
    public static void main(String[] args) {
        int n = 50;
        BigInteger result = calculateFactorial(n);

        System.out.println(n + "! = " + result);
    }
    private static BigInteger calculateFactorial(int n) {
        BigInteger factorial = BigInteger.ONE;
        for (int i = 1; i <= n; ++i) {
            factorial = factorial.multiply(BigInteger.valueOf(i));
        }
        return factorial;
    }
}
```

In this program:

- We use the BigInteger class to handle large numbers.
- The calculateFactorial method iterates from 1 to 50, multiplying the current value of factorial by the loop variable at each step.
- The final result is then printed to the console.

Compile and run this Java program to see the value of 50! printed
to the console. Keep in mind that the result will be a very large
number.

OK, if we ignore the annoying and entirely redundant bullet points at
the end, that's pretty impressive. I compiled and ran that program and it
printed:

50! =
    30414093201713378043612608166064768844377641568960512000000000000

Do you think the LLM wrote that code? Or did it find that code somewhere
on the internet and just reproduce it? Or was it some combination of
the two?

Likely, it was more the former than the latter, although I could not find
an exact copy. So the LLM probably pieced it together. I'm guessing that
this particular LLM is specially trained in Java and, unfortunately, the
bullet style of program documentation.

Let's try something a bit harder: *"Write a Java program that multiplies its
input by a succession of every other prime number and counts the number
of multiplications until the product exceeds a trillion."*

```
import java.util.ArrayList;
public class PrimeMultiplication {

    public static void main(String[] args) {
        long input = 2; // Initial input
        long limit = 1_000_000_000_000L; // Trillion
        int primeIndex = 0;

        while (input <= limit) {
            input *= getNextPrime(primeIndex);
```

```
            primeIndex += 2; // Move to every other prime number
        }

        System.out.println("Final product: " + input);
        System.out.println("Number of multiplications: " +
                            (primeIndex / 2));
    }

    private static long getNextPrime(int index) {
        ArrayList<Long> primes = new ArrayList<>();
        long num = 2;

        while (primes.size() <= index) {
            if (isPrime(num)) {
                primes.add(num);
            }
            num++;
        }

        return primes.get(index);
    }

    private static boolean isPrime(long num) {
        if (num < 2) {
            return false;
        }
        for (long i = 2; i <= Math.sqrt(num); i++) {
            if (num % i == 0) {
                return false;
            }
        }
        return true;
    }
}
```

I have to say that I'm quite surprised the LLM was able to parse my query and interpret it correctly enough to generate code that actually works. I'm also quite surprised at just how awful that code is. I mean, *it tests the number 4 to see if it is prime*. It *re-creates* all the prime numbers up to the index for each multiplication. This was not coded by a sane programmer. This was coded by a machine that was cutting and pasting code from a bunch of sources and gluing it together. Impressive? Yes.

Intelligent? No.

One more: *"Write a Java program that prints the 97th digit of pi."*

```
import org.apache.commons.math3.analysis.function.Constant;
import org.apache.commons.math3.util.FastMath;

public class PiDigit {

    public static void main(String[] args) {
        // Get the 97th digit of pi
        int digitIndex = 97;
        char piDigit = getPiDigit(digitIndex);

        System.out.println("The 97th digit of pi is: " +
                           piDigit);
    }

    private static char getPiDigit(int digitIndex) {
        // Calculate pi using Apache Commons Math
        double pi = FastMath.PI;

        // Convert pi to a string and get the desired digit
        String piString = Double.toString(pi);
        return piString.charAt(digitIndex);
    }
}
```

Um, no. That's not going to work. Again, no sane programmer would even suggest a solution like that. And that's the point. The LLM is not a sane programmer. The LLM is not sane at all. Indeed, applying the word *sanity* to an LLM is a category error. LLMs are neither sane nor insane, because they are not sentient.

But they can still be useful: *"What is the octal code for a Ctrl-L?"*

```
The octal code for the Ctrl-L (Control-L) character is \f or
\014. The Ctrl-L character represents the form feed control
character, which is used for various purposes depending on the
context, such as page breaks in printers or clearing the screen
in terminal emulators.
```

OK, TMI, but essentially correct. On the other hand, the octal code for Ctrl-L is not \f. In fact, it's not even \014. It is just 14_8. I didn't ask it for the C representation of the code; I just wanted to know the octal number. Over-specification can sometimes be as misinformative as under-specification.

Let's try another: *"What year was the Magna Carta signed?"*

```
The Magna Carta, also known as the Great Charter, was signed on
June 15, 1215, during the reign of King John of England. It was a
historic document that outlined certain legal rights and limited
the powers of the monarchy. The signing of the Magna Carta took
place at Runnymede, near Windsor, and it played a significant
role in the development of constitutional law and the protection
of individual liberties.
```

Once again, TMI. I would have been happy with "1215." Please don't give me a paragraph when I ask for a date.

"In Clojure, how do I transpose a two-dimensional table?"

In Clojure, you can use the map function along with the apply function to transpose a two-dimensional table. Here's a simple example:

```
(defn transpose [table]
  (apply map vector table))

(def example-table
  [[1 2 3]
   [4 5 6]
   [7 8 9]])

(def transposed-table (transpose example-table))

(println "Original Table:")
(doseq [row example-table]
  (println row))

(println "Transposed Table:")
(doseq [row transposed-table]
  (println row))
```

In this example, the transpose function takes a two-dimensional table as input and uses map and vector to transpose it. The resulting transposed table is then printed out for demonstration.

Make sure to adapt this code to fit the structure of your specific two-dimensional table if needed.

Yeah, that's the idiom right out of Stack Overflow. Lots of TMI. Honestly, I don't need the silly little example, and the ending comment is equally useless.

So, yeah, pretty useful as a search engine—but not a sane author. The output of LLMs does not pass the Turing test. If you present its output as though a human wrote it, you *will* get caught. Even the LLMs "know" that:

"Write a paragraph on why you will get caught it you present LLM output as if a human wrote it."

Presenting LLM output as if a human wrote it poses a risk of detection due to distinctive characteristics inherent in the AI-generated text. While an LLM excels at generating coherent and contextually relevant responses, it lacks the nuanced understanding and personal experience that a human writer possesses. The responses may occasionally exhibit inconsistencies, lack of real-world knowledge beyond its training data cutoff, or unusual patterns that astute readers or evaluators could identify. Furthermore, the LLM might inadvertently generate information or opinions that are outdated or incorrect. Moreover, the lack of a consistent personal voice and the absence of a genuine individual's perspective could raise suspicions. In scenarios where authenticity and credibility are paramount, presenting LLM output as human-generated may risk exposure, emphasizing the importance of transparency in communicating the use of AI-generated content.

THE DISRUPTION OF LARGE X MODELS

It's not hard to extrapolate from LLMs to large music models, or large artwork models, or large political speech models. The basic idea is the same. Mix a little neural networking with a little Markov chaining and build up a huge interlinked model by integrating the enormous amount of human contributions available on the internet, and you can have any kind of LxM you like.

Are these LxMs going to be disruptive? Sure. At least to some extent. People are going to try to use them for all kinds of purposes, from putting dead actors into modern films, to creating the next new Beatles hit record. And why shouldn't they?

Oh, there will be some legal maneuvering over the issue. The estate of Fred Astaire will probably have something to say about a new music video that shows Cleopatra dancing on the ceiling with *old Gum*[5] while the two sing a duet. But in the end, all of that will get worked out, and we'll see credit lines in movies that acknowledge the contributions of the estates of the AI-generated cast.

Are *we* going to be replaced by LCMs?[6] I hope some of the code snippets I've shown you dissuade you from that idea. Yes, LCMs will get better and better. Yes, your role as a programmer will change as a result. But that change will not supplant you.

LCMs are tools, just like C is a tool, and just like Clojure is a tool, and just like any IDE is a tool. And tools have to be *used* by humans.

Remember that the original programmers who coded in binary were very afraid that Grace Hopper's A0 compiler, as horribly primitive as it was, was going to replace them. And, in fact, the opposite happened. As the tooling got better, the higher the demand grew for more and more programmers.

Why? Why does the demand for programmers seem to grow without bound? Why does the number of programmers in the world double every five years?

The answer is, simply, that we have by no means exhausted the uses to which computers can be put. The number of potential applications is vastly greater than the number of existing applications.

But what is it about humans that LCMs could not replace? After all, if LCMs get good enough, the people who want new applications will simply ask the LCMs to write them—won't they?

Not a chance. And I explained why in the Why Are We Here? section at the beginning of this book. We are the detail managers. And no matter

---

5. I asked an LLM for Fred Astaire's nickname.

6. Large code models, like Copilot.

how smart AI and LCMs become, there will always be details that they can't manage—and that's where we come in.

It may be that, one day, we will direct the LCMs by using natural language. It may be that we'll point at the screen and say: "Move this field to the right by a quarter of an inch, and change the background to light gray." We may even say things like: "Rearrange this screen to look more like the screens of the Whoop-de-Doo application." We may use lots of new gestures and notations and symbology. *But we'll still be the programmers*, because we are the ones who deal with the details. And there will always, always be details.

HARDWARE 18

The hardware that our software runs on has changed quite dramatically since the early days of computing. Today is December 17, 2023. It took just under two centuries to get here from the gargantuan and unfinished Difference Engine. It's been only 80 years since the electromechanical behemoth of the Harvard Mark I, 71 years since the UNIVAC I, 60 years since the IBM 360, 54 years since the PDP-11, 40 years since the Macintosh, 35 since the laptop, 20 since the iPod, 17 since the iPhone, 13 since the iPad, and 9 since the Apple Watch.

It is possible to calculate the vast increase in computing power represented by that 200-year span. But the numbers wouldn't make sense to us, because they are well outside any scale that a human can conceive of. The number of multipliers is just too vast. But I'll give it a try.

Consider the Difference Engine. It could perform six subtractions in a second. My laptop is a billion times faster. That's 1E9.

The Difference Engine could store six numbers. My laptop can store 300 billion times that. That's 3E11.

The Difference Engine would have weighed 8,000 pounds. My laptop weighs 4[1] pounds. That's 2E3.

---

1. According to ChatGPT.

The Difference Engine would likely have cost £25,000 in 1820. Just that weight in silver would be worth about $10 million today, and the purchasing power is likely more on the order of $3 million. My laptop cost about $3,000. That's 1E3.

We're already up to 25 orders of magnitude, and we haven't considered ease of use, cost of operation, cost of maintenance, or a bunch of other factors I can't even imagine.

How big is 1E25? Well, it's pretty godawful big. If you laid out that many carbon atoms, end to end, they would span a distance of about 100 astronomical units—just about where *Voyager 2* is right now.

The point is that the change in computational power is nothing short of astronomical. But that growth rate has slowed.

Moore's Law

Sixty years ago,[2] George Moore, the director of R&D at Fairchild Semiconductor, predicted that the number of components on semiconductor chips would increase by a factor of 2 every year. Every year since then, that rule has more or less held. In 1968 a transistor spanned 20 µm. Now we are approaching 2 nm. Squaring that difference to get density yields an increase of 1E8 or ~2^{27}. That implies that density has only doubled once every two years. However, the chips themselves have gotten bigger over that period, so the actual number of components has increased closer to Moore's estimate.

Will this continue? Who knows? People can be pretty clever. But the challenges abound. A wire 2 nm across is only about 20 atoms wide, and is a wavelength well into the X-ray part of the spectrum. Across that distance, quantum tunneling effects can degrade the "insulation"[3]

---

2. 1965.

3. Can you even talk about "insulation" at that scale?

between wires. Suffice it to say that the ultimate limit to density looks pretty close.

Clock rates, on the other hand, stopped increasing 20 years ago. They got to about 3GHz and then hit a physical wall. This reality has not changed in 20 years, and does not appear likely to change in the future. So it looks like we're stuck here at 3 billion operations per second.

That means that in order to increase raw computational power, we're going to have to increase the number of computers and figure out how to connect them in an efficient way. That's why we've seen multiple cores on processor chips, and that's also one of the major reasons that cloud computing has become so important.

CORES

For a while, we thought that the number of cores on a processor would double every year or so. At first, we saw dual-core chips, then quad-core chips. But the exponential growth of cores has not appeared. There are a number of reasons for this, but perhaps the most significant is that those cores must communicate over an internal bus that is also limited to 3GHz. Caching can mitigate, but cannot eliminate, this limitation. Moreover, parallelizing algorithms is nontrivial, and often not possible.

THE CLOUD

Computers on the cloud have a similar kind of limitation. They must share information over the network. A 400Gbps network is pretty fast, but it's shared among many computers. And the parallelism problem remains.

THE PLATEAU

All these factors suggest that we either are on or are approaching an asymptote. Raw computational power can increase with the number of physical computers, but the amount of computational power accessible to any given application may be approaching a limit. It may be that there are applications beyond the power of our vast networks of von Neumann architecture machines.

But maybe quantum computers will come to the rescue.

QUANTUM COMPUTERS

The universe is a giant computer. No, I don't mean that we are all playthings in some transcendent teenager's video game. Rather, I mean that the universe operates according to physical laws that operate in real time. The universe, through those physical laws, determines the answers to questions that would require us to devote millions of cloud computing hours of simulation to solve.

For example, the universe solves the multibody gravitation problem of the solar system in real time. Wouldn't it be nice if we could use the universe as a computer to solve *our* problems?

Of course, we've used that strategy many times in the past. Analog computers simply use the physical laws of the universe that are *analogous* to the problems that we want to solve. All we have to do, in an analog computer, is set up those analogous laws to solve our problems and then let them operate.

That's a bit harder than it sounds, and it tends to make each analog computer specific to certain kinds of problems. Analog computers are not general-purpose machines. It would be extraordinarily difficult, for example, to set up an analog computer to behave like a word processor. In fact, it takes an analog computer with the complexity of the human brain to even conceive of a word processor.

Quantum computers are similar to analog computers. The idea is to set up a problem that is analogous to the way quantum particles behave, and then have quantum particles to solve that problem.

Again, this sounds easier than it is. First of all, it is hard—very hard—to maintain the necessary quantum states. It typically requires temperatures close to absolute zero, and very high orders of vacuum. Second, it is not at all easy to set up a device that is able to combine N quantum particles in a manner that maintains their quantum states for any useful amount of time. Lastly, there are relatively few problems that lend themselves to quantum solutions. So why are we so interested in quantum computers?

The laws of quantum mechanics (QM) offer a tantalizing possibility.

Quantum particles can exist in a superposition of states. If you set up a particle in a superposition of input states, and if you run that particle through a physical process that alters the state of that particle, the resultant particle will be in a superposition of all the possible output states. That's parallelism—with a catch. Yes, with a single operation, you can convert N input states in superposition to N output states in superposition; but when you measure the output state of the particle, the superposition collapses, and only *one* of the possible output states is revealed. So a quantum computer must be set up to cleverly take advantage of the inherent parallelism *without measuring it*. That's no mean feat.

One day we may see quantum computers that can be helpful for solving some interesting problems. But quantum computers are not the magic bullet that will cause computing power to regain the exponential growth we saw in the last half of the twentieth century.

THE WORLD WIDE WEB

It has been three decades since the World Wide Web was born. In that time, it has grown from a simple little text-oriented protocol to the massive JavaScript/HTML/CSS-driven behemoth that we all know and pretend to love.

But it's awful, isn't it? I mean, what we *want* to do on the Web and what the tools we use allow us to do are two very different things.

The Web was born to share text—nowadays, that's the last thing we want to do. We don't need another markup language. We don't need to know the style sheets. All we want is what's beyond HTML. Come on—sing along.

The future of the Web, from my point of view, will be based upon simple distributed processing. We will load programs into our workstations that communicate with servers using a nice data language.

Many websites work like this today, more or less. We send JavaScript into the web browsers and communicate with servers using JSON. More or less.

I envision something quite different. I think we'll eventually have Lisp engines running in our workstations and in our servers, and the data format exchanged between them will be Lisp. Because, remember, Lisp is not a programming language. Lisp is a data formatting language with an engine that can interpret that data as a program. So long as all the nodes in the network agree on that data format and that engine, the nodes will be able to share data and programs equally.

What this means is that there will be no difference between the web environment and the desktop environment. Indeed, the distinction will disappear. You won't use your favorite browser, because browsers won't exist. You won't have to fiddle with HTML or CSS or JSON, because those things won't exist either. You will simply be running programs in your workstation and on servers without any obvious dividing line.

In short, the Web will *disappear from our perception*. Consider, for example, the 1960s.

When I was growing up, a telephone was a device that sat on a desk or was hung on a wall. It had a telephone number that was associated with our *house*. I did not have a telephone number, *my house* did.

Talking on the phone tied me to a particular geographic location. Indeed, it tied me to an area roughly 10 feet in diameter. The phone, after all, was tied to the wall, and the length of the cord was relatively short. My father outfitted our wall phones with ultra-long cords so that we could almost reach any part of the kitchen while talking on the kitchen phone. We had to put the phone down if we wanted to open the far cabinet doors, though.

The telephone was divided into two parts: the base and the receiver. You held the receiver to your mouth and ear while the base remained on the wall or on the table.

When the phone rang, it was exciting! We didn't know who it was. To know who was calling, you had to answer and say "Hello." Therefore, when the phone rang, answering it was a priority. It might be important.

It might be gramma or my friend Tim or . . . So when the phone rang, we stopped whatever we were doing and answered it.

We memorized phone numbers. We knew the numbers of all our friends. We knew the phone numbers of businesses that we called frequently. My father used a label machine to put the phone numbers of most of our friends and frequently called businesses on the kitchen wall. We also had huge phone books that listed the numbers for just about everyone and just about every business in our calling area.

Your calling area was defined by your exchange and your area code. The amount you would be charged depended upon how far you called. If you called within your exchange, the cost was minimal. Calling outside your exchange was a toll call that cost significantly more. Calling outside your area was long-distance, and could be frightfully expensive. A very long-distance call—say, from Chicago to San Francisco (where my grandmother lived)—required the operator to get involved and create a special circuit connection. These calls were very, very expensive—and the quality was quite low.

We also had televisions in 1960. They were relatively large appliances that sat on the floor or on a table in one or two rooms of our homes. Usually there was one in the living room, and perhaps another one in the master bedroom.

Resolution was low, there was all kinds of interference, and you had to think about what direction your antenna was pointing. We had a little device that would rotate the antenna on our roof so that we could pick up Chicago or Milwaukee.

We had five channels to watch: WGN, ABC, NBC, CBS, and PBS. These were carried by local broadcasters. Shows came on at very specific times on very specific channels. They were listed in the *TV Guide*, a magazine you could subscribe to and have delivered weekly. You had to turn on the television before a show began and wait there for the show to begin. Anyone else who wanted to watch a show that was on at the same time had to use a different TV. Many, many siblings fought over who got TV rights.

Nowadays, *you* have a phone number. It moves with you. Wherever you go, your phone number follows you because you carry your phone with you.

In fact, you don't think much about phone numbers at all, because you carry a phone directory with you in your phone. You simply tell your phone to "Call Bob." You don't think much about distance either. Oh, you might be careful about calling to a different country, but area codes don't mean a thing anymore; they are just part of the phone number.

If you want a pizza delivered, you tell Siri to "Call Kaisers." If you want to check to see if the local Walgreens has Moose Tracks ice cream, you tell Siri to "Call the Walgreens in Libertyville." We still know about phone numbers, but for the most part, we ignore them. We expect they will all eventually *disappear from our perception.*

You watch TV on your phone. You don't usually have to wait for the show to come on; you just click on the show you want to watch and you watch it. Three siblings sitting on the couch can be watching three different shows on their phones while sharing popcorn out of the same bowl.

The point of this example is that in the 1960s, the infrastructure dominated the application. The phone numbers, the telephones, the TV show schedules, and the TVs themselves were all part of the infrastructure. There wasn't any good way to separate the infrastructure from the application.

Today the applications are almost entirely divorced from the infrastructure. You aren't aware of the cell towers. You aren't aware of massive telecommunications networks. Most users have no clue at all how it works. The infrastructure has *disappeared from our perception.*

This is what will happen to the Web. The infrastructure of the Web is currently very evident. We use browsers and type in or click URLs; we see tables and recognizable fonts. All that infrastructure will eventually disappear from our perception. For that to happen, HTML, CSS, and even browsers will have to fade away. What will be left will be programs running in computers communicating with each other—and I hope it's all in Lisp.

20 PROGRAMMING

What is programming going to be like in the future? Will we all be replaced by AI? Will we finally be able to program by drawing diagrams instead of writing code? Will we all be wearing augmented reality monocles and dictating code subliminally while sitting in massage chairs and sipping kale and mushroom smoothies?

My best guess about what programming will be like 50 years from now is to look at what programming was like 50 years ago. Fifty years ago, in 1973, I was writing if statements, while loops, and assignment statements into text files and then compiling and testing them. Today I write if statements, while loops, and assignment statements into text files and then compile and test them. Therefore, I can only assume that 50 years from now, if I live to be 120 and am still programming, I will be writing if statements, while loops, and assignment statements and compiling and testing them.

If I took you back in time 50 years, sat you in front of my programming station, and showed you how to edit, compile, and test programs, you'd be able to do it. You'd be horrified by the primitive hardware and the rudimentary language, but you'd be able to write the code.

Likewise, if someone transported me 50 years into the future and showed me how to use the programming tools of that time, I reckon I'd be able to write the code.

The hardware 50 years ago was radically more primitive than my MacBook Pro, because for the last 50 years we were riding the exponential curve of Moore's law. I think we have reached the end of that curve, so I have doubts that the next 50 years will see the 20+ orders of magnitude improvement that I experienced in the last 50. However, I am sure that the hardware will continue to improve, even if at a less than exponential rate. Thus, I would expect to be amazed, but not cowed, by it.

THE AVIATION ANALOGY

The first 50 years of air flight took us from fragile crafts made of wood, cloth, and wire to transatlantic commercial jets. That was a period of wild and crazy exponential growth driven by economics, politics, and war.

The second 50 years was a period of incremental improvement. The transoceanic commercial jets of today look very much like those early commercial jets. Oh, there have been significant improvements, to be sure. However, the difference between a Boeing 777 and the de Havilland Comet of the early '50s is a difference in details, not in kind or category, whereas the difference between the Wright Flyer and the Comet is categorical to the extreme.

I think our computer hardware is in the de Havilland Comet stage. The category has been established. The hardware of the next 50 years will improve that category, perhaps as much as the improvements between the Comet and the 777, but they are not likely to break out of that category.

PRINCIPLES

The last 50 years of software have seen little to no improvement in basic principles. The three major paradigms—structured, functional, and object oriented—were all in place by 1970, before the first 30 years of software had ended and before the last 50 had even started. Of course, there have been some worthwhile refinements—I consider the SOLID principles to be in that category. But the fundamentals from which those principles derive were already well established.

I do not expect to see a radical change in software principles in the next 50 years. The names may change, and a few things might get shuffled hither and yon. SOLID may give way to NEMATODE or some other reclassification of the principles. But whatever form the principles take in the next 50 years, they will still derive from the foundations laid before 1973.

That first 30 years of software, from 1940 to 1970, was akin to the period between the Wright Flyer and the Messerschmitt Bf 109. The foundations had been laid, but all the principles had not been named and enumerated.

METHODS

The last 50 years has been the period of methods. HIPO,[1] waterfall, spiral, Scrum, FDD, XP, and the whole Agile concept were created during the last half-century. Agile is the clear winner in that competition, and I expect that the next 50 years will see refinements, but no revolutions.

DISCIPLINES

The last 25 years have seen an increase in programming disciplines such as TDD, Test and Commit or Revert (T&&C||R), pair/mob programming, and continuous integration/continuous deployment (CI/CD). Virtually all of these disciplines were enabled by the improving technology. TDD and CI/CD would have been unthinkable in 1973. Pair/mob programming was not uncommon, but was not considered a discipline.

---

1. An old IBM technique: hierarchical input, process output.

I expect the next 50 years to be a period in which we extend and refine these disciplines. There have already been a number of publications that have moved the bar in this regard. One of the latest is Kent Beck's *Tidy First?*. It is among the growing list of such publications.

ETHICS

My guess, and my hope, is that the next 50 years of our nascent profession will give birth to a true set of professional ethics, standards, and disciplines. I've written much about this in previous works, and will likely continue to beat that particular drum.

At this point in time, ethics are barely mentioned in the software literature. But I believe that must change. Too much now rides on the ethical behavior of programmers.

Our whole civilization now depends, for its day-to-day existence, on software. If the software systems of the world were to suddenly shut down, I expect that the death toll in the weeks thereafter would dwarf that of any previous time in history.

Unfortunately, I expect that the stimulus that will drive an ethical revolution in software will be some kind of severe accident or malware. We've already seen too many of those, and with inevitably increasing severity. At some point, a threshold will be crossed, and the ethics, standards, and disciplines of a true profession will either be willingly adopted or be forced upon us. I hope for the former. I fear the latter.

REFERENCES

Beck, Kent. 2023. *Tidy First?: A Personal Exercise in Empirical Software Design*. O'Reilly Media.

AFTERWORD

I met Tom Gilb in Norway circa 2005. He is a tall and imposing figure with a sharp mind, an agile wit, and the gracious manners of a refined gentleman. He and his lovely wife entertained me for lunch in their cabin overlooking a beautiful fjord. He and I had many stimulating conversations.

Tom was around almost from the start. He has met and worked with many of the people I've written about in this book. I could think of no one better suited to close this book with an afterword.

REFLECTIONS ON THE CONTENT

I read the manuscript thoroughly, and like a good detail-oriented programmer, I had fun finding typos and other bugs in the manuscript to email back to Uncle Bob. Like a good programmer, he enjoyed it and fixed the "bugs."

This is a wonderful contribution to the history of computing! I know, because I have lived so much of it in parallel with Uncle Bob. I got my first job with IBM in Oslo in 1958 at the punched card IBM Service Bureau. And believe me, those plugs in the plugboards were programs, and those electromechanical IBM machines, some from before the war, were the forerunners of today's computers and programming. This book makes that historically clear.

I, like Uncle Bob, spent much of my career consulting, teaching, and going to computer conferences. The importance of this is that I got to meet and dine with many of the characters in this book. So this book is about my professional friends, and I can tell you that it is a faithful story. In fact, it is incredibly well-written and researched. That is how it *really* was.

PERSONAL ANECDOTES OR STORIES

Old people (I'm 83 in 2024) love to share their stories—if anybody wants to listen.

How many of us regret not asking our parents and grandparents for more stories of their past?

Uncle Bob, the characters in this book and I are your professional "elders." Call me "Grandpa Tom."

Not only are we old, but we have a huge variety of experience. We love to share our ideas as well as those of our friends and "elders."

We can save you a lot of grief. But maybe you prefer to learn the hard way.

We hope that by writing this down, we can get the wisdom to you sooner or later. Maybe decades from now, when you are more mature.

I cannot forget Grace Hopper, on stage, showing us the length of a light-nanosecond using 11.8 inches of knitting-wool string that she pulled from her purse. Then, using a 984-foot roll of wire, from a bag, she illustrated the length of a light-microsecond. She usually sat in the back of the audience, knitting and awaiting her turn to speak.

Later, I was asked to give the annual Grace Murray Hopper Lecture at South Bank University in London. She had held the talk personally for some years, telling us "what the future held," as was expected of her. But she, like me and Uncle Bob now, was not up to the travel then, and Zoom lectures were not an option. So I undertook the lecture. But I decided I could not "tell the future" like Grace could. So I based *my* lecture on eternally true *principles*, which would probably be true in 100 years, no matter what else happened in the real world[1] (a safer bet!). Principles like this one:

The invisible target principle

All critical system attributes must be specified clearly. Invisible targets are usually hard to hit (except by chance).

I felt guilty about breaching the "implied contract of future-telling," so I telephoned Grace and faxed a copy of my speech for approval. I was relieved that she was quite happy with it. She understood the power of good principles. But she seemed far more concerned with the aches and

---

1. Gilb, Tom. 1988. *Principles of Software Engineering Management* (Addison-Wesley); www .researchgate.net/publication/380874956_Ch_15_Deeper_perspectives_on_Evolutionary_Delivery _later_2001_known_as_Agile_in_Gilb_Principles_of_Software_Engineering_Management. The invisible target principle: All critical system attributes must be specified clearly. Invisible targets are usually hard to hit (except by chance).

pains of her old bones and limbs: a future she probably "predicted" for herself, and now me, and maybe Uncle Bob.[2]

I met Edsger Dijkstra at the doorstep of his home in Nuenen, Holland. I have just recently learned from a biographer that E.D.'s diary note for the day I met him described me as an "arrogant consultant." I wonder how many "Dijkstras" (units of arrogance, see earlier in this book) *that* is? The reader might also recall from earlier in this book how Dijkstra and Zonnefeld, using the dual-programming discipline, beat my old conference friend and client,[3] Peter Naur of Denmark, to completing a working ALGOL 60 compiler.

In an INCOSE (International Council on Systems Engineering) publication, I had suggested that *dual but distinct programs* might be a good idea for several reasons.[4] Two UK academics replied in the next issue that "They did not believe in the ideas of Gilb—about Distinct Software." They instead "believed in the structured programming (i.e., 'No Go To,' I assume) ideas of Dijkstra." Notice the term *believed*; no *science* for academics, just choice of religious direction!

So I was in Holland for business and invited myself to Dijkstra's. And on the doorstep, I asked him: "What do you think is the most powerful software paradigm: distinct software or your structured programming?" He thought for a moment and said, "You had better come in and define things more before we can discuss the subject." Good, I love "well defined." I am a programmer.

He then proudly told me how he and Jacob Anton "Jaap" Zonneveld had programmed their own "distinct" (NOT copied) versions of the ALGOL

---

2. Predict? Of course. Experience? Not so much. ;-)—Uncle Bob

3. He asked me to use my Planguage modeling methods to select a new computer for Copenhagen University.

4. Gilb, Tom. 1974. "Parallel Programming." *Datamation* 20 (10): 160–161, and many subsequent papers and books. See also my note with consequent influence on nuclear software at www.researchgate.net/publication/234783638_Evolutionary_development.

compiler, and had compared notes to detect problems like bugs. Using this, they beat Naur and the Danes to the first working ALGOL 60 compiler, as is related in this book.

I then said, "Professor Dijkstra, I think I have read most everything you have written, and I never saw any mention of dual and distinct programming." He replied, "No, of course not. I never documented that. You see, I am an engineer, and we understand such concepts of redundant systems very well. But I live in an academic computer science world, and they would not understand or appreciate such practical engineering methods. So to avoid confusing them, I kept it quiet!"

WOW![5]

One more story. Peter G. Neumann. Remember? Relating to his report of his father, dining in Munich next to *Hitler and his gang*, just before the Nazi-attempted revolution and Hitler's jailing,[6] and . . . more. Peter's art-dealer dad was smart and "rode outta town" ASAP.

This reminds me of a story from *my* dad (100 patents), who shared a lawyer with Tricky Dick Nixon, and overheard their common lawyer saying, "Let's run 'Dick for President,' because we can control him" (true story, but I digress!).

When Peter met me at a conference and realized I lived in Norway, he told me that in his family attic was an unpublished raw manuscript about his art-dealer father's experiences with his famous artist clients (circa 1920s) including, my favorite, Edvard Munch. There was a whole chapter about Munch. I immediately told the Munch Museum curator that they *must get it for the historical record*. I fear they did *not* act on this. And the last I heard is that it is still in the attic in Peter's family home!

---

5. See https://media1.tenor.com/images/9cac53aacc654f9987015ae7028614a4/tenor.gif?itemid =12339782.

6. Adolf Hitler is sentenced for his role in the Beer Hall Putsch of November 8, 1923.

So, in connection with this book, I emailed Peter (at Scientific Research Institute International, Emeritus, in his early 90s) and asked if the manuscript had been saved, and if so, could he please send me a copy or the original, which I would hand-carry to the Munch Museum curator (after I read it and copied it). Watch this space for this ongoing international historical drama![7]

But in connection with this book, I discovered that Peter did an interview in 2010 with the *New York Times*[8] titled "Killing the Computer to Save It."

Here is the opening statement:

> "Many people cite Albert Einstein's aphorism 'Everything should be made as simple as possible, but no simpler.' Only a handful, however, have had the opportunity to discuss the concept with the physicist over breakfast."

The only hint that the article, and two hours lunching with a genius, gives us of Einstein's "simplicity inclination" is this (and keep in mind, as the interview points out, that Neumann is big into music, and we know Einstein relaxed with a violin):

> "Dr. Neumann's college conversation was the start of a lifelong romance with both the beauty and the perils of complexity, something that Einstein hinted at during their breakfast.
>
> "'What do you think of Johannes Brahms?' Dr. Neumann asked the physicist.
>
> "'I have never understood Brahms,' Einstein replied. 'I believe Brahms was burning the midnight oil trying to be complicated.'"

I am very interested in complexity and simplicity, but this is not my book, so I will give you a *short* insight into my own complexity theory.

---

7. Peter responded that the manuscript is now at the Museum of Modern Art in New York.

8. See www.nytimes.com/2012/10/30/science/rethinking-the-computer-at-80.html?pagewanted=all& _r=0. (The article is free if you push past attempts at payment.) "Moving to the United States in 1923, Dr. Neumann recalls his father's tale of eating in a restaurant in Munich, where he had a gallery, and finding that he was seated next to Hitler and some of his Nazi associates. He left the country for the United States soon afterward." (Smart guy! Early adopter.)

People who think systems are complex and difficult to understand are just not equipped with the right tools, called technoscopes.[9] I just gave you about 100 ways to decode complexity.

Now, that simplicity quote caught my attention. Because in my PoSEM book,[10] on page 17, I cited it as "Einstein's Over-simplification Principle."

Years later, at a Requirements Engineering conference in Texas, a young man came up to me and asked if I could provide a proper source for the quotation. Of course I replied, "Well . . . everybody *knows* that Einstein said that" (like P.G. Neumann and *NYT* still thought in 2010, and both are very careful about sources, right?).

So the young man suggested that the answer would be in a book about Einstein titled *God Does Not Play Dice*. We drove an hour to a bookshop and bought the book, and I read it overnight (no digital scan available) and found . . . nothing.

Then, the ever-helpful young man (it's amazing what we do at software conferences!) suggested that a professor of his, at Princeton, used to take long walks with Einstein (shades of the Oppenheimer film scenes), so maybe *he* could find the source. So he called his professor during the conference and got the half-right answer: that it was *not* in Einstein's papers, it was in a May 17 *Newsweek* interview conducted near the last years of his Life (the *L* is a joke; keep reading).

Well, we never found that *Newsweek* issue. But we did find a *Life Magazine* article[11] printed just before Einstein died (I cannot bring myself to pretend familiarity by calling him Al. I always addressed W. Edwards Deming, when I took him to the ballet in London [really!], as Dr. Deming, not

9. See www.gilb.com/offers/YYAMFQBH.

10. Einstein's Over-simplification Principle: "Things should be as simple as possible, but no simpler." See www.researchgate.net/publication/225070548.

11. See https://books.google.no/books?id=dlYEAAAAMBAJ&pg=PA62&source=gbs_toc_r&redir _esc=y&hl=no#v=onepage&q&f=false.

Will, Bill, or Ed). It might be appropriate here to note that I had some illuminating private conversations with Dr. Deming on the PDSA cycle, related to Agile cycles, in 1983. But perhaps you should ask me about that at another time.[12]

You will not find the Einstein simplicity quotation there either. But Einstein clearly had sympathy for simplicity, just not that exact quote. (Are you up for a really shaggy dog story?)

Then I reread in 2010, years later, Marvin Minsky's (YES, the MIT AI Labs Minsky) *Society of Mind* (1986), and found the dubious Einstein simplicity quotation in it.

So I looked him up. I was astounded to know he was still alive. He died in 2016, with this headline: "Marvin Minsky, 'father of artificial intelligence,' dies at 88."

I asked if he could give the source for the Einstein simplicity quotation. Here is our correspondence:

"On Sun, Jun 6, 2010 at 5:13 PM, Tom Gilb <tomsgilb@gmail.com> wrote:

"Prof Minsky

"I just started rereading Society of Mind. I realized that your Einstein quotation is probably not correct and attributable to a checkable written source. I made the mistake myself.

"See the Calaprice book The Quotable Einstein, for her conclusion."

Minsky replied:

"What is this reference? Can you tell me her conclusion?

---

12. See T. Gilb, "Deeper Perspectives on Delivery," in *Principles of Software Engineering Management*. www.researchgate.net/publication/380874956_Ch_15_Deeper_perspectives_on_Evolutionary_Delivery _later_2001_known_as_Agile_in_Gilb_Principles_of_Software_Engineering_Management.

"When my book came out, an Einstein archive in Jerusalem asked me for the source, because they could not find it.

"I replied that I did not recall where I had heard it, but that I had known Einstein when I was at Princeton in 1950–1954, and perhaps had heard him say that—or something like that. Also, I could have made a mistake, because I had trouble understanding his very foreign accent. "So perhaps he said something simpler, but not *much* simpler.[13]

Oh, I wish I had said that too! But Minsky did.

Alice Calaprice saw this email. She had research access to all of Einstein's Princeton files! She told me Minsky must be a very humble man. He could have taken credit for hearing it from the Man himself, but deftly shied away. Fortunately for me! See below. (More shaggy dog story!)

I always wanted to say something as profound as *that*:

"Things should be as simple as possible, but no simpler."

Sounds like a software engineering principle to me, or is that not the gist of this whole book here?

Hmmm. Well, being as arrogant as Dijkstra, or perhaps even more, I have decided to claim that I, and I alone, said that. Prove me wrong, I dare you! Einstein did *not*! It is on page 17 of my 1988 copyrighted book! Beat that.

Believe me, I have a lot more shaggy dog stories, but they are in *my* books.

---

13. Emphasis mine (Uncle Bob).

Of course, if Minsky had had access to ChatGPT-4o, as I do 14 years later, he might have learned the truth, I found:

> "The quotation commonly attributed to Albert Einstein, 'Things should be made as simple as possible, but not simpler,' is a paraphrase rather than a direct quote. The closest verified source is from a lecture Einstein gave at Oxford in 1933, in which he said, "It can scarcely be denied that the supreme goal of all theory is to make the irreducible basic elements as simple and as few as possible without having to surrender the adequate representation of a single datum of experience.

> "This paraphrased version captures the essence of Einstein's philosophy on simplicity in scientific theories, emphasizing the importance of reducing complexity without oversimplifying. The popularized version likely evolved over time through repeated use and adaptation by others, becoming more concise and memorable."

We found this out years ago, without AI help. Well, with an internet search.[14]

REFLECTIONS ON THE CONTENT

This book—content, quality, density, and scope—is amazing, and yet Uncle Bob is clearly aware that it is just scratching the surface.

But he wants us to be aware of the early programming, hardware, and cost environment—the systems, not merely the code. And he does a great job at it.

Even I, who knew and know the people and lived a parallel life with Uncle Bob, found that I was constantly learning new and interesting things I did not ever know about my old friends and professional colleagues.

Heck, we are not very good about knowing our parents! Sorry, Mom and Dad!

---

14. See Einstein's 1933 Oxford Lecture text at www.jstor.org/stable/184387?origin=JSTOR-pdf.

AFTERWORD AUTHOR'S PERSPECTIVE

My perspective is that Uncle Bob has captured a period of history in a realistic and detailed way so that later generations can get some sense of "how it really was."

Re "simplification" (OK, another shaggy dog story coming up): One of my first "lowest man on the totem pole" jobs (like those Uncle Bob got to begin with) at IBM in 1958 was to go into a windowless room, they assumed for a few days, and count the physical stock of plugs for inventory.

These plugs were the basic tools for programming instructions to early computers. I figured out that the plugs of varying lengths and colors were each a variation of the same weight, so I sampled the weights of each color/length. Then, I weighed all of the plugs of each color and computed (manually on a Facit mechanical calculator) the total.

And I was, arrogantly, done in an hour or so. OK, so I was young, humble, and meek, and hoped they would let me out of the windowless room.

I have later found that I can usually simplify a given task by at least tenfold if I *redesign* the process or product. Engineers call this *design to cost*.[15]

DISCUSSION OF FUTURE TRENDS

Uncle Bob has done a good job of speculating about the future. Maybe as well as Amazing Grace. I would not dare to try to be clairvoyant, but this book is an interesting read, and a knowledgeable and experienced person's opinion.

---

15. "Cost Engineering: How to Get 10X Better Control over Resources and Value for Money" (https://tinyurl.com/CostEngFree), includes some really powerful software ideas forgotten by most, like Mill's IBM Cleanroom.

But as Uncle Bob knows and states: It is difficult to predict, especially about the future. This is related to the "ancient programming problem," discussed in many of the book's cases, about keeping a deadline for programming.

I have learned several powerful ideas about this, but I'll give you a summary (then you can go and read my free book, *Cost Engineering*).

- Conditions for cost estimates: You cannot understand costs until you understand the costs of your designs, and you cannot understand your designs unless you consider all your value objectives and constraints.[16]
- Design to cost: You can decide your own costs by "design to cost" better than by "cost estimation" when that estimation is based on the normally bad set of requirements combined with equally bad design engineering. Those bad inputs give you no basis for a reasonable cost-range estimate.
- Incremental adjustment to costs: The best way to control financial budgets and deadline calendar time is the Agile software process devised by Harlan Mills at IBM Federal Systems Division: the Cleanroom method.[17] Boy, was it disciplined!!! They were, with fixed penalty deadlines and a fixed-price lowest bid for state-of-the-art space and military software, "always on time and under budget." And it is a great learning and design adjustment cycle. The architect is in the loop!

This was "Agile as it should be." So the question is, why did *this* not get into the book?

---

16. Gilb, T. "Guides: A Broader and More-Advanced 'Constraints' Theory." *Theory of Guides* (ToG), 83 pages, August 2023, free. https://www.dropbox.com/scl/fo/4amgzl6wuieo8vfy4hgk0/h?rlkey =rkkszv3yrtrv0twoprdnnm5pl&dl=0.

17. Linger, Richard C., Harlan D. Mills, and Bernard I. Witt. 1979. *Structured Programming: Theory and Practice.* Addison-Wesley. The Harlan D. Mills Collection, a full book of great disciplined software engineering practices with an exceptional track record in practice. See Mills' entire library at https://trace.tennessee.edu/utk_harlan/9.

Short story: When Harlan Mills (regarded as a genius-level software engineer) read my 1976 book, *Software Metrics*, he snail-mailed me:

"Why isn't everybody doing this?"

Later, when I had brought him to Oslo to speak, I asked him how he had come upon the Cleanroom Evolutionary (i.e., Agile) method. On a slip of paper, while we both listened to another lecture, I ventured an answer:

"You saw the analogy to an intelligent rocket, trying to adjust to hit an evasive fighter."

He wrote back (I still have a photo of the scrap of paper):

"Yes, partly that."

And he smiled.

We are *still* asking that question (why isn't everybody doing metrics and engineering?). Rome was not built in a day, as they say.

An individual I respect at Snowbird (Agile Manifesto) has publicly debated me in *IEEE Software*[18] about metric viability. I feel like I am trying, like Dr. Semmelweis, to persuade reluctant medical doctors to decontaminate their hands.

---

18. Gilb, T., and Alistair Cockburn. 2008. Point/Counterpoint. *IEEE Software*, 25(2): 64–67. https:// ieeexplore.ieee.org/document/4455634. This department is part of a special issue on software quality requirements. The first article, "Metrics Say Quality Better than Words," is written by Tom Gilb. The second article, "Subjective Quality Counts in Software Development," is written by Alistair Cockburn. His (TG) book *Software Metrics* (Winthrop Publishing, 1976) was the inspiration leading to CMMI Level 4. Via Ron Radice and IBM CMM, www.dropbox.com/scl/fi/1zff9owastior8ybcu1rq/IEEE-Point -Counterpoint-Cockburn-2008.pdf?rlkey=4hkgrsvmin2s58l747p1d60py&dl=0.

CALLS TO ACTION, OR CLOSING THOUGHTS

Of course, students of computer science, software engineering, management, and the history of technology will benefit from including this book in their reading.

I hope this book inspires others in the software industry to write their own histories to enrich our available insights.

We all have a story to tell, and some of it is amazing.

REFERENCES

Gilb, Tom. 1976. *Software Metrics*. Winthrop Publishers.

Minsky, Marvin. 1986. *The Society of Mind*. Simon & Schuster.

Shiang, David A. 2008. *God Does Not Play Dice*. Open Sesame Productions.

GLOSSARY OF TERMS

2001: A Space Odyssey A 1968 science fiction epic written by Arthur C. Clarke and directed by Stanley Kubrick. The sentient computer on board a spacecraft goes insane and murders the entire crew except for one person, who disconnects him to the tune of "Daisy Bell." This movie set the standard for science fiction movies for decades.

ACM, Association of Computing Machinery Founded in 1947 as an unintended consequence of the Symposium on Large-Scale Digital Calculating Machinery hosted at Harvard by Howard Aiken.

ARRA (1 and 2) (1952) The first and second versions of the computer that Dijkstra was hired to work on at the Dutch Mathematical Center. The first was electromechanical and was a failure. The second used vacuum tubes and was a success. They were both called ARRA to hide the first failure. It was a binary machine with two working registers and 1,024 30-bit words of drum memory, and could execute ~40 instructions per second.

ARMAC (1956) An improvement to the FERTA. It could execute 1,000 instructions per second, because a small bank of core memory was used to buffer tracks on the drum. This machine had 1,200 tubes and consumed 10 kilowatts.

ASR 33 Teletype The Automatic Send/Receive Model 33 Teletype was the mainstay computer terminal from the late '60s to well into the '70s. It operated at ten characters per second and was typically driven by a byte-oriented serial bit stream. It had a keyboard, printer, paper tape reader, and paper tape punch. It continuously growled when turned on, and it sounded much like a jackhammer if it was printing and punching. The paper tape reader/punch was eight channels wide. The paper tape was yellow and oily (I think in order to keep the punch lubricated).

Automatic Computing Engine (ACE) (1950) Designed by Alan Turing in 1945, this machine was never (quite) built, but many smaller and derivative machines, such as the DEUCE, were. The pilot ACE was built at the National Physical Laboratory in 1950. It had just under 1,000 vacuum tubes, and 12 mercury delay lines that each held 32 words of 32 bits.

BCPL (1967) The Basic Combined Programming Language, created by Martin Richards and Ken Thompson, was a derivative of CPL (Cambridge Programming Language). BCPL was written for the IBM 7094. This is the language in which the first "Hello World" program was written.

Bletchley Park The English country house and estate that housed the Government Code and Cypher School in which Alan Turing and many others broke the German Enigma codes during World War II. This was the site of the Bombe electromechanical computers that they used for that effort. This is also the site of the Colossus vacuum tube computers used to decode the German "sawfish" codes.

Colossus: The Forbin Project A 1970 science fiction movie in which an American and a Russian supercomputer collaborate to take over the world and enslave the human race.

core memory Became common in the early '50s, and was nearly universal by the '60s. Cores were very small rings of ferrite (a mixture of powdered iron and ceramic) threaded upon a grid of wires. Current passed through the wires can magnetize the cores in one of two directions. The opposite current will reverse the magnetism, inducing a small current in a different wire that can be amplified and detected. Individual bits could be written and read in microseconds, so core memory was very fast for the day. There was virtually no limit to the number of cores, so very large memories could be created. Megabytes of RAM were made possible by core memory. Throughout the '50s and well into the '60s, core memory was expensive because the process to create it involved a fair bit of manual labor. Certain wires had to be threaded through the tiny cores by hand. But eventually, the process was automated and the cost gradually dropped from a dollar per bit to a penny per bit.

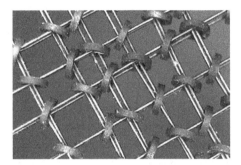

Core Wars A computer game created by D. G. Jones and A. K. Dewdney. It was popularized in the March 1984 issue of *Scientific American* (https://corewar.co.uk). The game simulates a simple computer in which two programs take turns executing one instruction at a time. The goal is for one program to cause the other to crash. I wrote a version of this in C for the Macintosh in 1985 (see https://corewar.co.uk/cwmartin.htm).

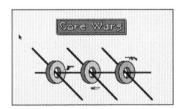

CP/M Control Program/Monitor. Released by Digital Research Inc. in 1974, this was one of the first commercial single-user floppy disk-based operating systems designed for microcomputers, specifically the Intel 8080. It had a very simple command-line interface that allowed users to copy files, list directories, and run programs.

CVSD Continuously Variable Slope Delta modulation. This was a strategy proposed in 1970 for encoding voice in a serial bit stream. A bit rate of 16–24kb/s was required to encode voice with a limit of ~3KHz. This allowed several bits per audio wavelength. Each bit represented either an increase (1) or a decrease (0) in the waveform. Sequential bits of the same polarity increased the amount of the increase or decrease. Thus, the slope of the waveform was continuously variable.

DECnet Digital Equipment Corporation released DECnet in 1975. It was a set of network protocols and software designed to connect PDP-11s together into a network. It continued to evolve throughout the '70s and well into the '80s as PDP-11s and VAXes became more and more popular. In the end, it was replaced by the TCP/IP protocols used on the internet.

DECwriter Released by Digital Equipment Corporation in 1970, the DECwriter was a keyboard/printer that was used as a console for many mini- and microcomputers. The printing mechanism was dot matrix and could print 30 characters per second on sprocket-fed paper. Typical paper width was 80 characters. It made the most satisfying "zipping" noise as it printed.

DEUCE (1955) Digital Electronic Universal Computing Engine. Built by English Electric, DEUCE was a cut-down version of Turing's ACE design. It contained 1,450 vacuum tubes. It had a Williams tube memory containing 384 words of 32 bits and a drum memory with 8K words. Access time was ~32 μs and 15 ms, respectively. IO was primarily punched cards. A total of 33 were eventually sold.

disk memory Thin disks with a magnetic coating, generally stacked up on each other like plates in a cafeteria. The disks were spun and the heads would move radially along the surfaces. The heads could read and write the magnetic data that was written in concentric tracks on the surfaces.

dotcom boom In the late '90s, the internet was becoming commercially viable. There were startups and business ventures galore. Investment money was easy to get. Any internet idea was worth $100 million. And then suddenly it was over, and the software market crashed hard. There were hints as early as mid-2000; but September 11, 2001, sounded the death knell. The world changed that day.

drum memory A form of magnetic memory that preceded disks. A drum is a metal cylinder with a magnetic coating on its surface. The drum spins beneath movable heads. The heads can read and write magnetic data on the drum surface. They can also move longitudinally along the long axis of the drum. Thus, data were written in circular tracks along the length of the drum. Heads could be positioned longitudinally and radially. The more heads, the faster the access time. Indeed, with many heads, parallel reading and writing was possible. Disks superseded drums because they take up a lot less physical space and are usually not as heavy.

EDSAC Electronic Delay Storage Automatic Calculator. The EDSAC was inspired by von Neumann's draft of the EDVAC and built by Maurice Wilkes at the University of Cambridge Mathematical Laboratory in 1949. It was very likely the second stored-program computer. This is the machine that so inspired Edsger Dijkstra when he took a class at Cambridge taught by Wilkes. The machine had 512 17-bit words stored in mercury delay lines. It had a cycle time of 1.5 ms and required four such cycles for a multiplication.

Educational Testing Service (ETS) Founded in 1947 and located in Princeton, NJ, ETS is the world's largest private educational testing and assessment organization. They hired me in the early '90s as a C++ and OOD consultant. Eventually, they hired Jim Newkirk and me to write the suite of software for the NCARB system.

EDVAC Electronic Discrete Variable Automatic Computer. The EDVAC was built at the Moore School of Electrical Engineering in Pennsylvania and was proposed by John Mauchly and J. Presper Eckert in 1944 with an initial budget of $100,000. It was delivered to the Ballistic Research Laboratory in 1949. It had 1,024 44-bit words stored in mercury delay lines, an average add time of 864 μs, and a multiply time of 2.9 ms. It contained 5,937 vacuum tubes and weighed nearly 9 tons. It was this machine about which von Neumann wrote his draft report. The popularity of that report caused the overall stored-program concept to be called a "von Neumann architecture."

email mirror In the '90s, an email mirror was an email address you could send to, and it would resend the message out to everyone on the mirror's list.

eXtreme Programming (XP) Invented by Kent Beck in the mid-'90s and popularized by his book *eXtreme Programming eXplained*,[1] XP is the best defined of all the Agile processes. It is composed of a set of about a dozen disciplines divided into three parts: business, team, and technical. It is this process that introduced such concepts as test-driven development, pair programming, continuous integration, and much more.

Ferrante Mercury (1957) An early commercial computer. It featured floating-point math and core memory with 1,024 words of 40 bits backed by four drums, each with 4,096 words. Core cycle time was 10 μs. Floating-point adds took 180 μs, and multiplication required 360 μs. It used 2,000 vacuum tubes and the same number of germanium diodes. It weighed 2,500 pounds.

FERTA (1955) A slightly better version of the ARRA (2). Memory was expanded to 4,096 34-bit words on drum, and the speed was doubled to ~100 instructions per second.

floppy disk Initially invented by IBM in the late '60s as the boot disk for the System/370, these disks were eventually used for minicomputers and, especially, microcomputers in the '80s. They started out as 8-inch disks made of thin mylar coated with a magnetic oxide. They were housed within a plastic sheath that allowed the disk to be spun at slow speed, and they allowed access by a read/write head. Later versions were reduced to 5.25 inches, and then 3.5 inches.

1. Addison-Wesley, 1999.

Forbidden Planet A 1956 science fiction movie (and my favorite movie of all time). Robby the Robot is a major character and has the persona of an English butler.

FTP, File Transfer Protocol Invented by Abhay Bhushan in 1971, this was the software and protocol that was used to transfer files across the internet. I used to use this to download PostScript files when reviewing the *Design Patterns* book.

GE DATANET-235 Introduced in 1964, this room-filling machine had a 20-bit word and could directly address 8K words. The core memory had a 5-μs cycle time. The machine had a 12-μs add time and could multiply or divide in ~85 μs. This machine was the data processing workhorse that often served as the back-end for a DATANET-30. Programming was primarily in assembler. This was also the back-end machine for the Dartmouth Time Sharing System running BASIC.

GE DATANET-30 Introduced in 1961, this was one of the first machines targeted at telecommunications. It was a room-filling general-purpose computer, but the internal hardware supported 128 asynchronous serial communication ports at rates of up to 2,400 bps. The serial data had to be assembled by the software one bit at a time, so much of the power of the machine was dedicated to that purpose. Fortunately, most data communications at the time were no faster than 300 bps (30 characters per second), leaving time for other processing. The core memory could be 4K, 8K, or 16K 18-bit words, and it had a cycle time of ~7 μs. Programming was primarily in assembler. This machine was the front-end for the Dartmouth Time Sharing System running BASIC.

GE DATANET-635 Introduced in 1963, this was a room-filling 36-bit word machine that could address 256K words. It had eight index registers and a 72-bit accumulator register. The core memory had a 2-μs cycle time. The arithmetic unit included fixed-point and floating-point mathematics. It could run COBOL, FORTRAN, and assembler.

GIER (1961) *Geodætisk Instituts Elektroniske Regnemaskine*. This was a Danish computer, and one of the first to be fully transistorized. The core contained ~5K words of 42 bits, and there were 60K words on the drum. It could run ALGOL, had a 49-μs add time, and weighed ~1,000 pounds.

Honeywell H200 Introduced in 1963, this was a very popular room-filling competitor of the IBM 1401. It was binary compatible with the 1401, but was more than twice as fast and had an extended instruction set. A 6-bit character-oriented machine that used decimal arithmetic, the H200 could run COBOL, FORTRAN, and RPG; was capable of addressing 512K characters; and had a cycle time of ~1 μs.

IBM 026 Keypunch Announced in 1949, these desk-size card punches were the mainstay keyboard-driven card punches for over 20 years. The keyboard sported uppercase letters, numbers, and some punctuation. Cards were automatically pulled from an input hopper and through the keyboard-driven punching mechanism, and then were stacked in an output hopper.

To: Uncle Bob...
Thanks for all the fun work over the MANY years!   Jennifer

IBM 2314 Disk Memory The 2314 disk pack was designed for the IBM System/360, but many other computer manufacturers created compatible disk drives. It was used between 1965 and 1978. The pack had 11 platters with 20 recording surfaces. It weighed about 10 pounds and was typically spun at 2,400 rpm. Memory capacity was on the order of 40MB.

IBM 701 Released in 1952, this 4,000 vacuum tube machine had up to 4K 36-bit words of Williams Tube memory. The memory cycle time was ~12 μs. Multiplication and division required 456 μs. Around 20 were built. Each weighed in at around 25,000 pounds and rented for ~$14,000/month. See Computer History

Archives Project ("CHAP"). "Computer History 1953 IBM 701 Rare promo 1953 first of IBM 700 Series Mainframes, tubes EDPM." Posted on YouTube on Apr. 6, 2024. (Available at the time of writing.)

IBM 704 Introduced in 1954, this room-filling vacuum tube machine had 4K 36-bit core memory. It had three index registers, an accumulator, and a multiplier/quotient register. It could do fixed-point and floating-point math. The floating-point add time was 83 μs. Both FORTRAN and Lisp were developed for this machine. Because of the large number (potentially thousands) of vacuum tubes in a 704 installation, the mean time between failure could be as low as 8 hours—which made compiling big FORTRAN programs a problem. A total of 123 were produced.

IBM 709 Delivered in 1958, this was an improved version of the IBM 704. It still used vacuum tubes. Core memory was 32K of 36-bit words, and it had an add time of 24 μs and a fixed-point multiply time of 200 μs. It was short-lived because the transistorized 7090 came out a year later.

IBM 7090/7094 First installed in 1959, this was a transistor-based but still room-filling version of the 709. Like the 709, core memory contained 32K of 18-bit words. The core cycle time was ~2 μs, and the processor was about six times faster than the 709. The 7094 was twice again as fast. These were mainstay machines for the early '60s. This is the machine depicted in the movie *Hidden Figures*. Thousands were produced, and each sold for around $2 million.

IBM Selectric typewriter Introduced in 1961, the Selectric became the mainstay business typewriter for several decades. It was also used as the heart of most IBM System/360/370 consoles. The printhead was a hemispherical ball with 88 embossed characters. The printhead moved across the paper, rather than the more traditional typewriter-moving paper carriage.

integrated circuit Though invented in the late 1940s, this device did not become commercially feasible until the late 1960s. An integrated circuit is a single "chip" of silicon upon which many transistors and other components are deposited through a photographic process. In the early days, this allowed dozens of transistors to be contained in a space of a few square millimeters. As the decades rolled by, Moore's law drove the transistor density through an exponential curve. Nowadays, the number of transistors per square millimeter is measured in the hundreds of millions. This increase in density radically reduced the price and the power consumption per transistor. Computers started using integrated circuits in the mid-1960s. Current laptop, desktop, phone, and other digital devices depend critically upon them. Our current digital environment would be impossible without them.

Intel 8080/8085 Released by Intel in 1974, the 8080 quickly became the industry-wide mainstay microcomputer. The 8080 was a single integrated circuit with ~6,000 transistors. An 8-bit processor with a 16-bit (64K byte) address space, it could be clocked at 2MHz and was typically connected to solid-state memory, as opposed to core memory. The 8085 came out a few months later. It could be driven at twice the clock rate, and had a few extra instructions, built-in serial IO, and some extra interrupts. Millions upon millions were sold.

Intel 8086/186/286 Released in 1978, this was one of the very first 16-bit micro-processors. The chip had ~29,000 transistors on board. The address space was banked, giving it access to a full megabyte, and the clock rate was 5–10MHz. This is the chip that was used in the original IBM PC. The 80186 was introduced in 1982. It had 55,000 transistors and could be clocked between 6MHz and 25MHz. It was intended for use as an IO controller, and therefore had a lot of IO-related goodies on board, including a DMA controller, a clock generator, and interrupt lines. The 80286 was also released in 1982. It had ~120,000 transistors and included memory management hardware, allowing it to access 16MB. It was therefore ideal for multiprocessing applications. It could be clocked between 4MHz and 25MHz.

JOHNNIAC (1953) John von Neumann Numerical Integrator and Automatic Calculator. A very early computer built by the RAND Corporation, it had 1,024 words of 40 bits stored in Selectron tubes—a form of electrostatic storage vaguely similar to Williams tubes. It was a simple single-address machine with one accumulator register and no index registers. It weighed 5,000 pounds.

Jurassic Park A good book by Michael Crichton, turned into a very good movie by Steven Spielberg in 1993. Scientists clone dinosaurs by getting DNA from mosquitos trapped in ancient amber. The dinosaurs escape and start eating people. Two kids save the day by hacking into a "Unix system" that was programmed by evil programmer Dennis Nedry.

LGP-30 (1956) Librascope General Purpose. An off-the-shelf computer of the day, this machine had 4,096 words, 31 bits each, stored on a magnetic drum. There were 113 vacuum tubes and 1,450 solid-state diodes.[2] It was a single-address machine with built-in multiply and divide. It had a clock rate of 120KHz and a memory access time of between 2 ms and 17 ms. It sold for $47,000.

Lost in Space A 1965 science fiction television show based very loosely on *The Swiss Family Robinson*. A family is lost in space and trying desperately to get home. The robot, built by the same engineers who built Robby the Robot from

---

2. Diode logic is a power-hungry and finicky way to make AND and OR gates.

Forbidden Planet, became iconic for saying "Danger, Will Robinson" and "It does not compute" while waving its corrugated arms around randomly.

M365 Created by Teradyne Inc. in the late '60s, this was an 18-bit single-address processor reminiscent of a PDP-8. The late '60s was a time when many companies decided to build their own computers rather than buy them. Teradyne was no exception. It was a lovely machine. The page size was 4K and the total memory space was half a megabyte—though we never used nearly that much. Oh, how I wish I could find one of the old instruction manuals. They were blue, and could fit in your shirt pocket.

Manchester Baby A small and very primitive vacuum tube computer built at the University of Manchester in 1948. Designed primarily as a vehicle for testing Williams tube memory, it was a 32-bit machine with 32 words of memory. Despite that limitation, it was probably the very first stored-program electronic computer to run a program. The design eventually grew into the Manchester Mark I, and then into the Ferranti Mark I, which was the first commercially available computer.

mercury delay line memory A very early form of memory used in the late '40s and early '50s. A delay line was a long tube full of liquid mercury, with a speaker at one end and a microphone at the other. Bits were pumped into the speaker and traveled acoustically through the liquid until they were received by the microphone, at which point they were electronically recycled back to the speaker. Both the speed of sound and the acoustic impedance of mercury depended upon the temperature. So the tubes were kept at 104°F (40°C) so that the impedance matched the piezoelectric speakers and microphones, and the speed was ~1,450 m/s. An 800-pound delay line, a meter in length, might store 500 bits with an access time of less than a millisecond.

Monte Carlo analysis The idea behind Monte Carlo analysis is pretty simple. One of the inventors of the technique, Stanislaw Ulam,[3] described it using the game of solitaire. He wanted to know, after the deck of cards was shuffled, what the odds of success were. Rather than try to calculate this using combinatorial

---

3. One of John von Neumann's oldest and best friends.

mathematics, one could simply play 100 games and count the successes. Of course, Ulam wasn't trying to solve solitaire. He was working on nuclear weapons at Los Alamos in 1946. He and John von Neumann used the technique to study neutron diffusion through a fissioning warhead. Because the work was secret, they gave it a clever code name: Monte Carlo.

MP/M-86 Multi-Programming Monitor Control Program. Released by Digital Research Inc. in 1981, this was a multiuser disk operating system for the Intel 8086 microcomputer. It could handle multiple terminals and multiple users concurrently, and had a very simple command-line language for copying files, listing directories, and running programs.

National Council of Architects Registry Board (NCARB) Founded in 1919, this is the organization that examines and licenses architects in the US. Their licenses are recognized in many other countries. NCARB contracted with ETS to create the suite of evaluation software that Jim Newkirk and I, along with several others, wrote in the mid-to-late '90s.

object-oriented database In 1989, the Object-Oriented Database System Manifesto[4] was written. It described an idea for storing objects on disk. Thus were born the many object databases that arose in the '90s. The main idea was similar to virtual memory. An object might be stored on disk, but the program should be able to access it as though it were in RAM. Many ingenious techniques were invented to achieve this. At the turn of the millennium, however, the idea kind of faded away.

PAL-III Assembler A paper tape assembler for the PDP-8 written by Ed Yourdon when he was a very young man working at Digital Equipment Corporation.

PDP-7 Introduced by Digital Equipment Corporation in 1965, this was a transistor-based minicomputer. It had a single-address instruction set, and core memory with a ~2-μs cycle time holding between 4K and 64K of 18-bit words. The internal clock rate was half a megahertz. It could sport a disk,

---

4. See www.sciencedirect.com/science/article/abs/pii/B9780444884336500204.

DECtape, ASR 33 Teletype, vector graphics display, and high-speed paper tape reader/punch. It weighed ~1,100 pounds and was the size of a restaurant freezer locker. These machines sold for $72,000. A total of 120 units were shipped.

PDP-8 Introduced by Digital Equipment Corporation in 1965, the PDP-8 became the mainstay minicomputer of the late '60s and early '70s. Many different models were produced. The original "straight" 8 was a transistor-based machine with core memory containing 4K of 12-bit words. Cycle time was ~2 μs, and the internal clock rate was half a megahertz. It was primarily programmed in assembler, but there was a FORTRAN variant and a BASIC-like interpreter called FOCAL. Over its life, there were several operating systems, but OS/8 was the most popular. The basic machine came with an ASR 33 Teletype. Other features included DECtape; a high-speed paper tape reader/punch; primitive disk drives; memory expansion up to 32K; and hardware multiply and divide. The minimal system cost ~$18,000. Well over 50,000 units were sold.

PDP-11 Digital Equipment Corporation released the first PDP-11 in 1970. In the end, ~600,000 were sold. The 11 had a 16-bit, byte-addressed architecture based on integrated circuits. Early memory was core, but changed to solid state as the decades passed. In the PDP-11, 64K bytes were directly addressable, and later models allowed for much more by using memory banks. The first model was the 20, which sold for $11,800. There were many other models, all the way up to the 70, which supported 4MB of solid-state memory and had built-in memory protect, floating point, and very fast IO. These systems were typically supported by disk memory, and used tape memory for backup.

Pharaoh While I was at Teradyne in the '70s, there was a game written in AL-COM named *Pharaoh*. I modified it heavily and spent a lot of time playing it. In 1987, I decided to write the game again, in C, for my Mac 128. Once complete, I uploaded it to CompuServe or something. It got around a bit. Most people hated it. Some liked it. You can download it at www.macintoshrepository.org /5230-pharaoh. At the time of this writing, a delightfully funny review from 2018 was available at: Tanara Kuranov (Gamer Mouse). "Gamer Mouse - Pharaoh Review - Macintosh". Posted on YouTube on Feb. 20, 2018.

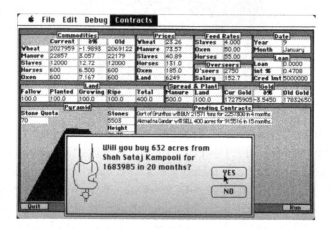

plugboard Many early machines were "programmed" by plugging electrical cords into appropriate holes within certain panels. Think of a telephone switchboard. Complex machines could have thousands of such interconnections.

PostScript Invented in 1984 by Adobe, PostScript is a so-called "page description language." Based upon Forth, this language was the common way to send print jobs from a computer to a laser printer in the late '80s and '90s. The computer would turn a print job into a PostScript program and send it to the printer. The printer would execute that program, which would cause the printer to print pages. Eventually, PDF replaced PostScript.

RAM Random-access memory. This is memory where the individual words (bytes) are directly addressable and accessible. Williams tube, core, and solid-state memory are examples. Delay line, disk, and drum memory are not RAM, because access must wait for the data to be positioned under the reader. Nowadays, the internal memory of all computers is RAM.

Rational Unified Process (RUP) Spurred by the dotcom boom and funded by Rational Inc., Grady Booch, Ivar Jacobson, and Jim Rumbaugh (the Three Amigos) collaborated to create a rich and diverse software development process. Rational started marketing the idea in 1996. RUP was eventually overtaken by the Agile movement, and primarily by Scrum and eXtreme Programming.

RK07 disk The RK07 disk drive was introduced by Digital Equipment Corporation in 1976. It was a common peripheral for the PDP-11, and it used 14-inch dual-platter removable disk packs that could hold ~27MB each. The platters spun at 2400 rpm, and access time was on the order of 42 ms, most of which was the 36-ms average seek time. Tracks on the three data surfaces were spaced 384 per inch. The disk drive itself weighed over 300 pounds and was the size of a kitchen dishwasher.

ROM Read-only memory. Typically, this is RAM that cannot be changed. There have been many varieties over the years. Nowadays, ROM is almost always an integrated circuit of some kind, in which the internal connections have either been burned or been programmatically altered. This is sometimes called PROM, which stands for programmable read-only memory. Some PROM can be erased through exposure to high-intensity ultraviolet light.

ROSE In 1990, Grady Booch wrote *Object-Oriented Design with Applications*.[5] The book presented a notation for describing object-oriented designs. This notation became very popular, and Grady's employer, Rational Inc., decided to create a CASE (computer-aided software engineering) tool to allow programmers to create such designs on SPARCstations. The name of that product was ROSE. I worked as a contractor on the ROSE team for a year in the early '90s.

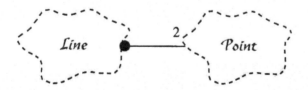

RS-232 An electrical standard from 1960 for serial communication. Often used to send and receive data between a computer and a data terminal or to send data from a computer to a printer, this standard was typically combined with a data format for the serial transmission of bytes or characters.

---

5. Benjamin-Cummings, 2000.

RSX-11M Released by Digital Equipment Corporation in 1974, this was a popular disk operating system for the PDP-11. It could manage multiple user terminals and multiple user processes concurrently. It had a relatively simple command-line language called MCR (Monitor Console Routine).

Short Circuit A 1986 science fiction comedy starring Aly Sheedy, Steve Guttenberg, and Fisher Stevens. A military robot gets his wires crossed and becomes sentient (sigh) and highly moral (double sigh).

SPARCstation Introduced by Sun Microsystems in 1989, the SPARCstation was a workstation computer the size of a pizza box. It came with a keyboard, a mouse, and (typically) a 19-inch color CRT monitor. It ran Unix—of course. The clock rate started at 20MHz and eventually climbed up to 200MHz. RAM was typically 20–128MB or more. The processor was a RISC (reduced instruction set computer) machine. This machine was the primary software workstation of the '90s.

ST506/ST412 Shugart (Seagate) Technology introduced the ST506 in 1980 and the ST412 a year later. These were small disk drives that had an internally contained 5.25-inch platter rotating at 3,600 rpm. They had a seek time of ~50–100 ms and a transfer rate of ~60–100kb/s. The ST506 could store 5MB, and the ST412 could store 10MB. They cost a little over $1,000, and weighed about 12 pounds. They were often used as microcomputer peripherals.

SWAC (1950) Standards Western Automatic Computer. Built by and for the National Bureau of Standards, the SWAC consisted of 2,300 vacuum tubes and had 256 words of 37 bits stored in Williams tubes. Add time was 64 μs, and multiply time was 384 μs.

T1 network Transmission System 1, introduced in 1962 by the Bell System. This was a long-distance digital serial communications strategy. A single T1 line transmitted bits at 1.544Mbit/s. It was used to carry digitized long-distance speech. Twenty-four channels of 64kbit/s speech could be multiplexed onto a single T1 line. In the late '80s and into the '90s, it was common for businesses to attach to the internet with a T1 line. Lease rates were in the thousands of dollars per month, but the data rate was worth it for large organizations. By the 2000s, the rate had come down to less than $1,000. And then, very quickly, other options became available.

thin film memory Similar in some ways to core memory, except that the magnetic material was vacuum-deposited as dots onto thin glass plates, and the drive and sense wires were overlayed using printed circuit techniques. Thin film memory was fast and reliable, but expensive.

transistor Invented at Bell Labs in the late 1940s, a transistor is a small solid-state device that can control the flow of electricity in a manner similar to a vacuum tube. Small changes on one input can result in large changes in output. Thus, these devices can be used as amplifiers and switches. Their small size and low power consumption revolutionized the computer industry in the late 1950s, and made the 1960s minicomputers possible. They are typically made from semiconductors, like silicon or germanium.

UART Universal asynchronous receiver/transmitter. A UART was an electronic device that converted byte-size data into a serial stream capable of being transmitted using RS-232. Incoming serial data were converted to individual characters, and outgoing characters were converted back into a serial stream of bits.

Unified Modeling Language (UML) Funded by Rational Inc., driven by the dotcom boom, and collaboratively created by Grady Booch, Ivar Jacobson, and Jim Rumbaugh (the Three Amigos) in the mid-'90s, this was a rich notation for depicting software design decisions. It replaced Booch's clouds with rectangles. I still find the notation useful from time to time nowadays. It was all the rage back then; but not so much anymore.

UNIVAC 1103 Released in 1953 and designed, in part, by Seymour Cray, this was a gargantuan, 19-ton machine that had 1,024 words of 36 bits held in Williams tube memory. It also had a drum memory that held 16K words. Both memories were directly addressable. This was a binary machine using one's complement arithmetic. It was programmed primarily in assembly, and there were several floating-point interpreters.

UNIVAC 1107 A room-filling, transistor-based machine introduced in 1962. There were 128 internal registers that used thin film memory that was six times faster than the 4-μs core memory cycle time. Core memory contained 65K of 36-bit words, and drum memory could hold 300K words. It was programmed in FORTRAN IV and assembler, and weighed just under 3 tons. A total of 36 units were sold.

UNIVAC 1108 A room-filling, transistor-based machine introduced in 1964. It used integrated circuits for its internal registers. The internal registers allowed for dynamic relocation of programs, and memory-protect hardware allowed for safe multiprogramming. Core memory had a cycle time of 1.2 μs and was organized into as many as four cabinet-size banks of 64K 36-bit words. A total of 296 were produced.

Usenet/Netnews A text-based social network invented by Tom Truscott and Jim Ellis in 1979. Usenet was transmitted over the internet using NNTP (Network News Transport Protocol), and into satellite (dial-in) machines using UUCP.

Topics were divided into many hundreds of newsgroups. Users would subscribe to the newsgroups they were interested in. Subscribers could read articles posted on those groups, and could respond or write new articles. New reader software, especially in Emacs, allowed articles and replies to be threaded. It was during the Usenet period that Godwin's law was created. I frequently participated in the comp.object and comp.lang.c++ newsgroups.

UUCP Unix to Unix Copy, a suite of computer programs and protocols that allowed files to be transmitted between Unix-based (and other) systems using telephone connections. In the late '80s and well into the '90s, this was the basis for dial-in satellite computers to access email and Usenet. Scheduled tasks in those satellite machines would periodically dial into a machine that had access to the internet. It would use UUCP to transfer all the queued-up email and news to that machine, and then download all the incoming news and email. Long daisy chains of machines using UUCP were common. Each would transfer to the next until they reached a machine on the internet backbone. Many of these dial-up connections were informally negotiated between friends and associates.

vacuum tube Invented in 1904 by John Ambrose Flemming, this simple device can control the flow of electric current. Small changes to one input can cause large changes in output. Thus, these devices can be used as amplifiers or switches. A small filament needs to be heated to red hot within the tube in order for the device to work. This makes the devices fragile, unreliable, and power hungry. This severely limits their use in computers. A computer with a few thousand tubes can have a mean time between failure measured in hours.

VAX 750/780/μ Digital Equipment Corporation introduced the VAX/780 in 1977. This was a room-filling, integrated circuit-based computer system. The processor was 32 bits, and with a 200-ns cycle time, it could execute half a million instructions per second. The instruction set was very rich. The memory had hardware mapping, and allowed for virtual memory paging and swapping. The machine was designed for multiuser and multiprocessing operations, and was a direct competitor to the IBM System/360. The operating system was VMS, a sophisticated disk operating system with virtual memory management and a wide variety of IO options. The 750 was introduced in 1980. This was a slower and smaller version of the 780, running at just over half the speed. The μVAX was introduced in 1984. Half again as slow as the 750, this little beast would happily fit under your desk (without any peripherals), and could be loaded with 16MB of RAM.

VT100 Introduced by Digital Equipment Corporation in 1978, this 80x24 monochrome cathode ray tube display and keyboard was the mainstay terminal for mini- and microcomputers for the better part of a decade. It weighed 20 pounds and cost less than $1,000. Millions were sold.

War Games A 1983 science fiction movie in which a young boy, played by Matthew Broderick, and his girlfriend, played by Ally Sheedy, hack into a government computer named WOPR (yeah, I know, the imagery . . .) and start a thermonuclear war between the US and the USSR. The teens have to track down the original programmer (whose password for the WOPR was his dead son's name,

"Joshua") to get him to convince WOPR (or Joshua) to stop the war. The movie ends in a game of tic-tac-toe. You can stop rolling your eyes now.

Wator A computer game devised and popularized by A. K. Dewdney in the December 1984 issue of *Scientific American*. The game is a simple predator/prey simulation between sharks and fish within a toroidal 2D ocean. I wrote a version of this game in C for the Macintosh and uploaded it to a bulletin board, or perhaps CompuServe, in 1984 or so. I have since written many other versions; the latest is in one of the chapters of *Functional Design*. The source code is available at https://github.com/unclebob/wator. You can get the original for the Mac 128 at www.macintoshrepository.org/3976-wator.

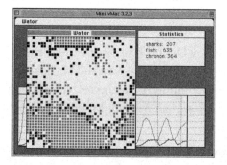

Whirlwind Developed at MIT in 1951, this was one of the first real-time computers. It was designed for controlling flight simulators, and had a parallel architecture. Core memory was invented for this machine: It had 5,000 vacuum tubes and 1K of core, and was 16 bits wide. It weighed 10 tons and consumed 100KW.

Williams tube (CRT) memory Some of you will remember the old black-and-white televisions from the '50s and '60s. The display was a cathode ray tube (CRT). This is a vacuum tube with an electron gun at the back and a phosphor screen at the front. The electron beam is moved across the screen by varying a magnetic or electric field near the gun. Where the beam hits the screen, the phosphors glow. Thus, a picture can be rasterized across the screen by varying the intensity of the beam as it rapidly plays across the screen. The electron beam leaves a region of charge behind on the screen. That charge can be sensed by measuring the current of the beam the next time it sweeps over that region. Thus, the screen can be used to "remember" bits of information. Since the beam can be immediately directed to any particular part of the screen, the memory is random access. Thus, it is much faster than mercury delay lines. However, the tubes degrade with time, and they are limited to around 2,000 bits of storage. Some Williams tubes had visible screens upon which the contents of memory could be seen firsthand. Alan Turing often read the results of his programs directly from memory by looking at such screens. Williams tube memory was common in the machines of the late '40s and early '50s, including machines like the IBM 701 and the UNIVAC 1103.

XI (1959) Successor of the ARMAC. This was a fully transistorized machine, with up to 32K 27-bit words. The first 8K of the address space was read-only memory and contained boot programs and a primitive assembler. The machine also had an index register. The memory cycle time was 32 µs, and the add time was 64 µs. It could therefore execute over 10,000 instructions per second.

Cast of Supporting Characters

Ackermann, Wilhelm (1896–1962) A German mathematician and logician who earned his Ph.D. at Göttingen. He helped David Hilbert with *Principles of Mathematical Logic*. He is perhaps best known among some computer scientists for the Ackermann function, which is sometimes used as a speed benchmark. He remained in Germany during the war and ended up as a high school teacher.

Aiken, Howard Hathaway (1900–1973) An American physicist educated at the University of Wisconsin at Madison. He earned a Ph.D. from Harvard and was the conceptual designer of the Harvard Mark I Automatic Sequence Controlled Calculator. A commander in the Navy Reserve, he convinced the Navy to fund, and IBM to build, the mammoth device. He then managed it, or rather commanded it, as though it was a naval vessel and he was her captain. This is the machine that Grace Hopper learned to program on.

Airy, Sir George Biddell (1801–1892) An English mathematician and astronomer. He was the Lucasian Chair of Mathematics from 1826 to 1828, and served as the seventh Astronomer Royal. He was one of Babbage's nemeses.

Amdahl, Gene (1922–2015) An American theoretical physicist, computer scientist, and entrepreneur, of Swedish descent. As a graduate student, he participated in building the WISC computer at the University of Madison. He joined IBM and worked on the 704 and 709, and became the chief architect of the System/360. He started Amdahl Corp. in competition with IBM, growing it to over $1 billion in sales by 1979. He went on to start several other successful ventures. He coined the term *Amdahl's law*, which defines limits on the advantages of parallel processing.

Beck, Kent (1961–) The inventor of eXtreme Programming (XP) and author of *eXtreme Programming eXplained*.[1] He also invented disciplines such as test-driven development (TDD) and test & commit || revert (TCR). He has been a powerful force in the software industry, writing many books, giving many talks, and promoting many beneficial ideas. He was one of the original founders of The Hillside Group, and gave strong support to the design patterns movement in the '90s.

Bell, Alexander Graham (1847–1922) A UK citizen who moved to Boston and invented the first practical telephone (unless you believe Ensign Chekov from *Star Trek*). He went on to commercialize the product and eventually founded Bell Telephone.

Bemer, Robert William (1920–2004) An American aerodynamicist and computer scientist. He worked for a while at Douglas Aircraft. At IBM, he invented COMTRAN, which was absorbed into COBOL. He worked for John Backus during the FORTRAN years and with Grace Hopper during the COBOL years. He is sometimes known as the father of ASCII, and he nearly got fired from IBM for proposing the concept of time sharing. While at the Rand Corporation, he was convinced by Kristen Nygaard to provide a UNIVAC 1107 in exchange for the rights to distribute SIMULA.

Berkely, Edmund Callis (1909–1988) An American computer scientist and cofounder of the ACM; founder of *Computers and Automation*, the first

---

1. First edition, Addison-Wesley, 2000.

computer magazine; author of *Giant Brains, or Machines That Think*;[2] and inventor of the Geniac and Brainiac computer toys. As an actuary at Prudential Insurance, he was instrumental in purchasing one of the early UNIVAC computers. He befriended Grace Hopper and wrote an "intervention" letter to help her through her alcoholism.

Blaauw, Gerrit Anne (1924–2018) A Dutch computer scientist, a devout Christian, and an associate of Dijkstra, Aiken, and Amdahl. He helped Dijkstra at the Dutch Mathematical Center with the ARRA and the FERTA, and went on to be a key designer of the IBM System/360. He made, and won, the case for an 8-bit byte.

Bloch, Richard Milton (1921–2000) An American computer programmer who worked with Grace Hopper on the Harvard Mark I. He became manager of Raytheon's computer division, VP of Technical Operations at Honeywell, VP of Corporate Development at Auerbach Corp., VP of the Advanced Systems Division at GE, and chairman and CEO of the Artificial Intelligence Corporation and the Meiko Scientific Corporation.

Böhm, Corrado (1923–2017) An Italian mathematician and computer scientist. He was the coauthor, with Giuseppe Jacopini, of "Flow Diagrams, Turing Machines, and Language with Only Two Formation Rules."[3] This paper helped Dijkstra formulate the rules of structured programming.

Booch, Grady (1955–) Author of several books, most famously *Object-Oriented Design with Applications*.[4] He collaborated with Ivar Jacobson and Jim Rumbaugh (together, they were known as the Three Amigos) to create the Unified Modeling Language (UML) and the Rational Unified Process (RUP). He served as the chief scientist at Rational Inc., and became a Fellow of the ACM in 1995, an IBM Fellow in 2003, and an IEEE Fellow in 2010.

---

2. John Wiley and Sons, 1949.

3. *Communications of the ACM* 9, No. 5 , May 1966.

4. Benjamin Cummings, 1990.

Boole, George (1815–1864) A self-taught English mathematician, philosopher, and logician, and inventor of Boolean algebra.

Brooks, Angela (1975–) My firstborn, and my faithful assistant for the last decade and a half.

Brooks, Frederick Phillips Jr. (1931–2022) An American physicist and mathematician. He earned his Ph.D. at Harvard under the supervision of Howard Aiken. He joined IBM in 1956 and became manager of development of the System/360 and the OS/360 software. He coined the term *computer architecture*. In addition, he was the author of *The Mythical Man Month*[5] and several other books. He also coined Brooks's Law—"Adding manpower to a late project makes it later."—as well as the term *second system effect* to mean the usually unsuccessful attempt to replace a small, simple system with a bloated and complex system.

Byron, Lord George Gordon (1788–1824) The father of Ada King, the Countess of Lovelace. He is considered one of Britain's greatest romantic poets and satirists. He was quite prolific, but is best known for the character "Don Juan" and *Hebrew Melodies*. He was also a major jerk. He cheated on everyone: his wife, his daughter, his other lovers, his bankers, and his creditors. I mean, this guy was a real worm. He did once hang out with Mary Shelly and inspire her to write *Frankenstein*, so perhaps that's a clue.

Campbell, Robert V. D. (1916–?) A lieutenant commander in the Navy during World War II. He was recruited as the first programmer of the Harvard Mark I. He worked with Grace Hopper, was later employed by Raytheon, and then became director of research at Burroughs. From 1966 to 1984, he worked at MITRE doing long-range planning for the Air Force. I could not find a date of death.

Cantor, Georg (1845–1918) A Russian mathematician and major contributor to set theory. The inventor of transfinite numbers, he was derided in his

---

5. Addison-Wesley, 1975, 1995.

time as a scientific charlatan and a corrupter of youth. David Hilbert doggedly defended him. The Royal Society eventually gave him their highest award in mathematics: the Sylvester Medal.

Church, Alonzo (1903–1995) An American mathematician and computer scientist. He is best known for lambda calculus, which he used to show that Hilbert's third challenge, to show that mathematics is decidable, was impossible. He beat Turing to this by just a few weeks. He was Turing's thesis advisor after that. The two created the Church–Turing thesis, which showed that lambda calculus and Turing's machine were mathematically equivalent, and that any computable function is computable by those means.

Coplien, James O. (Cope) (1955–) Author of *Advanced C++ Programming Styles and Idioms*[6] and many other books. He was a founding member of The Hillside Group to promote the design patterns community in the early '90s.

Cunningham, Ward (1949–) Is known as the father of software consultants. He was Kent Beck's mentor and an early proponent of Agile and eXtreme Programming (XP), pair programming, and test-driven development (TDD). He invented the wiki and created the very first online wiki (c2.com). He is someone who has an immense number of ideas that he gives away for free. Others have taken many of those ideas and run with them.

Darwin, Charles (1809–1882) A British scientist and naturalist. He proposed the theory of evolution through natural selection in a paper presented in 1859. Later that year he published *On the Origin of Species*. This book shook the world—and still shakes it today in certain circles.

DeCarlo, Charles R. (1921–2004) An American mathematician and engineer of Italian descent. He served in the Navy during the war. He became an executive at IBM and was involved with the FORTRAN team. Eventually, he became the well-loved president of Sara Lawrence College.

---

6. Addison-Wesley, 1992.

De Morgan, Augustus (1806–1871) A British mathematician and logician. He introduced the term *mathematical induction*. He formulated De Morgan's laws, and made contributions to probability.

Dickens, Charles (1812–1870) An English novelist famous for such novels as *Oliver Twist, Nicholas Nickleby, David Copperfield, A Tale of Two Cities,* and *Great Expectations*. But perhaps his most well-known character is Ebenezer Scrooge, the hero, and the villain, of *A Christmas Carol*.

Dirac, Paul Adrien Maurice (1902–1984) An English theoretical physicist and Nobel Laureate (the youngest in physics at the time). He was one of the Lucasian professors of mathematics at Cambridge. At Einstein's recommendation, he was invited to join the IAS at Princeton in 1931. He predicted the existence of antimatter and formulated the equations that describe fermions. That equation ($\iota\gamma \cdot \delta\psi = m\psi$) is inscribed on his memorial at Westminster Abbey and has been called the world's most beautiful equation. He had a massive influence on quantum mechanics and coined the term *quantum electrodynamics (QED)*. He was said to be as influential in physics as Newton or Einstein. He moved to Florida in 1970 and taught at Florida State University.

Eckert, John Adam Presper Jr. (1919–1995) An American electrical engineer. He codesigned, with John Mauchly, the ENIAC and the UNIVAC I. He cofounded EMCC (Eckert–Mauchly Computer Corporation), and he stayed with EMCC, which was bought by Remington Rand, which merged with Sperry Corp. and then Burroughs Corp., to finally become Unisys. He retired from Unisys in 1989 but remained a consultant until his death. He contended throughout his life that the von Neumann architecture should rightly be called the Eckert architecture.

Einstein, Albert (1879–1955) A German-born Nobel Prize-winning theoretical physicist. He is most famous for his two theories of relativity and the formula $E=mc^2$ (which is really $E^2=(mc^2)^2+(pc)^2$, but never mind that). He published five remarkable papers in 1905 (his "miracle year"). One was on the special theory of relativity, another proved the existence of atoms, and yet another proved the existence of the photon and the quantization of energy. He began an extended visit to the US in 1930. In 1933 he realized that, as a Jew, he could not return to Germany, so he stayed in the US, eventually taking a position at Princeton. A dedicated pacifist, it was he who signed the letter to Roosevelt encouraging the creation of the atomic bomb. Funny how that works.

Euclid (~300 BC) An ancient Greek mathematician who is considered the father of geometry. He was the author of *The Elements*, a series of books that established the foundation of geometry using the model of theorems derived from the logical application of five primitive postulates.

Faraday, Michael (1791–1867) A self-taught English scientist who delved into the topics of chemistry, electricity, and magnetism. Among many other things, he discovered the effect of electromagnetic induction and invented a primitive electric motor. Legend has it he demonstrated such a motor to the prime minister, who then asked him of what use it was. His response was that he didn't know, "but one day you can tax it."

Feynman, Richard (1918–1988) An American theoretical physicist. He made very substantial contributions to quantum mechanics. He is renowned for his lectures and books, and worked on the Manhattan Project in Los Alamos as a group leader of Hans Bethe's Theoretical Division. Together, he and Bethe developed the Bethe–Feynman formula for calculating fission yield. He assisted in establishing the calculation system using IBM punched card machines (Kemeny worked in this group). He also helped determine the cause of the 1986 Space Shuttle *Challenger* disaster.

Finder, Ken (~1950–) The person who hired me at Teradyne in 1976. He remained my boss, and mentor, for a decade or so. He taught me a lot of math, a lot of engineering, and a lot of common decency. It was he who invented the vector scheme for organizing the ROM chips in the 8085 COLT. He also managed the E.R. product.

Fitzpatrick, Jerry (~1960–) My good friend and coworker at Teradyne. He designed the Deep Voice card for E.R., and he wrote *Timeless Laws of Software Development*.[7] Nowadays, he is a software consultant.

Fowler, Martin (1963–) A friend, associate, and accomplished computer scientist and author. He was one of the key players in the eXtreme Programming (XP) and Agile movements. He has written and coauthored a plethora of very influential books, including *Refactoring*,[8] but my favorite by far is *Analysis Patterns*.[9]

Fulmer, Allen (1930–) An American educator. He received his MSEE and a BS in physics at Oregon State University. He is the inventor of the ECP-18 and the SPEDTAC educational computers. As a professor at Oregon State University, he helped introduce Judith Allen to computer programming and offered her a partnership in the ECP-18 venture.

Gödel, Kurt Friedrich (1906–1978) A German mathematician and logician. He tore down Hilbert's notion of the completeness and consistency of mathematics. He moved to Vienna in 1932 but was suspected to be a Jew sympathizer. In 1938, Austria became part of Germany, and he was found to be fit for service in the German army. So he and his wife traveled *east* across Russia, Japan, the Pacific Ocean, and North America to reach Princeton. That's the long way around, but Europe was embroiled in war by then. At Princeton, he and Einstein became close friends, and often took long walks together.

Goldbach, Christian (1690–1764) A Prussian mathematician, number theorist, and lawyer. He was a correspondent with Euler, Leibnitz, and Bernoulli, who made many contributions to the field. He is remembered today for his famous and still unproven conjecture that every even natural number greater than two is the sum of two primes.

---

7. Software Renovation Corp., 2017.

8. Addison-Wesley, 1999.

9. Addison-Wesley, 1997.

Goldberg, Richard (1924–2008) An American mathematician. He worked at IBM with John Backus on FORTRAN.

Goldstine, Herman Heine (1913–2004) An American computer scientist. He worked with John Mauchly to propose and then construct the ENIAC at Princeton. By chance, he met von Neumann on a train platform in 1944 and hinted at the ENIAC. He worked on the EDVAC and the IAS computers at Princeton, joined IBM in the late '50s, and became an IBM Fellow in '69.

Groves, Leslie Richard Jr. (1896–1970) A lieutenant general (honorary) of the Army who managed the building of the Pentagon and the Manhattan Project. He fell out of favor with Eisenhower due to his "rudeness, insensitivity, arrogance, contempt for the rules, and maneuvering for out-of-turn promotion." He left the Army and went on to become VP of Remington Rand, where he had to deal with the purchase of EMCC and the UNIVAC.

Haibt, Lois B. Mitchell (1934–) Graduated from Vassar and was a summer intern at Bell Labs. She joined IBM and learned to program the 704. She worked with John Backus on FORTRAN, and was the first IBM employee to hold a part-time, work-at-home position after starting a family. She worked off and on for IBM after that, and was also a contractor and consultant. She currently lives in Chicago.

Hamming, Richard Wesley (1915–1998) An American mathematician and Turing laureate who worked at Bell Labs concurrently with Dennis Ritchie, Ken Thompson, and Brian Kernighan. He worked at Los Alamos on the Manhattan Project, and helped to program the IBM punched card calculators. Later, at Bell Labs, he invented a scheme for specifying self-correcting error codes in digital streams (aka Hamming codes).

Heisenberg, Werner Karl (1901–1976) A Nobel Prize-winning German theoretical physicist and pioneer of quantum mechanics. He was at Göttingen with Hilbert and von Neumann. The "uncertainty principle" is named for him. He was a principle scientist in the Nazi nuclear weapons program despite the fact that he had been accused of being a "White Jew"—an Aryan who acts like a Jew. In 1939 he told Hitler that creating a bomb was possible, but would take years. The option was never actively pursued.

Herrick, Harlan Lowell (1923?–1997) An American mathematician employed by IBM for 30 years. He worked with John Backus on the first FORTRAN compiler.

Herschel, John (1792–1871) An English polymath and Babbage's good friend. He served as president of the Royal Astronomical Society. He cataloged thousands of double stars and many nebulae. He promoted the notion that science was inductive and based on observation. He made important advances in photography. He named many of the moons of Saturn and Uranus, and was the first to use Julian dates in astronomy.

Hickey, Rich (1971–) The creator of the Clojure language. He has been a popular and influential speaker at many conferences. One of my favorite talks of his is "Hammock Driven Development."[10] I first met him online in the comp.lang.c++ newsgroup. He went on to become the CTO of Cognitect, and then a Distinguished Engineer at Nubank, which purchased Cognitect in 2020. He has since retired, but I daresay we haven't heard the last from him—by a long shot.

Hopper, Vincent Foster (1906–1976) Grace Hopper's husband. A professor of English studies at New York University, he served in the Army Air Forces during World War II. He was a consultant for Barron's, and the author of several scholarly books.

Hughes, Robert A. (1925?–2007) An American mathematician who helped Lawrence Livermore National Laboratory set up physics problems on the UNIVAC I and IBM 701. He also worked with John Backus on FORTRAN.

---

10. ClojureTV. "Hammock Driven Development - Rich Hickey". Posted on YouTube on Dec. 16, 2012. (Available at the time of writing.)

Humboldt, Alexander von (1769–1859) A German polymath and proponent of science. He is the author of *Cosmos: A Sketch of a Physical Description of the Universe* (in German, *Kosmos – Entwurf einer physischen Weltbeschreibung*), in which he sought to unify the sciences and culture. His work eventually led to ecology, environmentalism, and even the study of climate change.

Iyer, Kris (CK) (1951–) A good friend and coworker at Teradyne, and later my boss at Clear Communications. He started at Teradyne in 1977 and the two of us worked very closely together on the SAC and the COLT for a couple of years. He and I translated the M365 COLT to the 8085.

Jacopini, Giuseppe (1936–2001) Coauthor, with Corrado Böhm, of "Flow Diagrams, Turing Machines, and Language with Only Two Formation Rules." This paper helped Dijkstra formulate the rules of structured programming.

Jacobson, Ivar (1939–) The first named author of *Object-Oriented Software Engineering*.[11] He collaborated with Grady Booch and Jim Rumbaugh (together, they were known as the Three Amigos) to create the Unified Modeling Language (UML) and the Rational Unified Process (RUP). He also worked at Ericsson on telephony.

Johnson, Stephen C. (1944–) An American computer scientist who worked at Bell Labs for over 20 years. The author of yacc (based on Knuth's work on LR parsing), lint, and spell, he became fascinated with computers as a boy when his father took him to the National Bureau of Standards and he saw the computer there. It was the size of a house, and was probably the SWAC. Later he worked for a number of startups, and was instrumental in creating the front-end of MATLAB.

Kay, Alan Curtis (1940–) An American computer scientist, jazz guitarist, and theatre designer. He worked at Xerox PARC and is the creator of Smalltalk. He coined the term *object-oriented programming*. He conceived of the

---

11. *Object-Oriented Software Engineering: A Use Case Driven Approach* (Addison-Wesley, 1992)

Dynabook concept (today we call that an iPad), and was instrumental in creating the Windows-Icon-Mouse-Pointer (WIMP) user interface.

King, William, Earl of Lovelace (1805–1893) The husband of Ada King Lovelace. He encouraged Ada's participation with Babbage, but grew frustrated with her severe gambling addiction. He reportedly left her upon hearing her deathbed confession of an affair.

Klein, Felix Christian (1849–1925) A German mathematician known for his work in non-Euclidian geometry and group theory. He "invented" the Klein Bottle—the three-dimensional analog of the Möbius strip. He established the mathematics research facility at Göttingen, and recruited David Hilbert, who eventually led it.

Knapp, Anthony W. (1941–) An American prize-winning mathematician. While working for Kemeny at Dartmouth, he traveled with Tomas Kurz to pitch GE to donate the computer system upon which BASIC and the Dartmouth Time Sharing System would be built. He earned his Ph.D. in mathematics at Princeton in 1965. He went on to become a professor at Cornell and then SUNY at Stony Brook. He is a prolific author of mathematical theory. One of his publications is on elliptic curves, upon which a number of cryptographic technologies, including Bitcoin and Nostr, are based.

Knuth, Donald (1938–) An American computer scientist and author of the famous compendium of books that every programmer should have and read, titled *The Art of Computer Programming*.[12]

Koss, Bob (1956–) An experienced teacher in C++ and object-oriented design in the mid-'90s. He was the third employee at Object Mentor Inc. Since we were both flying hither and yon teaching classes, we first met at O'Hare airport in Chicago and had our employment interview over a beer. He and I went through a lot of good, and tough, times together. He was a contributor to several of my early books.

---

12. Addison-Wesley, 1968.

Laning, J. Halcombe Jr. (1920–2012) An American computer scientist. He cowrote, with Zierler, an algebraic compiler (named George) for the Whirlwind at MIT. That language inspired Backus to create FORTRAN. He went on to work on space-based guidance systems for the Apollo program. He designed the Executive and Waitlist operating systems for the Lunar Module Guidance Computer. It was his design that saved the *Apollo 11* mission from the 1201 and 1202 errors. He went on to become deputy associate director of the MIT Instrumentation Laboratory.

Lasker, Emanuel (1868–1941) A world-renowned German chess player and mathematician. He earned his doctoral degree in mathematics at Göttingen; Hilbert was his advisor. He was the world chess champion for 27 years. He and his wife, both Jews, left Germany in 1933 as Hitler came to power. They accepted an invitation to live in the USSR. They left the USSR in 1937 to live in the US. Funny how that works.

Leigh, Augusta Maria (1783–1851) Lord Byron's stepsister and occasional lover. There is some evidence that her daughter Elizabeth was a product of that tryst.

Lindstrom, Lowell (1963–) A good friend and coworker at Teradyne and Object Mentor Inc. He was the business manager at OM from 1999 to 2007.

Lippman, Stan (1950–2022) The editor of *The C++ Report* at the time I started reading it. He worked closely with Bjarne Stroustrup in the very early C++ days. He was the author of a number of books, including the first author of *The C++ Primer*,[13] which was published in the late '80s and is now in its sixth edition. He went on to work at Disney, Pixar, and NASA.

Lyell, Charles (1797–1875) A Scottish geologist who authored *Principles of Geology*. He was a champion of gradualism, the idea that Earth changes very slowly due to consistent and slow physical processes.

---

13. Addison-Wesley, 1989.

Martin, Ludolph (1923–1973) My father. Born to a wealthy executive of an American steel company, he served in the Pacific during World War II as a Navy corpsman. He saw action in Guam and Guadalcanal. He promised God that upon his safe return he would devote his life to serving others. His inheritance was stock in the steel company, and it paid generous dividends and supported his upper-middle-class lifestyle, so he became a junior high school science teacher. The steel company went under in the '60s, and he was left trying to make ends meet on a teacher's salary. This drove him to drink, but he later joined AA and successfully fought back that horrible addiction. He died at the age of 50, leaving few assets behind. His is a story of riches to not-quite rags, and of the courage to take arms against a sea of troubles and overcome them. I see him every day looking back at myself in the mirror.

Martin, Micah (1976–) My secondborn. He is the cofounder of 8th Light Inc., as well as cofounder of cleancoders.com and Clean Coders Studio. I hired him as an apprentice programmer at Object Mentor Inc. in the late '90s. He went on to become a senior programmer and an accomplished teacher.

Mauchly, John William (1907–1980) An American physicist. He codesigned, with J. Presper Eckert, both the ENIAC and the UNIVAC I. He also was a founding member and president of the ACM, and founder of Mauchly Associates, who introduced the critical path method to the industry.

McCarthy, John (1927–2011) An American mathematician and computer scientist of Lithuanian and Irish descent. A Turing laureate, he was something of a child prodigy who skipped his first two years at Caltech, only to be kicked out for not attending physical education. He went back after a stint in the Army and got his BS in math. He attended a lecture by John von Neumann at Caltech, and it changed his life. He was the (somewhat inadvertent) inventor of the Lisp language.

McClure, Robert M. (dates unavailable) Worked at Bell Labs and was the inventor of the TransMoGrifier (TMG), an early compiler similar to yacc. A version of the TMG was used to build the B language, which, over time, became C.

McIlroy, Malcom Douglas (1932–) An American mathematician, engineer, and programmer. He worked at Bell Labs with Dennis Ritchie, Ken Thompson, and Brian Kernighan. He was a very early user of Unix on the PDP-7. He invented the *pipe* concept that Thompson built into Unix, and later participated in the design of languages such as Snobol, PL/1, and C++.

McPherson, John C. (1911–1999) An American electrical engineer who, during the war, helped set up the punched card computing facility at the Ballistics Research Lab in Aberdeen. He became director of engineering and VP at IBM. He participated in the planning of the SSEC, and was involved in the FORTRAN project with John Backus.

Menabrea, Luigi Frederico (1809–1896) An Italian statesman, military general, and mathematician. As a young man, he attended Babbage's lecture concerning the Analytical Engine in Turin. He was eventually charged by Giovani Plana to write down notes from that lecture. It was these notes that Ada translated to English, and then added her own famous notes to.

Meyer, Albert Ronald da Silva (1941–) A doctoral student at Harvard with Dennis Ritchie. He is currently a Hitachi America emeritus professor of computer science at MIT.

Meyer, Bertrand Dr. (1950–) The inventor of the Eiffel language and the Design by Contract discipline. He is the author of *Object-Oriented Software Construction*[14] and was the originator of the open–closed principle. His writings were deeply influential in the early days of object-oriented programming. He is a French academic who has held positions at several European universities.

---

14. Prentice Hall, 1988.

Millbanke, Ann Isabella (Annabella) (1792–1860) The wife of Lord Byron—albeit briefly. An educational reformer and philanthropist, who was also a horrible mother to her daughter Ada, she was gifted in mathematics and was known to her husband as his "princess of parallelograms."

Minkowski, Hermann (1864–1909) A German mathematician and professor, and one of Einstein's professors. Hilbert considered him his "most dependable friend." He made significant contributions to general relativity and conceived the concept of four-dimensional space-time.

Moore, Gordon (1929–2023) Cofounder and chair emeritus of Intel Corporation. He is famous for Moore's law, in which he stated, in 1965, that the density of integrated circuits would double every year for the next ten years.

Morris, Robert H. Sr. (1932–2011) An American cryptographer and computer scientist who worked at Bell Labs with Doug McIlroy. He was one of the earliest users of Unix on the PDP-7. He wrote the original crypt utility for Unix, and he and Doug McIlroy used TMG to create an early version of PL/1 (named ELT) for the Multics project.

Naur, Peter (1928–2016) A Danish astronomer and computer scientist. He won the Turing Award in 2005. He worked on ALGOL 60, and revamped John Backus's notation and got it adopted by the ALGOL committee. That notation became known as BNF, which originally stood for Backus Normal Form but was renamed by Donald Knuth to Backus–Naur Form.

von Neumann, Klára Dán (1911–1963) A Hungarian-American mathematician and John von Neumann's wife. She was one of the first true computer programmers. She worked at Los Alamos, and she used the MANIAC I for nuclear calculations. She also used the upgraded ENIAC to do Monte Carlo simulations for nuclear and meteorological applications.

Neumann, Peter Gabriel (1932–) An American mathematician and computer scientist. He worked at Bell Labs and helped invent the name *Unix (UNiplexed Information and Computing Service)*.

Newkirk, James (Jim) (~1962–) My good friend, and my business partner during the '90s. He was the primary mover of the NCARB project. He and I cofounded Object Mentor Inc. Prior to that, we worked together at Teradyne and Clear Communications.

Noether, Amalie Emmy (1882–1935) A German-Jewish mathematician described by Einstein and others as the most important woman in the history of mathematics. Her most famous work is Noether's theorem, in which she showed that all symmetries in nature correspond to conservation laws. She was a leading member of Göttingen's mathematics department, working with Hilbert and Klein. She left for Bryn Mawr College in Pennsylvania in 1933 as the Nazis came to power.

Nutt, Roy (1930–1990) A programmer who worked on FORTRAN with John Backus. He was the cofounder of Computer Sciences Corporation (CSC).

Oppenheimer, Julius Robert (1904–1967) An American theoretical physicist known as the father of the atomic bomb. He was the scientific director of the Manhattan Project at Los Alamos, became director of the IAS at Princeton in 1947, and was stripped of his security clearance out of fear that he had communist leanings.

Ossanna, Joseph Frank Jr. (1928–1977) An American electrical engineer and computer scientist. He helped come up with the word processing scheme to purchase a PDP-11 for Unix. He wrote nroff and troff and was a very early Unix evangelist.

Pauli, Wolfgang Ernst (1900–1958) An Austrian theoretical physicist, Nobel laureate, and one of the early contributors to quantum mechanics. He was the originator of the Pauli exclusion principle, and was also known for the "Pauli effect," in which experimental equipment would break in his mere presence. He proposed the existence of the neutrino, but did not name it. He was a patient of, and then a collaborator with, Carl Jung. He joined the IAS in Princeton in 1940.

Peel, Sir Robert (1788–1850) Twice the Prime Minister of the United Kingdom (1834–1835, 1841–1846), who also served as Chancellor of the Exchequer, and Home Secretary. Founder of the Metropolitan Police Service and, therefore, considered the father of modern policing in the UK. With regard to Charles Babbage, he once said: "What shall we do to get rid of Mr. Babbage and his calculating machine?"—1842.

Phillips, Charles A. (1906–1985) A colonel in the US Air Force and director of Data Systems Research at the DoD. He was the first chair of the Conference on Data Systems Languages (CODASYL), the group that created COBOL. He coined the phrase "Do not fold, spindle, or mutilate!"

Plana, Giovani (1781–1864) An Italian astronomer and mathematician. He was chair of the astronomy department at the University of Turin. He invited Babbage to Turin to present his thoughts on the Analytical Engine. He promised to publish notes of that presentation, but life got in the way and he eventually assigned that duty to Luigi Menabrea.

Plauger, Philip James (Bill) (1944–) An American physicist, computer programmer, entrepreneur, and science fiction author. He is the founder of Whitesmith's Ltd., where it is said he "invented" pair programming. He is the coauthor, with Brian Kernighan, of *Elements of Programming Style*.[15]

Richards, Martin (1940–) A British computer scientist at Cambridge who worked with Ken Thompson to create the BCPL language.

Roget, Peter Mark (1779–1869) A British physician and theologian and publisher of *Roget's Thesaurus*.

---

15. McGraw Hill, 1974.

Rumbaugh, James (1947–) First named author of *Object-Oriented Modeling and Design*.[16] In that book, the Object Modeling Technique (OMT) is described along with a notation that was common in the '90s. He collaborated with Grady Booch and Ivar Jacobson (together, they are known as the Three Amigos) to create the Unified Modeling Language (UML) and the Rational Unified Process (RUP).

Russell, Bertrand Arthur William (3rd Earl Russel) (1872–1970) A British mathematician and philosopher. He is famous for Russell's Paradox, which presented a significant challenge to the reduction of all of mathematics to a few postulates and a set of theorems using pure logic. He was coauthor with Alfred North Whitehead of *Principia Mathematica*, a major work that used type theory with some success. He won the Nobel Prize in Literature. A pacifist for most of his life, his initial approach to the rise of the Nazis was appeasement. But by 1943, Hitler had convinced him that war was sometimes the lesser of two evils. Funny how that works.

Sayre, David (1924–2012) A groundbreaking crystallographer and leader in diffraction imaging. He worked with John Backus on FORTRAN; Backus referred to him as second-in-command. He worked at IBM for 34 years and was a pioneer in virtual memory operating systems and X-ray diffraction and microscopy. (This guy was no slouch.)

Schmidt, Doug Dr. (~1953–) The editor of *The C++ Report* for a time, before handing the reins to me. He was active in the design patterns community and a frequent speaker at software conferences. He was the initial author of the ACE framework. He has gone on to lead a rather stellar academic career (see www.dre.vanderbilt.edu/~schmidt/).

Schrödinger, Erwin Rudolf Josef Alexander (1887–1961) An Austrian physicist who made significant contributions to early quantum mechanics, for which he won the Nobel Prize. He is remembered in popular culture for inventing the paradox of Schrödinger's Cat. He left

---

16. Prentice Hall, 1991.

Germany in 1933 out of his disdain for antisemitism, but the fact that he lived with both his wife and his mistress made it hard for him to find a permanent position elsewhere in Europe. He moved to Austria, but had to recant his disavowal of Nazism; he subsequently recanted that recantation when challenged by Einstein. He and his wife eventually fled to Italy.

Seeber, Robert Rex Jr. (1910–1969) An American inventor. He worked for Howard Aiken on the Harvard Mark I, and then at IBM, where he was a computer architect. He invented the SSEC, and hired John Backus, who thought it was cool.

Shelley, Mary Wollstonecraft (1797–1851) Author of *Frankenstein* and friend of Lord Byron.

Sheridan, Peter B. (?–1992) A research scientist at IBM who worked with John Backus on FORTRAN.

Snyder, Elizabeth Holberton (Betty) (1917–2001) An American computer scientist. An original ENIAC programmer, she was employed by EMCC and helped create the UNIVAC I. She invented the SORT/MERGE compiler and became supervisor of advanced programming for the Navy's Applied Math Lab. She participated in the COBOL definition, and later, at the National Bureau of Standards, she participated in the F77 and F90 FORTRAN specifications.

Somerville, Mary (1780–1872) A Scottish scientist, writer, and polymath; a friend of Annabella Byron; and an occasional tutor of Annabella's daughter Ada. It was she who introduced Ada to Babbage. She studied the relationship between light and magnetism, and the motion of the planets. She participated in the prediction of the existence of the planet Neptune based on orbital perturbations of Uranus. She was published in the *Proceedings of the Royal Society*. She was also a friend of Michael Faraday, who collaborated with her on some experiments.

Strachey, Christopher S. (1916–1975) A British computer scientist who worked at Standard Telephones and Cables (STC) during the war, using differential analyzers. Later, interested in computers, he wrote a game of checkers for the Pilot ACE (a cut-down version of the ACE), but failed to get it working in that limited environment. In 1951, with the help of Turing, he got it working on the Manchester Mark I. He later got the Ferrante Mark I to play a few tunes, including "God Save the King" and "Baa Baa Black Sheep." In 1959 he wrote the seminal paper on time sharing.

Stroustrup, Bjarne (1950–) A Danish mathematician and computer scientist, and inventor of C++. He was inspired by SIMULA 67 while studying in Aarhus and Cambridge.

Szilard, Leo (1898–1964) A Hungarian physicist and inventor. He conceived of (and patented) the nuclear fission chain reaction in 1933, and worked with Enrico Fermi on controlled nuclear fission. He drafted the letter that he and Einstein sent to Roosevelt encouraging the building of the atomic bomb. He thought that the demonstrated existence of such a weapon would convince Germany and Japan to surrender.

Teller, Edward (1908–2003) A Hungarian-American Jewish nuclear physicist. He received his Ph.D. under Heisenberg at Leipzig. The father of the hydrogen bomb, he left Germany in 1933 as the Nazis came to power. He bounced between England and Copenhagen for two years and then moved to the US. Oppenheimer recruited him to Los Alamos, where he worked on the Manhattan Project. Never a pacifist, he always advocated for nuclear power, both for peace and for defense. He was one of the first to identify the risk of climate change due to the burning of fossil fuels. He joked that Jane Fonda's protest against nuclear power after the Three Mile Island accident caused his 1979 heart attack. The man was a card.

Ulam, Stanislaw Marcin (1909–1984) A Polish-Jewish mathematician, nuclear physicist, and computer scientist. He was the coinventor, with

John von Neumann, of Monte Carlo analysis. He worked on the Manhattan Project and was codesigner of the Teller–Ulam hydrogen bomb. Eleven days before the Nazis invaded Poland, he and his 17-year-old brother, Adam, boarded a ship bound for the US. The rest of his family was killed in the Holocaust.

Veblen, Oswald (1880–1960) An American mathematician and a professor at Princeton. He helped organize the Institute for Advanced Study (IAS), and worked to obtain funding to recruit top scientists from Europe to the IAS. In this he was remarkably successful, though Hitler helped a lot. He supported the proposal to build the ENIAC.

Watson, Thomas John Sr. (1875–1956) An American wheeler-dealer who, in 1914, after several other nefarious adventures, became president of a division of the Computing-Tabulating-Recording Company (CTR) and in 1924 renamed it to International Business Machines (IBM). If you want to read a really interesting story, you could do worse than to study this scoundrel and supreme businessman.

Weyl, Hermann Klaus Hugo (1885–1955) A German mathematician and theoretical physicist. He earned a Ph.D. at Göttingen under the supervision of David Hilbert. He was a colleague of Einstein and Schrödinger in Zurich. In 1930 he took over for Hilbert at Göttingen, but left for Princeton in 1933 when the Nazis took power. He made many significant contributions to mathematics and particle physics.

Wheatstone, Sir Charles (1802–1875) An English scientist and inventor who studied electricity and was the first to measure its speed. He made major contributions to many fields, including telegraphy, optics, and electrical theory.

Whitehead, Alfred North (1861–1947) An English mathematician and philosopher. He was coauthor, with Bertrand Russel, of *Principia Mathematica*. Later in his career he focused more on metaphysics, and was a proponent of the notion that reality is not based upon material existence, but on a sequence of dependent events.

Wigner, Eugene Paul (1902–1995) A Hungarian-American Nobel Prize-winning theoretical physicist and mathematician. He was one of Hilbert's assistants at Göttingen. He and Hermann Weyl introduced group theory into physics. He participated in the meeting that resulted in Einstein's letter to Roosevelt encouraging the building of the atomic bomb, and later worked on the Manhattan Project. He accepted a position at Princeton in 1930 along with John von Neumann.

Wirth, Nicklaus Emil (1934–2024) A Swiss electronics engineer and computer scientist. He created the Pascal programming language and was the author of many fine books, my favorite of which is *Algorithms + Data Structures = Programs*.[17] It was he who, in 1968, retitled Dijkstra's article about GOTO and published it as a letter to the editor in *CACM*[18] titled "Goto Statement Considered Harmful."

van Wijngaarden, Adriaan (1916–1987) A Dutch mechanical engineer and mathematician who ran the Mathematical Centre during the creation of the early computers (ARRA, FERTA, ARMAC, and X1). He hired Dijkstra after meeting him at the Cambridge course on the EDSAC. He participated in the definition of ALGOL, but did not write any of Dijkstra's and Zonneveld's compiler.

Yourdon, Edward Nash (1944–2016) An American mathematician, computer scientist, software methodologist, and inductee to the Computer Science Hall of Fame. He founded Yourdon Inc., a consulting company that promoted the structured programming, design, and analysis techniques in the '70s and '80s.

---

17. Prentice Hall, 1976.

18. *Communications of the ACM*, vol. 11, no. 3, March 1968.

Zierler, Neil (?–) An American computer scientist. He cowrote, with J. Halcombe Laning, an algebraic compiler (named George) for the Whirlwind at MIT. That language inspired Backus to create FORTRAN. He participated in the creation of Lisp at MIT. He is currently doing research in applied mathematics at the Center for Communications Research at Princeton.

Zonneveld, Jacob Anton (Jaap) (1924–2016) A Dutch mathematician and physicist. He became a scientific assistant at the Dutch Mathematical Centre and worked with Dijkstra on the first successful ALGOL 60 compiler. He later went on to direct a software research group at Philips's NatLab.

INDEX

C

C#, 181, 331, 334

C++
  advent of, 196
  author's interest in, 298
  author's work with, 302, 311
  B language and, 24
  data types and, 334
  origination of, 183
  SIMULA 67 and, 181
  SIMULA and, 168

C-10 language, 97–98, 101, 104
Calaprice, Alice, 379
call management systems, 288
calls, ARRA, 143
Campbell, Robert, 79, 83, 414
Cantor, Georg, 46, 414
Carew, Mike, 286
Cartesian coordinate plane, 16
CASE (computer-aided software engineering), 305
CDS (Craft Dispatch System), 295–296, 298
cell phones, xxii, 6, 198
central limit theorem, 59
Central Office Line Tester (COLT), 272, 273, 281, 284
central processors, 61, 338
ChatGPT, 198, 380
chemistry industry, 332
chroma-key, 323
Church, Alonzo, 51, 187, 415

C language
  assembler, 236
  author's introduction to, 282–283
  author's work with, 292, 293
  B and, 24
  creation of, xxi, 232–235
  data types and, 334
  innovativeness of, 327
  int in, 146

popularity of, 196
similarity with other languages, 331
Unix and, 211
classes/subclasses, 48, 180
Clean Code, 320–321
Clean Coders Inc., 324
Clear Communications, 301–302
clock rates, 357
Clojure, 334, 349–350, 352
cloud computers, 357

COBOL
  creation of, 108–112
  physical architecture and, 146
  success of, xxi, 113
  users as focus of, 112–113

C.O.D.E., 313, 315

code
  binary vs. assembler, 327
  Clean Code, 320–321
  code generator programs, 129
  Difference Engine, 25
  editing magnetic tape, 263
  historic changes in, 367
  magnetic tape source code, 262
  Mark I, 89–90
  need for writers of, 7
  octal, 250, 349
  provable, 163
  source code control, 274–275
  source code statement, 162
  Speedcoding, 120–123
  UNIVAC, 95–98
COLT (Central Office Line Tester), 272, 273, 281, 284
COLT Measurement Unit (CMU), 284
Columbia University, 117

.comments, invention of, 78
communism, 54, 72
Compatible Time-Sharing System (CTSS), 221, 222
compilers
  algebraic, 107
  BASIC, 192
  beginnings of, 99–100
  data checks by, 333–335
  FORTRAN input to, 127–129
  Grace Hopper and, 77, 90, 103, 106
  IBM 370, 268
  IBM 704, 124
  Kurtz/Kemeny's work on, 191
  M365, 264
  SIMULA, 169, 170, 174, 178, 179, 180
  Type A compilers, 103–105
  XI, 147–150
completeness proof, 47–49, 55
complexity, 376–380
computer-aided software engineering (CASE), 305
computers
  accuracy for early, 24
  ALWAC III-E, 206
  Analytical Engine, 30–33
  ARRA, 138–143
  ASCC (Harvard Mark I), 79
  Babbage's prototype for, 15, 30–33
  cloud computers, 357
  computer revolution, 195
  ECP-18, 204, 250–251
  expense of early, 104, 108, 123–124
  Ferranti Mercury, 169
  growing power/capacity of, 4
  human, 23, 66